The Media in France

The Media in France presents a comprehensive overview of the history, present and future prospects of the French media and considers the successes and failures of French media policy from 1945 to the present day.

Raymond Kuhn investigates the history, politics and economics of the press, radio and television from the days of state intervention and monopoly provision to current trends towards de-regulation and pluralism. He also discusses the importance of the 'new media' of cable and satellite broadcasting. In particular he explores the changing interrelationship between media and state, as ownership and direct interference decline while the state remains a key part of the media landscape in its policy making and regulatory roles.

This up-to-date, accessible textbook is essential reading for all students of French, European and Media Studies.

Raymond Kuhn is Senior Lecturer and Head of the Department of Political Studies at Queen Mary and Westfield College, University of London. He is the editor of *The Politics of Broadcasting* and *Broadcasting and Politics in Western Europe*.

The Media in France

Raymond Kuhn

London and New York

First published 1995
by Routledge
2 Park Square, Milton Park, Abingdon, Oxon, OX14 4RN

Simultaneously published in the USA and Canada
by Routledge
270 Madison Ave, New York NY 10016

Transferred to Digital Printing 2005

© 1995 Raymond Kuhn

Typeset in Times by
Florencetype Ltd, Stoodleigh, Devon

British Library Cataloguing in Publication Data
A catalogue record for this book is available from the British Library

Library of Congress Cataloging in Publication Data
Kuhn, Raymond.
 The media in France/Raymond Kuhn.
  p. cm.
 Includes bibliographical references and index.
 1. Mass media–France. I. Title.
P92.F8K84 1994
 302.23'0944–dc20   94–9595

ISBN   0–415–01459–X (hbk)
       0–415–01458–1 (pbk)

To Agnes and Roman

Contents

Tables

Acknowledgements

I should like to thank the members of my department at Queen Mary and Westfield College, University of London, for their support during the writing of this book. I am also grateful to Dr Peter Morris of the University of Nottingham for his advice and friendship.

Others whom I should like to thank include: Professor Trevor Smith, my former head of department and currently Vice-Chancellor of the University of Ulster; Dr Ian Campbell, my Ph.D. supervisor at the University of Warwick; and Dr Vincent Wright of Nuffield College, Oxford.

I am grateful to those at Routledge who waited patiently for this book to come to fruition. They include Jane Armstrong, Rebecca Barden and Sue Bilton. Brigitte Lee did an excellent job as copy editor.

I should like to acknowledge the financial assistance provided by the Nuffield Foundation, the University of London Central Research Fund, the ESRC/CNRS and the British Academy, all of which provided small but invaluable sums of money to enable me to make short research trips to France to conduct interviews and obtain published material.

I owe an immense debt of gratitude to my partner, Kerstin, for her unfailing humour and encouragement.

Finally, I wish to thank both my parents for all their love and help over the years. This book is dedicated to them.

Abbreviations

AFP	Agence France-Presse
ARD	Arbeitsgemeinschaft der öffentlich-rechtlichen Rundfunkanstalten Deutschlands
BBC	British Broadcasting Corporation
BSB	British Satellite Broadcasting
CFDT	Confédération Française Démocratique du Travail
CGE	Compagnie Générale d'Electricité
CGT	Confédération Générale du Travail
CLT	Compagnie Luxembourgeoise de Télédiffusion
CNCL	Commission nationale de la communication et des libertés
CNN	Cable News Network
CSA	Conseil Supérieur de l'Audiovisuel
CTPP	Commission for the transparency and pluralism of the press
DBS	Direct broadcasting by satellite
DGT	Direction Générale des Télécommunications
EDF	Electricité de France
EEC	European Economic Community
ENA	Ecole Nationale d'Administration
EU	European Union
FLN	Front de Libération Nationale
FM	Frequency modulation
FR3	France Régions 3
GATT	General Agreement on Tariffs and Trade
IBA	Independent Broadcasting Authority
INA	Institut National de l'Audiovisuel

ITV	Independent Television
NATO	North Atlantic Treaty Organization
NRJ	Nouvelle Radio Jeune
OAS	Organisation Armée Secrète
OFI	Office français d'information
ORTF	Office de Radiodiffusion-Télévision Française
PAL	Phase Alternate Line
PCF	Parti Communiste Français
PTT	Post, Telegraphy and Telephony
RAI	Radiotelevisione Italiana
RTF	Radiodiffusion-Télévision Française
RTL	Radiodiffusion-Télévision Luxembourg
SECAM	Séquentiel couleur à mémoire
Sept	Société d'édition de programmes de télévision
SFP	Société Française de Production
SLII	Service des liaisons interministérielles pour l'information
Sofirad	Société financière de radiodiffusion
TDF	Télédiffusion de France
TDF1	Télédiffusion de France 1
TDF2	Télédiffusion de France 2
TF1	Télévision Française 1
TGV	Train à grande vitesse
TVS	TV South
UK	United Kingdom
US	United States
VAT	Value added tax
VCR	Video cassette recorder

Introduction

The mass media of press, radio and television form an integral part of the political, economic and social life of contemporary France. They play a key role in the process of political communication, sometimes operating as an apparently passive conduit for the transmission of information, but more usually adopting a more pro-active stance in the selection and construction of news and the provision of comment. Not only are the media the most convenient means by which elites communicate both with each other and with the general public; they are also political actors in their own right, with the capacity to bring issues on to the news agenda and to mobilize public opinion in support of a particular point of view. In short, the French media are both the main arteries of a sophisticated system of political communication and major players within that system.

The media are also important economic actors. Growing public consumption of media product has been stimulated by an increase in its supply, particularly in the audiovisual sector. The broadcasting media expanded enormously in the 1980s as a result of government decisions to legalize private local radio and encourage the establishment of new television channels. Advertising expenditure in the media experienced impressive levels of growth during the same decade, as did levels of employment in the media and related sectors of the economy. Several French media companies have very high annual turnovers, while some also have an important stake in foreign media markets. Though still lagging behind some other industrialized countries in terms of media growth, by the 1990s France was well on the way to having a well-developed media sector of the economy.

It was also becoming a media-rich society. The extent to which the media have established themselves as important forces in French society can be gauged by a cursory examination of some statistics. In 1987 approximately 10 million daily newspapers, 69 million weekly newspapers and magazines, and 63 million monthlies were produced in France. There were 50 to 60 million radio sets in use, 27 million television sets and more than 6 million video-recorders. One of the leading writers on the French press estimates that in the late 1980s around 55 per cent of the population regularly read a daily newspaper, 72 per cent listened to the radio and 70 per cent watched television.[1] Survey evidence suggested that in the same period the average French citizen devoted about 20 minutes per day to reading a newspaper, almost two hours to watching television and between one and two hours to listening to the radio.

Yet while the growing penetration of the media into various aspects of daily existence is one of the most notable phenomena of postwar France, the qualitative impact of this trend is difficult to ascertain with any certainty. Intuitively one suspects that the media must be powerful forces in French politics and society. It seems reasonable to assume that consumption patterns, lifestyle trends and value systems have all been affected by the relentless progress towards media saturation. None the less, the power of the media in producing specific effects is hard to demonstrate unequivocally and almost always impossible to quantify. Academic studies have examined the links between media exposure and all manner of political and social behaviour, from voting preferences to violent crime. Theories purporting to reveal the omnipotence of the media are challenged by counter-theories claiming to show the very finite limits to their power. In the end, however, the precise contribution of media usage to an explanation of attitudinal or behavioural change in postwar France remains a matter of intensely fascinating, but ultimately inconclusive, speculation. The media may indeed be powerful, but exactly how powerful is a subject of conjecture.[2]

The functions performed by the media in contemporary France also give rise to different and contradictory interpretations. There is no consensus on this issue, which, like the debate on media effects, is a battleground for the exposition of rival academic and ideological perspectives. For some the media are primarily ideological weapons which are manipulated for the purpose of social control. They are part of a process whereby the contradictions of power relations in society are resolved to the economic and political benefit of a power elite or ruling class. For others the media are primarily independent actors in a political system characterized by electoral competition and the diffusion of power. Press, radio and television act on behalf of the electorate, keeping them informed of elite decisions and acting as a check on the abuse of power. In this debate, any assessment of the effectiveness with which the French media perform certain functions will depend to a large extent on the nature of the observer's own value system. As McQuail argues, there is no agreed version of what functions the media perform since this 'would require an agreed version of society'.[3]

The complexity of this issue is self-evident. Several of the analytically distinct media functions overlap in practice, while some functions appear to be performed more successfully by some media than by others. Most confusingly, some media functions seem to be in direct contradiction with others, making generalization difficult, if not impossible. What follows, therefore, is not intended to be a comprehensive checklist. Rather it is a brief overview of some of the more important functions which have been, or more accurately may have been, performed by the French media in the postwar period.[4]

First, and perhaps least controversially, the French media perform an important *information function*. They are a primary source of news for the French public, informing them of key local, national and international events. They also provide necessary background material and analysis to help their users understand and interpret the 'reality' presented to them. Press, radio and television are the three most important information sources on events taking place outside the boundaries of the household and its immediate environs. Without them, the information base of French citizens would be overwhelmingly dependent on knowledge gained through interpersonal (as opposed to mass) communication, and knowledge of a world beyond the local commune would be at best fragmentary. This information function is carried out by all the French media to some extent, though clearly it is given greater emphasis and is more successfully performed by some media outlets than by others.

Second, the French media fulfil a vital *communications function* as links for the transmission of all sorts of messages within and between different strata of society: among the social, economic and political elites; between different sections of the public; and, finally, between the elites and the public in both directions. In this last role the media carry messages from opinion formers both to the public as a whole and to specific groups in society. In this top-down communication role, the media are frequently used (or exploited) by elites for the purpose of public persuasion (or manipulation). The advertising of consumer goods by commercial companies is an example of top-down communication. So too is the increasing use of the media by political elites for the purpose of image projection, most clearly evident during election campaigns. At the same time, the media may also serve as a means for the public to exert influence on elite opinion. Grass roots pressure groups which use the media to seek to influence policy makers would be a good example of such bottom-up communication. Some media messages involve communication in both directions. For instance, the media-friendly activities of a pressure group such as Greenpeace are designed both to influence policy makers and to raise public awareness on environmental issues.

Third, and more debatably, the French media may perform a *watchdog function*, acting on behalf of the public as an independent check on elite behaviour. This may take the form of a newspaper article highlighting bureaucratic inefficiency, a radio phone-in condemning professional impropriety or a television programme exposing political corruption. In carrying out this function, the media can help make power-holders such as politicians, bureaucrats and commercial companies accountable to the public, helping to empower the latter as voters, service-users and consumers. The media's attachment to this watchdog function is not as deeply entrenched in France as in some other liberal democracies, notably the United States, where the practice of investigative journalism is deeply rooted. None the less, some French media outlets see this function as an integral part of their civic responsibilities, even if the adverse coverage given to an issue or personality may at times look like a self-serving exercise in muckraking.[5]

Fourth, the media in France may perform an important *socialization/legitimation function*. In carrying out this role the media are normally assisted by other agencies of socialization/legitimation, including the educational system, the family, peer groups, religious institutions and voluntary associations. With the support of these other agencies, the media help shape popular attitudes, values, norms and beliefs with regard to the functioning of society in general and the operation of the political process in particular. The potential of the media in this respect makes them important political actors. For the holders of economic and political power, control of the press, radio and television may be crucial for the popular mobilization of support for political institutions and for the legitimization of power relations in society. Conversely, the media have the potential to act as a destabilizing force, sapping a regime's legitimacy and even in extreme circumstances contributing to its collapse.

Fifth, the contemporary French media perform an important *entertainment/cultural function*. Some media act as vehicles for the popular dissemination of 'high culture', a means of spreading the French cultural canon throughout society. In so doing, they may succeed in promoting a feeling of pride in the great works of French music, art, literature, theatre and cinema. At the same time, much of the mass media play a key role in reflecting and shaping popular culture. Pop music, romantic fiction and television soap operas and game shows form a large part of the stock in trade of contemporary mass media output. The precise cultural impact of the mass media may be open to debate. Yet irrespective of whether one is talking about the television dramatization of a Zola classic or radio coverage of a pop concert, there can be no doubt that without the mass media the entertainment and cultural intake of the French population would be hugely different from what it currently is.

Finally – and here the problems of generalization become overwhelming – some of the media may perform a *nation-building function*, while others (or the same media at different times) emphasize a feeling of difference and may encourage social and political divisions. Some media outlets (such as national television) and some media content (such as coverage of a presidential address or of a French football victory) tend to unite the nation in a collective ritualistic celebration. While the media's performance of this nation-building function is a frequent feature of developing societies, it can also be found in postwar France. Centralized state control of television by the Gaullists in the 1960s, for instance, was intended to reinforce the legitimacy of the one and indivisible (Fifth) Republic as the embodiment of the national will, just as the prefectoral system of 150 years previously had been used to bind the nation under the control of the Napoleonic Empire. Conversely, some media outlets (such as the provincial press) and some media content (such as coverage of regional folk festivals or separatist political movements) may contribute to a feeling of difference within the nation or even, in extreme circumstances, subvert the claims of nationhood altogether.

In any case, whatever functions are attributed to the French media, none of them is performed in a vacuum. Rather, they are carried out within a variety of specific contexts or bounded environments. The particular configuration of the French media system at any point in time is itself a crucial variable in this respect. Important elements of the media system which may influence the capacity of the press, radio and television to carry out their functions (however defined) include, *inter alia*: the level of media penetration and consumption in society; the balance between private and public ownership and control of the media; the sources and levels of media finance; the relative market weighting of local, regional and national media; the supply of and demand for quality and popular media content; the extent to which the media are regulated; public levels of confidence in media practitioners and media content; and the degree of political and commercial independence of the media.

The French media interact in a highly complex, varied and dynamic system. A popular provincial daily, a privately owned pop music radio station and a public service television channel have different resources, gear their product for different audiences, work to different professional norms and operate within different regulatory environments. Consider some of the main elements of contrast within the French media system. Whereas *Le Figaro* can trace its origins back to the mid-nineteenth century, the NRJ radio network came into existence only in the 1980s. Some media, such as the TF1 television channel, serve a nationwide audience; others, such as the many provincial daily newspapers, cater for a local or regional readership. While the France 2 television channel is subject to a host of public service norms, the pay-television channel, Canal Plus, is very lightly regulated. The former state monopoly broadcasting organization, the ORTF, was run by a director general who was appointed by the government, with the result that its news coverage was politically suspect; conversely, the satirical newspaper *Le Canard enchaîné* prides itself on its political independence and publishes scathing critiques of alleged abuses of power by government ministers and other politicians. The weekly news magazine *L'Express* receives over half its income from advertising; in contrast, Radio France is funded principally through licence revenue, while some cable channels are financed mainly from viewer subscription. These and other differences between the various media players affect not just the content, but also the style, presentation and form of media product – as well as its cost to the consumer.

The structure and operation of the media system in France are themselves influenced directly and indirectly by a whole series of variables. While many of these are interrelated in practice, they can be distinguished for analytic purposes. *Geographical, demographic and linguistic factors* comprise one set of variables. Even though France is by no means self-sufficient in media product, it is still a large enough and sufficiently well populated country with its own national language to support a highly developed indigenous media system. Compare the French situation with that of Canada, which is a huge but thinly populated country whose mainly Anglophone inhabitants live for the most part alongside a common border with the United States. As a result, many Canadians rely heavily on American media product, especially television programming. In Europe, small countries such as Belgium, the Netherlands and Ireland are major users of non-domestic television product both in the form of programme imports on their national stations and direct audience usage of foreign channels via terrestrial transmission, cable and satellite. Even in an era of growing internationalization of media technology, capital and product, France possesses a media system with solid national roots.

Technological factors make up a second set of variables which have influenced the evolution of the French media system. New methods of production and distribution in the late nineteenth century ushered in an era of expansion in the press, while the introduction of new printing technology in the 1970s and 1980s had important consequences for the economics and employment practices of the publishing industry as a whole. More efficient use of the FM waveband facilitated the explosion of private local radio stations in the early 1980s. The huge potential of fibre optic technology and switched star networks for the provision of a wide range of interactive services persuaded the French state to invest in an ambitious national cable project at the beginning of the same decade. Simultaneously, the state also provided public resources for the construction and launch of a direct broadcasting satellite, TDF1, to ensure that France would not be left out of what was hoped would be a lucrative hi-tech market for satellite hardware.

Third, the French media system has been affected by *economic factors*. The economic condition of the media sector is linked to the general performance of the economy as a whole, with the latter having a notable impact on the supply of, and demand for, media services. In a period of economic downturn, for instance, the state and commercial companies are less likely to invest in new media hard- and software, media advertising budgets decline and consumers have less money to spend on media entertainment. For example, the budgetary problems faced by the French government in the mid-1980s led to a cutback in the state-sponsored cable programme announced with such a flourish only a few years earlier.

More particularly, the economic situation of the media sector has obvious implications for the output – and even survival – of different media players. The collapse of the commercial television channel, La 5, in 1992 was the result of the company's inability in a highly competitive audiovisual market to generate an audience of the requisite size or socio-economic composition to attract sufficient advertising and thus make itself financially viable. Various schemes to launch a mass circulation national daily newspaper in France have foundered in the face of negative financial projections. In the 1980s some private local radio stations went under because of their inability to raise sufficient advertising revenue, while others recognized 'economic reality' and became part of *de facto* nationwide networks. The budgetary constraints within which the public sector television channels Antenne 2 and FR3 had to operate in the late 1980s had deleterious consequences for the companies' programming, audience ratings and staff morale. Indeed, the costs of television production had massive consequences for programme output across the whole of the French broadcasting system as certain programme genres (for example, home-produced fiction and drama) declined, while others (such as variety shows and feature films) increased.

The *changing nature of French society* is a fourth factor which has influenced the configuration of the media system and the output of the various media players. For example, the demand by a new generation of women for equal rights has been sympathetically reflected in the content of many women's magazines. New publications (such as *Cosmopolitan*) aimed at the target group of young, independent women have come on to the market to join well-known titles such as *Marie-Claire*. Other new weeklies and monthlies have been published to cater for contemporary lifestyles: magazines for computer junkies, car buffs and hi-fi freaks now compete with those covering more traditional leisure pursuits, including the venerable *Le chasseur français*, established in 1885.

In a consumer society which places a high premium on leisure activities, a lot of media product is designed for entertainment purposes as consumers seek to distract themselves from the more mundane aspects of their existence. The impact of the entertainment imperative has not just been reflected in the expansion of those media sectors specifically geared for this purpose (such as pay-television and music radio stations). It can also be seen in public service media outlets and in programme genres such as news, where the need to entertain the audience has become an important constraint on the behaviour of media practitioners.

One social group which is now better catered for than ever before by the entertainment-oriented media is French youth, a development which reflects their economic importance as consumers. The expansion in the audiovisual media has allowed radio stations and television channels to target the 15–34 age group. Many local radio networks transmit music designed to appeal predominantly to this section of society, while the short-lived television channel, TV6, successfully attracted young viewers with its output of pop music and video-clips.

Geographical and linguistic factors, technological developments, economic conditions and changing social patterns have all played a part in shaping the structures and operations of the French media. The single most important set of variables, however, is to be found in the realm of French politics. Both the historical evolution and contemporary development of the French media have been indelibly marked by the influence of *political factors*. Four features of French politics are particularly worthy of note in this regard.

The first of these is the chronic regime instability from which France has suffered since the 1789 Revolution.[6] The constitutional issue has rarely been far off the top of the political agenda in post-revolutionary France. In the absence of agreement among French political elites on the basic groundrules of the constitution, French politics has frequently presented a tragi-comic spectacle of high ideological rhetoric combined with low-level political accommodation and bargaining, especially in cases of resource allocation by the state.

In such a political environment the media have often been able to act to stimulate popular discontent with the regime on behalf of a disaffected social group or political party and to present politics as an essentially amoral and cynical 'pork barrel' activity. It is highly likely that as well as contributing directly on occasions to regime collapse, the media have often played a part in undermining the legitimacy of the political system through their critical coverage.[7] After the Fifth Republic was established in 1958, it is understandable that the implantation and consolidation of the regime was a constant source of concern for de Gaulle and his supporters. Not surprisingly they used their control of television to try to mobilize popular support for Gaullist institutions in the face of opposition from the Communists (over the new constitution in 1958), from the extreme Right (over decolonization from Algeria in the early 1960s) and from the post-war political elites (over the 1962 constitutional amendment to elect the President by direct universal suffrage).

Second, the French political landscape has traditionally been scarred by a number of deep and troublesome criss-crossing faultlines. These have both destabilized regimes and exacerbated executive instability by making it difficult for the government to build cohesive, enduring parliamentary coalitions to support executive policy decisions. In addition to disagreement over the constitutional question, these divisions have centred on issues such as the role of the Church in political life and in particular its institutional relationship with the state; the incorporation of working-class representatives from both organized labour and political parties into a decision-making process dominated by an objective alliance of peasant–bourgeois interests; and the thorny and for a long time apparently intractable problem of decolonization, especially from Algeria.[8] In general the press system has reflected and perhaps even exacerbated the fissures of this divided society, with newspapers taking up the cudgels on behalf of one tendency or another.[9]

Reflecting this societal disunity, the French party system has traditionally covered a wide ideological spectrum of opinion organized in an assortment of clubs, movements and parties, many of which have had only a short and tempestuous lifespan.[10] It is not the existence of a multi-party system in itself which has been crucial in influencing political behaviour, however impressive the sheer number of political parties has frequently been. What has been more significant historically is the large ideological spectrum covered by the different parties. This has resulted in the party system frequently being characterized by a high degree of polarized pluralism, including the presence of anti-system parties.[11] Even during the Fifth Republic, which has witnessed a reduction in the degree of ideological polarization in the party system, inter-party rivalries have been intense.[12] Faced with such a complex party system, state broadcasting during the post-war period has tended to articulate the views of the political party or coalition in power, rather than try to present a balanced and impartial account of political debate. Governments feared giving access to their opponents because there was no agreement on the rules of the political game which would set accepted boundaries to party conflict. The postwar British concept of a consensual middle ground cutting across the two-party division and underpinning a public service approach by broadcasters to political coverage has been an alien one in French party politics.

Third, in contrast to this pluralism in the party system, the state has been organized on highly centralized lines. Originating in the pre-revolutionary period of the *ancien régime* and reinforced during the Napoleonic empire, the centralized Jacobin state largely confined itself to the minimalist functions of territorial defence and economic protectionism until the collapse of the Third Republic. The Second World War changed this, producing a postwar state which, whatever the political complexion of its governing parties, intervened massively in the management of the economy, the provision of welfare and the dissemination of culture. Even the liberalization and privatization programmes of the conservative and Socialist governments in the second half of the 1980s failed to undermine the primary role of the state in many facets of French economic, social and cultural life. State subsidies to the press and centralized state monopoly control of broadcasting were only two aspects of the wide-ranging role of the French state in the postwar media.

Finally, during the Fifth Republic a powerful presidency, usually supported by a stable and durable majority in Parliament, has been established at the apex of the policy-making process. While de Gaulle concentrated mainly on foreign and defence matters, his successors at the Elysée have extended the presidential domain to include domestic policy. The President of the Fifth Republic has generally been able to impose his will on the various legislative initiatives in the media field. For example, the decision in 1974 to abolish the ORTF was made by President Giscard d'Estaing, while the initiative to set up two commercial television channels in the mid-1980s came from President Mitterrand. Sometimes the President has been willing to delegate power to one of his ministers. During de Gaulle's presidency, for instance, the Minister of Information drafted the 1964 broadcasting statute. He also ensured that television news was pro-Gaullist in content and tone through a combination of partisan political appointments and close supervision of editorial decisions. However, since the early 1970s the guiding hand has generally emanated from the Elysée.[13]

The point to stress here is not just that the French media have evolved against the backdrop of these political factors. It is rather that the development of the press, radio and television has been strongly conditioned by them. The key political actor in this context, and one whose role must be central to any analysis of the media in France, is the state. The multiple linkages between the state and the media since the Liberation include the following:[14]

1 **The ownership of radio stations and television channels**. Up until 1982 the state had a monopoly in the ownership of the broadcasting media. This state monopoly was entrusted to a single broadcasting corporation until 1974 and then to separate radio and television companies. In addition, through its participation in the holding company Sofirad, the state indirectly owned a share in several peripheral radio stations such as Europe 1, while through its stake in Havas it had a controlling interest in Radiodiffusion-Télévision Luxembourg. Private ownership of the broadcasting media was introduced only during the 1980s.

2 **The formulation of media policy**. Through its policy-making role and specifically by means of legislation the state determines the rules by which the media operate. Since the Liberation there have been several major statutes on broadcasting (1964, 1972, 1974, 1982, 1986 and 1989) and three important pieces of legislation on the press (1944, 1984 and 1986), plus a plethora of supplementary decrees, ordinances and policy documents. During the postwar period these state-sponsored measures have ranged from macro-initiatives which have radically altered the configuration of the media system (such as the establishment of commercial television channels) to micro-measures targeted at specific aspects of media performance (such as programming obligations for television, the allocation of political broadcasts during election campaigns and rules covering the

provision of a minimum broadcast service during industrial action by broadcasting personnel). The state has also introduced measures designed to prevent concentration of ownership in the media, has passed a privacy law covering press activities and in the 1980s established three consecutive regulatory authorities to supervise the functioning of the broadcasting system.

3 **Control of media finance**. The state gives financial subsidies to the press. Through its control of the banking sector it has also been able to play an influential role in the reorganization of press groups and the restructuring of the newspaper industry.[15] Up until recently the state held a controlling interest in France's largest advertising agency, Havas, and was a major purchaser of advertising in the media. The state sets the level of the licence fee for public sector radio and television. It was the state which allowed the introduction of advertising on television in 1968 and set statutory limits on its contribution to broadcasting turnover. Finally, in the 1950s and 1960s the state played a highly interventionist role in the spending decisions of the state broadcasting organization.

4 **The power of appointment to key decision-making posts**. For most of the postwar period the state appointed the director general of the state broadcasting corporation and controlled (or at least influenced) other key managerial and editorial appointments. During the 1980s and early 1990s the state controlled the majority of appointments to the broadcasting regulatory authorities. In addition, the state has consistently enjoyed close links with the media through a system of interlocking personnel.[16]

5 **The capacity to influence the news agenda through the primary definition of issues, media manipulation and censorship**. The French state has sought to define the media agenda and influence the content of political information in the press, on radio and on television. For a time it controlled the principal news agency in France, Agence France-Presse. It has utilized an impressive array of weapons to try to ensure that media coverage of its activities is favourable and supportive. These have ranged from the primary definition of issues by means of press releases and ministerial statements to outright censorship and seizure of publications. Such intervention has been particularly crucial (though not always successful) at politically sensitive periods such as the 1968 'events', the Rainbow Warrior scandal and the French military involvement in the Gulf War.

6 **The use of the media to further other state policy goals**. The state has used its powerful position in the media sector to assist the implementation of its objectives in other policy fields. For instance, in the 1980s the state made decisions about investment in the new media of cable and satellite

to ensure that their technological development would be in accord with the goals of French industrial policy. In the 1960s the state used its monopoly control of broadcasting to influence television programme output so that it conformed with the general thrust of state cultural policy.

In the light of the key role played by the postwar state in the French media, it is tempting to paint a picture of state omnicompetence and even omnipotence in this area. However, an account of the French media system in terms of state domination of the press, radio and television, exercised through a combination of direct and indirect, overt and covert controls, needs to be severely qualified. A simple state power thesis is too static and monolithic, failing to account both for change in the relationship between the state and the media over time and for conflict within the state apparatus.

Far from being static, the links between the state and the media are dynamic and subject to constant change. For example, the links between the state and television are very different in the 1990s from what they were in the 1960s. Though still a key player in the media system, the state does not have the field to itself. Non-state actors are now active on the media scene, constraining the exercise of state power. The ownership of newspapers, much of local radio and a large share of the television market is in private hands. In terms of ownership the past decade has witnessed a marked decrease in the role of the state, following the abandonment of the broadcasting monopoly in 1982. Not only has private local radio been legalized and commercial television channels established, but a major television channel (TF1) was removed from the public sector and privatized in 1987. Commercial companies have also taken a major stake in the cable industry as network operators. Under the original 1982 cable plan the state also devolved some powers of control to local authorities. This was a decentralizing initiative without precedent in the audiovisual field, which for so long had been marked by a strong attachment to the centralist Jacobin tradition.

Advertising as a source of revenue has also increased in importance with the commercialization and privatization of radio and television. Control of the licence fee remains a powerful tool for the state *vis-à-vis* public sector radio and television, but it is no longer a weapon which can be brandished over the whole of the broadcasting media. The state's power of appointment has also been eclipsed both by the growth of private sector media and the establishment of regulatory authorities in the audiovisual field. While sometimes the regulatory authorities have acted as transmission belts for decisions taken by the state authorities and at other times have been simply ignored, they have still to some extent curtailed the power of the state to appoint political sympathizers to key decision-making posts in public sector broadcasting. Finally, the growth in the media in the 1980s, especially in radio and television, has of itself weakened the capacity of the state to exert control over content. As the number of information sources has expanded, it has become both more difficult and less rewarding for the authorities to control the output of any single source.

As for the coherence of the state apparatus, the French state is internally divided and riddled with conflict. Sometimes this assumes a party political form, as in the period of Right–Left *cohabitation* between 1986 and 1988 or the Giscardian–Gaullist conflict of the late 1970s. More frequently, conflict manifests itself as a struggle between ministries or administrative agencies, as in the internecine strife over new media policy in the 1980s between the state transmission company, TDF, and the telecommunications wing of the PTT ministry, the DGT.

As an alternative to the state power thesis, it might be argued that the defining characteristic of the relationship between the state and the French media has not been unwavering state dominance, but rather the withdrawal of the state from an initial monopoly position, followed by economic and political liberalization of the media as ownership and control are taken over by private interests. From this perspective the history of the French press and broadcasting reveals an early period of state domination, followed by a marked relaxation of state intervention and control once the medium has reached maturity, as happened with the press in the late nineteenth century and broadcasting in the 1980s.[17] However, the argument that the history of the French media is one of inexorable liberalization from state control is not wholly persuasive either. For example, this model is particularly inapplicable to the case of radio. Though radio was officially a state monopoly during the inter-war years, in practice the existence of several private stations was tolerated. State control of radio was not effectively established until the advent of the collaborationist Vichy regime. Moreover, with regard to the press, state intervention in the immediate postwar period brought an end to an era in which newspapers had been remarkably free from government controls.

The liberalization thesis appears to be more relevant if the analysis is confined to the period since 1945. In the immediate postwar years the state became heavily involved in the media, as owner, regulator, financial controller, source of patronage, primary definer of issues and censor. In contrast, during the 1980s the state transferred its ownership of much of the audiovisual media into the private sector, while its role as censor had also declined in significance. However, two caveats are important in this context. First, even when applied only to the period since 1945, the liberalization thesis needs to be qualified. While the role of the state may have lessened on some dimensions, it clearly has not on others. The state may have less of an ownership stake in the media, but it remains a powerful regulator and primary definer. It is important, therefore, to distinguish between different forms and degrees of state intervention and control.

Second, inasmuch as economic and political liberalization have taken place, it cannot be taken for granted that this process will continue or that it is irreversible. Different political circumstances, such as a regime crisis, could well result in a return to a more interventionist role for the state.

The book aims to provide the reader with an overview of the structures and functioning of the French media system, particularly emphasizing key aspects of the complex interrelationship between the media and the state. Its central focus is on the period since the Liberation, though in the chapters on the press and radio historical material from the period before 1944 is also included. The book is principally organized by media sector (press, radio, television and the new media), with the four chapters on television being divided chronologically. Chapter 1 provides a general introduction to the press, highlighting the history and economics of the daily newspaper sector. Chapter 2 examines two key features of the politics of the press: its linkages with the state and with political parties. Chapter 3 looks at the development of radio from its origins at the end of the First World War to the emergence of private local radio networks in the late 1980s. The next four chapters focus on television, tracing its evolution from the end of the Second World War up to the early 1990s. Chapter 4 examines television during the de Gaulle presidency; chapter 5 covers the Pompidou and Giscard d'Estaing presidencies; chapter 6 concentrates on the period of the first Socialist government (1981–86); and chapter 7 deals with the period since 1986. Chapter 8 looks at the new media of cable and satellite. In the Conclusion some common threads of the analysis are drawn together and key issues on the media policy agenda in the 1990s are examined.

Chapter 1

The press: history and economics

With a total of 2,913 separate titles published in 1990, the press in contemporary France encompasses a wide spectrum of printed material.[1] It includes local, regional and national newspapers, published daily and weekly, catering for a variety of tastes, interests and points of view. It also comprises specialist magazines and periodicals, which seek to satisfy the myriad demands for information, education and entertainment of a variegated, heterogeneous society. The geographical, social and cultural diversity of France is to a large degree reflected in the richness of its press. So too are different shades of economic, party political and ideological opinion. Taken at face value, the press industry in France produces a very broad range of products – from simple local freesheets to glossy international magazines – from which consumers can make their choice. As a result, the French press appears to be a system of bewildering complexity, whose main characteristics tend to militate against the formulation of simple overarching generalizations.

Yet at the same time there is evidence of countervailing trends to offset this initial picture of apparently healthy pluralism. Faced with competition in a media-rich environment, some sections of the press have contracted and gone into decline. In key sectors there has been a clear tendency towards concentration of ownership and in many parts of France domination of the market by a single regional newspaper is the norm. A small number of companies, most notably the Hersant group, have spread their tentacles to control broad swathes of the press and publishing industries. Moreover, the diversification strategy followed by several of these groups has included attempts to extend their controlling interests to incorporate other media.[2] As a result, the issue of control of information by a few multimedia companies has come on to the policy agenda, raising important questions about their political and economic power.

Indeed, much of the postwar policy debate on the press in France has reflected the tension between the desirability of promoting pluralism and diversity on the one hand and the recognition of the weight of economic factors working in favour of concentration and rationalization on the other.

What is taken to be the optimal balancing point in this equation reflects the different ideological views of media practitioners and policy makers alike. In particular, the nature and extent of state intervention to remedy perceived defects in the operation of the market remains a thorny issue on which, predictably, it has proved impossible to achieve political or media consensus.

This theme is one of several covered in this and the following chapter on the press. This first chapter begins with a historical overview of the development of the press from the late eighteenth century to the present day, charting the rise and decline of the press as a mass medium of communication. The main focus in this section (as throughout chapters 1 and 2) is on daily newspapers. The second section examines those economic features which have exerted a significant impact on the configuration of the postwar press system. The short concluding section places the press within the context of the French media system as a whole, emphasizing both the complementarity and competition between the press and the audiovisual media.

THE HISTORY OF THE PRESS

The golden age of the French press: 1870–1914

The press is by far the oldest of the mass media in France. The first periodical was published in 1631, while the first daily newspaper, the *Journal de Paris*, appeared in 1777. Unprecedented political freedom in the period immediately following the 1789 Revolution, combined with low publishing costs, resulted in a rapid growth in the number of newspaper titles.[3] As a result, domestic politics began to be covered more fully than ever before, while at the same time a tradition of overtly partisan journalism started to take root. Once the initial revolutionary fervour had died down, however, many of these newspapers disappeared as a climate of reaction set in. The 1848 Revolution led to another huge surge in the number of newspaper titles published. Again, however, many of them did not survive for long. Some gave up the ghost even before the short-lived Second Republic (1848–51) was replaced by the repressive regime of the Second Empire (1851–70). Others were suppressed soon after the *coup d'état* of December 1851.

Apart from these two short periods after the 1789 and 1848 Revolutions, none of the other regimes which governed France prior to the establishment of the Third Republic (1870–1940) was particularly beneficial towards the press.[4] It was not until the last quarter of the nineteenth century that the press began a period of unprecedented development during which it achieved the status of a medium of *mass* communication. More particularly, in the years between the collapse of the Second Empire in 1870 and the outbreak of the First World War in 1914, the daily newspaper press underwent a massive expansion in both the number of different titles published and the size of its total readership.

Even a brief examination of the relevant aggregate statistics on the daily press reveals the phenomenal extent of the growth during this period. In 1870 the total print run of daily newspapers was 1,420,000, which represented the publication of a mere 37 dailies for every 1,000 members of the population. In the same year there were 36 Paris-based and 100 provincial daily titles. In contrast, by 1914 there were as many as 80 different Paris dailies and no fewer than 242 provincial daily titles (see tables 1.1 and 1.2). Moreover, during the same period the total print run of daily papers had reached 9,500,000, which represented an impressive total of 244 daily papers for every 1,000 inhabitants. This spectacular market penetration enabled France to occupy first place in Europe for the number of daily newspapers produced per capita (Great Britain sold only 160 per 1,000 inhabitants in 1914), due in no small part to the fact that French newspapers were among the cheapest in the world. Little wonder then that for many commentators this period represented the golden age of the French press.[5]

This historic growth was attributable to the fortuitous combination of various factors – technological, economic, social and political – which by the outbreak of the First World War had placed the French press at or near the top of the international league table. For example, during the nineteenth century major technical advances were made in the composition, publishing and distribution of newspapers, all of which helped transform the press from an artisanal craft into an industrial enterprise. Whereas previous technical developments had been limited to incremental improvements to the existing arrangements, by the late nineteenth century the scope and pace of change had brought about a paradigmatic shift in production and distribution methods. A whole new era in newspaper publishing had begun.

The invention of the rotary press was part of this technological leap forward. It greatly speeded up the process of printing, with the result that by the 1860s 16,000 sheets per hour could be printed, compared with only 2,000 sheets per hour 40 years previously. Innovations in typesetting and the spread of electrical power also played an important role in improving newspaper production.[6] The advent of the telegraph facilitated the collection and transfer of information, while the expansion of the railway network – particularly during the Second Empire – was crucial in improving distribution.[7] In short, major technical advances in the publishing industry and transportation infrastructure lay at the heart of the late nineteenth-century flourishing of the newspaper press in France.

At the same time the period saw the emergence of enterprising industrialists and financiers. Recognizing that progress in technology could be harnessed to create a new popular market for newspapers, they regarded the press as an economic sector ripe for commercial development and

Table 1.1 Number of daily newspaper titles 1788–1990

Year	Paris	Provinces	Total
1788	2	1	3
1803	11		
1812	4	4	8
1815	8		
1825	12		
1831–32	17	32	49
1846	25		
1850		64	
1852	12		
1863	16	60	76
1867	21	57	78
1870	36	100	136
1880	60	190	250
1885		250	
1908	70		
1910	73		
1914	80	242	322
1917	48		
1924	30		
1939	31	175	206
1946	28	175	203
1952	14	117	131
1972	11	78	89
1975	12	71	83
1980	12	73	85
1983	13	74	87
1985	12	70	82
1987	12	67	79
1990	11	62	73

Blanks indicate that numbers are unavailable

Sources: P. Albert, *La presse française*, Paris, La documentation française, 1990, p.32; SJTI, *Tableaux statistiques de la presse1990*, Paris, La documentation française,1992, p.86.

exploitation.[8] With the aid of mass production techniques, the industrialization of the publication process led to a lowering in the cover price of newspapers, which in turn helped boost sales. In 1863 the sale of *Le Petit Journal* at 5 centimes a copy led to the introduction into the market of what were to become mass circulation newspapers, 'specifically designed for the masses and not for those interested in politics'.[9] By 1880 *Le Petit Journal* had a circulation of 582,000, four times that of its nearest rival and more than a quarter of all the Paris dailies put together.[10]

Meanwhile growing literacy rates and the spread of education in the latter part of the nineteenth century under the aegis of the Jules Ferry legislation led to a greater public demand for information, comment and

Table1.2 Daily newspaper print-run figures 1788–1990 (in '000s)

Year	Paris	Provinces	Total	Number of copies per 1,000 inhabitants
1788	4	0.5	4.5	0.2
1803	36			
1812	35	3	38	1.3
1815	34			
1825	59			
1831–32	83	20	103	3
1846	145			
1850		60		
1852	160			
1863	200	120	320	8.5
1867	763	200	963	25
1870	1,070	350	1,420	37
1880	2,000	750	2,750	73
1885		1,000		
1908	4,777			
1910	4,920			
1914	5,500	4,000	9,500	244
1917	8,250			
1924	4,400			
1939	5,500	5,500	11,000	261
1946	5,959	9,165	15,124	370
1952	3,412	6,188	9,600	218
1972	3,877	7,798	11,675	221
1975	3,195	7,411	10,606	200
1980	2,913	7,535	10,448	195
1983	2,877	7,241	10,118	185
1985	2,777	7,109	9,886	178
1987	2,713	7,030	9,743	176
1990	2,741	7,010	9,751	173

Blanks indicate that numbers are unavailable

Sources: P. Albert, La presse française, Paris, La documentation française, 1990, p.32; SJTI, Tableaux statistiques de la presse 1990, Paris, La documentation française, 1992, p.86.

entertainment, which the press rushed to satisfy. Papers increased their number of pages, while their content widened to cover a broader range of social and cultural topics as well as the more traditional political material. Numbers entering the journalistic profession grew as the press became an important source of employment.

The new mass circulation papers which sprang up around this time included Le Petit Parisien, which after the turn of the century became the biggest-selling newspaper in France (and indeed the world) with a print run of 1.5 million copies by 1914. In fact, four papers (Le Petit Journal, Le Petit

Parisien, Le Matin and *Le Journal*) enjoyed a combined circulation of 4.5 million before the First World War. In addition to these mass circulation papers, a whole new generation of smaller-scale newspapers sprang up, while many existing ones took advantage of the growth in public demand to increase their circulation. These included quality newspapers serving an elite market, as well as newspapers with a strong partisan political commitment. The local and regional press also benefited from expansion. By the late nineteenth century large regional papers were already becoming a feature of the French press system, with fierce competition taking place between different newspapers in the main towns across the country.

Political developments also played a part in helping to bring about a regulatory framework more sympathetic to the expansion of the press at this time. For example, the provisions of the 1881 press statute, which guaranteed freedom of opinion and the right to publish, were indicative of a major change of attitude on the part of the state authorities towards the print media.[11] Moreover, this change in press legislation coincided with the implantation in France of a political system of parliamentary democracy based on (male) universal suffrage, a measure which in itself provoked greater interest among the citizenry in political information.[12] While to a large extent, therefore, the impetus behind the development of the newspaper press in the late nineteenth century lay in a combination of technological, economic and social changes, a new political climate also made an important contribution.

The inter-war years

The First World War brought the golden age of the French press to an inglorious end. During the conflict the government instituted a system of ferocious censorship to boost national morale. However successful this policy may have been in the short term in mobilizing popular support for the war, the brainwashing propaganda campaign appeared to alienate a large section of the newspaper readership. At the same time the press had to cope with an adverse combination of economic circumstances which seriously affected newspaper production and distribution: an acute shortage of labour, severe restrictions on the supply of paper, troublesome transportation problems, a marked reduction in advertising revenue and a general increase in production costs. While the mass circulation papers were better able to withstand these adverse conditions, many newspapers were not so resilient and were forced to close down.

Between the two world wars there was a marked decline in the number of daily newspaper titles published. The number of Paris dailies had dropped to 31 by 1939, while their provincial counterparts had fallen back to 175. In contrast, the total daily newspaper print run had edged up to 11 million by 1939, almost all of which was due to the expanding circulation of the provincial dailies. The big regional papers in particular were becoming more important players in the newspaper market. By the outbreak of the Second World War parity between the Paris and provincial dailies had been attained, with total print runs of about 5.5 million each.

The powerful position enjoyed by press barons came to the fore during the inter-war period. The most successful of these was the textile manufacturer Jean Prouvost, a future owner of *Le Figaro*, who made a spectacular entry into the newspaper market with his 'straightforward commercial approach'.[13] In 1930 he purchased the daily evening paper *Paris-Soir* which at the time had a derisory circulation. Through a combination of sensational reporting, serious journalism, pictures and sports coverage, the paper became a major success story with a print run of well over 1.5 million by 1939. Prouvost also launched a successful weekly women's magazine, *Marie-Claire*, in 1937. Finally, just before the outbreak of the Second World War, he took over the sports magazine *Match* and turned it into a weekly news magazine, which a few years after the war was re-launched with the slightly new title of *Paris-Match*. As an illustrated weekly news magazine *Paris-Match* was to constitute 'one of the most glaring successes of the postwar French press'.[14] The Prouvost formula for success, however, was not typical in a decade punctuated by economic crisis and political scandals. Though the total circulation of daily papers increased gradually between the wars, the per capita growth was small. Moreover, comparison with Great Britain showed the extent to which the French press was falling behind in international terms. Whereas 261 newspapers per 1,000 inhabitants were sold in France in 1939, in Britain the corresponding figure had already reached 360.

Vichy and Resistance

Inevitably the Second World War entailed massive dislocating consequences for the French press, as the population came to terms with the psychological shock of military defeat, the grim reality of Nazi occupation in the North and the vainglorious pretensions of the Vichy regime in the South. It is tempting to present a simple picture of a wartime society divided between the antithetical reactions of collaboration and resistance. In fact, however, these polar opposites were only two among a range of several possible responses to the unfurling of events between 1940 and 1944. A wait-and-see attitude (*attentisme*) was particularly widespread in French society. However, the official and clandestine press tended to emphasize the simplistic duality rather than reflect the complexity of reactions to the issues of German occupation, Pétainism and de Gaulle's call to continue the fight against the Nazi invader. If the press is rarely an accurate mirror of any society, during the Second World War the propaganda of the French press grossly distorted the range and strength of public opinion.

In terms of press organization, the fall of France in 1940 led to many of the Paris papers such as *Le Temps* and *Paris-Soir* fleeing to the provinces, most notably to Lyons. Others simply stopped publishing altogether. With the country divided into two zones, several Paris papers operating in the southern zone found themselves deprived of their natural readership in the capital. Along with the local and regional dailies, they also had to counter a whole series of production difficulties, as well as being subject to severe Vichy censorship.[15] After the German invasion of the southern zone in 1942, most of the Paris dailies which had earlier moved south abandoned publishing. In the northern zone the officially sanctioned press was naturally dominated by collaborationist papers for the whole period after 1940.[16]

During the war the influence of the pro-Vichy and pro-Nazi press was to some extent offset by the publication of clandestine newspapers (as well as by BBC radio broadcasts from London) sympathetic to the views of de Gaulle and the Resistance.[17] This clandestine press was a vital means of spreading the ideals of the Resistance, mobilizing support for its activities and maintaining a sense of solidarity.[18] The launch of a clandestine newspaper was a major gesture of defiance against the authorities, and those who took this initiative ran a great risk of discovery and punishment. Kedward describes the decision to set up a clandestine newspaper as a significant act of political engagement.

> The commitment which this involved was a decisive step in moving from attitudes to action, and the process of distribution necessitated new contacts and wider liaisons. The ripples of revolt began to spread. Producing a newspaper was a well-established political reflex in France, and should not be seen as an avoidance of more effective action. . . . It was now a means of creating and sustaining new groups of activists, and having to do it secretly meant that increasing numbers of recruits were rapidly introduced to the problems and risks of clandestine activity.[19]

Using the press as a means of political participation to influence public opinion was not an innovation of the Resistance movement. The founders of clandestine publications during the Second World War were corresponding

> closely to precedents in French history when struggle for public opinion had issued in a flood of publications. This was to happen in 1941 as it had in the Dreyfus Affair of the 1890s, the last years of World War 1, and the middle years of the 1930s, and those who created newspapers or information sheets were perpetuating patterns of behaviour which extended well beyond their own individual or group experience.[20]

It is no coincidence that the three main Resistance movements in the southern zone became known by the name of their newspapers: *Combat*,

Franc-Tireur and *Libération (sud)*, while in the occupied zone the same was true of the Paris-based movements *Libération (nord)* and *Défense de la France*.[21] The Socialist party paper *Le Populaire* appeared as a clandestine paper in 1942. The Communist party newspaper *L'Humanité* re-emerged clandestinely in October 1939, though until June 1941 when Nazi Germany declared war on the Soviet Union it 'never ceased demanding the authorisation to publish legally' and for a time even 'encouraged the French workman to fraternise with German soldiers'.[22]

The number of different clandestine titles was impressive, as was the political spectrum covered: Catholic, Socialist, Communist and Gaullist among others. Moreover, the clandestine press became well organized and highly professional in its operations.

> In April 1942 Jean Moulin set up a *Bureau d'information et de presse* under the direction of Georges Bidault, ex-editor of *L'Aube*, which set out to link the clandestine press of both zones. On the directing committee professional journalists from the southern zone were in the majority. . . . The Bureau later began to issue daily bulletins from which the rest of the clandestine press gathered much of its news. In organizational terms it was a recognition of the vital significance of journalism and communication in the growth of the Resistance and a rationalization of the underground press as a sector of activity on its own, manned by professionals.[23]

As the defeat of the Nazis came to seem the likeliest outcome of the war, the clandestine press formed a national federation at the end of 1943.[24] In agreement with the Resistance organizations and the Provisional Government, this federation was to help shape the content of legislation on the press after the Liberation. Thus, the press system which emerged in France in the immediate postwar years was to a very large extent determined by the wartime experience and in particular owed much to the ideas of the Resistance.

The press since the Liberation

The immediate post-Liberation period saw a sharp increase in the total print run of daily newspapers in comparison with pre-war figures: over 15 million in 1946 compared with 11 million in 1939. The explosion in circulation figures can be explained by an enormous hunger for information after the famine of the war years, the pace of institutional and political change, and the flourishing of new social and economic ideas. Most of this increase benefited the provincial press, whose print run went up from 5.5 million in 1939 to over 9 million in 1946. Overall, however, there was some shrinkage in the number of different daily newspaper titles. The number of Paris dailies dropped slightly from 31 in 1939 to 28 in 1946, while the total of provincial dailies remained constant at 175. Yet in general, despite – or as a result of – all the changes which had taken place in the press system at the end of the Second World War, the daily newspaper market was in an apparently healthy condition in 1946. Circulation figures for daily newspapers had never been higher, while the large inter-war drop in the number of newspaper titles had been virtually halted (see tables 1.1 and 1.2).

Many new newspapers were established in the months following the Liberation, with party political papers particularly in evidence in this initial postwar period.[25] With the majority of prewar newspaper owners discredited and their assets sequestrated, France now witnessed nothing short of a revolution in the ownership and control of its press. Newspapers founded in 1944 included new national dailies such as *Le Parisien libéré* and *France-Soir* which was the postwar embodiment of the clandestine Resistance paper, *Défense de la France*. *Le Monde* too was set up in 1944 to provide France with a newspaper of reference in the style of the pre-war *Le Temps*. The ranks of the provincial press also welcomed a host of newcomers after the Liberation. They included *Nice-Matin*, *Le Provençal*, *Le Midi libre*, *Sud-Ouest*, *La Voix du Nord* and *Ouest-France*, to name but a few of the major regional dailies. New personalities, including Emilien Amaury, Hubert Beuve-Méry, Gaston Defferre and Pierre Lazareff, entered into the operations of the French press, many of them coming straight from the ranks of the Resistance.[26]

This postwar boom was short-lived. Sales began to decline, the number of titles shrank and the ethos of the Resistance quickly evaporated.

As interest in news subsided and the economy stagnated, the new papers were forced gradually either out of business or into the hands of people willing to apply new capital to their development. In 1947 a month-long printers' strike led to the loss of scores of papers, and the sudden miracle of a 'decapitalized' press was over, together with much of the spirit of the Resistance. Many of the pre-war press-owners, including Prouvost, who had been banned from owning papers at the Liberation, returned to their businesses, and France ceased to be among the major newspaper-consuming countries of the world.[27]

Following the high point of 1946 the daily newspaper press entered a period which was generally marked by either decline or stagnation, punctuated by sporadic bursts of growth. The number of Paris-based daily titles decreased from 28 in 1946 to 11 in 1990, while the number of provincial daily titles shrank from 175 to 62 over the same period. Total print-run figures for daily newspapers peaked at just over 15 million in 1946, but then quickly dropped back to under 13 million the following year. This downward trend continued with the result that, by the end of the 1940s, total daily newspaper print run had declined to around 11 million. Since then it has exceeded 13 million only in 1968 (the year of the famous 'events') and it fell below 10 million in four consecutive years in the mid-1980s (see tables 1.3 and 1.4).

Within this overall picture of daily newspaper sales figures it is important to note peaks and troughs. The print run of Paris dailies declined until 1952, stayed between 3.5 and 4.5 million until 1967, touched 5 million briefly in 1968 and since then has been on a steady decline. Total print-run figures of Paris dailies in the 1980s exceeded 3 million in one year only – 1981 – the year of François Mitterrand's first presidential election victory. The provincial daily press witnessed a similar decline between 1946 and 1952, saw its print run hovering between 6.5 and 7.5 million until the mid-1960s, touched over 8 million in 1967 and 1968 and since then has never fallen below 7 million.

A study of daily newspaper consumption in France is revealing. The French in general are poor consumers of the daily newspaper press compared with the British, Americans, Japanese, Scandinavians and most Northern Europeans, though they do come ahead of the Italians, Spanish, Greeks and Portuguese (see table 1.5). In fact, in most parts of France, the majority of households do not regularly take a daily newspaper.[28] The greater Paris area shows a particularly low level of newspaper consumption, with only just over one in four residents reading a newspaper every day.[29] Daily newspaper readership across the country shows the following sociological characteristics: a higher proportion of men than women, more elderly than young or middle-aged, and a slightly larger percentage of rural and small town inhabitants than city dwellers.

The poor sales performance of daily newspapers in France appears much worse when one takes into account the increase in the population and the spread of higher education during the postwar period. In 1990 a population of over 56 million read fewer papers than a population of 39 million did in 1945.[30] Regular reading of a daily newspaper has been on the decline for some time: from 59.7 per cent of French people in 1967 to 55.1 per cent in 1973, 46.1 per cent in 1981, 45 per cent in 1983 and a meagre 41.3 per cent in 1988.[31] This situation is in part attributable to the constant increase in sales price, especially evident since the 1970s.[32] The rise in the price of French newspapers has far outpaced general price inflation and has made them considerably more expensive than those in Britain and many other European countries.[33] Weaknesses in the distribution network have also been put forward as an explanatory factor, particularly the limited development of direct delivery to households.[34] In addition, there is evidence of a declining trust on the part of readers in newspaper content and less willingness than previously to believe in the independence of journalists.[35] A particularly worrying statistic for newspaper owners is that in 1988 only one in four of the 15–24 age group regularly read a daily newspaper – a 50 per cent decline in 20 years. The problem here may be the emergence of widespread aliteracy – a growth in the number of

Table1.3 Number of daily newspaper titles 1945–90

Year	Paris	Provinces	Total
1945	26	153	179
1946	28	175	203
1947	19	161	180
1948	18	142	155
1949	16	139	145
1950	16	126	142
1951	15	122	137
1952	14	117	131
1953	12	116	128
1954	12	116	128
1955	13	116	129
1956	14	111	125
1957	13	110	123
1958	13	110	123
1959	13	103	116
1960	13	98	111
1961	13	96	109
1962	13	96	109
1963	14	94	108
1964	14	93	107
1965	13	92	105
1966	14	91	105
1967	12	86	98
1968	13	85	98
1969	13	81	94
1970	13	81	94
1971	12	81	93
1972	11	78	89
1973	12	75	87
1974	13	73	86
1975	12	71	83
1976	13	71	84
1977	15	72	87
1978	15	72	87
1979	13	72	85
1980	12	73	85
1981	12	73	85
1982	13	74	87
1983	13	74	87
1984	13	70	83
1985	12	70	82
1986	12	67	79
1987	12	67	79
1988	11	65	76
1989	11	64	75
1990	11	62	73

Source: SJTI, *Tableaux statistiques de la presse 1990*, Paris, La documentation française, 1992, p.86.

Table1.4   Daily newspaper print-run figures 1945–90 (in '000s)

Year	Paris	Provinces	Total
1945	4,606	7,532	12,138
1946	5,959	9,165	15,124
1947	4,702	8,165	12,867
1948	4,450	7,859	12,309
1949	3,792	7,417	11,209
1950	3,678	7,256	10,934
1951	3,607	6,634	10,241
1952	3,412	6,188	9,600
1953	3,514	6,458	9,972
1954	3,618	6,559	10,177
1955	3,779	6,823	10,602
1956	4,441	6,958	11,399
1957	4,226	7,254	11,480
1958	4,373	7,294	11,667
1959	3,980	6,930	10,910
1960	4,185	7,170	11,355
1961	4,239	7,087	11,326
1962	4,207	7,198	11,405
1963	4,121	7,434	11,555
1964	4,107	7,617	11,724
1965	4,211	7,857	12,068
1966	4,391	7,831	12,222
1967	4,624	8,005	12,629
1968	5,034	8,039	13,073
1969	4,596	7,572	12,168
1970	4,278	7,587	11,865
1971	4,244	7,750	11,994
1972	3,877	7,798	11,675
1973	3,707	7,506	11,213
1974	3,831	7,509	11,340
1975	3,195	7,411	10,606
1976	2,970	7,197	10,167
1977	3,185	7,391	10,576
1978	3,173	7,370	10,543
1979	3,041	7,468	10,509
1980	2,913	7,535	10,448
1981	3,193	7,629	10,822
1982	2,779	7,332	10,111
1983	2,877	7,241	10,118
1984	2,707	7,200	9,907
1985	2,777	7,109	9,886
1986	2,885	7,109	9,994
1987	2,713	7,030	9,743
1988	2,942	7,155	10,097
1989	2,828	7,093	9,921
1990	2,741	7,010	9,751

Source: SJTI, *Tableaux statistiques de la presse 1990*, Paris, La documentation française, 1992, p.86.

Table1.5 Number of copies of daily newspapers per 1,000 inhabitants

Country	1960	1970	1979	1984	1986	1987
Australia	358	321	336	296		
Belgium	285	260	228	223	187	185
Canada	222	218	241	220		
Denmark	353	363	367	359	358	356
Finland	359	392	480	535		
France	252	238	196	185	176	175
Germany (West)	307	326	323	350	341	345
Great Britain	514	463	426	414	403	398
Greece					134	132
Italy	122	144	93	96	111	116
Japan	396	511	569	562		
Netherlands	283	315	325	310	312	314
Norway	377	383	456	501		
Portugal					30	30
Spain					78	78
Sweden	490	537	526	521		
USA	326	302	282	268		

Blanks indicate that numbers are unavailable

Sources: P. Albert, *La presse française*, Paris, La documentation française, 1990, p.34; J.-M. Charon, *La presse en France de 1945 à nos jours*, Paris, Seuil, 1991, p.396.

people who, although they *can* read, do not see reading as a pleasurable activity.[36]

One of the most notable aspects of the French press since 1945 has been the dominance of provincial daily newspapers over those produced in Paris.[37] This phenomenon dates from the Liberation, though the trend in favour of the provincial press was established long before. During most of the nineteenth century the market share of the provincial dailies varied between 20 per cent and 38 per cent of total daily newspaper sales. By the outbreak of the First World War this share had risen to 44 per cent, while by the start of the Second World War the provincial and Paris newspapers each took 50 per cent of the daily market.[38] While during the inter-war period the Paris dailies had larger circulation figures than their provincial counterparts, the latter were catching up and achieved market dominance after the Liberation.

Moreover, in contrast to some other developments in the press since the Liberation, this superiority of provincial over Paris-based newspapers has never been reversed. In 1988, for example, of the 10 million total print run of daily newspapers in France, over 7 million were provincial papers and less than 3 million were Paris dailies. Whereas in 1946 provincial dailies accounted for just over 60 per cent of total daily newspaper print run, by 1970 this had risen to just under 64 per cent. Ten years later it had further increased to over 72 per cent and it remained around the 70 per cent mark during the 1980s.[39]

In 1976 for the first time a regional paper, *Ouest-France* (Rennes), became the biggest-selling daily in France. Its circulation in 1991 was 794,000. (The top-selling Paris daily, *Le Figaro*, had a circulation of 423,000 in the same year.) Other high-circulation regional dailies included *La Voix du Nord* (Lille, 371,000), *Sud-Ouest* (Bordeaux, 367,000), *Le Progrès* (Lyons, 387,000) and *Le Dauphiné libéré* (Grenoble, 293,000). In 1991 11 regional dailies had a circulation of 200,000 or more (compared with five Paris dailies), including four exceeding 350,000 (see table 1.6). In 1990 the top 11 regional dailies together accounted for well over 50 per cent of the total print run of the provincial daily press.

The legacy of the Second World War helped the provincial press in its battle against the Paris papers. The wartime division of the country into an occupied and an unoccupied zone, with the capital firmly under Nazi control, increased the importance of the provincial press over its Paris counterpart.[40] Another factor working in favour of the provincial press was that in the immediate postwar period, when rationing was still in force, local and regional newspapers were the major source of information regarding the availability of food supplies in the locality. Yet however important these features of the press during the war and its immediate aftermath, they clearly cannot account for a trend which was already in evidence before 1939, nor explain the postwar consolidation of the unchallenged dominance of the provincial press.

The great importance attached to regional identity in France has no doubt contributed to the powerful position of the provincial press. Strong identification with heterogeneous sub-national cultural traditions and communities helps underpin the strength of provincial newspapers in their competition with the Paris dailies. Despite the creation of ever faster and more efficient communication and transportation networks, many French people cling tenaciously to their local roots, taking a great interest in information relevant to events and personalities in their particular locality or region. The provincial papers are well placed to satisfy this demand, with their extensive coverage of local and regional information, ranging from news to classified advertising.

The status of locally based political *notables* may also have helped the provincial press by concentrating public attention on local political figures and issues. In the parliamentary systems of the Third and Fourth Republics, deputies and senators frequently acted as champions of local and regional interests in Parliament, using their influence in the national political sphere to secure both protectionist legislation for local interest groups and the allocation of state resources to their local fiefdoms. If successful, they were rewarded with favourable press coverage in their constituencies. Even in the presidential system of the Fifth Republic, during which parties have become more disciplined and the national party organizations have increased their power at the expense of local party structures,

Table1.6 Circulation of regional daily newspapers in 1990 and 1991 (in '000s)

Newspaper	1990	1991
L'Alsace (Mulhouse)	125.8	126.0
L'Ardennais (Charleville)	27.3	27.2
Le Berry républicain (Bourges)	37.5	37.6
Le Bien public (Dijon)	52.2	51.5
Centre-Presse (Poitiers)	21.4	23.1
Centre-Presse (Rodez)	25.0	25.2
La Charente libre (Angoulême)	40.2	40.3
Le Courrier de Saône-et-Loire (Chalon)	44.6	80.6
Le Courrier de l'Ouest (Angers)	109.0	107.5
Courrier picard/Courrier de l'Oise	80.4	81.6
Le Dauphiné libéré (Grenoble)	296.4	293.2
La Dépêche du Midi (Toulouse)	233.4	228.2
Les Dernières Nouvelles d'Alsace	223.3	223.2
La Dordogne libre (Périgueux)	4.7	n/a
L'Echo républicain (Chartres)	34.0	33.8
L'Eclair (Nantes)	15.6	14.8
Eclair-Pyrénées (Pau)	10.0	10.0
L'Est Eclair (Troyes)	31.6	31.5
L'Est républicain (Nancy)	246.3	243.1
L'Eveil de la Haute-Loire (Le Puy)	14.1	14.2
Havre libre	24.9	24.6
Le Havre-Presse	17.5	17.4
L'Indépendant (Perpignan)	73.5	73.5
Libération-Champagne (Troyes)	14.0	13.2
La Liberté de l'Est (Epinal)	31.9	31.9
La Liberté du Morbihan (Lorient)	8.9	7.8
Lyon-Matin	38.2	36.5
Le Maine libre (Le Mans)	55.1	54.9
Le Méridional-La France (Marseilles)	68.8	64.7
Le Midi libre (Montpellier)	185.1	184.6
La Montagne (Clermont-Ferrand)	246.9	224.0
Nice-Matin	253.1	261.1
Nord-Eclair (Roubaix)	99.3	101.0
Nord-Littoral (Calais)	7.2	7.3
La Nouvelle République du Centre-Ouest	267.1	266.4
La Nouvelle République des Pyrénées	17.2	n/a
Ouest-France (Rennes)	795.4	794.1
Paris-Normandie (Rouen)	114.3	112.1
Le Populaire du Centre (Limoges)	55.7	55.2
La Presse de la Manche (Cherbourg)	27.9	27.6
Presse-Océan (Nantes)	83.0	82.0
Le Progrès (Lyons)	351.1	386.7
Le Provençal (Marseilles)	158.9	156.9
Le Provençal-Le Soir (Marseilles)	15.1	14.8
Le Républicain lorrain (Metz)	192.9	193.9
La République du Centre (Orléans)	63.2	62.4
La République des Pyrénées (Pau)	29.3	29.4
Sud-Ouest (Bordeaux)	370.0	367.2

Table1.6 Continued

Newspaper	1990	1991
Le Télégramme de Brest	186.4	186.3
L'Union (Reims)	110.4	110.9
Var Matin République (Toulon)	78.6	76.2
La Voix du Nord (Lille)	372.2	371.2
L'Yonne républicaine (Auxerre)	40.4	40.4

n/a = not available

Sources: E. Ducarroir, 'Evolution de la diffusion des quotidiens et principaux périodiques français de 1987 à 1990', Médiaspouvoirs, no.24, Paris, 1991, p.166; E. Ducarroir, 'Evolution de la diffusion des quotidiens et principaux périodiques français de 1988 à 1991', Médiaspouvoirs, no.28, Paris, 1992, pp.150–151.

representatives with a strong local base remain key political actors. For example, since French politicians are permitted to hold posts simultaneously at different levels of the political system (a practice known in France as le cumul des mandats), the local mayor is frequently a politician of national importance, none more so than the mayor of Paris, Jacques Chirac.[41] At the same time national politicians generally seek to legitimize their position through control of a local power base. The result is less of a disjunction in France than in Britain between the local and national political levels, a situation which has helped buttress the role of the provincial press as an important source of news and political information.[42]

The strength of the provincial press means that in terms of circulation it is difficult to speak of a national daily press in France. The Paris daily newspapers sell predominantly in the greater Paris area, which happens to be the weakest region for the consumption of daily newspapers (Paris and provincial titles combined).[43] In contrast, in the French provinces it is local and regional newspapers which overwhelmingly dominate circulation to the virtual exclusion of the Paris dailies. In Brittany, for example, the region with the highest consumption per household of daily newspapers, almost 60 per cent of households regularly took a local or regional daily paper in 1986 compared with under 4 per cent which took a 'national' one produced in Paris. Outside the greater Paris area and Picardy, in no region of France did Paris dailies regularly penetrate over 10 per cent of households.[44] However, though this situation may seem very odd to British eyes, long accustomed to the dominance of the national press, it is worth noting that in this respect it is Britain rather than France which is more the exception in Europe. The French situation is also more similar to that existing in the USA, where national dailies are weak and regional city newspapers are strong.

The sales superiority of daily provincial newspapers does not mean that the Paris press has a lower status or exerts little influence. Whereas in some other European countries, such as Italy and Germany, large non-metropolitan urban centres publish high-quality, prestige newspapers, this is not the case in France. As far as the publication of elite opinion-forming newspapers is concerned, there is no French equivalent of Milan or Frankfurt. On the contrary, despite their comparatively low overall circulation, in many respects the Paris dailies are the dominant players in the French press system. Whereas the provincial dailies may be important sources of information for the mass of society, it is the Paris dailies which reflect the concerns of the elites. In particular, the quality Parisian dailies such as *Le Monde*, *Le Figaro* and *Libération* exercise a strong influence among key economic and political decision makers, as well as acting as a major forum for the discussion of new ideas in social and cultural matters. This privileged position of the Paris press among the elites is scarcely surprising, given that the capital is the centre of French political, economic and cultural life. Despite the decentralist initiatives of the Socialist government in the 1980s, the politico-administrative system is still characterized by a high degree of centralization. At the same time a tradition of anti-provincialism among French intellectuals has ensured the privileged position of Paris as the source of new ideas.

None the less, one consequence of the circulation dominance of provincial dailies in France is the striking absence – to British observers at least – of a mass market popular national daily on the lines of *The Sun* or the *Daily Mirror*. The polarization in Britain between large circulation, downmarket tabloids and small circulation, quality broadsheets simply does not exist in France. Before the First World War there were four mass circulation French dailies, while in the 1950s *France-Soir* regularly sold over 1 million copies. However, there is at present no newspaper in France with a circulation of a million or over, while the sales figures of the Paris dailies are low for papers with pretensions to national status (see table 1.7).[45]

Various proposals to launch a cheap, mass circulation national daily have been discussed from time to time. The Hersant, Hachette and Maxwell press groups, for instance, all separately considered such a project during the 1980s. However, in each case the obstacles to its realization proved insuperable. High investment costs; the competitive state of the media advertising market; the lack of enthusiasm shown by advertisers and advertising agencies; competition from an expanded television system, private local radio and a healthy regional press; and the problematic status of such a speculative venture in the business strategies of the media firms concerned – all worked against any of the projects ever coming to fruition.[46]

THE ECONOMICS OF THE PRESS

A central theme running through the above historical overview has been the strong influence of economic factors in shaping the configuration of the contemporary press system in France. This section examines in more detail

Table1.7 Circulation of major Paris-based daily newspapers (in '000s)

Newspaper	1981	1987	1988	1989	1990	1991
La Croix	118	103	104	104	104	102
Les Echos	61	89	96	104	110	113
L'Equipe	223	227	231	268	301	312
Le Figaro	336	433	432	429	424	423
France-Soir	429	334	255	240	257	246
L'Humanité	141	108	109	n/a	84	71
Libération	70*	165	195	180	182	183
Le Monde	439	362	387	382	386	380
Le Parisien	343	366	385	405	384	388
Présent	–	8*	8*	n/a	n/a	n/a
Le Quotidien de Paris	65*	40*	30*	n/a	n/a	n/a

* Estimated circulation; n/a = not available

Sources: P. Albert, *La presse française*, Paris, La documentation française, 1990, p.116; E. Ducarroir, 'Evolution de la diffusion des quotidiens et principaux périodiques français de 1987 à 1990', *Médiaspouvoirs*, no.24, Paris, 1991, p.165; E. Ducarroir, 'Evolution de la diffusion des quotidiens et principaux périodiques français de 1988 à 1991', *Médiaspouvoirs*, no.28, Paris, 1992, p.149.

the impact of certain key economic variables on the structure and functioning of the press in the period since the Liberation.

Concentration of ownership

One striking feature of the postwar press is concentration of ownership and control, which is directly linked to the economic difficulties of the newspaper industry and the corporate strategies of the major press groups.[47] Concentration in the postwar French press is evident at three different levels.

First, there has been a decline in the number of different daily newspaper titles.[48] Titles which have disappeared in the postwar period include the original *Libération* (unconnected with the present newspaper of the same name) which folded in 1964, *Paris Jour* (1972), *Combat* (1974), *L'Aurore* (which merged with *Le Figaro* in 1980), *Le Matin* (1988) and *La Truffe* (1991).[49] While there may be a variety of specific reasons why a particular newspaper does not survive in the marketplace, in general the size and social status of the readership are the two key variables. A newspaper's income comes overwhelmingly from a combination of sales and advertising. Revenue from sales depends on the circulation figures and the cost of the paper to the individual reader, while advertising income is determined by the size and attractiveness of the paper's readership to advertisers. In circumstances of a declining readership for daily newspapers since the late 1960s and a very competitive advertising market, there has been limited scope for new entrants to stake a claim. This is particularly the case as the entry costs of a new title on to the market are very high. Since the immediate postwar boom only one new national daily newspaper has been established, survived and made a major sales impact – the current *Libération*. The success of *Libération*, however, is the exception which proves the rule. Other projects have either never left the drawing board or, once launched, have failed to secure an enduring niche in the market.[50] The combined total of 73 Paris and provincial daily newspaper titles in 1990 was the lowest postwar figure and only just over half the number of daily titles published in 1950.

Second, concentration of ownership is evident in the provincial press, with several big regional dailies dominating the market in their respective circulation areas. In many parts of France the surviving regional titles have successfully eliminated their major rivals. Though they do not constitute a monopoly in the strict sense of the term, since they are still in competition with smaller departmental papers and the Paris dailies, these big regional papers have secured a strategic position in their sub-national markets. Several of them have formed important regional press groups, centring on the major regional title and including other smaller titles in the region, thereby absorbing previously independent papers into a powerful press chain. Examples of this phenomenon include the Sud-Ouest group (which also owns *La France*, *La Charente libre*, *La Dordogne libre*, *Eclair-Pyrénées* and *La République des Pyrénées*); *La Montagne* (which has a stake in *Le Populaire du Centre*, *Le Berry républicain* and *Le Journal du Centre*); *Ouest-France* (which has interests in *La Presse de la Manche*, several local weeklies and a company which publishes free newspapers) and *La Dépêche du Midi* (which is a major shareholder in *La Nouvelle République des Pyrénées* and *Le Petit Bleu*).[51] Pacts have also been made between different regional newspapers not to penetrate into one another's established circulation area. Finally, advertising agreements to minimize competition and strengthen their hand *vis-à-vis* advertisers are common among different titles in the same region.[52]

This means in effect that in many regions of France there is very limited competition between provincial papers. In general, the daily provincial newspaper market is characterized by the following features: a large regional paper exercises a quasi-monopolistic position in its circulation area, while inside the region (and at its edges) it comes up against pockets of resistance where a smaller but strongly rooted daily paper competes against it and sometimes even comes out on top.[53] Examples of a major regional daily based in a large town or city dominating the region as a whole include: *Ouest-France* (Rennes), *La Voix du Nord* (Lille), *L'Est républicain* (Nancy), *Le Progrès* (Lyons), *Le Dauphiné libéré* (Grenoble), *Le Midi libre* (Montpellier), *La Dépêche du Midi* (Toulouse), *Sud-Ouest* (Bordeaux), *La Nouvelle République* (Tours) and *La Montagne* (Clermont-Ferrand). *Ouest-France*, for example, is by far the major daily newspaper in Brittany and certain neighbouring departments in Normandy and the Pays de la Loire; while *Sud-Ouest* is the biggest-selling newspaper in the Aquitaine region from Bordeaux right down to the Spanish border. However, in some towns and departments within these regional fiefdoms a smaller title may exercise a *de facto* local monopoly. For example, in the Finistère department in the extreme western tip of Brittany *Ouest-France* is outsold by *Le Télégramme*, while *La République du Centre* (Orléans) outsells *La Nouvelle République* in the Loiret.[54]

Third, concentration of ownership has become more apparent with the increasing importance of national press groups. For a time both the 1944 press legislation and the strength of the big regional independents acted as a barrier to the emergence of powerful national press groups in France. The press was also an unattractive sector of economic activity for large financial and industrial companies. Moreover, since up until the 1980s the state stoutly defended its monopoly in broadcasting, newspaper owners were not allowed to diversify into the audiovisual sector. With only publishing and advertising offering them potential fields for diversification, press groups tended to operate on a small scale.

This picture has changed to a significant extent, with concentration of ownership in the newspaper industry becoming popularly associated with the name of one man: Robert Hersant. In the mid-1970s Hersant's stake in the French press came to public attention at a time when other press groups such as those owned by Amaury and Prouvost were running into severe financial problems. Hersant was already the owner of several provincial newspapers such as *Nord-Matin*, *Le Havre-Presse* and *Paris-Normandie*. The failure of other press barons allowed him to purchase *Le Figaro* from the ailing Prouvost group in July 1975. A year later he added *France-Soir* to his growing stable of titles, this time from the Hachette group. In 1978 the Paris daily *L'Aurore* was purchased from Boussac, with the result that the Hersant group now owned three Paris dailies. This allowed it to acquire a national dimension and for the first time in France to combine Paris and provincial dailies under the same corporate umbrella. Hersant himself became a symbol of the power of press barons and was vilified by many on the French Left. The Hersant empire continued to grow as more regional newspapers came under its control. In 1982 it purchased *Le Dauphiné* and in 1985 *Le Progrès* and *L'Union* (Reims) were added. It has been estimated that in the late 1980s the Hersant group controlled around 22 per cent of the print run of provincial daily papers and almost one third of that of Parisian dailies, which constituted an impressive share of the newspaper market by any standard.[55]

It is important, however, not to exaggerate the levels of concentration in the French press. By European standards national press groups are relatively weak in France in terms of both total circulation figures and market share. Despite all the publicity surrounding the extension of the

Hersant empire, the French press is less dominated by large press groups than are several of its counterparts in the European Union (EU). In Britain in the 1980s the four main press groups accounted for over 50 per cent of turnover (and a much higher proportion of the national daily newspaper sector). In Germany 70 per cent of the periodicals market was controlled by four main groups, while in Italy two groups between them accounted for about 40 per cent of press market share. By contrast, in France the top ten groups accounted for only 50 per cent of press turnover and the top 30 for 75 per cent.[56]

Paradoxically, the existence of strong, well-entrenched quasi-monopolies in the different French regions has mitigated concentration of the press at the national level. Prosperous, powerful and proud of their independence in their own fiefdoms, regional press groups have frequently and successfully resisted attempts by Paris-based groups to gain control and establish *de facto* national chains of regional newspapers. One consequence of this is that French press groups are not big players at the European or international level and are in general ill-equipped to move into supranational or global markets.

The press and advertising

Advertising is a vital source of revenue for the French press. In 1988 it was estimated that 40.5 per cent of press revenue (excluding freesheets) came from advertising, with just under 60 per cent coming directly from sales.[57] In 1990 advertising made up 43.7 per cent of total press turnover.[58] However, as this was an overall average figure, it disguised huge disparities across different sectors: provincial dailies, Paris dailies, weeklies, technical press and freesheets. The daily newspaper sector as a whole took nearly half of its income from advertising, with the provincial dailies receiving 43.6 per cent of their revenue from this source.[59] Some periodicals received up to 80 per cent of their income from advertising, while in the case of freesheets it was 100 per cent.

While at first glance such figures may appear impressive, they have to be placed in the historical context of the underdeveloped role of advertising in the French economy. Since the nineteenth century the contribution of advertising to French economic life has been considerably lower than in many other industrialized countries, including Britain and the USA, and this was still the case up until quite recently (see table 1.8). Moreover, the share of media advertising expenditure secured by the French press has been smaller than its equivalent in some other EU countries. For example, the British press took just under 65 per cent of media advertising spend in 1990, while the West German press secured over 75 per cent (see table 1.9). This means that the French press has had to secure a higher proportion of its income from sales than several of its European counterparts.[60]

Table 1.8 Advertising expenditure in 1986

Country	$ per inhabitant	% of GDP
Belgium	77.89	0.55
France	81.02	0.62
Germany (West)	133.26	0.88
Italy	53.73	0.78
Japan	150.81	0.70
Spain	76.84	1.15
Sweden	130.78	1.13
Switzerland	213.04	1.06
United Kingdom	145.63	1.37
United States	424.07	1.60

Source: B. Jouanno, 'L'Europe en chiffres', *Médiaspouvoirs*, no.12, Paris, 1988, p.143.

Table 1.9 Media share of advertising in selected European countries in 1990 (as % of total media advertising budget in each country)

Country	Press	Television	Posters, radio and cinema
France	56.2	25.0	18.8
Great Britain	64.1	29.6	6.3
Germany (West)	77.1	14.2	8.7
Italy	43.2	47.9	8.9
Spain	55.0	30.5	14.5

Source: Y. Lorelle, *La presse*, Paris, Retz, 1992, p.141.

The historical weakness of the advertising sector in French economic activity altered in the 1980s with a huge expansion in media advertising throughout the decade (see table 1.10). Advertising expenditure tripled between 1979 and 1987, while advertising spend per capita increased from 229 francs in 1976 to 1,042 francs in 1988.[61] All sectors of the press benefited from this huge growth in advertising, with the Paris dailies and the freesheets coming off best (see table 1.11). However, though the press took advantage of this advertising surge, its dominant position in the market continued to be eroded by other media. The percentage share of the press in media advertising maintained its decline during the 1980s as a result of a huge increase in competition from radio and television. By the beginning of the 1990s the press as a whole was taking just over 55 per cent of total media advertising spending compared with around 80 per cent in 1967, the last year in which advertising was prohibited on state television (see table 1.12).

Table 1.10 Total advertising expenditure in France 1980–91 (in billions of francs)

1980	20.3	1986	44.8
1981	23.1	1987	52.0
1982	27.3	1988	58.3
1983	32.3	1989	65.0
1984	36.5	1990	70.2
1985	40.0	1991	72.3

Sources: E. Ducarroir, 'Le marché publicitaire français en 1990', *Médiaspouvoirs*, no.23, Paris, 1991, p.211; E. Ducarroir, 'Le marché publicitaire français en 1991', *Médiaspouvoirs*, no.28, Paris, 1992, p.140.

Table 1.11 Trends in advertising expenditure by media 1984–90 (annual % changes)

Medium	1984–85	1985–86	1986–87	1987–88	1988–89	1989–90
Press	+10.5	+13.0	+14.0	+13.0	+14.0	+ 8.5
Paris dailies	+11.5	+21.5	+21.5	+19.0	+22.0	+ 8.0
Provincial dailies	+ 7.0	+ 8.0	+12.0	+ 9.5	+ 7.0	+ 2.3
Magazines	+11.0	+10.5	+ 9.5	+ 9.5	+12.0	+ 7.5
Specialist	+10.5	+12.0	+13.5	+17.0	+14.5	+11.5
Freesheets	+17.5	+23.5	+21.0	+17.0	+22.0	+13.3
Television	+16.5	+27.0	+36.0	+27.0	+13.5	+10.0
Posters	+10.0	+12.5	+10.0	+11.0	+11.0	+10.5
Radio	+13.0	+ 6.0	+ 1.0	+12.0	+ 6.0	+ 6.0
Cinema	+ 2.0	+ 3.0	–20.0	– 6.0	+ 1.5	+ 9.0
Total media	+11.5	+14.5	+16.0	+15.5	+13.0	+ 9.0

Sources: E. Ducarroir, 'Le marché publicitaire français en 1988', *Médiaspouvoirs*, no.15, Paris, 1989, p.172; E. Ducarroir, 'Le marché publicitaire français en 1991', *Médiaspouvoirs*, no.28, Paris, 1992, p.141.

While a contracting share of a growing advertising cake might have been tolerable to the press, alarmingly the advertising surge itself came to an end in 1991 (see table 1.13). This was the first time since 1978 that the advertising market had not grown in real terms. This left the press in receipt of a declining share of an advertising market in recession, with no immediate prospect of an economic upturn. The advertising revenue of the press sector as a whole fell by 7.5 per cent, which was a shock for an industry whose dependence on advertising had grown from 35.9 per cent of turnover in 1983 to 43.7 per cent in 1990. The Paris newspapers which had been major beneficiaries of the expansion in the 1980s were particularly adversely affected in 1991, with a year-on-year fall in advertising revenue of 17 per cent. After a poor year in 1990 (only a 2.3 per cent increase on 1989), the

Table 1.12 Media share of advertising in France 1982–92 (as % of total media advertising budget)

Medium	1982	1983	1984	1985	1986	1987
Press	58.0	59.5	59.0	59.0	58.0	56.9
Television	16.0	16.5	16.5	17.0	19.0	22.4
Posters	15.0	13.5	13.5	13.0	13.0	12.2
Radio	9.0	8.5	9.0	9.0	8.5	7.4
Cinema	2.0	2.0	2.0	2.0	1.5	1.1
	1988	1989	1990	1991	1992*	
Press	55.7	56.4	56.2	53.7	51.1	
Television	24.5	24.6	24.9	27.2	29.4	
Posters	11.7	11.4	11.5	12.0	12.0	
Radio	7.2	6.8	6.6	6.5	6.9	
Cinema	0.9	0.8	0.8	0.6	0.6	

* estimated

Source: *Médiaspouvoirs*, nos.31–32, Paris, 1993, p.286.

Table 1.13 Trends in advertising expenditure by media 1990–92 (annual % changes)

Medium	1990–91	1991–92
Press	− 7.5	− 5.5
Paris dailies	−16.9	−18.4
Provincial dailies	− 8.5	− 5.7
Magazines	− 6.0	− 0.9
Specialist	− 7.0	− 5.6
Freesheets	− 3.0	− 4.9
Television	+ 6.0	+ 7.0
Posters	+ 1.0	− 1.2
Radio	− 5.0	+ 5.5
Cinema	−24.0	+ 2.9
Total media	− 3.0	− 0.8

Source: *Médiaspouvoirs*, nos.31–32, Paris, 1993, p.286.

provincial press saw its advertising revenue fall back by 8.5 per cent. Every sector of the press was affected, leaving press owners to hope that the downturn was only temporary.

The financial impact of advertising on the press has varied enormously, not just between different sectors but also between different titles in the same sector. For example, in 1988 it was estimated that among the Paris dailies *Le Figaro* attracted more than 70 per cent of its income from advertising, *Le Monde*, 45 per cent, *Le Parisien*, 28 per cent, *Libération*, 20 per cent, *L'Humanité*, only 11.5 per cent and *La Croix*, a meagre 8 per cent. The weekly news magazine *L'Express* was 60 per cent funded from advertising, whereas the Sunday newspaper *France-Dimanche* received only 6 per cent of its revenue from this source.[62] Some newspapers shun advertising completely, notably the satirical weekly *Le Canard enchaîné*. *Libération* originally sought to do the same, but changed its policy in 1982. This wide disparity in the contribution of advertising to a title's turnover can largely be explained with reference to the strategies of advertising agencies. Niche marketing by advertisers has led to an emphasis on up-market newspapers and on magazines, especially those aimed at women. In contrast, ideologically committed newspapers, such as the Communist party daily *L'Humanité*, are not favoured by advertisers.

While it is relatively easy to provide statistical information on the contribution of advertising to the finances of the French press, it is much more difficult to evaluate its qualitative impact. One possible economic consequence on the press system as a whole has been to aid the movement towards concentration, with advertisers supporting those titles which are already winning circulation battles. On the issue of press content – the extent to which dependence on advertising shapes the press agenda and influences issue coverage – it is difficult to come to any hard and fast conclusions. As in other European countries the spread of colour magazines and weekend supplements in newspapers has resulted in a blurring of the traditional distinction between advertising material and journalistic coverage. This has been most evident in features articles covering travel, holidays, cars and consumer durables. However, it is hard to demonstrate that dependence on advertising has had a notable impact on newspapers' information content.

State aid to the press

Income from advertising and sales is supplemented in France by a system of state aid to the press. This was introduced after the Second World War as part of a package of measures which increased the role of the state in press matters.[63] The creation by the state of a system of financial assistance had the avowed objective of fostering pluralism among newspaper titles and encouraging access for readers to different sources of information. The dominance of the inter-war press by capitalist financiers was anathema to those groups which dominated French politics after the Liberation. In their eyes the market had failed both to provide real choice and to reflect the diversity of opinion in French society. Market forces, it was argued, by emphasizing a paper's ability to attract advertisers as well as readers, resulted in a restricted range of newspaper titles and a lack of diversity in press content. The establishment of a state subsidy scheme was designed to counter what were regarded as the undesirable consequences of the operation of a free market in the press.

State aid to the press in France takes the form of both direct financial support and indirect subsidies, with the latter much the more important of the two (see table 1.14). Indirect support comprises tax concessions on profits for investment purposes (e.g. the purchase of new equipment), a reduced VAT rate on sales, various tax allowances and exemptions, and reductions in certain state tariffs (post, telegraph and telephone).[64] Direct financial assistance is more exceptional. This includes a support fund for daily newspapers with low levels of advertising revenue. Because of the nature of the conditions governing this type of aid, in 1986 only five Paris newspapers benefited: *La Croix, L'Humanité, Libération, Le Matin* and *Présent.* By 1991 only *La Croix* and *L'Humanité* among the Paris dailies still received direct state aid. Direct aid also covers state assistance for the transportation of newspapers by state railways. Finally, financial support in the form of the subsidization of distribution costs is given to the French press to help sales abroad.

Though it is difficult to make exact calculations, it has been estimated that state aid accounts for between 12 per cent and 15 per cent of the total turnover of the French press, and nearer 20 per cent of turnover in the case of an average daily newspaper. Among western countries France is ranked second only to Italy for the amount of state aid to the press (see table 1.15). In the light of these figures, it is reasonable to ask how effective and desirable

Table 1.14 State aid to the press in France 1985–91 (in millions of francs)

Type of aid	1985	1986	1987	1988	1989	1990	1991
Direct aid	171	171	173	201	239	273	278
Indirect aid	5,190	5,104	5,037	5,132	5,276	5,554	5,838*
Total state aid	5,361	5,275	5,210	5,333	5,515	5,827	6,116

* estimated

Sources: P. Albert *La presse française*, Paris, La documentation française, 1990, p.72; SJTI, *Tableaux statistiques de la presse 1990*, Paris, La documentation française, 1992,

Table 1.15 Direct state aid to the press in selected European countries in 1986 (in millions of francs)

Belgium	21.5
Denmark	8
France	200
Great Britain	–
Italy	860
Netherlands	64
Spain	200
West Germany	–

– = no state aid given

Source: J.-M. Charon, *La presse en France de 1945 à nos jours*, Paris, Seuil, 1991, p.397.

the system is. Criticisms of state aid have focused both on the principle and the practicalities of its operation. The objection on principle is that such aid unjustifiably distorts the mechanisms of the free market, making newspapers less likely to take risks, to be dynamic and entrepreneurial, and to respond to changing social and economic circumstances. However, this objection does not seem to be very strongly held among French political elites, even in circles sympathetic to economic liberalism in general.[65]

Criticism has been more commonly directed at the way in which the system functions in practice. In this context, the key question is: does state aid as currently operated help newspapers which have a weak financial base but a significant information function? The answer, according to critics, is that it does not, or at least not well enough. To avoid possible charges of political bias and at the same time not alienate powerful press groups which benefit from the current arrangements, the system of aid is politically neutral. However, it has been argued that this concern with neutrality and formal equity, however understandable it may be, has thrown state aid off course. By appearing to help all, state aid to the press is too indiscriminate, not differentiating between the needy and the already well-off. Indeed, the system may even be perverse, with unintended consequences which run counter to the principles which underpin its operation. It may actually help the better-off newspapers. For example, the mechanism of postal aid helps only those papers with big postal distribution, which tend to be the papers which are already commercially successful. A paper may be receiving 80 per cent of its income in advertising and still be eligible for state assistance. This means that state aid is available and of great benefit to newspapers which are already prospering in the marketplace. At the same time, the system is limited in scope. For example, there is no state aid, either in the form of subsidy or preferential loans, to help in the foundation of new newspapers. Overall, therefore, the system tends to favour the status quo rather than encouraging new initiatives.[66]

The impact of new technology

The introduction of new technology has had some impact on the economics of the press in France and more significant consequences for labour relations in the industry. It has radically changed the way in which information is produced and distributed at every stage of the publishing process, turning newspaper offices and print works into high-technology enterprises. Old-fashioned printing installations have been replaced by new modern ones, such as the one established in 1989 at Ivry on the outskirts of Paris by *Le Monde* in association with Hachette and *Le Parisien*. However, it was the provincial press, with their multiple editions in different localities, which first realized the benefits to be gained from the transition to new technology, while the Paris press followed in their footsteps.

This technological revolution not only changed the work practices of journalists by speeding up the process of information production, storage and retrieval. More crucially, it challenged the tight grip on the newspaper publishing industry of the print workers, whose trade union organization can be traced back to the eighteenth century. The leading print union, the Fédération du Livre, secured important concessions in the period immediately following the Liberation. In this it was helped by its affiliation to the Communist-dominated trade union confederation, the Confédération Générale du Travail (CGT), at a time when the Communist party was part of the postwar governing coalition.

> Since 1944 (the union) had obtained for itself and its members three advantages. . . . First, the union controlled the hiring of labour in the printing plants in the Paris region. The system was a closed shop; workers without a Syndicat du livre card could not be hired. The role of the union went even further; each week it designated which of its members would be assigned to work on which newspaper. Second, it had successfully negotiated extremely favourable working conditions. Its members were required to work only five hours a day and could set production targets far below the capacities of modern machinery. And third, members' salaries were exceptionally high.[67]

For a long time newspaper bosses were not actively opposed to these arrangements, as they permitted a considerable degree of flexibility in the management of the workforce. At any given time the union would supply each company with the number of workers required, with the result that both management and labour were engaged in a conspiracy of inefficiency at the expense of the consumer. During the 1970s, however, the decline in newspaper profits and the possibility of introducing new printing techniques which would lower production costs persuaded some newspaper owners that change was required.

Naturally the print union fiercely opposed management attempts to modernize the printing process, regarding these as a challenge to its own extraordinary authority within the industry. Tension between management and workers heightened against a background of increasing economic difficulties for the press. The inevitable clash pitted the union against the press boss Emilien Amaury. He owned *Le Parisien libéré*, which with a circulation of around 750,000 at the time was the number one morning daily paper, second only to *France-Soir* overall. In March 1975 Amaury decided to abandon the newspaper's Paris printing plant and move operations outside the region. This was accompanied by an announcement of massive redundancies, with management indicating that only 170 people rather than the 560 employed in Paris would be required for future production. The union regarded this decision as an act of provocation and demanded the reinstatement of the great majority of the employees of the Paris plant.

The print workers' dispute at *Le Parisien libéré* lasted two and a half years, during which time distributors of the paper were attacked and the union staged spectacular media events including occupations of the Paris Stock Exchange, Notre-Dame cathedral and the ocean liner *France*. During the 29 months of the conflict there were 12 solidarity strikes which affected much of the newspaper industry, though ironically *Le Parisien libéré* itself continued to be published as its replacement staff were not members of the union.

During the prolonged conflict the paper's circulation fell drastically, down to 300,000 by 1977, imposing a huge financial burden on the Amaury press group. Shortly following Amaury's death at the beginning of 1977, an agreement backed by the government was reached between the two sides, with the union largely capitulating to management demands. Despite some gains, the print union was the major loser from the conflict, forced to abandon the closed shop and compelled to accept the introduction of new technology and new work practices. In return the management agreed to the retraining of some employees to work on the new technology. The management had won, but the cost had been high and the newspaper never fully recovered from the conflict.

The path blazed by Amaury has been followed by most newspapers since. Yet while the introduction of new technology has revolutionized publishing methods and work practices, the impact on the economics of the press system has been less marked. The cost of newspaper publishing remains high in France. More than half the costs of daily newspapers (even higher in the case of the Paris dailies) go on raw materials, distribution and self-promotion – areas where new technology has made little or no impact.[68] Overall, new technology has not had a major influence in reducing the costs of entry into the newspaper market. It has certainly not reversed the decline of the daily newspaper sector as measured by the number of titles and their circulation figures.

THE PRESS AND THE AUDIOVISUAL MEDIA

The aim of this short concluding section is to situate the press within the context of the media system as a whole and to evaluate its role in an era dominated by the broadcasting media, particularly television. It is tempting to attribute responsibility for many facets of the decline of the postwar press, such as the falling circulation figures of daily newspapers, to the rise of television. If expenditure by consumers on the media were constant and time allocated to their overall use fixed, then the introduction of television and its expansion over the years might easily account for the problems facing the press in the early 1990s.

Certainly these two media have not developed independently of each other. One of the most obvious interactions between the two can be found in the existence of a healthy market of television listings magazines and of weekly television supplements provided with many newspapers. It may be somewhat ironic that the television listings magazines are one of the highest-selling sectors of the press.[69] In 1986 there were no fewer than 19 separate titles with a combined circulation of over 11.5 million copies. The main titles in 1991 included the market leader *Télé-7 jours* (circulation of just under 3 million); *Télé star* (2 million); *Télé poche* (1.6 million); *Télé loisirs* (1.3 million); *Télé Z* (1.6 million); and *Télérama* (just over half a million copies).[70] The total circulation of television listings magazines is currently higher than that of Paris and provincial daily newspapers combined. In addition, two main weekly television supplements (Hersant's *TV Magazine* and Hachette's *TV Hebdo*) have a combined circulation of 6.5 million via newspaper sales.

Yet the causal link between a television system in expansion and a daily newspaper press in decline is both oversimplistic and difficult to prove. In several other European countries the rise of television has not had such deleterious consequences for newspaper sales, which suggests that the two media can be complementary as well as competitive. Moreover, when television was being established as a mass medium in France in the 1960s, the print run of daily newspapers actually increased, peaking in 1968. It was not until 1975 that the total daily newspaper print run again fell below the 11 million mark, a total it had failed to achieve in seven separate years during the 1950s when television had scarcely made any impact in France. Finally, the magazine sector, which covers a wide range of general and specialist interests, has performed well in the television age. All of this would tend to suggest that television cannot be held responsible for the problems of the press. None the less, it may well be the case that the routinization and expansion of television (and radio) in the late 1970s and 1980s have adversely affected daily newspaper sales, even if a direct link is hard to prove.

Certainly the press and audiovisual media now interact in a variety of ways, with the press becoming a more integrated player than before in an increasingly complex media environment. Four aspects of this interaction are particularly worthy of note. The first is that the low per capita circulation figures of daily newspapers in France mean that the press is potentially a much less important information source and opinion-forming agency for the mass of the French citizenry than are other media. At the same time French newspapers may be less influential in shaping social and political attitudes and behaviour than their counterparts in several other European countries, including Great Britain. The decline of the newspaper press from its postwar peak has certainly increased the importance of the broadcasting media as an information source. Moreover, the dominance of the newspaper market by *provincial* dailies means that television (and to a lesser extent radio) is the main source of national and international news for the majority of French people. In contrast, despite the spread of local radio and regional television in the 1980s, the press remains of paramount importance as a source of local and regional news for large sections of the French population.

Second, the expansion of the audiovisual media has had a qualitative impact on the information role carried out by the French press. In the broadcasting era newspapers can no longer hope to be first with the news. They have to tailor their content and adopt marketing strategies which take account of this change. Some Paris newspapers (such as *Le Monde, Le Figaro* and *Libération*) complement broadcast output by providing more in-depth coverage, explanation and analysis than is commonly available on radio and television. Other papers (such as *Le Parisien* and *France-Soir*) have tended to concentrate on human interest stories, sport, sensationalism and interviews with celebrities, often television stars. The regional dailies strive to differentiate themselves from other media by stressing their implantation in the local community, covering local and regional issues and thus avoiding head-to-head competition with nationally oriented television. Frequently, regional dailies publish separate editions for different localities to emphasize their local roots. At the same time most newspapers have continued to emphasize those functions which the press does well and which radio and television have greater difficulty in performing. One of the most important of these is classified advertising, which despite the advent of electronic data services remains a financially very rewarding preserve of the press.

Third, the press has become more fully integrated into the media system as a whole through the practice of cross-media ownership. This is a relatively new departure, since before 1982 broadcasting was a state monopoly and therefore out of bounds to private entrepreneurs. Fearful of losing readers and advertisers to private local radio and commercial television during the 1980s, several press groups (including Hersant) sought to diversify and transformed themselves into multimedia enterprises. Paris newspapers such as *Le Monde* and *Libération* acquired an interest in the running of private local radio, while various regional newspapers became involved in related media activities such as telematics, freesheets, private local radio, publishing and television.[71]

Finally, the press has had to compete more fiercely for a slice of the media advertising market. Before 1968 the main competition faced by the press came from billboards and the peripheral radio stations such as Europe 1 and Radio Luxembourg. Even when advertising was introduced on state television in 1968, it was kept within a fixed percentage statutory limit of total television resources. However, the importance of advertising as a source of revenue for state television increased in the 1970s. With the establishment of commercial television channels in the 1980s and the concomitant expansion of private local radio, daily newspapers have had to fight more fiercely against other media for advertising revenue. For example, since 1970 the regional daily press has lost over half of its non-local (i.e. national) advertising to magazines and television. Overall, despite the fact that newspapers and television are regarded by some advertisers as complementary rather than competitive media, the fact remains that the position of the press in this area is much less protected than it was even ten years ago.

Yet the problems of certain sectors of the press, notably daily newspapers, cannot be laid at the door of other media. Many of them, such as chronic undercapitalization, are self-imposed. Nor will declining sales be reversed by new technology or state aid. Moreover, if the growing dependence of daily newspapers on advertising is now exposed because of the combination of increased media competition and a decline in company advertising expenditure, then this sector of the press will have to respond positively. The task of the press is to improve its productivity, distribution, marketing and content so as to attract new readers, especially among the younger age groups. The success, not to mention the continued existence, of several daily newspapers will depend on how well they realize these goals.

Chapter 2

The press: politics

For a long time the principal means of mass communication in France, the press has traditionally provided coverage of both domestic and foreign politics. It has been a prime source of information and comment on political issues at local, regional and national levels, while increasingly covering European and international political developments as well. The press has played an important role in shaping public opinion and mobilizing electoral support. It has also helped to set the political agenda by focusing on certain personalities, events and issues, while ignoring or marginalizing others. A few newspapers and magazines have at times acted as a neutral forum for debate; others have been the committed mouthpieces of a single political movement or party; most have articulated a clear political line on major events and lent their support to candidates during election campaigns. Frequently the press has become an active participant in the political process rather than merely an interested commentator on events.

Although its significance as the main source of news and political information may have diminished, first with the arrival of radio and then, more importantly, with the advent of television, the press has not been totally eclipsed by the incursion of the broadcasting media into coverage of politics. Certain daily papers and weekly news magazines continue to fulfil an important role as opinion formers among the national political and economic elites. Meanwhile, the provincial press is still the major provider of news and comment on local and regional matters. No local politician would willingly seek a conflict with his or her regional newspaper for fear of the electoral retribution it might bring.

This chapter does not pretend to be a comprehensive survey of the political role of the press in France. Various topics either not covered or only touched upon in this chapter include the use of the press by interest groups, the capacity of the press to set the political agenda, the depoliticization of the provincial press, the role of the press in election campaigns and the extent of press influence on elite and mass political behaviour. The omission of these topics is not to underestimate their importance, and a study focusing specifically on political communication in France would want to address these issues among others. The aim of this chapter, however, is more modest. It sets out to examine two aspects of the complex interrelationship between politics and the press which are fundamental to an understanding of the operations of the French media system. The first section examines the multifaceted role of the state, concentrating on its functions as regulator, censor and primary definer. The second section explores the main linkages between the press and political parties, with particular emphasis on the issue of parallelism between newspapers and parties since the Liberation.

THE PRESS AND THE STATE

In a political culture and system where the ethos and practice of statism have been historically well entrenched, it is scarcely surprising that the state has played – and continues to play – a key role in matters concerning the press. In the previous chapter, we saw how the postwar state has been actively concerned with the funding of the press through a system of financial aid. This is only one aspect of the state's role as an enabler in press matters. Another is the way in which the state guarantees to all publications, whatever their content and circulation, access to the press distribution network.[1]

Other aspects of the state's relationship with the press have stronger historical roots. The role of *regulator*, carried out via legislation and rule making, is a traditional state function. So too is that of *censor*. Whatever the official legal framework in place, the authorities have frequently sought to control and censor press coverage, especially at politically sensitive moments when the government, or *a fortiori* the regime, was perceived to be in crisis. The state has also engaged in the manipulation of the press through its authoritative status as a *primary definer* of issues on the media agenda.

In the performance of these different functions (enabler, regulator, censor and primary definer), the postwar state has frequently created the impression of giving with one hand, only to take away with the other. For example, it has introduced measures to foster a diverse and pluralistic press through the implementation of anti-trust legislation and the provision of financial aid. Yet conversely, it has often shown itself willing and able to intervene in press content, for example by manipulating journalists and in extreme cases through outright censorship. This apparent contradiction in the objectives pursued by the state in press matters (a pluralistic versus a controlled press) may demonstrate a cynical attempt by a unified authoritarian state to hide its largely repressive tendencies behind a benevolent enabling façade. Alternatively, it may be indicative of the inherent tensions in the relationship between the state and the media in a political system based on liberal democratic norms and values. It may also be evidence that the state is not a monolithic entity and that different state agencies pursue different, and even mutually incompatible, policies in their relationship with the media.

The state as regulator

Through its control of the legislative process the state lays down the regulatory framework within which the French press operates. Legislation may be more or less restrictive, more or less liberal depending on the constitutional framework of the regime, the ideological complexion of the authorities and the latter's interpretation of the prevailing political situation. Since the beginning of the implantation of the press as a mass medium in the late nineteenth century, three major phases of press legislation stand out from the plethora of legal rules and administrative decisions: the 1881 statute, the 1944 ordinance and the 1984/86 statutes. These were all introduced in specific historical circumstances, addressed the organization of the press with particular concerns in mind and as a result produced quite contrasting legislative emphases.

The 1881 press statute

The 1881 statute may be viewed either as the culmination of an uneven process of liberalization whose origins can be traced back to the 1789 Revolution or as a reaction to the practice of state control of the press which was evident during the greater part of the nineteenth century. The passage from 1789 to 1881 was certainly not a straightforward tale of gradualist, ameliorative reform in state–press relations. In fact, the pattern of governmental attitudes and behaviour towards the press varied considerably during this period. In general the picture was one of prolonged periods of domination by an interventionist and often censorial state, punctuated by rather short periods of relative press freedom from state control. As a result, prior to 1881 the French press was more often than not subject to severe governmental restrictions on its freedom to report and publish.

Of course one should be wary of simple generalizations in this regard. It is not wholly accurate to depict the relationship between the state and the press before 1881 as a continuous period of domination by the former of the latter. In general, it is true that as the press expanded and became more politically partisan during the nineteenth century, the relationship between it and the state was strained. The authorities frequently sought to block the development of a free press through the use of restrictive and even repressive measures. Yet as one leading commentator on the period has pointed out, there was not a constant battle between tyrannical governments on the one hand and radical journalists and liberal politicians on the other.[2] Several newspapers were quite happy to accept the rules as set by the government. This was not altogether surprising, since a tight system of state control did present some advantages for newspapers. 'Under the old system of licensing (pre-1789) an author had been safe once the censor had permitted him to publish; with a so-called "free press", an author could live in fear of reprisal from offended parties.'[3] Moreover, state restrictions on the press were at times in tune with public opinion, which frequently adopted a conservative position on the issue of wider freedom for the press.[4]

Yet while the relationship between the state and the press from 1789 to 1881 was complex and dynamic, rather than simple and static, the picture of an authoritarian state still retains a large degree of validity. Consequently, when a republican regime was restored in the 1870s, its supporters made press reform an early priority. This was one key area in which the Republicans could differentiate themselves from the Bonapartists and Monarchists. One of the earliest acts of the Government of National Defence was to declare that the professions of printing and publishing were free. In so doing, the new regime was seeking to encourage the growth of a democratic political culture to support the new republican institutions:

> the chief task of the republicans, now that they had abandoned the social utopias of an earlier generation, was to educate the people of France to play a responsible part in democratic government, and a free press was obviously one of the chief requisites for such a task.[5]

It was, however, more than a decade before press liberties were fully embodied in a new law.[6] In 1875 the government began the process of revising the legislation on the press. After five years of discussion, Parliament abolished 42 former laws, containing 325 separate clauses, which had been passed over 75 years by ten different regimes. This maze of rules and regulations was swept aside to be replaced by a comprehensive piece of legislation – the Law on the Liberty of the Press of July 29 1881 – which began with the words 'Printing and publishing are free'.[7]

The main features of the 1881 legislation were as follows.[8] First, the publication of newspapers and periodicals could be undertaken without obtaining the government's prior authorization and without depositing caution money. Instead all publishers just had to present their names to the authorities and deposit two copies of every edition. Second, no power was given to either the administrative or judicial authorities to suspend or suppress a newspaper or periodical. Third, as far as press offences were concerned, the hated *délits d'opinion* disappeared once and for all. There were to be no more prosecutions for the vague offence of inciting to hatred and contempt of the government; for attacks on the idea of property, on freedom of worship or on the respect due to the laws; or for outrages against the government or the Republic. The Chamber decided to retain a limited concept of 'press offences', the list of which was greatly reduced and all of which were to be tried by jury in the assize courts; libel was severely reduced in scope, and fair reporting of all parliamentary or legal proceedings was exempted from libel prosecution; and incitement by the press to commit offences was no longer indictable if the offences were not actually committed, except in the case of murder, theft or arson. A small list of offences was left, including outrage to public morals, provocation to racial violence and defamation of the courts, the armed forces, members of the government, public officials, ministers of religion (who were public officials), members of juries and witnesses. It was also forbidden to insult the President of the Republic, the memory of the dead, heads of foreign states or ambassadors. Finally, the 1881 statute instituted a right of reply for persons who wished to make a correction or criticism of an article in which they were featured. According to Smith, 'the new law was to be the most liberal ever devised' and 'the new legal position made it possible for a mass press to take root in Paris and throughout France earlier than in any other country of Europe.'[9] Thomson also attributes great significance to the 1881 legislation: 'This important but neglected law, modified inevitably during the First World War, remained the basis of all press freedoms until the end of the Third Republic.'[10]

Yet there was also a negative side to this newly discovered press freedom. Loosed from the shackles of state censorship and regulation, the press did not always exercise the social responsibility necessary if liberty were not to be abused. 'The abolition of censorship in 1881 gave the press a free rein, almost untrammelled even by libel laws. . . . All this meant that the papers could get away with a great deal. . . .'[11] In these circumstances liberty could easily degenerate into licence, with balanced, moderate coverage losing out to sensationalist and even malevolent reporting as the press abused the latitude allowed it 'to slander and incite to violence with almost total impunity'.[12] This aspect of press behaviour was to become especially marked in the final years of the Third Republic and was to contribute to the destabilization of the political system when economic crisis and political scandal rocked the regime. In particular, in the 1930s the 1881 law

> was open to the charge it gave excessive license, for it made possible the vicious personal attacks and incitement to violence of such publications as the *Action française*. The French press of the 1930s certainly tolerated a degree of scurrility, violence, and financial corruption which were abuses of the freedoms laboriously won in the course of the previous century.[13]

The 1944 ordinance

As France emerged from the ravages of the Second World War, it was clear that the end of the conflict marked a political and economic watershed for the country. The military defeat of the Nazis inevitably led to the final collapse of the Vichy regime, and this was accompanied by a nationwide revulsion against the reactionary ideals of Pétainism and the collaborationist activities of its supporters. The pre-war parliamentary system of the Third Republic and the political forces which had dominated it were also discredited for their humiliating failure to prevent the invasion and occupation of France. Popular demand for institutional change was manifested in the referendum of October 1945 in which there was a massive 96 per cent vote against the re-establishment of the pre-war political system. In effect, this meant that France would yet again acquire a fresh constitution and new political institutions.

The Fourth Republic was finally established in October 1946, though only after the divisions between the major political forces on the constitutional issue had exposed the fragile nature of the postwar coalition. The political system after 1944 was dominated by those forces which had played an active role in the Resistance: the Communists, the Socialists and the Christian Democrats, plus the leader of the Free French, General de Gaulle. Lacking a party base in Parliament, De Gaulle was able for a time to exert personal authority in his capacity as Prime Minister. However, it was the two political parties of the Left working in harness with the Christian Democrats in the governmental coalition known as Tripartism which set the policy agenda and controlled decision making until the expulsion of the Communists from government in May 1947.

The Tripartite government quickly introduced a series of major economic and social reforms. These included wide-sweeping nationalization measures whereby key industries including coal, gas, electricity and the Renault automobile company were brought under state control. Major banks were also nationalized and a programme of indicative planning was introduced.[14] The growing role of the state in social welfare provision and economic management represented the practical embodiment of the ideals of the Resistance Charter which had set out collectivist guidelines and objectives for France's postwar government. The new emphasis on the central role of the interventionist state also borrowed from aspects of the Vichy regime's wartime use of planning.

As both a major industrial concern and an important medium of political communication, the French press was a natural target for this wave of enthusiasm for reform. Many in the Resistance were critical of the pre-war newspaper industry and wanted to vent their wrath on those press owners, the so-called 'big bosses', who had dominated the press before the war. Their attention, however, was not confined to a mere settling of personal accounts, though that certainly formed part of their revanchist agenda. More importantly, proponents of reform wanted to address what they regarded as the structural weaknesses of the pre-war press system which had allowed it to become dominated by capitalist entrepreneurs. They concentrated therefore on the organizational framework of the press and on the liberal ethos which had underpinned its operation since 1881. In short, rather than just the ritual sacrifice of those proprietors who had abused their freedom to publish under the Nazis and Vichy, a full-scale reorganization of the press was considered essential by the parties in power after the Liberation.

The sum of the changes introduced in the immediate postwar period amounted to nothing short of a wholesale revolution in the French press system. As part of the clean sweep of the press, punitive measures were employed against newspapers accused of collaboration. Legislation forbade the reappearance of titles which had appeared under German control. As a result, of the 206 daily newspapers which had been published in France in 1939, only 28 were able to resume operations after the war.[15] The property and equipment of many pre-war publishing houses were put under sequestration before being transferred to newspapers which had been sympathetic to the Resistance. At the same time, the old pre-war press groups were eliminated and a new press system was reconstituted from independent companies. Small press groups including Catholic and Communist ones established themselves in the new system.

The concern of the postwar government to reform the press system found embodiment in legislation – the ordinance of August 26 1944 – the main provisions of which were designed to guarantee pluralism, prevent concentration of ownership and introduce transparency into the financial dealings of the press. Inspired by the ideological dominance of the political agenda by the collectivist ideals of the Resistance, the 1944 reform sought to establish a more positive framework to protect the press from economic pressures which might limit its independence. It aimed to make patterns of ownership and control more visible through a combination of measures which compelled newspapers to declare their economic interests and make public their financial situation. In particular, the ordinance made it illegal for the same person to be the publishing boss of more than one daily newspaper.

The 1944 ordinance was a very different piece of legislation from the press statute of 1881. The laissez-faire provisions of the nineteenth-century legislation were now perceived as an inadequate means of ensuring pluralism in ownership and diversity in content. In its emphasis on the need for new legislation to secure these objectives, the postwar government was trying to make a clean break with the liberal paradigm instituted over 60 years previously. The 1881 legislation had been introduced at a time of expansion and as a counter to the previous practice of excessive state control. In the eyes of the postwar government the inadequacies of this free market approach had been exposed during the inter-war period. Whereas in 1881 the concern of the legislators had been to promote the liberty of the press by protecting it from *political* control by the state, in 1944 the emphasis was placed on removing *economic* threats to press freedom from capitalist entrepreneurs.

In 1944 state intervention was not supported as a means of impeding editorial freedom. It was not intended to mark a return to nineteenth-century censorship and governmental interference in content. Rather it was advocated as a prerequisite for the effective functioning of the market by improving the conditions of competition. The state, it was argued, could help the market work more fairly and effectively. At the same time the government hoped that the result would be a press system more sympathetic to the viewpoint of progressive forces in French society, most notably the parties of the Tripartite coalition. Thus, a mixture of altruism and self-interest lay behind the introduction of the new legislation.

Overall, the role of the state in the organization of the press was massively increased after the Liberation. New radical legislative provisions, the establishment of a national press agency, Agence France-Presse (AFP), and the institution of a system of financial aid were all indicative of the state's desire to play a more pro-active role in the affairs of the press than had been the case prior to the outbreak of the Second World War. Not surprisingly, this emphasis on a strong role for the state in press matters has not been without its critics. For example, in comparing what he terms 'the French model' unfavourably with the more laissez-faire regimes in Germany and Great Britain, Charon puts forward a liberal critique of the excesses of statism. He argues that the powers taken by the French state in press matters have facilitated political control, prevented the implementation of decisions which were desirable on economic grounds and made essential rationalization in the newspaper industry more difficult than it would otherwise have been.[16]

It has also been argued that the ideals of the Resistance were utopian and their fulfilment soon undermined by the re-emergence of hard-nosed economic realities. According to this interpretation of events, the 'political phase' of the postwar press was very short-lived. State regulation and financial aid may have tempered some of the less desirable aspects of market competition, but the parties of the Resistance were unable to impose their values on the functioning of the press. Within a few years of the end of the war many newspapers had gone out of business. The inexperience of some of the new press owners played a part in this retrenchment. Economic factors also came into play. As the price of newspapers increased, the circulation figures of some fell, while those of others went up. Advertising tended to go to those papers whose circulation was already healthy, thereby giving a further downward push to the weaker papers. Meanwhile, readers preferred to read newspapers of a general information character rather than party political papers with their ideologically partisan content.[17] Another reason why the objectives of the 1944 legislation were not fully realized was that many politicians themselves became press owners and had no interest in seeing its provisions tested in court amid a blaze of critical publicity. In general, the period of the Fourth Republic saw a move away from the fulfilment of the ideals of the Liberation. The further the experience of the Resistance receded into the background, the more economic factors and commercial concerns asserted their importance.

Yet this does not mean that the innovations of the Liberation were a total failure. Whatever its limitations in practice, the 1944 legislation did have some impact in checking a tendency towards concentration of ownership and the emergence of large press groups in the postwar period. What evolved was a market system in which the state played an important but by no means all-embracing role in aiding diversity.

> If this revolution was not as durable as its promoters in the Resistance or in exile had hoped, at least it did for a time make a *tabula rasa* of the past, put in place new titles, men and organizations and defined a different regime from that of 1881. Developments since the Liberation have profoundly transformed this new press; economic factors have favoured concentration. The constraints of commercial journalism have rendered inoperative many of the prescriptions of 1944 and 1945. The resistants were able to give an opportunity to a very wide spectrum of newspapers and journalists: they could not guarantee to each the same success.[18]

The 1984 and 1986 statutes

In 1981 the Left came to power for the first time in the Fifth Republic. The postwar era had witnessed a process of concentration in the French press as many newspapers disappeared from circulation, regional papers built up quasi-monopolies in their circulation areas and a combination of mergers and takeovers resulted in the emergence of important national press groups, none more so than that dominated by Hersant.[19] The growth of the Hersant group during the 1970s and early 1980s was clearly anathema to the Left, since the group's newspapers strongly backed the policies and candidates of the Gaullist component of the mainstream right-wing coalition. Justifying their case by emphasizing the desirability of a pluralist press and the consequent need for measures against concentration of newspaper ownership, the Socialist government launched a fierce attack on the Hersant empire in 1983. As the 1944 legislation was deemed to be inadequate to tackle the problem, the Socialists decided to introduce a new press law, which soon became known as the 'anti-Hersant law'. With shrewd prescience President Mitterrand was apparently sceptical of the merits of such an initiative, fearing that the resultant controversy might backfire against the Socialists.[20] The weight of opinion in the Socialist parliamentary group, however, carried the day in favour of change.

The passage of the bill through Parliament was accompanied by stormy scenes: 'the most virulent, unrelenting obstruction of any bill in the history of the Fifth Republic'.[21] Backed by Hersant's newspapers, the conservative opposition in Parliament resolutely opposed the bill and mounted a fierce parliamentary campaign to sabotage the Socialists' reform proposals. The Socialists argued that a pluralistic press required limits on ownership if diversity of information were to be guaranteed. The Right argued that the freedom to publish was a property right and should not be interfered with by a government for partisan purposes. It also pointed out that while the legislative proposals would damage the Hersant group, they would leave untouched the regional monopoly of the Socialist minister, Gaston Defferre, in Marseilles. Subjected to massive amendment in parliamentary committee and by the government itself, the legislation was eventually adopted thanks to the large Socialist majority in the National Assembly.

In October 1984 a new press law was promulgated, but only after the Constitutional Council had so altered its provisions as to make it virtually useless as a weapon against Hersant. The law's anti-trust focus relied on a fixed market ceiling, i.e. maximum percentages of total circulation for daily newspapers that any one press group could acquire. The central provision of the 1984 statute was that no single press group could control more than 15 per cent of the total circulation of national dailies or 15 per cent of the total circulation of regional dailies; if a press group owned both national and regional newspapers, the ceiling was 10 per cent in both sectors. The statute also created a Commission for the transparency and pluralism of the press (CTPP) and introduced measures to clarify the details of newspaper ownership.[22]

The ruling of the Constitutional Council, however, prohibited the application of the statute's anti-trust provisions to existing situations, both letting Hersant off the hook and making it legally impossible for any other press group to rival Hersant. It also weakened the role of the proposed CTPP, 'gutting the CTPP's powers to force compliance in the event of future violations'.[23] In sum, the Constitutional Council destroyed the legislation as it had been passed by Parliament, effectively neutering the Socialist government's reform. As a result, the 1984 legislation was without consequence for the activities of the Hersant group.

By March 1986, when the Right returned to power, the Hersant press group controlled more than 38 per cent of the national market and more than 26 per cent of the regional one, including an absolute monopoly in the nation's largest multi-paper regional market, the Rhône Valley. In comparative terms, the percentage of the total French market controlled by Hersant is greater than that controlled by any press group in any western democracy.[24]

Despite the fact that the 1984 press statute was to all intents and purposes a dead letter, the new right-wing majority which emerged after the 1986 parliamentary elections was determined to rescind it. Arguing that the Socialist legislation was profoundly anti-liberal and had been targeted in an *ad hominem* fashion at the Hersant empire, the conservative government of

Prime Minister Chirac introduced new legislative proposals which became law in August 1986. The 1986 press statute replaced both the 1944 and 1984 texts in their entirety. While the original bill abolished fixed ceilings on press group holdings, these were reintroduced in Parliament in an attempt to head off a negative ruling from the Constitutional Council. A ceiling of 30 per cent of total daily newspaper circulation was introduced on the market share of any single press group. The distinction between national and regional markets was now abandoned, and ownership of weekly or monthly publications was not considered relevant to the calculation. Curiously, the Hersant group's market share at the time fell somewhere between 28 and 29 per cent![25] The statute also abolished the CTPP set up less than two years previously.

As in 1984 the Constitutional Council was asked to rule on the constitutionality of the 1986 press reform. It accepted that the higher ceilings and the abolition of the distinction between national and regional markets did not weaken pluralism, but criticized the wording of the act and compelled the government to revise the text. This it did in the autumn of 1986 along with a revision of its statute on broadcasting. The cumulative effect of this was the establishment of an elaborate anti-trust regime governing the whole communications sector (press, broadcasting and new media) and imposing limits on the development of multimedia groups.[26] The Council had become a key player in the legislative process on the press and audiovisual media in the 1980s and its interventions became the subject of intense political controversy.[27]

The 1986 legislation revealed how the approach of the state to the issue of press regulation has evolved over time. For much of the nineteenth century the state controlled the press through a range of censorship devices. After 1881 it adopted a position of laissez-faire liberalism until the end of the Second World War. In the immediate postwar atmosphere favourable to statism, it followed a policy of trying to control the market via strict regulations. Some of this interventionist ethos still survives in anti-trust legislation on concentration of ownership and in the array of financial aid measures funded by the state.

However, it now seems clear that much of the spirit of the 1944 legislation has been largely abandoned as anachronistic. Elite attitudes to the press have also altered in the postwar period. In 1944 the press was regarded as a different entity from other businesses because of its political and cultural importance. By the early 1990s this view was much less in evidence. Information was more likely to be regarded as an economic product like any other, while the dominant view among state officials was that communication groups should be regulated in as similar a manner as possible to other commercial enterprises. A minimally regulated market rather than an interventionist state was deemed to be the optimal means of ensuring pluralism and diversity in the press.[28]

The state as censor

With the origins of the practice pre-dating the 1789 Revolution, censorship has traditionally been one of the main roles played by the French state in its relationship with the press. Though direct censorship of press content is more the exception than the rule in contemporary France, the tradition has not entirely died out. Instances of press censorship still occur, while during the postwar period the state has also directed its censoring activities to the output of the broadcasting media.[29]

For most of the nineteenth century the state employed a range of mechanisms to seek to ensure a compliant press. Before the 1789 Revolution the press had been strongly controlled by the monarchical regime. Many newspapers were official or semi-official and censorship was commonplace. The king employed no fewer than 121 censors in 1763.[30] The 1789 Revolution radically, but temporarily, changed this situation. The system of press control and prior censorship was rendered defunct as the shackles of monarchy were cast off. Article 11 of the 'Declaration of the rights of man and the citizen' defined the new principle of press freedom:

> The free expression of thought and opinions is one of the most precious rights of man: all citizens, therefore, may speak, write (or) publish freely, subject to the penalties for any abuse of this freedom in cases determined by the law.

However, while the practice of the very early years of the Revolution may well have reflected this liberal commitment, the principle never properly took institutional root. 'Press liberty was not compatible with external or internal warfare, and France was now subjected to both.'[31]

The outbreak of war had devastating consequences for the domestic political environment and for press freedom, with first the royalist and then the Girondin press becoming the victims of Jacobin orthodoxy.[32] Press freedom was one of the casualties of the warped application of revolutionary ideals in the period dominated by terror. Newspapers were closed down and journalists imprisoned or executed as dissidence was rooted out under the aegis of revolutionary probity. At the same time, official patronage and subsidy were increased, 'aimed at creating a compliant press to disseminate revolutionary propaganda'.[33] In the immediate aftermath of Thermidor, as a reaction against the terror, a substantial degree of press freedom returned. Under the Directory, the Consulate and the Napoleonic Empire, however, the press once again became the object of strict government control.

Napoleon in particular understood the importance of the press as a link between state power and public opinion.

> On his accession to power, Bonaparte was to waste little time in refining the machinery bequeathed to him by his predecessors, and returning the political press to the kind of government control that it had experienced

under the *ancien régime*. In this he did not innovate, but merely built on the legacy inherited from the last two years of the Directory, of censorship, police control and complete distrust of editorial freedom.[34]

In 1811 a government decree allowed only four political newspapers to publish in Paris. Meanwhile, in the provinces the papers could cover politics only through extracts from the *Moniteur*, an official government newspaper after 1800.

The fall of the Empire in 1814 brought little substantive change. Between 1814 and 1830 press freedom was restricted by the use of various devices: advance authorization which allowed the state to permit the functioning of only those newspapers which it was prepared to tolerate; censorship which permitted the banning of articles or even whole issues; and stamp duty which penalized the circulation of newspapers with a political content. Even when the July Monarchy (1830–48) abolished prior censorship, different legislative measures could be employed to regulate and control the press, including the payment of caution money by newspapers and the imposition of restrictive libel laws 'in such a way that they strangled the republican and legitimist press'.[35]

The demise of the short-lived Second Republic heralded the start of one of the most repressive regimes on press matters – the Second Empire.

[In] December 1851 the Minister of the Interior transmitted to the prefects arbitrary power to prevent newspapers from commenting unfavourably on the *coup d'état* [which had brought the Second Republic to an end]. In Paris the police took possession of the offices of all leading newspapers. . . . The more notorious opposition journals . . . were obliged to cease publication until further notice, and the rest could only appear if they agreed to refrain from comment on the *coup d'état*.[36]

The tendency of monarchism and of Bonapartism to assert firm control of the press, to hamper opposition and to hem round all publication with complex restrictions reached a height with new legislation introduced in 1852. Preliminary authorization to publish, which required the founders and publishers of all journals dealing with 'politics or social economy' to get prior permission from the Minister of the Interior, was restored. New offences were added and prefects were given discretionary power to warn, suspend, or suppress newspapers and to punish journalists for activities which were displeasing to the government but which could not be described as offences in law. Since no drawing could be published without permission of the Prefect of Police, there was direct censorship of illustrated papers.[37] The 1852 legislation

combined all of the crippling restrictions attempted over the previous thirty years: newspapers now had to reacquire permission every time they underwent a change of staff; no foreign papers were allowed in

France; huge caution moneys were imposed on all political papers; stamp taxes and postage rates were raised; publication of 'false news' was forbidden; it was forbidden to print the name of a suspended journal; two offences within two years led to automatic suspension, and all trials relating to these laws were held without juries; for good measure, officials had power to prosecute journalists who wrote material displeasing to the authorities even if it was not indictable under the law.[38]

These measures had an immediate impact. By 1865 only 250 political journals were appearing in the provinces, as compared with some 430 in 1851. Radical papers which had been suspended after the *coup d'état* did not dare to reappear; moderate papers which had ventured into politics in 1848 now returned to literature or commerce; and legitimist and orléanist papers, either from fear of socialism or fear of the press law, supported the government of Louis Napoleon.[39]

Towards the end of the Second Empire a significant move was made towards a more liberal framework for the press with the press law of 1868 which abolished the need for preliminary authorization for the establishment of a newspaper. However, it was not until the Republicans came to dominate the parliamentary regime of the Third Republic in the 1880s that liberalization was finally achieved with the enactment of the 1881 statute.

Yet even this highly liberal piece of legislation did not put an end to state censorship, which was particularly in evidence at times of national crisis. During the First World War, for example, the government severely censored the press in the interest of keeping popular morale high. Moreover, from a sense of patriotic duty much of the press for much of the time was more than happy to comply with government directives and presented a highly misleading and optimistic picture of events at the front.[40]

On the eve of the Second World War, before hostilities had actually been declared, the French government moved to ban the publication of the Communist press, including the party daily *L'Humanité*. The Fall of France in 1940 was followed by the introduction of censorship by the Vichy state in the southern zone. Kedward describes the mechanisms of Vichy control of the press as follows:

The principal source of information for the press, L'Agence Havas, was taken over by Vichy and renamed Office français d'information (OFI). Repeated instructions and *notes d'orientation* were sent out from the OFI not only telling newspapers what not to print, but also telling them how they must refer to the government decisions and in particular to the person of Pétain. . . . The Vichy government did not initiate press censorship, since it already existed under Daladier and Reynaud, but by adding compulsory propaganda to negative censorship it made it necessary for all newspapers to submit to government control or to cease publication altogether.[41]

During the postwar period the major occasion for press censorship was the Algerian war of independence (1954–62) which pitted an indigenous Muslim nationalist movement (organized in the Front de Libération Nationale – the FLN) against the nominally Christian French colonial power. All the elements were present for a bloody conflict over who should govern Algeria. From 1954 to 1958 various Fourth Republic governments poured troops into North Africa in an attempt to retain Algeria as an integral part of France. At the same time the professional army and the European settlers in Algeria (*les pieds noirs*) feared that a sell-out of French interests was being prepared. The settlers were afraid of losing their economic power and prosperous lifestyle, while the army wanted to make up for the débâcles of Dien Bien Phu in Indochina (1954) and Suez (1956). Defence of French Algeria bound these two groups in common cause against the alleged treachery of the Fourth Republic authorities. De Gaulle and his supporters used these two groups for their own political purposes of bringing about the collapse of the regime and replacing it with new institutions in which the executive dominated the legislature, the President controlled the government and de Gaulle ruled France.

The establishment of the Fifth Republic in 1958 marked in retrospect a change in French government policy on Algeria with the beginning of the slow and tortuous path towards an independent Algerian state. This was not to take place for another four years, however, during most of which time the French government proceeded with the war against the FLN. In the last few months of the conflict it also found itself fighting against supporters of *Algérie française*, grouped together in the terrorist organization known as the Organisation Armée Secrète (OAS). It was the OAS – a motley collection of disaffected politicians, aggrieved military officers and self-interested *pieds noirs* who were prepared to die, but more importantly kill, in their desperation to keep Algeria French – which carried out numerous abortive assassination attempts on de Gaulle in the early 1960s, one of which was fictionalized in Frederick Forsyth's best-selling novel, *The Day of the Jackal*.

In contrast to the two world wars, the Algerian conflict was not a war of national survival, even if some of the protagonists on the French side in Algeria viewed it in such a light. However, it was certainly a war of regime survival in the case of the Fourth Republic and, arguably, in the case of the Fifth as well. In any event it was a struggle which the French were desperate to win. Torture by the French military in Algeria was tacitly condoned in Paris, as the French state waged a savage war of repression against supporters of the FLN. This physical battle was complemented by a propaganda war fought by the authorities in Paris to win the hearts and minds of the French people in support of official government policy.

Censorship of the media was an integral part of the government's approach. Censorship was employed not primarily for the purposes of military security, which would have been justifiable, but rather to bolster morale at home and prevent opposition to the official perspective on the conflict from becoming too vocally persuasive. The leftish intellectual weekly, *France-Observateur*, was suppressed repeatedly, as was *L'Humanité*.[42] Knightley describes the means employed by the authorities to harness the media in support of official policy as follows:

> [France] was forced to employ a campaign of censorship, repression, and intimidation of correspondents, so as to keep from the French public – and the rest of the world – the truth about the nature of the war in Algeria.
>
> All publications in Algeria were put under the control of the Prefecture, which was given the right to veto any material prior to printing. In France, the authorities used an obscure section of the criminal code to seize all the issues of *Les Nouvelles de Bordeaux*, the first paper to suffer what was to become a popular form of suppression and financial punishment. . . . There was a wave of arrests of journalists. . . . French newspapers that failed to follow the government line were attacked for being unpatriotic, traitors to France. . . . There appeared no limit to the government's determination to suppress news that it did not like and to discredit or destroy professionally any correspondent who resisted this policy.[43]

Keane's description of French government policy on media coverage of the Algerian war supports Knightley's view:

> During the transition from the Fourth to the Fifth Republic, amidst mounting public tension and fears of an army takeover spearheaded by General de Gaulle, the press was routinely threatened, censored and seized. Editors were notified by the government that 'France' was in danger. Ministers briefed journalists about precisely what could and could not be reported, insisting that such briefings were strictly confidential. Direct bans were imposed on certain kinds of information, such as news of house arrests, expulsions and the use of anti-guerilla tactics. In Algeria itself, *L'Express*, *Libération* and *L'Humanité* were banned totally for various lengths of time. Most liberal and left papers were seized numerous times in metropolitan France. Since seizure amounted to blocking the distribution of a publication *after* it was printed, even if a censored article were replaced, the entire print run had to be repeated, leading to a doubling of costs of production. Newspaper publishers were subject to extensive bombing campaigns by 'unidentified attackers', and journalists were arrested and convicted on charges of disclosing military secrets and 'attacking the morale of the army'.[44]

The most infamous use of government censorship during the Algerian war concerned the publication in 1958 of the book *La Question*, written by

Henri Alleg, who had been editor of the *Alger Républicain* from 1950 to 1955. This newspaper, which according to the book's introduction was the only daily in Algeria which opened its columns to all aspects of Algerian democratic and national opinion, was banned in September 1955. An internment order was made out against most of the contributors to the paper, with Alleg himself going into hiding. He was arrested in June 1957 by French paratroopers and kept in detention for a month in a building on the outskirts of Algiers, during which time he was questioned under torture with unbelievable brutality and sadism. The book is a passionate and disturbing account of his detention and torture.

When the book was first published in France, it sold 60,000 copies in the first two weeks. When *L'Express* published a long article by Jean-Paul Sartre on the book, the entire issue was seized by the Paris Police by order of the Minister of the Interior. The government obviously feared any favourable publicity being given to the book by authoritative figures in French political and intellectual circles. An issue of *France-Observateur*, containing extracts from the book, was also seized, as were copies of the book itself. According to the book's publisher, this was the first time that a book had been seized in France for political reasons since the eighteenth century.[45]

Towards the end of the war, French state officials also censored press reporting of the deaths of Muslim demonstrators at the hands of the French police during a demonstration in Paris in 1961. When supporters of the FLN marched on central Paris to protest at a curfew, the police banned all journalists before attacking the protesters with appalling savagery. A Channel 4 documentary broadcast in 1992 claimed that up to 200 peaceful Algerian demonstrators were killed during the demonstration. Details of the slaughter only emerged a few days later when corpses started bobbing up in the Seine. Even then, the French press failed to give the incident the coverage it undoubtedly merited, though it is not wholly clear whether this was because of censorship or a racist-inspired lack of sympathy with those who had been killed.[46]

The picture of a press virtuously seeking after truth, but coming into conflict with a government ruthlessly committed to, and wholly successful in, implementing effective censorship in defence of *Algérie française*, is scarcely a balanced picture of events. The reality of the state–press relationship during the Algerian war was much more complex. First, as in the First World War, many French newspapers were perfectly content to promote the government's line on the war, even at the cost of ignoring reports of torture committed by the French military in Algeria. Many newspapers engaged in selective self-censorship, not as a pre-emptive move to avoid being censored by the authorities, but because they were prepared to act as a media conduit for the official perspective on the conflict. This might have been because they were in genuine sympathy with the official perspective on the war or, even if they had doubts on this issue, because they did not wish to alienate that section of their readership which backed the government line. Self-censorship was frequently based on commercial rather than political considerations. Second, Talbott argues that government censorship was not as harsh as it might have been:

> the government could have squeezed the press much harder. It bolted no newspaper's doors, smashed no printing presses, left no writers rotting in jail. The authorities feared that the controversy over torture would not only diminish support for keeping Algeria French but further antagonize an already unhappy army. They may have wanted to take sterner measures against critics of the Algerian policy, but they resisted the temptation. The laws respecting freedom of the press were bent and strained but not trampled under.[47]

Third, the government was not always successful in ensuring that censorship was effectively applied against those sections of the press which sought to present a different agenda from the official one. Alternative and oppositional views of the conflict did feature in the French press, qualifying the official perspective or even countering it head on. *France-Observateur*, *L'Express* and *Témoignage Chrétien* among others published reports and articles which called into question the government's defence of its case in Algeria. Finally, it should be noted that government censorship was not confined to articles sympathetic to the FLN or hostile to the French military. When official government policy changed from one of a defence of *Algérie française* to one of support for self-determination for the Algerian people, the French government put pressure on the press to refrain from publicizing the viewpoint of the OAS. Pressure was exerted not to report

> anything to do with those of its members who were French army officers or any details of the vicious underground war it was waging with the barbouzes [underground government agents engaged in a bloody struggle with the OAS]. Any correspondent who interviewed the OAS chief, General Salan, would be expelled . . . and in January 1962 the European edition of *Time* was seized because it carried a picture of Salan on its cover.[48]

The state as primary definer

In addition to its roles as enabler, regulator and censor, the French state is a primary definer of issues covered by the press (and the broadcasting media). The primary definition of issues can be analytically differentiated from censorship, though in extreme cases the former may merge with the latter. Whereas censorship is an overt exercise of naked power, primary definition is a more subtle form of media management and manipulation. It covers low-level activities such as the issuing of press releases about official events and the use of public relations techniques. It also includes different kinds of misinformation and disinformation, from leaks and planted stories to propaganda. The concept of primary definition can be satisfactorily explained with reference to two features of developed media systems: first, the routinization of the news production process in an age of sophisticated mass communications technology and highly bureaucratic media organizations; and second, the legitimacy which is conferred on certain individuals, groups or institutions as authoritative sources of information because of their social status, technical expertise, economic power or political position.[49]

The collection and dissemination of news by the press (and other media) is a complex process, much of which has been routinized to enable the system to function efficiently. In an organizational culture often characterized by severe time constraints, the selection of news stories by the press is not, and cannot be, random. Rather it is made with reference to criteria of newsworthiness, which, far from being neutral, are ideologically and culturally determined. Media practitioners are generally socialized into the corporate culture of the organization so that the production process functions smoothly. In such an environment there is a natural tendency on the part of editors and journalists to make considerable use of official sources, which are themselves geared up to provide information in ways which the press finds user-friendly. These official sources enjoy good formal links with the media, for example through the use of full-time press officers. They also usually benefit from strong informal links with editors and journalists on the political/media network. As a result, official sources are generally perceived by the press as a regular and reliable source of news copy and this position allows them to shape the media agenda and issue coverage.

At the same time, because they possess some form of authority, primary definers are usually essential purveyors of information if the press is to have what it regards as a complete account of events. Whereas many individuals and groups in society are excluded or marginalized in the process of news construction, primary definers enjoy a privileged insider position. It is not just the mechanics of news collection or their superior resources which make official sources prominent in this process. It is their status, expertise, wealth and power. The possession of any one of these (and *a fortiori* a combination of them) legitimizes their views in the eyes of the media and makes their views an integral component of the press version of reality.

The French state's role as primary definer has a long historical pedigree, stretching back to the Revolution and before.[50] In the early 1830s state management of the press was institutionalized through the establishment of Havas as an international press agency. Exercising a quasi-monopoly on the supply of information in France, especially in the realm of foreign affairs,

Havas was used by the state to control the quantity, range and quality of news provided to newspapers and their readers.[51] In the twentieth century, inter-war governments went so far as to subsidize newspapers from secret funds in return for favourable coverage. 'Journalists shamelessly presented themselves at the end of the month at the Ministry of the Interior for their "envelopes".'[52] This was part of a widespread corrupt practice in which newspapers accepted money from industrialists and politicians among others in payment for sympathetic treatment. 'The French government, far from disapproving of this bribery, took an active part in it, in the hope of deriving short-term political advantage itself.'[53]

While in the Fifth Republic such crude financial transactions have disappeared, the political executive has a number of other ways in which it can influence press reporting. The President and his advisers ('the Elysée'), the Prime Minister and his staff ('Matignon') and the other government ministries are key primary definers for the contemporary French press. On major domestic and foreign policy issues, from the fight against inflation to the war in the Gulf, their input helps to structure the way in which an issue is covered. To help ensure that the official version of events dominates press coverage the political executive is assisted by a range of support staff and official bodies, including public relations personnel and media advisers, presidential and governmental spokespersons, press offices and governmental information agencies. An assortment of 'spin doctors' are dutifully wheeled out to provide the required 'angle' for a press story. Sometimes editors and journalists will go along with the official line because they are in sympathy with the government's policies, sometimes because not to do so would disadvantage them in the competition for readers. The executive's perspective on events, therefore, usually has little difficulty in finding a channel in most of the press.

The executive also stages special events to help structure the media agenda, including presidential press conferences, interviews with journalists and television appearances by the President and his ministers. Perhaps the most dramatic media event in the Fifth Republic was the mysterious disappearance of President de Gaulle during the upheaval of 1968. This was an unusual case where the head of state seized the political initiative not through the normal device of a press conference, which would scarcely have competed in newsworthiness with the disturbances in the streets of Paris, but by creating a spectacular media event – his own disappearance from the political stage – which was bound to dominate the front pages of the nation's newspapers and focus public attention back on the General.

The Elysée, Matignon and government ministries are not the only primary definers for the press. Other state actors include the bureaucracy, particularly top civil servants and officials with specialist technical knowledge; the military, which acted as an important propaganda medium during the Algerian war; and the police. Outside the state apparatus, mainstream political parties, 'insider' pressure groups, i.e. those which are regarded as representative and responsible, financial institutions and individuals occupying positions of authority may also act as primary definers. Conversely, many other actors in the political process, such as non-mainstream parties and 'outsider' pressure groups, find it difficult to compete with primary definers in either resources or legitimacy. As a result, they have difficulty in finding an outlet for their views in much of the press.

The importance of primary definers in helping to structure the agenda of the press and its issue coverage does not mean that the media are involved in a conspiracy of collusion and compliance. Nor does it follow that primary definers *determine* the media agenda or the manner in which issues are treated. In part this is because in a pluralistic society primary definers will often be in competition with one another, most obviously when mainstream political parties ferociously compete to impose their own agenda on the media during election campaigns. In addition, since primary definers are in reality rarely monolithic entities, this also inhibits their capacity to determine press coverage. This is certainly true in the case of the French state which is frequently internally divided on the formulation and implementation of policy in any specific field, divisions which are often evident to the media and exploited by them in the interest of public information. This may lead to embarrassment for state authorities as disagreements are exposed and fought out under the glare of the media's spotlights.

Sometimes the conflicts are based on party political divisions within the governing coalition. This was the case in the 1970s when the Gaullists and Giscardians frequently fought over policy, while in the early 1980s the Communist party became an increasingly sullen and disenchanted participant in the government of the Left. The most obvious example of party political conflict at the very apex of the state was the period of *cohabitation* between the Socialist President Mitterrand and the Gaullist Prime Minister Chirac between 1986 and 1988. Yet even when the government appears united, there are often dissenting voices prepared to use the press for the furtherance of their political career.

Nor does the press depend solely on primary definers for constructing its agenda. Other non-primary sources are normally used, especially by the quality press, in an attempt to cover a story from different angles. Some newspapers even go further by encouraging journalists to question officially released material and submit it to critical scrutiny. The apotheosis of this approach is the practice of investigative journalism, made famous in the USA by Woodward and Bernstein's exposure in the *Washington Post* of President Nixon's involvement in the Watergate scandal. Though the Watergate investigation is by no means typical of the relationship between the press and the authorities in the USA, far less in France, it does illustrate the difficulties that even the most illustrious primary definers may face in their attempts to impose their agenda or their news angle on the press. This is most obviously the case with those sections of the press which pride themselves on their 'alternative' status and which are automatically sceptical of anything emanating from official sources – the satirical newspaper *Le Canard enchaîné* being the most obvious example in France.

Even in France, where the practice of investigative journalism is poorly implanted in the professional journalistic culture and is constrained by strong privacy legislation, there have been several occasions when the view of the press as the quiescent mouthpiece of the primary defining state stretches credulity to breaking point. During the 1968 'events', for example, the official perspective, which tended to emphasize the law and order dimension of the protest and attribute responsibility for the disturbances to the Communist party, was echoed by some but by no means all of the press. In the late 1970s President Giscard d'Estaing had great difficulty first in keeping the Bokassa diamonds affair out of the press once it had been revealed in the iconoclastic weekly, *Le Canard enchaîné*, and then in imposing the Elysée version of events once the story had broken in the mainstream media. President Mitterrand faced a similar problem in covering up the Rainbow Warrior fiasco and, once it had become public knowledge, in having the official version of events swallowed by the press. In short, even with the odds stacked in its favour, the state cannot always rely on the official perspective dominating press coverage all of the time.

THE PRESS AND POLITICAL PARTIES

According to Seymour-Ure, there are three main reasons why the relationship between newspapers and political parties is generally worthy of study:

> First . . . there have been very obvious historical associations between press and party systems. The growth of competing political parties in nineteenth-century Europe was widely paralleled by the rise of newspapers supporting them – in Britain, France, Germany, Russia and Scandinavia, for example. . . . In the second place, the press in widely varying types of political system is given a role explicitly or implicitly that connects it to party. . . . A third reason . . . is that the functions of parties are highly compatible with the capabilities of newspapers.[54]

The relationship between the press and political parties in France has altered dramatically during the postwar era as a result of changes in both the political and media systems. First, the importance of political parties has considerably altered in the period since the end of the Second World War. During the Fourth Republic parties were by far the main political actors, dominating government, Parliament and the electoral process. Not for nothing did de Gaulle contemptuously dismiss the Fourth Republic as 'le régime des partis'. In contrast, the Fifth Republic has witnessed a marked decline in the significance of parties. The Gaullist constitution of 1958/62, the institution of a powerful presidential office and the development of television as a mass medium have all played a part in weakening the hold of parties on French political life. Party loyalties in the 1990s are weaker than they used to be, with fewer French voters identifying with a political party than in the past. Moreover, even among those voters who still consider themselves to be party supporters, partisan identification is generally more pragmatic and conditional than before. The sub-cultures which both reflected and contributed to the strength of parties have disappeared, including the Communist sub-culture which helped the party through its cold war isolation in national politics during the 1950s. French voters have become less members of political families and more consumers in the electoral marketplace.

Second, the press itself has changed since the Liberation. The decline in the number of different newspaper titles and the emergence of strong market leaders in different regions has encouraged many provincial newspapers to downplay any strong party political views for fear of alienating sections of their readership. The commercial desire to maintain circulation figures and widen their market appeal has encouraged many regional papers to eschew partisan commitment in favour of a more anodyne approach to politics. In some cases the political sympathies of regional papers have been clear. Under Gaston Defferre's ownership, *Le Provençal* in Marseilles was naturally sympathetic to the policies of the Socialist party and in particular to those of the city's mayor – Gaston Defferre! Some regional dailies such as *La Dépêche du Midi* (Radical) and *La Voix du Nord* (Socialist) still retain a vestigial link with their political origins, while *Nord-Matin* was pro-Socialist until its takeover by the Hersant group. However, these are the exceptions among the provincial press, which overall tends to be socially conservative and politically circumspect.

Whereas during the early years of the Fourth Republic party political newspapers emerged to take a significant share of the market, in the 1950s the same papers began a process of near terminal decline. Different types of newspapers came to dominate sales, with looser (or no) links with political parties and a less partisan approach to political reporting. With the exception of the Communist press, the readership of most newspapers in France is politically heterogeneous. Among the non-Communist press few, if any, large circulation newspapers have a readership drawn mainly, far less exclusively, from supporters of a single political party. As in Britain, many French readers use papers more for entertainment and general information than for specific political purposes.

This does not mean that the French press and political parties are independent entities, occupying separate spheres of activity and functioning without any form of interaction. Newspapers and political parties in France do interact, but they do so in different ways and to varying degrees.

The model of press/party linkages outlined by Seymour-Ure is useful in this respect. He argues that the connection between individual parties and newspapers can be measured by reference to three characteristics of parties: (1) organization; (2) goals (programmes and tactics); and (3) members and supporters. A newspaper is defined as 'paralleling' a party if it is closely linked to that party by organization, loyalty to party goals and the partisanship of its readers.[55] Employing this model in the context of the present study, it is possible to reach some preliminary conclusions about the nature of the connection or parallelism between newspapers and parties in postwar France.

When, immediately following the Liberation, there was an explosion of new press titles coming on to the market, political party newspapers were strongly in evidence. Initially, advance authorization to publish a newspaper was given only to those papers emanating from the Resistance or controlled by political parties. Parties owned newspapers based in both Paris and the provinces, with each current of the Resistance movement represented. In 1946, for example, the Communists controlled 51 major daily papers, the Socialists 34 and the Christian Democrats 27. In general these official party newspapers did not survive for very long. The Christian Democrat daily (*L'Aube*) folded in 1951, while the Socialist party daily (*Le Populaire*) eventually gave up the ghost in 1966 after years of decline – it had lost nine in ten of its readers between 1947 and 1958.[56] The Gaullist party daily (*La Nation*) disappeared in 1974, though it had survived until then only thanks to a hidden governmental subsidy. Despite its derisory circulation, *La Nation* was politically important because its editorials were given prominent coverage in radio and television news programmes during de Gaulle's presidency. The Communist paper *Ce Soir* disappeared in 1953. Attempts to set up ideologically committed newspapers in the wake of the 1968 'events' were also short-lived. *Rouge, Le Quotidien du Peuple, L'Humanité rouge* and *Combat socialiste* all failed to achieve large enough sales or attract sufficient advertising income to maintain themselves in existence.

At the same time daily newspapers which have adopted an editorial line too overtly sympathetic to a single political party have also run the risk of market failure. This was the case, for example, with *Le Matin* (originally published under the title of *Le Matin de Paris*). Launched as a new national daily by the management of *Le Nouvel Observateur* in 1977, *Le Matin* supported François Mitterrand's Socialist party. However, following its failure in the 1980s to carve out a market niche for itself in competition with *Le Monde* and *Libération*, it ceased publication at the beginning of 1988. The conservative evening daily *J'informe*, launched in September 1977 to support the governing right-wing coalition and to compete against the pro-Mitterrand *Le Monde*, was a particularly notable failure in this regard. It ceased publication in December of the same year with a circulation of only 20,000 and a loss of 30 million francs. The virtual absence of official party dailies and the weak position of newspapers which slavishly follow a single party line mean that strong, direct links between political parties and mass circulation newspapers are now rare in France.

There is one notable, if declining, exception to this generalization: *L'Humanité*, the official daily newspaper of the French Communist party (PCF). Under all three criteria proposed by Seymour-Ure, *L'Humanité* very closely parallels the PCF. In terms of organization *L'Humanité* fits the ideal type of a party paper since it is effectively controlled by the party. The paper's editor is a member of the PCF politburo; the party appoints the paper's editor and other senior executives, many of whom are party office-holders; the party exercises critical surveillance over the contents of the paper; there is a high level of party membership among journalists; and the training of journalists is directly controlled by the party.

Given its organizational links with the PCF, *L'Humanité* clearly supports the electoral and ideological goals of the party. This is a classic case of extreme newspaper loyalty to party objectives. The paper frequently contains articles by party members, party officials and often the general secretary himself, all of which articulate the party line. When the party line changes, for example from a dalliance with 'Eurocommunism' in the 1970s to a pro-Soviet, ouvriériste approach in the 1980s, the content of *L'Humanité* alters accordingly. The paper acts as a Leninist transmission belt for the articulation of party policy, rallying the faithful, mobilizing the core electorate and condemning any signs of dissent among the militants. *L'Humanité* was particularly important to the party during the cold war era of the 1950s, when the PCF was politically isolated and other media, including state radio, were resolutely anti-Communist.

Finally, for parallelism between a newspaper and political party to be complete, the paper's readership ought not to include supporters of any other party.[57] *L'Humanité* more than adequately satisfies this criterion, since the paper's readership is overwhelmingly made up of members and supporters of the PCF. *L'Humanité* preaches entirely to the converted. Unfortunately for both the party and its newspaper, however, the Communist faithful – as measured both by party membership and electoral support – have declined in numbers since 1945. The paper lost half its readership between 1947 and 1958, while in recent years its circulation has plummeted in conjunction with the sinking electoral fortunes of the party. Its 1991 circulation of just over 70,000 copies testifies to the precarious nature of its existence.

At the opposite end of the spectrum of newspaper/party parallelism from *L'Humanité* is the national daily, *Le Monde*. This Paris-based newspaper has no organizational connection whatsoever with a political party. In fact, it is in the category of newspapers whose principles explicitly require non-partisanship, with the result that the paper presents an image of total independence from party views. *Le Monde* has even sought to institutionalize its independence by diversifying its share ownership and giving a large stake to the newspaper's staff, especially its journalists. *Le Monde* regards its institutional independence of party not as incidental to its activities but as a fundamental aspect of its operations. In terms of content, this means that the paper aims to adopt an essentially non-partisan approach to political coverage:

> Essential to this idea is the notion of balance. Partly this implies broad, comprehensive coverage of national and international affairs. More literally it involves an obligation that is most explicit in formal political contests, like general elections or parliamentary debates, to give a balanced coverage of the activities and views of all sides. . . . The notion of balance, further, attributes rationality to the reader and assumes it in the paper.[58]

This does not mean that *Le Monde* takes no interest in party politics. In fact, quite the reverse is the case. The paper provides in-depth coverage of national and international politics, with detailed background articles which are highly analytic and eschew the human interest approach of many other newspapers. The paper's serious, even dry, approach has been exemplified by the dense nature of the layout and the lack of photos. Nor does *Le Monde* always succeed in its posture of total detachment from political partisanship. Ideologically, the paper is committed to socially progressive and politically left-of-centre goals, described by its founder Hubert Beuve-Méry as 'social liberalism or liberal socialism'.[59] Though the paper does not have regular editorials, it still makes its political views known. *Le Monde* does not operate in either an ethical or an ideological vacuum, as can be seen from its critical coverage of Le Pen and the National Front in the 1980s. Moreover, even within the context of mainstream French politics, it can reveal its political sympathies, as was evident in its sustained critique of the Giscard d'Estaing presidency in the late 1970s.

The commercial success of *Le Monde* for much of the postwar period is ample testimony to the fact that the decline of party political newspapers cannot be equated with a simple depoliticization of newspaper content. Quickly establishing its reputation as the top people's newspaper in France, *Le Monde* substantially increased its circulation up until the early 1980s. The arrival of the Socialists in government and the success of *Libération* in attracting young readers dented *Le Monde*'s circulation figures for much of the rest of the decade. In 1985 a rescue plan was launched by the managing director, André Fontaine, to rid the paper of its growing deficit. The plan was a notable success and the paper's circulation stabilized in the late 1980s, albeit at a lower level than ten years previously.

In between the two antithetical cases of *L'Humanité* and *Le Monde* are numerous daily newspapers which exhibit a range of different linkages with political parties. In Seymour-Ure's model a wide spectrum of press–party relationships is possible. First, various organizational links are located between the extremes of party control on the one hand and total independence on the other. These include: papers organizationally distinct from a party but in fact fully under its control; financial subsidies to papers by parties; papers controlled by groups or individuals closely or loosely associated with parties; control of papers by individuals following a political career; papers linked *informally* with parties through the personal support of their proprietors; and papers owned by strong but 'non-activist' sympathizers. Second, between the extremes of total loyalty to party goals and independence from them lies the great mass of papers more or less loyal to party. In some cases there is an obvious link between organization and goals, in that it would be difficult to envisage a situation in which a newspaper linked organizationally to a party was disloyal to that party's policy objectives. However, organization and goals do not always go hand in hand. Some papers manifest great loyalty to party goals even when they enjoy complete organizational independence. Finally, with regard to the party membership/newspaper readership link, a paper's readers may adopt a variety of positions on their paper's party preference (if it has one), ranging from unconditional support to total opposition and including mild sympathy or antipathy between these polar opposites. Most papers tend not to have a readership that is overwhelmingly loyal to the paper's party preference.[60]

Most French daily newspapers occupy this vast middle ground in terms of their organizational links with political parties, their support for party goals and the overlap between party supporters and readers. *Le Figaro*, for example, is not controlled by a political party, but it is clearly partisan in terms of its coverage of domestic politics. Its owner, Robert Hersant, was for a time a Gaullist deputy in the French Parliament and the paper shows strong sympathies for the Gaullist party. In 1988 it supported the presidential candidacy of the Gaullist party leader Jacques Chirac against those of his right-wing rival, Raymond Barre, and the incumbent President, François Mitterrand. Another Gaullist deputy, Bertrand Cousin, was for a time part of the paper's management team and Gaullist politicians such as Alain Peyrefitte have been regular contributors. In September 1988 the left-wing journalist from *Le Nouvel Observateur*, Franz-Olivier Giesbert, was appointed editor of *Le Figaro* in place of Max Clos. This was symptomatic of a toning down of the paper's partisan commitment, but it did not signify an abandonment of its liberal conservative traditions.[61]

Libération supports a political line significantly different from that of *Le Figaro*. First published in 1973 as a leftist paper, *Libération* failed to exceed a circulation of much above 30,000. It was relaunched on May 13 1981, a few days after Mitterrand's historic presidential election victory, under the editorship of Serge July. Less committed than its predecessor to extreme left-wing politics, the paper quickly established a reputation for its political, social and cultural reporting. Based on a mixture of critical news and investigative journalism its circulation increased steadily during the 1980s to peak in 1988 at just over 195,000. With the majority of the paper's capital owned by its employees, *Libération* successfully competed with *Le Monde* in the 1980s as a serious, opinion-forming, left-of-centre newspaper. It was particularly popular with younger readers and students, probably more due to its style and tone than its political leanings. Whereas *Le Monde* became rather stuffy and conservative in the 1980s, *Libération* was more iconoclastic and in tune with the tastes and mood of young French people, for example in its support for feminism and environmental concerns.

France-Soir is another part of the Hersant group and like *Le Figaro* espouses a political line sympathetic to the Gaullists. It is a more down-market newspaper than its stablemate, competing for a readership with a similar audience profile to that of *Le Parisien*. Its circulation has declined from over 1 million in the late 1950s and early 1960s to around 250,000 in the early 1990s. Among the other main Paris dailies, *La Croix* is sympathetic to the reformist tendencies within Roman Catholicism. *Le Parisien* (formerly *Le Parisien libéré*) is a tabloid devoted to human interest stories, sport, etc., with a largely downmarket readership. *Le Quotidien de Paris* is sympathetic to the mainstream Right. *Les Echos* is a financial daily, rather like the British *Financial Times*. *L'Equipe* is devoted wholly to sports coverage. Finally, *Présent* is an extreme right-wing newspaper with a derisory circulation.[62]

The decline and demise of the party political daily newspapers has been partly compensated for by the success of non-party political weekly magazines, such as *L'Express*, *Le Nouvel Observateur* and *Le Point*. These magazines also fill a gap left by the lack of quality Sunday newspapers which in Britain, for example, provide a source of political analysis and commentary. These French equivalents of the American weeklies *Time* and *Newsweek* all have creditable circulation figures (see table 2.1). In 1988 *L'Express* had a higher circulation than any Paris daily paper, including *Le Figaro* and *Le Monde*. *L'Express* has veered between support for the Centre–Left and the Right during the Fifth Republic, becoming more right-wing under the ownership of Sir James Goldsmith in the 1980s. *Le Point* is vaguely centrist, while *Le Nouvel Observateur*, the successor to *France-Observateur*, has generally been sympathetic to the Socialist party.

While the links between *individual* press titles and political parties are revealing of important changes in both media and political systems since the Liberation, they tell us little about the extent of parallelism between the press *as a whole* and the party system in the Fifth Republic. Do the circulation figures of French daily newspapers accurately reflect the levels of electoral support for the political parties they champion? Or, as in Britain, is there 'a yawning gap . . . between editorial and electoral opinion'?[63]

Table 2.1 Circulation of political weekly magazines (in '000s)

Magazine	1981	1987	1988
L'Express	507	555	554
Le Point	336	311	320
Le Nouvel Observateur	385	340	370
L'Evénement du jeudi	n/a	150	177
Le Canard enchaîné	469*	396*	423*
Valeurs actuelles	113	96*	90*

* estimated circulation figures; n/a = not available

Source: P. Albert, *La presse française*, Paris, La documentation française, 1990, p.133.

Because of the circulation dominance of provincial dailies, it is difficult to come to any hard and fast conclusion on this issue. Many of the big regional papers in France do not adopt an overt party political stance in the way that national dailies in Britain do. In addition, newspapers may alter their party support following a change of ownership.

Though in the absence of detailed content analysis one can make only a tentative assessment on this question, evidence would suggest that editorial opinion across the whole of the press system does not accurately reflect the range of electoral opinion. In the 1960s the Gaullists argued that much of the provincial press was against them, though they were the dominant electoral force in French politics at the time. In the 1960s and 1970s the Communist party regularly obtained around 20 per cent of the vote, but it was never supported by 20 per cent of nationwide newspaper circulation. The Socialist party under Mitterrand's leadership in the 1970s was also disadvantaged in terms of its newspaper support. So, too, in the 1980s was the National Front. Jean-Marie Le Pen's electoral score of 14.38 per cent of the vote in the first ballot of the 1988 presidential election was not reflected in favourable editorial columns (though, paradoxically, the amount of space given the party in newspaper articles in the 1980s may well have overstated its electoral importance). In general it is likely that newspaper support for political parties over the past fifteen years has overstated the electoral support for the mainstream Right, especially as the Hersant press empire has grown. If this is correct, then the press system as a whole does not accurately reflect the range of electoral opinion in contemporary France.

Chapter 3

Radio

Of the three principal mass media in postwar France, radio may seem at first sight to be the least important. The long-established role of the press has given it a prominent status in the contemporary media system, particularly at the local and regional levels. Meanwhile television, though a relative newcomer in comparison with the press, enjoys a ubiquity and pervasiveness which have made it by far the most prominent national medium of information and popular entertainment. In contrast to these two apparently dominant media, radio may seem to occupy a fairly minor position in the mass communications hierarchy.[1]

Yet it would be impossible to do full justice to the role of the media in twentieth-century France without an examination of the contribution made by radio. In part this is because during the inter-war period radio enjoyed a monopoly in the broadcasting field. Even after the Liberation, it was by far the senior of the two broadcasting media during the late 1940s and 1950s. Two indicators out of many illustrate the superiority of radio over television during the first decade and a half of the postwar period. First, whereas over 80 per cent of French households possessed a radio in 1961, less than 20 per cent had a television set.[2] Second, of 340 tenured journalists employed in the state broadcasting organization in 1960, no fewer than 310 worked in radio.[3] Up until the early 1960s, while television was still finding its feet, radio was the established broadcaster, already transmitting to a mass audience.

In many ways radio was also the forerunner of television, not just in the obvious sense of preceding it chronologically as the first broadcasting medium, but more importantly in the way in which it influenced the contribution of television to the social, cultural and political life of France. Television did not develop in a vacuum. It came into existence and then matured in a broadcasting environment which had been shaped for at least a generation by the monopoly influence of radio. Though the pre-eminence of radio was to be first challenged and then overturned by television, the visual medium – especially in its formative years – was to depend greatly on the rich legacy bequeathed to it by its predecessor.

For example, radio helped to shape the attitudes of the political elites towards the information function performed by the broadcasting media. These views, frequently ill-founded and sometimes coloured by deep-rooted prejudice, were then carried over and applied to television. During the 1930s and the Second World War it was radio which first alerted French politicians to the potential of broadcasting as both a means of communication and a propaganda weapon through which to try to hold sway over the mass audience. As a result, a whole generation of French politicians, seduced by the apparent power of radio, were later to lust after and covet partisan control of television.

Radio is also of historical importance because it was the broadcast medium on which many politicians first acquired new communication techniques which they later transferred to television. Foremost among these was General de Gaulle, who was to learn and then perfect his skills as a broadcast performer through his interventions on BBC radio during the Second World War. After becoming President of the Fifth Republic in 1958, de Gaulle became adept at using television to project an image of authority and build up popular support for his regime. It was on radio, however, that he served his broadcasting apprenticeship, leaving an indelible mark on French political life. There cannot be many countries in the world where streets, squares and even roundabouts are named after a radio broadcast. Yet such is the case in France, where de Gaulle's initial appeal over the airwaves of the BBC on June 18 1940 has acquired mythical status in the annals of the Resistance movement and become part of the collective historical memory of the French nation.

The transfer of communication skills across the broadcasting divide was not confined to politicians. Several top television engineers and technicians began their careers in radio before taking up employment in television.[4] So too did many journalists and producers. Well-known figures in the postwar French media – including Pierre Desgraupes, Pierre Dumayet, Jacques Sallebert, Armand Jammot and Guy Lux among others – first cut their broadcasting teeth on the medium of radio before moving into the exciting new world of television.[5] This movement has continued ever since, though it has long become a two-way process, with top media personnel swapping back and forward between radio and television in a closed, incestuous version of media musical chairs. Programme formats, such as game shows, have also been lifted from radio and adapted to the specific exigencies of the visual medium.[6]

Finally, radio exercised a profound influence on the institutional development of television. Since television was initially perceived by many to be 'radio with pictures', it seemed only natural to tack the former's organization on to the corporate structures already in existence for the management of radio. In France the organizational framework of the state monopoly, which was to have such wide-reaching consequences for the development of television after the Second World War, was first established for the management and regulation of radio services. Nor was France by any means unique among industrialized countries in this respect; in fact, the French experience emulated that of many of its European neighbours. In Britain, for instance, the BBC was initially given monopoly control of the development of television mainly because it was already in charge of running the nation's radio services.

It is tempting to relegate the contribution of radio to the secondary role of a mere training ground or organizational blueprint for television. This would be tantamount to reducing radio to the subsidiary status of a medium which, though historically important, had become barely relevant once it had been supplanted by television as the main means of broadcasting. This would be a grave error. While the role of radio has undoubtedly changed during the television age, the medium has never been wholly supplanted by television. In fact, in many ways it has successfully repulsed the challenge and emerged strengthened from the contest. During the post-war era, for example, the amount of time devoted to radio listening in France has remained remarkably stable, despite a large increase in television viewing since the 1950s (see table 3.1). Nor is this trend peculiar to France. In spite of the popularity of television, a similar continuing commitment to radio listening can be found in several other European countries (see table 3.2).

The resilience of radio in the television age can be partly explained by developments in transmission and reception technology. The increasing use of the FM waveband has greatly improved sound quality, while the spread of transistor radios, hi-fi stereo tuners, walkman radios, radio alarm clocks and car radios is a notable feature of contemporary lifestyles and leisure

Table 3.1 Average amount of time per day spent listening to the radio by French adults 1950–89 (in minutes)

Year	Minutes	Year	Minutes
1950	118	1978	117
1964	106	1979	109
1968	110	1980	118
1969	102	1981	130
1970	104	1982	126
1971	100	1983	121
1972	96	1984	118
1973	99	1985	119
1974	110	1986	124
1975	110	1987	115
1976	111	1988	128
1977	113	1989	124

Source: J. Durand, 'L'évolution des audiences de la radio et de la télévision au cours des quarante dernières années', *Médiaspouvoirs*, no. 21, Paris, 1991, pp.133, 140 and 143.

Table 3.2 Average amount of time per day spent listening to the radio by European adults 1989–90 (in minutes)

Switzerland	174
Netherlands	169
Great Britain	159
Germany, West	154
France	131
Portugal	90
Spain	73

Source: N. Funès, 'Qui écoute la radio? Une comparaison internationale', L'Etat des Médias, Paris, La Découverte, 1991, p.199.

patterns (see table 3.3). Not only have these developments helped radio achieve virtual saturation point in terms of its market penetration, with 98 per cent of French households possessing at least one radio set in 1989. More importantly, they have changed the nature of listening habits, providing the possibility of continuous audience exposure to radio programmes and making the medium more portable and individualistic than television.

Table 3.3 Radio ownership in France (expressed as a % of total population)

Type	1964	1969	1974	1979	1984	1989
Radio	90.9	92.1	94.3	95.7	96.7	98.0
(with FM)	6.5	20.7	30.4	48.7	76.7	92.8
Fixed set	65.5	40.8	27.6	36.2	57.7	51.9
Transistor	46.5	72.7	85.4	86.5	69.8	82.5
Car radio	4.9	10.3	26.6	41.0	51.7	63.9
Radio alarm clock						63.3
Walkman radio						19.4

Sources: C. Méadel, 'Mesures de la radio', *Médiaspouvoirs*, no.24, Paris, 1991, p.161; N. Doucant, 'Le public de la radio', *Médiaspouvoirs*, no.21, Paris, 1991, p.163.

A purely statistical analysis of radio ownership and listening patterns can provide an indication of the enduring importance of radio in the television age. It fails, however, to convey the full extent of the political and social impact of radio, which can be evaluated only through a qualitative appreciation of the medium's contribution and influence. For example, radio has continued to occupy centre stage at key moments in postwar French history and it has also become an integral medium of contemporary popular culture, especially among the young.

One instance of radio's political significance was the attempted putsch led by four army generals in April 1961 in the final months of the Algerian war. Fiercely opposed to de Gaulle's policy of self-determination for Algeria, elements of the professional army staged a revolt to bring about the collapse of the Gaullist regime. In France de Gaulle appeared on television in military uniform to condemn the putsch. In the barracks in Algeria, however, the conscript troops listened to the President on their transistor radios as he unequivocally condemned the uprising, appealed to them to support the legitimate institutions of the Fifth Republic and ordered them to use every means possible to ensure the failure of the rebellion. The effect of this broadcast was described by Werth in these terms:

> It was later said that this broadcast produced in Algeria what was called a 'transistor victory' for de Gaulle. The hundreds of thousands of French conscript soldiers there had, through their transistor radios, listened to this broadcast, and the effect had been overwhelming; they were determined to resist the 'foursome'. Countless officers who had wavered, decided against embarking on an adventure which might end very badly for them. It was obvious to them that de Gaulle was a man who would stand no nonsense.[7]

The conscripts thus opted for loyalty to de Gaulle and refused to support the attempted *coup d'état*. The revolt ended a few days later with the unforgettable sight of the soldiers of the crack paratroop regiment returning to their barracks in disgrace, singing at full voice the Edith Piaf hit *Non, je ne regrette rien*. De Gaulle's radio broadcast had helped save the embattled Fifth Republic.[8]

Seven years later, radio played a key role in almost toppling the same regime, before once again serving de Gaulle as the means to come to its rescue. When youth and worker protest movements seemed on the verge of bringing about the collapse of the Gaullist state in 1968, it was over the radio (and not television) that the French were kept most immediately informed about what was taking place in the Latin Quarter in Paris. With state television largely ignoring the protest, radio rushed in to fill the broadcasting information gap. In fact, the 1968 'events' provided radio with an excellent opportunity to demonstrate the multifaceted nature of the medium.

First, it fulfilled a traditional function as a means of mass communication, informing listeners across the length and breadth of France about the student protest, the barricades and the police repression. This led to a wave of public sympathy for the demonstrators, especially in the early days of May. Second, radio acted as a narrower channel of communication between the student leaders and their followers, in effect assisting in the organization of the revolt. In this context the speed of radio news and the widespread use of transistor radios by the demonstrators were important elements in the mobilization of the protest both in Paris and in provincial university towns. Third, radio provided the communication link for an interpersonal dialogue to take place between the university authorities and the student leaders in the search for a negotiated compromise. One of the most famous instances of this was the conversation between the student leader Alain Geismar and vice-rector Chalin during the night of May 10–11, conducted 'live' over the airwaves of Radio Luxembourg.[9] Finally, radio provided the means for de Gaulle to restore order, reassert his authority and reinforce the legitimacy of the Fifth Republic. His speech at the height of the crisis on May 30 1968, condemning totalitarian communism and announcing the premature dissolution of the National Assembly, was deliberately not broadcast on television. It was an attempt to use radio at a time of evident regime crisis to evoke and recreate the mood of June 18 1940. Followed by a massive demonstration in support of the Gaullist regime, the President's radio broadcast appeared to be a major factor in changing the political situation in his favour.

During the 1968 'events', therefore, radio performed several different communication functions, often simultaneously. It was a principal source of information and comment for the mass audience, helping to set the parameters of news coverage and shape public opinion on the issues of university reform and police violence among others. In this respect radio demonstrated a clear superiority over television in its coverage of the protest. Second, it was an agent for the mobilization of a relatively narrow targeted audience (the students) by a small elite group (the student leaders), thereby laying itself open to the Gaullist charge of not just reporting the demonstrations, but of helping to foment the protest. Third, radio acted as a forum for debate and negotiation between the two principal protagonists in the dispute – the authorities and the protesting students. Finally, the medium was the means by which the legitimacy of the institutions of the Fifth Republic was re-established and Gaullist law and order reimposed.

It is clear that in 1968 French radio did not just passively report or comment on the 'events' as they unfolded. It actively participated in them, sometimes at the risk of creating a media event to serve its own appetite for news and sensation. To its traditional function of political reporter was added the role of political actor and, in the eyes of some, of *agent provocateur*. To put it another way: French radio did not just cover the story in 1968; it became part of the story and at times even dominated the plot.

With the return to political 'normality' and the continuing expansion of television after 1968, radio faded into the media background for a time. However, it was to become the subject of increasingly fierce political controversy in the late 1970s, as it assumed the vanguard role in the assault on the state broadcasting monopoly. Embodying the spirit of 1968 in their challenge to state authority, the pirate stations presented themselves as alternative sources of information to the official broadcasting media. For example, the Green movement first came to public attention during the

Giscard d'Estaing presidency largely because of the publicity surrounding its illegal broadcasts on the pirate station Radio Verte. Like de Gaulle's first BBC broadcast in 1940, Radio Verte's initial transmissions were heard by very few listeners. However, not only were they a sign of the growing green consciousness in France, they were also the first toll in the death knell of the state broadcasting monopoly.

In the summer of 1979 radio again dominated media coverage when the Socialist party leader, François Mitterrand, was among those charged with breach of the monopoly over his involvement in the party's pirate station, Radio Riposte. The place of radio in the French media system became an issue in the run-up to the presidential contest between Valéry Giscard d'Estaing and Mitterrand in 1981, thus providing further evidence of the extent to which radio had again successfully forced its way on to the political agenda. It was never to be off that agenda during the 1980s as local private stations were legalized, private networks established and different regulatory regimes implemented.

It was as a result of developments in radio provision (not television) that the state broadcasting monopoly first began to crack and then disintegrate. Radio not only paved the way for the major, controversial changes in the French television system of the 1980s. The abolition of the monopoly at the start of the Mitterrand presidency also opened up a new competitive era for French radio, raising the public profile of the 'old' broadcast medium and giving it a renewed lease of life. By taking advantage of technological innovations, social change and political developments, radio has successfully adapted to the television age, carving out new markets and occupying a key position in the radically altered French media environment of the 1980s and 1990s. It has continued to perform functions which television has been either reluctant or unable to fulfil, for example in targeting specific audience groups for advertisers. Radio has sometimes been a complementary medium to television, catering for tastes and social groups which have not been adequately served by the latter. It has also been an effective competitor for the mass audience at certain times of the day (notably the morning breakfast schedules) and in certain areas of programming (such as news and music). In short, far from being an anachronism, French radio has continually proved itself capable of redefining its mission. In so doing, it has ensured that it is a medium not just of historical import, but also of contemporary significance.

THE EARLY YEARS OF RADIO

Prior to the outbreak of the Second World War French radio had the formal status of a state monopoly. In fact, however, several privately owned local stations operated during the 1920s and 1930s. According to the provisions of legislation introduced in 1923, the state was guaranteed a monopoly 'in the transmission and reception [sic] of radioelectric signals of any kind'. In practice, however, revocable licences were granted to several private radio stations giving them permission to broadcast, provided that they did not interfere with the transmission of the programmes of state radio. In 1928 13 private radio stations had their authorization to transmit confirmed,[10] while in the same year 14 state stations were broadcasting.[11] During the inter-war period, therefore, the French state tolerated the coexistence of both public and private radio stations operating at the local and regional levels.

The early French radio stations developed in almost anarchic conditions, punctuated by attempts on the part of the postal administration to establish overall regulatory control.[12] The first radio station to broadcast was Radio-Tour Eiffel, which was established in 1921 as a state station linked to the Ministry of Posts.[13] The first private radio station to transmit officially was Radio-Paris (originally called Radiola), which had the backing of the national syndicate of radioelectric industries.[14] Funded by shareholder subscriptions and discreet advertising, it began broadcasting at the end of 1922, only a few months before the state's monopoly in radio was officially sanctioned in legislation. Like the pirate stations during the Giscard d'Estaing presidency, the pioneer private stations did not always wait for official authorization for their transmissions.

However, in contrast to the late 1970s, the state's broadcasting monopoly was not rigorously enforced. Indeed, in 1926 a decree was promulgated regulating the operations of the private stations. The state was content to allow private radio to function, provided that it retained overall control. Yet private radio was tolerated by the authorities only as a provisional concession; it was not allowed to broadcast as of right. The state's decision to allow private radio transmissions 'was dictated by a double powerlessness to contain the explosion of the phenomenon and to respond to the demands of the listeners'.[15]

Inter-war legislation on radio constantly sought to address the issue of the uneasy relationship between the private and public sectors. During this period there was strong competition in Paris between the different public and private stations, such as Radio-Tour Eiffel, Paris-PTT and Radio-Paris. Rivalry between stations was also fierce in the provinces. The private stations broadcast mainly entertainment programmes and were funded principally from advertising revenue. Some also received subsidies from municipal and local councils, as well as from local chambers of commerce. The public service radio stations were also funded in part from advertising up until 1933 when the radio receiving licence was introduced.[16] This was designed to give a solid funding base to the state sector at a time when radio was just beginning to establish itself as a medium of mass communication: by 1938 there were over 4 million radio sets in France, compared with only 1.9 million at the start of 1935.

The development of privately managed, commercial broadcasting in France (and elsewhere on the European continent) was of particular concern to the BBC in Britain. English-language commercial programmes were broadcast to British listeners from stations such as Radio-Toulouse, Radio-Paris, Radio-Normandie and Radio Luxembourg.[17] In the early 1930s gramophone record companies sponsored programmes which were broadcast to Britain from private stations in France.[18] Competition to the BBC was especially strong on Sundays, when British listeners preferred the delights of a continental regime to the more staid offerings of the domestic sound broadcaster.

Apart from Radio Luxembourg, Radio-Normandie was the most popular of the foreign stations for British listeners. The French station was able to give a good service to the whole south coast area of England, with the result that its potential British audience was larger than its French equivalent.[19] According to the BBC's official historian, Asa Briggs, 'many of the programmes put across by Radio-Normandie were of a distinctly American type. Three American "soap operas" followed each other in a row, for example, on five days of the week in 1939'.[20] Repeated efforts by the BBC in the 1930s to persuade the French government to control these sponsored programmes in English all failed, as France chose to defend commercial radio interests (including those of Luxembourg) in international decision-making forums, much to the chagrin of the Reithian-inspired BBC.[21]

The BBC was by no means alone in having to deal with competition from private radio. French newspaper owners were even more concerned, as they faced up to the challenge posed to the political influence and economic viability of the press. One response, prefiguring that adopted by press groups in adjusting to the legalization of private local radio in the 1980s, was to acquire their own stake in the new medium. For example, in 1925 Le Petit Parisien was the first paper to establish a radio station. Later Jean Prouvost, the owner of Paris-Soir, established Radio-37; and in 1927 Senator Paul Dupuy, boss of the newspaper Le Petit Parisien which owned Le Poste Parisien, was appointed chairman of the recently established federation of private stations.[22]

As competition between public and private radio stations intensified, news bulletins became part of the programme output of radio, posing problems of political balance and impartiality. Worried about losing readership, the press in general was opposed to radio coverage of politics. However, as newspaper owners were unable to prevent this development, they adapted to the new circumstances by advising listeners to their stations to purchase their company's newspapers so as to complement the news diet from radio.

Radio also began to make an impact on French political debate, with the medium first being used in an election campaign in 1932. Miquel argues that until 1932 there was a general consensus among the political elite on the desirability of the 'neutralization' of radio news output.[23] However, this view altered as the decade progressed. Radio was used by the Popular Front leaders Blum and Thorez during the Left's successful election campaign of 1936. Some French politicians, such as Pierre Laval who had a stake in Radio-Lyon, took an active interest in the new medium's development. As French politics became marked by scandal, social conflict and political extremism during the late 1930s, Daladier also sought to use radio as a political weapon. With the signing of the Munich agreement in 1938, 'radio became the official organ of a government at war, an effective weapon in its hands to group the nation around a determined policy'.[24] In 1938–39 the government's political control of radio grew, culminating in 1939 in a request by the Daladier government that the private stations should retransmit the news of the public network. From an initial position of rejection of the new medium, French politicians had come round to a recognition of its importance as a means of information and electoral propaganda.

Overall, though, before the outbreak of the Second World War French politicians did not really appreciate the potential of radio. In general, they adopted a negative approach, more intent on preventing radio from being hostile to them than on using it positively to their own advantage. The role played by radio in the Second World War altered this perception for good. As war approached, radio was to become a weapon in the national struggle for survival. A new generation of politicians learnt to use radio for their own partisan political objectives and made it a powerful instrument to be utilized in times of peace as well as war.

RADIO'S WARTIME ROLE

It was the outbreak of the Second World War which really thrust radio into a position of political prominence in France. The potential of radio as a medium of propaganda came to light with the advent of the war and was exploited by all sides in the conflict. 'In the north, the Germans requisitioned all radio installations whether public or private, while in the south, the Vichy government created a public organisation, National Broadcasting, which exercised a monopoly in that zone and which formed a vital part of its propaganda services.'[25] From 1940 to 1944 France was the scene of a verbal battle over the air involving radio stations articulating pro-Nazi, pro-Vichy and pro-Resistance sentiments.[26] Pétain frequently used radio to try to rally support for the Vichy regime, while de Gaulle broadcast over the BBC as the symbol of French resistance. The military and political conflict of the Second World War thus found a reflection in a battle of the airwaves as each side strove to impose its views through the medium of radio.

Before the Fall of France radio had already come under government control, with friends of Prime Minister Daladier occupying key positions in the broadcasting system.[27] During the phoney war, radio broadcast optimistic, morale-boosting messages about the preparedness of the French forces to face the enemy. The optimism proved groundless and the propaganda backfired. Not only were the French forces defeated militarily, but the German propaganda machine successfully undermined the national will to fight:

> When the crisis came, [French radio] alternated between wild exaggeration and deliberate evasion. . . . At the same time, the desperate efforts which had been made to jam those German stations which were broadcasting in French were futile and generated increased animosity as the German armies advanced. . . . Before Paris was handed over to the Germans – appropriately enough by radio – and before Radio Stuttgart gloatingly broadcast a list of French radio employees who had been singled out for punishment as 'enemies of the Reich', the French radio, itself in a state of near collapse, had begun to ignore news from Britain.[28]

News from Britain, however, could not easily be ignored. Listening to the BBC radio news in French had become popular among the middle and professional classes since the time of Munich. While at first there was little general listening to the BBC in France, for many people listening to British broadcasts was the first act of resistance. In the early months of the war 'the initials BBC [quickly became] part and parcel of the daily vocabulary of French citizens' and it was from the BBC that the French first heard the news of the terms of the French armistice.[29] As the Second World War progressed, the BBC became one of the authentic voices of French resistance.

Most tellingly, it was the BBC which afforded de Gaulle the opportunity to present himself as the embodiment of resistance to the armistice, the Nazi occupation and the Vichy regime of Pétain.

> It was in Britain, in the studios of the BBC, that a new system of French broadcasting was born. Brigadier de Gaulle made his historic broadcasts to the people of Occupied France from British soil. It is uncertain whether many people heard him, certainly in the early months when millions were fleeing from their homes and the Germans had attempted to confiscate every single radio receiver in the northern part of France. Nonetheless, the political personality of de Gaulle, which was decades later to be the foundation stone of the broadcasting structure, was created at that moment by the transmitters of the BBC. It was at that time that he first realised, more powerfully and more skilfully than any other world leader, the political potential of broadcasting and its particular applicability to the chaotic conditions of the French nation.[30]

Though some politicians were already becoming fascinated with the power of the radio medium, de Gaulle was virtually unique among the military in appreciating its significance. His first and most famous broadcast, the appeal of June 18 1940 from the London studios of the BBC, was a call to his compatriots to continue the struggle against the Nazis.

> General de Gaulle dated the beginning of a 'new life' from that moment: 'as the irrevocable words flew out upon their way I felt within myself a life coming to an end'. Separated as he was from his own people, many of whom at first had never heard of his name, he acknowledged through his *Memoirs* that broadcasting, which he first approached in 1940 as a novice, had provided him with 'a powerful means of war'.[31]

The broadcast has been described as 'an extraordinary intervention'[32] and 'the act which established his prestige beyond dispute'.[33] In his biography of de Gaulle, Lacouture argues that

> Charles de Gaulle was to make more accomplished speeches, but he had immediately struck an oratorical tone in which the most classical tradition was enriched by the possibilities of the microphone, while at the same time he produced some phrases that, pending the utterance of others still more splendid, were to last in his hearers' memories.[34]

Yet it is also the case that in the early days

> even to many of the French who found themselves in London at the time, his broadcasts seemed impossibly pretentious, while to people in France his first period of resistance was hardly more than a curious, tantalizing piece of unsubstantiated news. Only for a few was it a meaningful call to action.[35]

> The first de Gaulle speech was a landmark mainly in retrospect. On 17 June, Pétain had made his first broadcast to the French nation, announcing his taking over of political power, and his intention to sue for the end of hostilities. It was in the light of this speech that the British War Cabinet ... decided ... that General de Gaulle should be allowed to broadcast a talk. ... How many listeners heard him is uncertain. What is certain is that they were a tiny fraction of Pétain's audience a day earlier.[36]

None the less, in recognition of de Gaulle's mastery of radio and as a sign of the importance the Gaullists attached to their wartime origins, for a long time during the Fifth Republic one of the symbols of Gaullism was the four beats of 'London calling'.[37]

The flexibility of radio allowed BBC broadcasts to France to fulfil diverse functions during the war. They served as a means of information, providing the French audience with news about the progress of the conflict; as an agency of propaganda, mobilizing popular opposition and resistance to Vichy and the Nazis, such as in the famous V campaign in 1941; as a form of narrowcasting, transmitting personal coded instructions to very specific audiences of Resistance groups on the ground, for example in the run-up to D-Day in 1944; and as a unifying echo of national celebration, such as in the coverage of de Gaulle's entry into a liberated Paris.

The BBC did not, of course, have a monopoly as a mass medium during the war. It had to compete with Vichy radio and the German media, while the Resistance movement within France was also served by its own clandestine press (and after the Liberation of Paris by clandestine radio as well). 'By 1942 the Vichy media and the clandestine [resistance] press made up two completely separate and contradictory sources of information, with the German media in the occupied zone constituting a third, and the BBC gaining an increasingly dominant position as the fourth.'[38] While there is little evidence that the German station, Radio-Paris, ever secured a hold on French listeners, Radio-Vichy was different.[39] In the summer of 1940 there was widespread support for Pétain, and Vichy broadcasts, particularly Pétain's broadcasts, were listened to with genuine interest.[40]

The role played by radio during the war was a decisive factor in the formulation of broadcasting policy by the political forces active in the Resistance, since it was decided during this wartime period that the radio services would be nationalized following the Liberation.[41] Since private radio was considered incompatible with the public service role which fell to radio in 1944,[42] the private radio stations which had been allowed to broadcast up until the outbreak of hostilities were compelled either to cease broadcasting altogether or to transmit from outside French territory – an option which the peripheral stations were to choose after the war (see the next section). After the Liberation all private station licences were cancelled and the installations belonging to the private radio companies were requisitioned by the state,[43] though some staff from the pre-war private stations obtained posts in the new state service.[44] The Vichy laws on broadcasting were reinstated after temporary repeal.

Thus the role played by radio during the conflict was to have a spillover effect on French broadcasting policy once peace had been restored and in particular was to have a crucial impact on the postwar organization and development of both radio and television. Politicians emerged from the steep learning curve of the war not just conscious of radio's power, but also determined to harness that power for their own political purposes. This meant creating structures for broadcasting which would facilitate the achievement of those goals which were at the heart of the postwar coalition's political programme. Within the coalition a state monopoly represented the optimal organizational framework for broadcasting.

1945–78: STATE RADIO AND THE PERIPHERAL STATIONS

French radio emerged from the war ripe for reorganization. Not surprisingly the medium had expanded only very gradually during the conflict: from just over 4 million radio sets in 1938 to 5.5 million in 1946. In comparison, the UK had almost twice as many radio sets as France in the first year after the end of the war.[45] The main concern for French politicians, however, was not so much to encourage consumer demand for radio, but to ensure that the medium would serve the objectives of the postwar state. The main provision of the immediate postwar legislation was the confirmation of broadcasting as a state monopoly with public service goals, placed under the responsibility of a Minister of Information. The Liberation government thus legitimized the framework within which broadcasting in France was to develop and attain maturity: a state monopoly with a formal public service role, but in practice closely subordinated to the political interests of the government of the day.[46]

The Second World War had clearly highlighted the propaganda potential of broadcasting. This had the unfortunate consequence of linking two separate ideas (state monopoly and political control) in the minds of French politicians. The legal framework of the state monopoly became inextricably bound up with the practice of partisan control of the broadcasting media by the authorities. This fusion of state monopoly and government control was evident under the wartime Vichy regime. It was to continue under the Fourth Republic (1946–58), during which representatives of various political forces (Socialists, Radicals, Christian Democrats and assorted conservatives and independents) all sought to exploit both the established medium of radio and the newcomer, television, for their own political ends.

The relationship between the authorities and state radio in the early months following the Liberation has been described by Eck as follows:

> In the months which followed the Liberation, circumstances did not encourage the State to loosen its hold on an essential tool. It was necessary to settle the legality and authority of the provisional government, finish the war, prepare for the first elections, face up to economic problems and establish France's position with regard to the Allies. In such a context, radio was an instrument of government and it seemed normal that those who governed should come to explain their plans and tasks, as well as their policies.[47]

During the Fourth Republic political control of broadcasting worked especially to the detriment of the Communists and the Gaullists, including General de Gaulle himself. The Communists were expelled from the Tripartite Centre–Left coalition in May 1947. Because of their close ties to the Soviet Union and the prevailing cold war climate of the 1950s, they were regarded thereafter, not least by the Socialist party, as an untrustworthy and even alien political force. For his part, de Gaulle had strongly criticized the constitutional provisions of the new regime and condemned the weakness of the executive and the dominance of the political parties, whose squabbling was to contribute to governmental instability, political immobility and a negative image of France abroad. Both de Gaulle and the Communists, therefore, were regarded by the legitimist political parties as hostile not only to the government in power, but more fundamentally to the regime itself, i.e. as anti-system forces. Their electoral progress would be detrimental not just to the success but even to the very existence of a political system which faced severe problems of economic reconstruction at home and military involvement abroad in colonies such as Indochina. To try to minimize their impact on electoral opinion and the policy agenda, de Gaulle and the Communist party were largely denied access to state broadcasting.[48]

Both de Gaulle and the Communists suffered from a lack of radio exposure in which to air their views, while the latter were also the victims of cold war anti-Communist propaganda broadcasts such as *La Vie en rouge* and *Paix et Liberté*.[49] De Gaulle himself was denied access to state radio between 1947 and 1951. In contrast, Paul Ramadier 'made extensive use of the radio to explain his strict economic policy and to denounce the Communist threat, with at least nine talks from February to July 1947'.[50] During the Fourth Republic, therefore, radio was used to help legitimize the political system and the various parties which controlled it. Political control of radio was largely confined to news and current affairs content, patronage appointments and the desire to ensure the financial stability of the state broadcasting organization. Government ministers and parliamentary deputies were little concerned with general programming which, in keeping with the service's public service mission, frequently aimed to educate as well as entertain and to be 'an active cultural intermediary' between the audience and 'the intellectual and artistic elite'.[51] However, if intellectuals and commentators discussed political topics too overtly or in a manner displeasing to the authorities, they ran the risk of giving offence and suffering the consequences. For example, the programme 'La Tribune des *Temps Modernes*', which had featured Jean-Paul Sartre as a contributor, was taken off the air in late 1947 because of its anti-establishment tone and content. More generally, however, the chronic instability of Fourth Republic governments and their multi-party coalition composition tempered the worst effects of partisan control of broadcasting to some extent, at least until the escalation of the Algerian war.

Under Guy Mollet's Socialist government, which included François Mitterrand in its ministerial ranks, measures were taken at the time of the Algerian war to suppress anti-government views in news broadcasts. After 1958 Gaullist ministers, criticized by the opposition for their exploitation of the state broadcasting services, frequently retorted by referring to the censorship of which they had been the victims during the Fourth Republic and to the doctoring of the news during Mollet's premiership. The lack of new legislation to regulate government-broadcasting relations did nothing to ameliorate the situation in the 1950s. Of 16 bills drawn up on the subject of state broadcasting during the Fourth Republic, none was passed or even went to the vote.[52] However, even new legislation would probably have been insufficient of itself to restrain politicians from interfering in news programming when the regime ran into terminal difficulties over the Algerian question. With the political system fighting for its life over its handling of the Algerian issue, the temptation to use state radio as the mouthpiece of government policy was overwhelming. As a result, the official perspective on the conflict dominated state radio coverage.

Between 1945 and 1974 public service radio was organized as part of the state broadcasting organization – Radiodiffusion française (1945–49), Radiodiffusion-Télévision Française (RTF) (1945–64) and finally the Office de Radiodiffusion-Télévision Française (ORTF) (1964–74). When the unitary structure of the state corporation was dismantled in 1974, public service radio became the responsibility of a separate programme company, Radio France. During the second half of the 1970s Radio France managed three main national radio networks (France-Inter, France-Culture and France-Musique) which, taken together, provided approximately the same sort of programme mix as that covered by the BBC national radio networks 2, 3 and 4 in Britain. France-Inter was the mass audience station, while the other two networks with their high cultural output attracted comparatively small audiences. Under the 1974 legislation, Radio France Internationale (the equivalent of the BBC's external services) was also run as an integral part of Radio France.

Right up until the early 1980s, the state monopoly in the provision of radio services was enshrined in all major pieces of postwar legislation on French broadcasting. In theory, this meant that only state radio could transmit from within French territory. No privately owned or commercially managed competition was allowed under the provisions of the various pieces of legislation which applied to broadcasting in the period before Mitterrand's presidential election victory in 1981. In practice, however, the situation was much more complicated. The monopoly status of state radio in the postwar period did not go unchallenged, with strong competition coming from the so-called peripheral radio stations (radios périphériques) such as Europe 1, Radio Luxembourg, Radio-Monte-Carlo and Sud-Radio.[53]

As a result, the state radio services did not enjoy the same privileged monopoly position vis-à-vis their listeners as did the state television channels with French viewers. In fact, between 1948 and 1968, state radio progressively lost more than half of its listeners to the peripheral stations.[54] While up until the mid-1970s the public service station France-Inter had always led in the radio ratings war, it was never again to occupy the pole position, losing out first to the peripheral stations and later to the private local radio networks.[55] Competition for audiences in radio, which had been such a notable feature of the pre-war system, was also a characteristic of the postwar arrangements, despite the legal framework of the state monopoly up until 1981.

The peripheral radio stations transmitted quite freely from just outside French territory to audiences in France. Producing their programmes in their headquarters and studios inside France, they then relayed them to their transmitters on the other side of the French border without any interference from the state. In fact, in the early 1970s one of the peripheral stations, Radio-Monte-Carlo, was even allowed to construct a transmitter on French soil at Roumoules in southern France.[56] The state was cooperating in the breach of its own monopoly!

For French audiences these peripheral stations provided additional sources of news, music and entertainment. They contributed to political information by staging debates between politicians, including campaign debates in the run-up to municipal, parliamentary and presidential elections.[57] *Club de la presse* was created on Europe 1 in 1976 and quickly established itself as an important media forum for political discussion.[58] Its combative interview format featuring an invited politician and a panel of journalists was emulated by other radio networks. The peripheral stations were in general less hidebound, more informal and unashamedly more commercial and populist than state radio, which as a public service broadcaster still possessed a strong sense of a cultural and educative mission.[59]

Their news was also considered by many to be less subject to governmental control than the output of France-Inter, which in the 1960s and early 1970s was widely perceived as suffering from too close a link with the Gaullist authorities. To some extent the reputation of the peripheral stations for more reliable and impartial news output than the state station was accurate, as was evident in their coverage of the May 1968 'events'. In reporting the student demonstrations and protests, the public service radio station France-Inter certainly enjoyed more leeway than state television. For example, in sharp contrast to the state television channels, France-Inter covered the university crisis from the beginning. It was almost always the lead item on its news bulletins from early May onwards. However, the manner of covering the crisis was partisan: even though 'live' reports of the demonstrations were frequently sympathetic to the student cause, demonstrators were rarely invited to put their case directly. Moreover, France-Inter journalists were quickly forbidden by André Astoux, assistant director general of the ORTF, to broadcast 'live' reports, despite the disagreement of the head of radio news at France-Inter, Jacqueline Baudrier. As a result, more balanced coverage of the 'events' took place only when the station was taken over by journalists in the second half of May and management was pushed aside.[60]

The really important radio actors in 1968 were the peripheral stations. The clashes between the police and the demonstrators were vividly and dramatically described by radio journalists broadcasting 'live' from the streets of the capital. The student leaders of the protest, such as Daniel

Cohn-Bendit and Alain Geismar, were quickly transformed into media stars. The mobile telephone links between the radio cars and the studios proved such an effective means of transmitting information and mobilizing the protest that they were shut down by the authorities on May 23 on the pretext that the police needed the frequencies. They were permitted to function again on May 30 on the occasion of the demonstration in support of General de Gaulle, which was given extensive radio coverage.[61] The reporting of both Radio Luxembourg and Europe 1, therefore, easily outshone that of France-Inter. Their active role in covering the 'events' led to their condemnation by Prime Minister Pompidou, who accused them of exacerbating the tense situation, and by the Minister of the Interior, Christian Fouchet, who baptized Radio Luxembourg *radio-barricades*.[62]

The infringement of the state monopoly by the peripheral radio stations prior to 1982 was, however, more apparent than real. Despite their dependence on advertising revenue, their commercial orientation and their less partisan news coverage, the peripheral stations were by no means independent of the French state. Through a holding company called Sofirad, the state owned important and frequently majority shareholdings in all the peripheral radio stations, with the exception of Radio Luxembourg (in which, none the less, it had a stake via the Havas company). As a result, while these stations provided strong competition for audiences for the state radio services, their own finances were closely controlled by the state. It has been argued that one of the main functions of the peripheral stations, given the absence of commercials on state radio, was to absorb the demand for national advertising on radio.[63]

As far as state control of peripheral radio was concerned, ten of the 12 members of Sofirad's board of governors, including the chairman, were appointed by the government. The post of chairman, was of course, a political appointment of considerable importance. Pierre Lefranc, a former member of de Gaulle's *cabinet*, held the post until 1973. He was replaced by Denis Baudouin, one of Pompidou's personal advisers on media policy and the head of the President's press service. In 1977 Baudouin left Sofirad to become head of communications in the entourage of former Prime Minister Chirac, who had just been successfully elected mayor of Paris and was starting to prepare his assault on the Elysée in 1981. Baudouin's departure left the way open for President Giscard d'Estaing to appoint a new chairman loyal to him personally – Xavier Gouyou-Beauchamps, former head of the Elysée press service. In short, by the exercise of political patronage in appointments to the top post in Sofirad, the French government effectively controlled the organization.

Through Sofirad the French government retained the power of appointment to the key managerial and editorial posts in most of the peripheral radio stations. One of the clearest examples of governmental intervention in the running of peripheral radio occurred in October 1974, when Maurice

Siegel was dismissed from his post as director general of Europe 1, with the complicity of the then Prime Minister, Chirac.[64] Though undoubtedly the most spectacular, Siegel's dismissal was only the first in a process by which the holders of key posts in all the peripheral radio stations were changed during the Giscard d'Estaing presidency. The President placed personal supporters at the head of Sofirad, Havas, Radio-Monte-Carlo and Radio Luxembourg.[65]

During the Giscardian presidency, therefore, the authorities were keen to ensure that the peripheral radio stations would be loyal to the President. Persons sympathetic to Giscard d'Estaing, either out of conviction or for purely career reasons, were given key posts in the management and news staffs. While direct censorship was rare, pressure and 'advice' were more common. In the eyes of some employees, including its chief political correspondent, Europe 1 had a pro-Giscardian bias which in the late 1970s operated to the detriment of both the Gaullists and the Left.[66]

In the summer of 1981 the incoming Socialist government replaced these Giscardian sympathizers in the peripheral stations with persons more likely to favour the new administration.[67] Pro-Socialist commentaries tended to replace pro-Giscardian ones.[68] Generally during the Mitterrand presidency the authorities sought to influence appointments both indirectly through control of Sofirad and directly through pressure from the Elysée.[69] In short, while the peripheral radio stations were never legally a part of the state radio monopoly, they could still be legitimately regarded as an integral component of the state's overall control of broadcasting, at least up until the mid-1980s when their privatization became the order of the day.

PIRATE ATTACKS BREACH THE MONOPOLY

During the second half of the Giscard d'Estaing presidency, the main challenge to the state monopoly in radio came not from the national peripheral networks, but from small pirate stations transmitting from within French territory on a localized basis. The establishment of these pirate stations was a result of the interaction of different factors: improvements in radio transmission technology; the absence of local radio stations (either public service or commercial); the rise of new social and political movements in the aftermath of the 1968 'events' and their exclusion or marginalization from state radio and television; a new approach on the part of mainstream political parties (notably the Socialists) to the issue of the state monopoly; and legislative intransigence on the part of the Giscardian government.[70]

The push from technological change is the easiest to comprehend. The pirate stations sprung up in France during 1977–78, when technological advances had made the transmission equipment cheap to buy and easy to operate. The example of community radio in the United States, and more significantly, of the private radio stations in Italy, provided models of decentralized radio for the French to imitate. Radio amateurs in France looked across the Alps to the situation which had resulted from the Constitutional Court's decision in 1976 to render the state broadcasting monopoly at the sub-national level null and void. In Italy hundreds of small-scale private radio stations had come into being, representing different social, political and cultural groups and operating in a totally deregulated broadcasting environment. As a result, the state broadcasting corporation, RAI, found itself facing unfettered competition from local radio (and television) stations whose output was not subject to any controls.[71]

The diversity of the Italian experience was in sharp contrast to the highly regulated and limited choice available in France from the national state and peripheral networks. The tradition of centralized control of broadcasting meant that there was no local radio in France at this time. Regional radio, which had become part of the responsibilities of the regional broadcasting company FR3 after the 1974 reform, covered a much wider geographical area than local radio stations would have done. In any event, the contribution of regional radio to the total broadcast output was extremely limited, being largely confined to insertions into predominantly national programming. Regional radio represented a minimalist supplementary output to national state radio rather than providing a fully fledged complementary or competitive service.

Yet even if local or regional radio had been provided by Radio France, this would scarcely have defused the challenge from non-mainstream social and political movements. These were less intent on gaining access to state broadcasting than posing an effective challenge to the state monopoly in the hope of bringing about its demise. Largely excluded from access to the centralized and politically controlled state radio (and television) services, small, highly motivated social and political groups retaliated by setting up their own alternative broadcast media. In so doing they were acting firmly within the tradition of *contestation* which had been so much in evidence during the 1968 protest by students and workers. The demands made in 1968 for the decentralization of decision making, for the abolition of hierarchies based on power and wealth and for a greater emphasis on workers' self-management (*autogestion*) found an echo less than a decade later in the activities of the pirate stations. Their output represented both a challenge to state power and the means of communicating that defiance to a wider audience.

The first pirate station to begin broadcasting was Radio Verte, which was set up in Paris in the spring of 1977 as one of the mouthpieces of the growing environmentalist movement. Several green radio stations were set up soon afterwards in other parts of France and their example was copied by feminists, gays, regionalists and ethnic minorities among others. The total number of pirate stations probably exceeded 100 by early 1978, though given the rapidity with which some stations were set up and then disbanded, it was impossible to estimate their numbers accurately. Pirate radio was essentially an urban phenomenon. The Paris region alone had about 20 stations, while in provincial France the pirate stations were concentrated mainly in major towns and cities.

This overt challenge to the state monopoly compelled the government and the mainstream political parties to clarify publicly their positions on this contentious issue. The political parties had differing reactions to the new phenomenon of the pirate stations. Divisions of opinion were apparent not just between Right and Left or among the partners of the broad coalitions of government and opposition. Frequently parties were internally split as well. The Gaullists were now moving away from the largely uncritical support of the state monopoly which they had advocated during the de Gaulle and Pompidou presidencies. This change of heart was no doubt partly due to the fact that, after 1974 (and more particularly after Chirac's resignation from the premiership in 1976), they no longer controlled state radio and television, which had become an area for the exercise of Giscardian patronage and power.

The President's own supporters were divided, with some Giscardians even setting up their own station (Radio Fil Bleu) in Montpellier.[72] Launched in July 1977, Radio Fil Bleu at first looked as if it might be a trial balloon to test the strength of the monopoly legislation. In the event of a victory of the Left in the 1978 general election and the transfer of the state broadcasting services to Socialist–Communist control, the Giscardians might need the fallback position of an independent local radio sector. However, it seems more likely that there was simply a conflict of opinion within the Giscardian party on this issue and that the Radio Fil Bleu initiative reflected largely local political concerns. The President himself clearly favoured the maintenance of the state monopoly. In adopting this position he was mindful of the stance taken by much of the provincial press, which had consistently opposed the establishment of any independent radio on French soil for fear that this would adversely affect the circulation figures and advertising revenue of local and regional newspapers.

Divisions between and within the two main parties of the Right were reflected by shifting and often inconsistent policy stances adopted by the parties of the Left. Traditionally both the Socialist and Communist parties had been ardent supporters of the principle of the state monopoly, while at the same time fiercely critical of its alleged partisan misuse by the Right. By 1978, however, neither appeared as committed to the principle as in the past. In the case of the Socialist party, increasing disenchantment with the concept of the monopoly could be traced back to the 1974 presidential election campaign, during which the Socialists alleged that their candidate,

Mitterrand, had been unfavourably treated in comparison with Giscard d'Estaing. Yet several leading Socialists still remained attached to the concept of the monopoly as the best means of ensuring a public service broadcasting system, while many also feared opening up broadcasting to private interests which might be hostile to the policies of the Socialist party.

The Communist party favoured the legalization of local radio, but under the control of municipal authorities. This policy option was particularly favourable to the Communists after their victories with the Socialists in the 1977 municipal elections. Naturally, such a proposal was anathema to the social and political movements who had been behind the establishment of the original pirate stations. They had not opposed centralized state control of broadcasting just to have it replaced by party political control at the local level.

The government and the main political parties were clearly caught out by the phenomenon of pirate radio. Taken unawares by the pace of technological change, policy advisers embarked on a fast learning curve to help them appreciate its opportunities and constraints. Prior to the 1978 general election, the Giscardian government reacted fairly circumspectly, jamming the transmissions of the pirate stations without in the main taking those responsible for the illegal broadcasts to court. However, following the victory of the governing right-wing coalition over the Socialist–Communist opposition, the government reacted in a more draconian fashion. Not only did it confirm the illegality of the pirate stations, but it took steps to close them down by force. With its electoral mandate renewed, the Giscardian government decided to defend the state monopoly at all costs and in July 1978 it introduced supplementary legislation to buttress the provisions of the 1974 broadcasting statute.

The future of the pirates looked bleak. Disunity among the pirate radio pressure groups campaigning for a change in the law did not help matters. One group favoured the creation of local commercial stations, while another regarded commercial radio as little better than the state monopoly. In particular, the means of financing local radio split the lobby groups into warring camps, with the anti-advertising ideological purists lined up against the pro-advertising pragmatic realists. In addition, the local radio pressure groups were weakened by internal disunity, lacked any formal organic links with both the main broadcasting trade unions and the parties of the opposition, and were not regarded as responsible interlocutors by the Giscardian government. Yet the repressive legislation failed to stem the demand for alternatives to state radio as pressure for change continued unabated. Some stations carried on transmitting despite the tougher sanctions and new ones were established in flagrant defiance of the authorities. Two of the best known broadcast in Longwy, a Lorraine steel town badly affected by the recession in the world steel industry. One was set up by the local branch of the CGT trade union confederation (Lorraine

Cœur d'Acier) and the other by its CFDT (Confédération Française Démocratique du Travail) counterpart (Radio SOS Emploi).[73]

The most famous of the new pirate stations was Radio Riposte. This station was established by the Socialist party in protest against government interference in the state broadcasting media. Though transmitting only infrequently, Radio Riposte became front page news in the French press in the summer of 1979 when the Socialist party headquarters in Paris were forcibly invaded by police searching for the transmission equipment. As Socialist deputies wearing their tricolour sashes were caught in the glare of press cameras, several prominent members of the party, including Mitterrand himself, were summonsed to appear in court for infringement of the state monopoly. As the 1981 presidential election approached, the broadcasting issue was once again placed firmly on the political agenda.

THE LEGALIZATION AND EXPANSION OF PRIVATE LOCAL RADIO

After Mitterrand's presidential election victory in May 1981 many new radio stations sprang up, competing with each other for restricted airwave space, particularly in Paris. They included local stations serving a restricted geographical area, community stations catering for a particular social group and thematic stations offering a specialist programme output. The first problem which the new Socialist government had to deal with concerned the legal status of these previously outlawed pirates. The government met with strong criticism, not least from within the Socialist party itself, for what was widely viewed as a backing down from the policy the party leadership had advocated when in opposition. Though sympathetic to the many small stations which had sprung up in the latter half of the Giscard d'Estaing presidency, once in government the Socialists' initial response was scarcely encouraging for those pressure groups campaigning for the legalization of independent local radio. For a time the new regime even continued the repressive Giscardian practice of jamming certain stations, explaining that it did not want large commercial enterprises ideologically hostile to the Mitterrand regime to take advantage of the fluid political situation to set up their own networks.

New legislation was introduced in the autumn of 1981 as a stop-gap measure prior to the full-scale reorganization of broadcasting due the following year. The government's proposals, however, were regarded as unnecessarily timid by the most representative of the local radio pressure groups. In particular, the decision not to allow the local stations to derive income from commercial advertising angered many of the stations' operators. They argued that, without this source of revenue, the small stations, which the government allegedly wished to promote, would not be able to continue broadcasting.[74]

None the less, the state monopoly in radio provision was comprehensively smashed. After 1981 the floodgates were opened to an apparently infinite number and astonishing variety of small, privately run, local stations. By the end of 1983 it was estimated that up to 850 were operating quite legally. As a result, many different groups in French society now enjoyed privileged access to local radio. Alternative social, cultural and political groups, religious organizations, newspaper and magazine publishers, community associations, scouts and music lovers all took advantage of the new freedom. Though municipal radios as such were not allowed, town councils also joined in. Radio-Tour Eiffel, backed by the Gaullist mayor of Paris Jacques Chirac, was probably the best-known example of this type of station. Like the pop music pirates in Britain in the 1960s, the new local stations satisfied a demand previously left unfulfilled by both the state radio company and the peripheral networks. Despite poor transmission quality in several cases, the new stations proved extremely popular with French listeners eager to obtain something new from their radio sets.

The Socialists' comprehensive reform of broadcasting – the 1982 statute – allowed for the establishment of local radio outside the control of the state programme companies Radio France and FR3. Limited to a transmission capacity of up to 30 kilometres, these private stations were still forbidden to receive income from commercial advertising. Financial aid was to be provided by means of a state subsidy. To prevent the formation of commercial oligopolies, no person or group was allowed to manage or financially contribute to more than one private station. A new regulatory authority (the High Authority for Audiovisual Communication) was given responsibility for the allocation of local radio licences so that there would be no Italian-style anarchy of the airwaves in France.[75]

The Socialist government's policy marked a clear break with the past. The explosion in local radio in the early 1980s, comparable in scale to the growth in the press after the Liberation, could no longer be repressed as Giscard d'Estaing had tried to do. It had to be accommodated. This the Socialists were willing to do, in part because the monopoly was now regarded as an anachronism and in part because legalization of private local radio fitted in with the government's commitment to the decentralization of power to the regions and localities. The Socialist government viewed private local radio as an important element of a more pluralistic and decentralist broadcasting system. Its legalization marked a step in the direction of diversity in broadcast outlets and hence a perceptible relaxation in the state's hold over the broadcast media. However, legalization posed political as well as purely techno-administrative problems. Two in particular dominated the debate in the early 1980s: the allocation of frequencies and finance.[76]

One test of the political independence of the High Authority was the manner in which it approved the allocation of local radio licences. Its task was not an easy one since there was a limited number of available frequencies on the FM waveband and demand often exceeded supply, especially in the Paris area. In some cases the Authority obliged different applicants to share the same frequency (with each being given a specific time slot) in an attempt to maximize access. While in general this task was completed with remarkable smoothness, there were some difficult cases. In the heavily politicized atmosphere of French broadcasting, some of the decisions of the High Authority were naturally the subject of controversy as applicants tried to ensure that their demands were met. Not surprisingly, some groups complained of political discrimination by the High Authority.

On one occasion – the case of Radio Solidarité – the Authority's attempt to rebut this charge met with perverse results. The station's chairman was the conservative politician and former Minister of Information Philippe Malaud, and its output was strongly sympathetic to the right-wing opposition. Originally the station had been allocated a frequency at the very edge of the spectrum. After a series of vociferous complaints, however, the High Authority allocated Radio Solidarité a frequency nearer the centre of the waveband which it found more acceptable. Immediately other stations protested against this alleged favourable treatment. As a result, in trying to be seen to act impartially and counter accusations of political bias, the High Authority found itself accused of being partisan.

The second aspect of the Socialist government's policy on private radio which came in for criticism was the continued ban on commercial advertising as a source of finance. This meant that many stations had to eke out a hand-to-mouth existence helped by voluntary subscriptions and donations. Conscious of their financial plight, the government also allocated funds taken from the advertising budgets of the state radio and television companies. None the less, starved of revenue, some radios had recourse to secret advertising of commercial products, a practice which the authorities had great difficulty in controlling.

The government initially argued that to allow advertising would be to run the risk of a commercial ethos, ideologically hostile to the Socialist regime, dominating this non-state sector of the media. More prosaically, it is also likely that the Socialists were worried about the possible effects on the state broadcasting sector if advertising were allowed on private local radio. With the introduction of advertising on the regional television channel, FR3, following the 1982 reform, all three state television channels now derived some income from advertising. The government feared the deleterious effects on the finances of state television if advertising revenue had to be spread too thinly among a host of recipients. Paradoxically, therefore, in the first phase of private local radio in France, while much of the state broadcasting sector (though not Radio France) was supported by advertising, private radio was not. One of the classic dividing lines between a public and private service, the source of finance, was fudged.

Finance was undoubtedly the main problem facing the private stations between 1982 and 1984. Once the initial flood of enthusiasm had evaporated and audiences tired of the amateurism of many of the local stations' programme output, some stations ceased to function because of their lack of resources. Pressure on the government to change its policy increased and in 1984 the Socialists gave way, amending the 1982 statute to allow private local radio to accept advertising. 'So began a process of commercialisation which was to accelerate and change the landscape of French broadcasting.'[77]

The decision to allow advertising was a reflection of the institutionalization of private local radio in France. It no longer had an experimental status, but was rather an integral part of the broadcasting system. Its success, especially among young listeners, meant that advertisers and advertising agencies wanted to use the stations to reach this attractive target audience who were not major consumers of other media. Many of the stations themselves needed advertising to upgrade their activities on to a more professional footing. With the financial base made more secure, private local radio continued to expand: by the end of 1984 around 1,000 private local radios had been authorized to transmit and by the middle of the decade the estimated figure was over 1,500.[78]

While in Britain the BBC/IBA television duopoly at the national level was mirrored in the organization of local radio during this period, in France a very different system was emerging. In only a few localities was there a public service local radio station managed by Radio France. In many areas, however, there were a variety of private radios competing with each other for listeners and for space on the crowded waveband. Yet this picture of a healthy pluralistic local radio system subject to minimal content regulation did not endure. The established national players – Radio France and the peripheral networks – mounted their own counter-offensive to recapture their audiences. More importantly, in defiance of the legislation, *de facto* networks of private local stations were formed in a struggle for market domination and, in some cases, mere survival. These networks radically changed the nature of private local radio in France, ensuring that the system would come to be dominated by a few big players. Among them was the network which became the sensation of the mid- to late 1980s: NRJ.

NRJ AND THE AGE OF PRIVATE NETWORKS

Ten years after the decision to legalize private local radio, about 1,700 stations were operating in France. The system, however, had undergone a qualitative change. Non-profitmaking community radios were now in the minority: a mere 400 in 1991. There were 1,200 commercial radio stations, of which 300 were independent and 900 were part of a regional or national network. By the early 1990s, therefore, networks had become the main players on the FM waveband.

The establishment of networks was facilitated by the use of satellite technology for programme transmission. A central programming station could distribute a programme via telecommunications satellite to its affiliated stations or transmitters, which in turn relayed the entire programme or part of it locally on FM. Technology was not the only factor, however, in helping the establishment of networks. Competition for audiences and advertisers encouraged many local radio stations to seek the protection of a network arrangement and as the networks grew they could use their economic muscle in the battle against the small independents. The growing professionalization of the FM band and the audience's expectations in terms of programme presentation also worked against the long-term survival of many of the local independent stations, with their tradition of voluntary amateurism.[79]

The best-known network is NRJ (Nouvelle Radio Jeune), pronounced *énergie*, a Paris-based music station which began transmission in July 1981. In other parts of France stations took the name and adopted the format of the Paris station. This was initially done through franchising arrangements, with the Paris station providing programming advice and technical assistance in return for a share of the stations' advertising revenue. This produced an NRJ network across France, rivalling the pull of the national peripheral stations (see table 3.4).[80] With a programme output of virtually non-stop music, NRJ proved especially popular with listeners in the 12–25 age category, an important consumer group for advertisers because of its high level of disposable income (see table 3.5).

Table 3.4 Number of NRJ stations

1983	1
1984	12
1985	28
1986	42
1987	50
1988	85
1989	110

Source: B. Clarens, 'Parcours sans faute de Jean-Paul Baudecroux, entrepreneur de radio', *Médiaspouvoirs*, no.15, Paris, 1989, p.100.

In 1984 this audience also showed that it could exert political muscle. When NRJ infringed the provisions of the 1982 legislation by massively exceeding the statutory limits on transmission power, it ran into problems with the High Authority who suspended its licence. Hundreds of young NRJ listeners, transistor in hand, came out on to the streets to voice their opposition against the decision and support their favourite radio. Twenty-six years after the 1968 May 'events', radio was at the heart of another noisy

Table 3.5 NRJ listening figures (as % of total radio audience)

Year	Greater Paris region	Rest of France
1983	8	–
1984	12	–
1985	18	–
1986	23	7.6
1987	18	10
1988	20	11.2
1989	n/a	10.6

n/a = not available; – = not applicable
Source: B. Clarens, 'Parcours sans faute de Jean-Paul Baudecroux, entrepreneur de radio', *Médiaspouvoirs*, no.15, Paris, 1989, p.100.

protest by French youth on the streets of Paris. On this occasion, however, the demonstration was not intended to campaign for university reform or protest against police violence, far less bring about a change of society. The aim of this new generation was to keep a pop music radio station on the air – and they succeeded in doing just that.

Since the mid-1980s NRJ, under the management of Jean-Paul Baudecroux, has gone from success to success and the NRJ formula has become the model for many other FM radio stations to emulate. NRJ has opened up a second radio network, Chérie FM, for listeners in the 25–45 age category and has expanded into a powerful media group.[81] It had a stake in the commercial television channel TV6 before the reallocation of franchises in 1987, became active in the telematics field and has its own record production company. In a French version of the Disney corporation, NRJ has also moved into merchandising, promoting its own brand of school gear and sportswear as well as its own version of the Renault 5 car.

The growth of FM radio during the 1980s had knock-on consequences for other players in the French media system. The newspaper press grew anxious at the arrival of new competition and, having failed to prevent the implantation of advertising-funded local radio, decided to increase their participation in the ownership and management of stations. Faced with the challenge from private local radio (and commercial television), press groups sought to buy into these new initiatives. Several regional papers established their own radio stations – for example, the Sud-Ouest group had three local stations in the mid-1980s, including Radio 100 in Bordeaux.[82] In Paris newspapers and magazines of opposing political tendencies shared the same frequency in the early 1980s.[83] Overall, however, private radios supported by press groups have not been commercially successful, as several newspapers encountered problems in their attempt to diversify into new media markets. This in turn explains the marked reluctance of many regional dailies to become involved in local television projects.

The main media players affected have been the traditional national radio networks of Radio France, notably France-Inter, and the peripheral stations, such as RTL and Europe 1. At the beginning of the 1980s the state radio service had belatedly attempted to draw off some of the heat from the threat of the pirate stations by setting up experimental public service local radio stations of its own. It also created Radio 7, which was targeted at the youth audience, and thematic stations, such as France-Info and Radio Bleue, to widen its market profile.[84] By 1990 Radio France had 47 local, decentralized stations (the equivalent of BBC local radio), covering almost 50 per cent of the national territory.[85] In the eyes of their defenders, these public service local radio stations are the only ones to offer a real, local, quality news service and to give a prominent place to locally produced programming.[86] However, the audience figures for Radio France's local stations are low, while the Radio 7 venture was later abandoned as a failure.

The audience ratings of the peripheral stations were also adversely affected by the growth of the FM networks. In 1986 the government granted the peripheral stations access to the technically superior FM frequencies, releasing them from their previous confinement to long wave. Either through direct ownership or as programme supplier, the peripheral stations have effectively set up their own FM networks. Europe 2 supplies programmes to a 'network' of local stations; RTL created a network called Maxximum; and in 1989 Radio-Monte-Carlo bought the Nostalgie network. The main independent networks responded to this challenge by each taking control of a second, smaller, network to offer advertisers complementary audiences.[87] As well as setting up new local stations and FM networks, Radio France and the peripheral stations have also modified their programme schedules and formats in a fiercely competitive battle for audiences.

Listening patterns have changed dramatically since the advent of private local radio. First, the arrival of stations such as NRJ has led to an overall growth in the popularity of radio among young listeners, with 15–34-year-olds constituting 40.3 per cent of the total radio audience though they represent only 37.6 per cent of the population. Especially popular are the FM networks devoted to music: NRJ, Europe 2, Skyrock and RFM. The same age group comprises 62.3 per cent of the audience of private local radios as a whole and an impressive 70.2 per cent of NRJ's audience.[88] Second, the audience share of the different stations has evolved to the benefit of the independent networks. In the first semester of 1990, for example, the peripheral stations attracted only 37.8 per cent of the audience, the FM networks and the private local radios 37.7 per cent, and Radio France a mere 17.5 per cent.[89]

The growth of radio in the 1980s also posed a series of problems for the regulatory authorities, who were themselves suffering the consequences of governmental turnover and political interference. After the change of government in 1986 the High Authority was abolished and replaced by the

National Commission for Communication and Liberties (CNCL) which in turn gave way to the Higher Audiovisual Council (CSA) in 1989.[90] The short reign of the CNCL resulted in political criteria becoming more important in the decision to grant or withhold a private local radio licence. 'In the Paris area [the CNCL] decisions caused the disappearance of almost every station of left sympathies.'[91] The 1986 legislation introduced by the Chirac government (and since modified in 1989 and 1990) also recognized the existence of private local radio networks. The main aim of the legislators and regulatory authorities in the late 1980s was to contain network power within certain prescribed limits, for example through the enforcement of anti-concentration measures.[92]

In an attempt to preserve what was left of the pluralism in the radio system of the early 1980s, the CSA has divided applications for private radio licences on the FM waveband into five categories.[93] These range from non-commercial community stations at one end of the spectrum to generalist national radio stations (i.e. the traditional peripheral stations such as Europe 1 and RTL) at the other. Between these two extremes lie three classifications of commercial radio: independent local or regional stations, local or regional stations affiliated to or franchised by a network (such as Skyrock, Fun Radio and Europe 2), and national thematic stations (such as NRJ, Chérie FM, Superloustic and Maxximum).[94] Since good transmission is one of the keys to the success of FM radio, the allocation of frequencies by the CSA has provoked further economic and political battles involving in particular powerful communications groups (such as Hachette, Hersant and Filipacchi) which are tending to dominate the market.[95] It still remains an open question whether this attempt by the CSA to achieve a balance and complementarity of radio provision in a given region will succeed. Once again, the battle between regulatory constraints and market pressures has been joined, with the suspicion that, as in the past, commercial criteria and the powerful network players will dominate.

RADIO IN THE 1990s

The past fifteen years have witnessed radical changes in the field of radio in France. From small illegal experimental radio stations have emerged professionally run private local radios, frequently organized in nationwide networks. Of course, there are still private local radio stations in France which are more reminiscent of the early Giscardian era. But they are not the norm. The system has evolved from illegal, and therefore unregulated, pirate stations through various learning stages to what may be regarded as a reasonable attempt to create conditions for minimal pluralism. The sum of these changes has been 'to increase competition, massively open up radio broadcasting to the private sector . . . displace the centre of gravity of radio output to the FM wave band . . . multiply the supply of programmes a hundred-fold, fragment the audience into small targeted segments and turn radio listening into a solitary activity on personal stereos or the car radio where everyone has their own receiver and is able to listen to their chosen station'.[96]

Competition between the different radio stations and networks in France has become intense. At one level radio as a whole has to compete with a range of other media, including the press, public sector and commercial television channels and the new electronic media of cable and satellite. At the same time expansion within the radio sector has resulted in a fierce jockeying for market dominance to win audiences and advertisers. The market in radio supply is still relatively open and entry costs are lower than in the daily newspaper press or television. None the less, it has become extremely difficult for newcomers to establish themselves in a tight competitive market. With a few exceptions the era of the small artisanal station of the early 1980s has gone. In its place there is now a system dominated by highly professional companies, targeting listeners on the basis of sophisticated market research and seeking to retain, if not increase, their audience share. The overall result has been an oligopolization of the private radio sector in France.

Along with the dominance of the major networks has come an undoubted professionalism which embraces an increased emphasis on promotion and marketing, greater attention to transmission quality and detailed consideration of programme formats, presentation and scheduling. This professionalism also covers a concern with cost efficiency in all aspects of the business and the maintenance of harmonious relations with key advertisers.[97] The main FM networks are investing abroad and lobby organizations have been formed to represent the interests of the FM radio sector.

Professionalism, however, is not synonymous with diversity and pluralism. With oligopolization has come a certain sameness in programme output. The dominant format is a combination of music and news. There is an evident lack of choice in much of the programming across different stations, many of which for reasons of cost leave little space for local expression either in terms of news coverage or programme production.[98] Many of the stations have become little more than vehicles for delivering targeted audiences to advertisers.

This poses various problems. The first – a purely commercial one – is whether the market can support all the different stations and networks transmitting music aimed at the 15–25-year-old age group.[99] It is already being asked whether there are not too many FM networks now operating in France. Though audience share for FM radio has been increasing towards 40 per cent of the total radio market, advertising revenue has not kept pace. In this respect radio is the poor relation of the French media, taking only 6.6 per cent of total expenditure on media advertising in 1990. Only NRJ, Europe 2 and Skyrock attract more than 5 or 6 per cent of the audience and these three (plus Nostalgie) were the only stations to make a profit in the early 1990s.[100] Networks may fail, as Kiss FM did in March 1991, or mergers take place. Companies may continue to get their fingers burnt, as did Crown Communications Group, which decided in 1992 to sell its stake in the network RFM because of disappointing audience and advertising figures.[101]

Even if many, though not all, of the networks are commercially successful, this is scarcely the only criterion by which to judge the French radio system of the 1990s. Questions will continue to be asked about the relative uniformity of programme formats and the levels of ownership concentration, as well as the old chestnuts of programme quality and standards. Hare has also emphasized the twin dangers of marginalization/exclusion and stereotyping inherent in a system which places so much stress on delivering a particular type of audience to advertisers. In perceiving their audience purely as consumers, Hare argues, FM stations will tend to exclude social groups with low levels of purchasing power and at the same time present a one-dimensional concept of the listener as consumer, ignoring or downplaying other facets of the audience's social identity.[102]

In conclusion, Lewis and Booth are surely correct when they write that

> what was originally a political initiative has been overtaken by a different dynamic. French local radio has to be seen in relationship to a sophisticated consumer environment in which sound plays multiple roles: it is both a link in a chain of products *and* assists in the construction of a 'discipline of leisure' *and* for a post-modern generation which has rejected the text, it provides the context for living.[103]

In short, what began as vehicles of political protest and alternative culture have been replaced by suppliers of a consumer-friendly lifestyle.

Chapter 4

Television under de Gaulle

Compared with some other industrialized countries, such as the United States and Great Britain, France was slow to enter the television era. Though French television was officially established in 1935 and regular transmissions began after the Second World War, it was not until the late 1950s that a significant mass audience began to emerge. There were a variety of reasons for the relatively slow market take-up of television in postwar France.[1] The low standard of living of many French people, the initial high cost of sets and the belief that television was a non-essential luxury item helped keep consumer demand down. At the same time, many intellectuals and opinion formers manifested a barely disguised contempt for the medium, which on the basis of the American experience they regarded as a vehicle for all that was worst in mass culture.[2] On the supply side, the weakness of the French electronics industry delayed the production of sets. Most crucially of all, financial constraints within the state broadcasting services, which were still geared up primarily for radio broadcasts, meant that the transmission network and programme output of television were slow to expand and attract a large nationwide audience.[3] As late as 1957 only five major urban areas could receive television programmes. The result was that during the 1950s the new medium failed to penetrate into many French households (see tables 4.1 and 4.2). Ownership of a set was confined to a select few, while many were introduced to television viewing in cafés and télé-clubs.[4]

By contrast, in the following decade the take-off of television sales was impressive. The number of households which owned sets steadily increased, from just under 2 million in 1960 to just over 10 million in 1969 (see table 4.3). Whereas in 1958 well under 10 per cent of French households possessed a television set, by 1964 this had climbed to 40.3 per cent and by 1969 to 69.7 per cent.[5] The amount of time spent watching television by the average French adult also increased from 57 minutes per day in 1964 to 107 minutes in 1969, almost wholly because of the expanding market penetration of the medium rather than radical changes in individual viewing habits.[6]

Table 4.1 Number of television sets per 1,000 inhabitants in selected European countries

Country	1955	1960	1965	1972
France	3	41	133	237
United States	170	310	362	474
Great Britain	95	211	248	305
West Germany	5	83	193	293

Source: P. Albert, *La presse française*, Paris, La documentation française, 1979, p.25.

Table 4.2 Percentage of households with a television set

Country	1958	1963
France	6	25
Great Britain	33	80
West Germany	6	38
Italy	5.5	28

Source: J. Beaulieu, *La télévision des réalisateurs*, Paris, La documentation française, 1984, p.145.

In line with this increase in consumption, the supply of television programming grew in the 1960s. A second national channel was established in 1964, with 20 per cent of the population covered by its transmitter network on launch date, 50 per cent in 1966 and 82 per cent by 1969.[7] Colour television arrived in 1967. Daily programme schedules were lengthened with the result that the total amount of television programming doubled during the decade (see table 4.4). These measures were designed not just to raise viewing figures and widen choice, but also to boost sales of television sets. In a virtuous economic circle the extension of the television networks and the availability of more television programming stimulated consumer demand for sets, which in turn provided more revenue through the licence fee to the state television services for the expansion of programme provision. Along with ever-lengthening television schedules came a growth in the number of staff employed in the state broadcasting corporation and an increase in the proportion working for television (see table 4.5). By the end of the 1960s the ORTF was one of the European giants in television production, programming and transmission, ranking alongside other public service broadcasting organizations such as the BBC in Britain, the RAI in Italy and the ARD in West Germany.

The spectacular growth in television supply and consumption during this period can easily be measured by the use of statistical data. The *qualitative* influence of television, however, remains a matter of evaluation and even speculation. The political role of the medium in the 1950s appears to have been minimal. For example, Rioux argues that during the Fourth Republic

Table 4.3 Television licence fee holders 1950–69

Year	Number of licence fee holders	% of French households with television	
1950	3,794		
1951	10,558		
1952	24,209		
1953	59,971		
1954	125,088	1.0	(December)
1955	260,508		
1956	442,433		
1957	683,229	6.1	(September)
1958	988,594		
1959	1,368,145		
1960	1,901,946	13.1	(April)
1961	2,554,821		
1962	3,426,839	23.1	(April)
1963	4,400,278	27.3	(April)
1964	5,414,276	39.3	(April)
1965	6,493,943	40.8	(April)
		45.6	(December)
1966	7,484,294	51.7	(December)
1967	8,335,752	58.0	(December)
1968	9,277,499	61.9	(December)
1969	10,153,180	66.4	(December)

Sources: ORTF, *ORTF 73*, Paris, Presses de la Cité, 1973, p.698; J. Bourdon, *Histoire de la télévision sous de Gaulle*, Paris, Anthropos/INA, 1990, p.303.

'governments still had not taken stock of the full power of the image', with the result that television played little part in French political debate.[8] As far as its impact on social life is concerned, Wylie comments in his study of life in a Provençal village that in 1959

> television seems to have atomised still further the social contacts of the people of Peyrane, which were already badly fragmented in 1950. However, the Peyranais who watch television instead of playing boules with their neighbours and gossiping about village affairs no doubt feel as though they have more in common with Frenchmen in general who are also watching the swimming meet in Paris. This is only one example of many influences which act upon the people of Peyrane to increase their sense of integration with the rest of France today.[9]

If accurate, Wylie's impressionistic assessment of the effect of television on this rural community would attribute to the medium responsibility for fragmenting social contact at the *local* level and simultaneously promoting a feeling of *national* cohesion. However, the evidence for this, or indeed any, generalization about the impact of television on French society in the 1950s is at best patchy.

Table 4.4 Annual number of hours of television transmission 1958–69

1958	2,451	1964	4,011
1959	2,651	1965	4,614
1960	2,760	1966	4,885
1961	2,881	1967	5,208
1962	2,914	1968	5,232
1963	2,937	1969	5,980

Source: J. Bourdon, *Histoire de la télévision sous de Gaulle*, Paris, Anthropos/INA, 1990, p.307.

Table 4.5 Number of permanent staff at the (O)RTF 1960–70 (excluding journalists and musicians)

1960	7,547	1966	10,522
1961	9,489	1967	10,815
1962	10,624	1968	11,195
1963	10,297	1969	11,638
1964	10,102	1970	12,324
1965	10,122		

Source: J. Bourdon, *Histoire de la télévision sous de Gaulle*, Paris, Anthropos/INA, 1990, p.305. (Originally compiled from different sources, the above table is indicative of a general trend only.)

Ten years later, the situation had dramatically altered. By the end of the 1960s television had displaced the press and radio as the principal medium of national and international information. At the same time it had substantially modified the political communications process. It had also become the primary source of domestic entertainment and the single most important mass disseminator of culture. It was held responsible for various social phenomena, such as the decline in cinema attendance and, more controversially, the disruption of family life and the promotion of violence. Though in any specific context the precise extent of its influence on attitudes and behaviour was difficult to assess, there can be little doubt that by the time General de Gaulle resigned from the presidential office in April 1969, television had become the most powerful mass medium in French history.

This chapter concentrates on key features of the relationship between the state and television during the de Gaulle presidency (1958–69). The state completely dominated French television throughout this period. In its capacity as *policy maker and regulator* the state was responsible for drafting and implementing the major piece of legislation on television, the 1964 ORTF statute. This reaffirmed the state's *monopoly of ownership* in the broadcasting field. In its role as *financial controller* the state set the level of the licence fee, revenue from which made up virtually all of the broadcasting organization's income until 1968. In that year it was also the state which decided that advertising would be introduced on television. The state translated its formal powers of appointment into a *source of political patronage* whereby Gaullist sympathizers were nominated to key decision-making posts in broadcasting. This was part of a wider system of political patronage whereby the upper echelons of state and para-state agencies were occupied by Gaullist supporters. The state exerted its power to act as a *primary definer* of television's political agenda and was not averse to taking on the role of *censor* of news output. The political content of television was strictly controlled by the Gaullist authorities to ensure that coverage would further the realization of their electoral and ideological objectives. The state also used television to pursue its general *cultural policy* goals: the medium was to help disseminate the glories of French culture to a mass audience. Finally, as the *formulator of industrial policy* the state directed key aspects of television's technical development so that these conformed to broader objectives of the government's industrial policy.

TELEVISION AND THE CONTESTED GAULLIST REGIME

The linkages between the state and television during de Gaulle's presidency can best be understood with reference to the political context of a regime struggling to legitimize itself. Television and the Gaullist Fifth Republic did not just take root and mature simultaneously. Their respective developments were closely interrelated. From the outset the Gaullist authorities badly needed television to help in the implantation and legitimation of the new political system. This it did by providing de Gaulle and his supporters with a platform from which they could bypass intermediary bodies such as Parliament, traditional political parties and interest groups to address the nation directly. The medium thus fitted in perfectly with de Gaulle's personal vision of how France should be governed, by furnishing a direct link between the President and the people.

Naturally, the Gaullist conception of television's political role included the desire to ensure as favourable coverage of their policies as possible. In this respect the Gaullist authorities behaved no differently from any other government in the television age. All governments want to use television to mobilize public opinion in their favour. Yet couched in such general abstract terms, this is an unsatisfactory explanation of the significance de Gaulle and his supporters attributed to television during his presidency. It scarcely accounts for the crucial role which was accorded the medium as an integral part of the political process, nor for the tenacity which the Gaullists showed in keeping tight control of television news output.

Nor is it sufficient to talk purely in terms of the continuation of a French tradition of partisan political control of broadcasting in the postwar period. Missika and Wolton are correct in stating that 'the subordination of public service television to government policy was less a novelty than the continuation of habits which were already more than a quarter of a century old'.[10] Moreover, the practice of governmental manipulation of radio which had been used to keep de Gaulle off the air during the Fourth Republic undoubtedly goes some way to explaining the Gaullists' understandable desire for revenge once they arrived in power in 1958. Yet an explanation of the links between the Gaullist state and television simply in terms of an entrenched practice or party political revanchism is of itself scarcely adequate.

The essential point to grasp is that the Fifth Republic under de Gaulle was a contested regime. It was a political system which faced constant attacks on its legitimacy. These challenges came both from outside the mainstream political process (for example, extreme right-wing terrorism in the early 1960s and student/worker protest in 1968) and from inside (for instance, the party political opposition to the presidentialization of the regime in 1962). In particular, the relationship between television and the state must be explained with reference to three specific features of Gaullist rule: first, the inauspicious circumstances in which the Fifth Republic came into existence in 1958, followed by the prolongation of the war in Algeria for another four years; second, the widespread opposition from the traditional political elites to de Gaulle's proposed constitutional amendment in 1962; and finally, de Gaulle's presidential domination of the political system combined with his personal mastery of the audiovisual media.

The combination of these three features of Gaullist rule into a contextualizing framework for understanding the relationship between the state and television during de Gaulle's presidency is not an attempt to excuse or justify the practice of government control of political information on television. Rather the objective is to situate the linkages within a specific national and historical context in which the nature of political conflict was very different from that which was to be found in Great Britain or the United States at the time. Television was not just an electoral weapon to be used by the Gaullists in the normal party political battles of a stable liberal democracy in which all the players accept the rules of the game. Rather it was a key ideological tool to be wielded unmercifully in the process of legitimizing the contested political system of the Fifth Republic. For the Gaullists television was indispensable in the construction of a popular consensus in support of the new institutions.

The nature of the regime transition from Fourth to Fifth Republic was the first feature of Gaullist rule which influenced the relationship between state and television. The Fourth Republic collapsed in 1958 over its failure to resolve the apparently intractable conflict in Algeria. The parliamentary regime's short existence came to an end in chaotic conditions, exemplified by a breakdown of governmental authority, deep divisions between the parties in Parliament and low levels of popular legitimacy. It was in an atmosphere in which civil war or a military *coup d'état* seemed more likely developments than a peaceful resolution of the crisis that General de Gaulle returned to power after 12 years of self-imposed exile. A precondition of his acquiescence in once again taking up national political office was the drafting of a new constitution, which de Gaulle considered essential for France's long-term political stability.[11]

Though the 1958 Constitution provided France with institutions based on a blueprint drafted by de Gaulle, of itself it could not guarantee the exercise of strong executive authority. In the early years of his presidency de Gaulle lacked power bases in key areas of the political system. He did not have the unconditional backing of a majority party in Parliament, nor were the Gaullists well represented in local government. During the first four years of the Fifth Republic, therefore, de Gaulle governed through the exercise of his charismatic authority. This highly personalized form of rule was facilitated by television, which allowed de Gaulle to speak directly to the French people (*la France profonde*) and rally them behind his regime. Just as rulers in developing countries frequently use television for nation-building purposes, so de Gaulle exploited the medium to transcend the fragmentation in French society and the divisions at the level of parliamentary representation to put together a popular coalition supporting the institutions of the Fifth Republic. In so doing, de Gaulle was continuing a practice of direct popular appeal to the nation which had been used by Napoleon and Louis Napoleon in the nineteenth century.[12] Indeed, in the early years of the de Gaulle presidency this use of television by a charismatic leader led some commentators to regard Gaullism as a contemporary manifestation of the Bonapartist tradition in French politics.

The Algerian conflict, which dominated the political agenda of the regime in its early years, provided a further incentive for the Gaullist government's control of television. Paradoxically, de Gaulle's tenure of the presidential office appeared to be contingent on the continuation of the war. As long as the conflict persisted, de Gaulle was essential to the governance of France and the maintenance of the democratic political process. Yet de Gaulle knew that the defence of French Algeria was an anachronism, which was sapping the country's economy, undermining its credibility among the international community and preventing it from playing a more fruitful role in the EEC. Hence, he began the slow and tortuous process of educating the French people towards the acceptance of a policy of French withdrawal. In particular, de Gaulle used television to convince the French electorate of the wisdom of his policy of self-determination for Algeria. Meanwhile, an attempted putsch against the regime, various assassination attempts on de Gaulle's life and numerous terrorist outrages by pro-*Algérie française* extremists testified to the fragility of Gaullist rule. Until the policy of French withdrawal had been implemented, control of television could be justified by the Gaullists as an essential measure in a period of *de facto* national emergency.

The ending of the war in 1962 did not, however, have an immediate impact on the relationship between the state and television. This was due in large part to the re-emergence of the constitutional issue on to the political agenda. In fact, the major conflict over the Constitution of the Fifth Republic came not in 1958 but in 1962, when de Gaulle's controversial proposal to introduce direct popular elections for the presidency met with a barrage of opposition from the traditional political elites. This challenge to the regime from within the mainstream political process was the second feature of Gaullist rule which confirmed the ideological importance of television for the President and his government.

With the notable exception of the Communists, most of the political forces of the Fourth Republic had supported de Gaulle's return to power in 1958. However, they had done so only because of the regime's inability to deal with the Algerian problem. With this issue off the agenda by 1962, they were now free to argue that de Gaulle was no longer indispensable to political stability and that political life could return to something more akin to Fourth Republic parliamentary 'normality'. They were fiercely opposed, therefore, to what they regarded as an anti-republican move in the direction of a more overtly presidential style of regime.

At the same time the resolution of the Algerian conflict meant that de Gaulle could no longer rely solely on the exercise of his personal authority to maintain himself in power. The goal of establishing a more solid institutional basis for the presidency could be achieved by the introduction of direct elections which would increase the legitimacy of the office. The stakes were high in the autumn of 1962 as the Gaullists sought both to amend their own Constitution by popular referendum and deliver the President a parliamentary majority in the subsequent general election. Mobilization of the electorate had to be effective and for this once again television had a key role to play.

The electoral majority in favour of the constitutional amendment institutionalized a powerful presidential office in France. After 1962 the Gaullists had to ensure that it did not fall into the hands of their opponents. The Gaullists were afraid that the election of a non-Gaullist President (or a parliamentary majority opposed to the President) would lead not just to conflict over policy, but to a constitutional crisis which might result in the downfall of the Fifth Republic itself. In the opinion of the Gaullists, their regime had constantly to be protected from its implacable enemies. A foreign policy emphasizing national grandeur and a defence policy based on an independent nuclear deterrent might win popular approval. Control of state television would improve the Gaullist chances of turning that approval into electoral success.

The ideological spread and intensity of the party political opposition to Gaullism helped confirm the government's media strategy on regime implantation. As no consensus existed among the parties regarding the basic principles on which the Fifth Republic was founded, the party in power was understandably reluctant to open up television to political views which called the legitimacy of the institutions – *its* institutions – into question. The Gaullist case was strengthened in their eyes by the fact that the leading opposition party of the Left was not a social democratic or labourist force, but rather the Communist party which in the early 1960s was still under the pro-Soviet, Stalinist leadership of Maurice Thorez. Even after the death of Thorez in 1964, the Communist party was never regarded by the Gaullists as a fully legitimate opposition party. The dominance of the Left by the Communists was a useful electoral weapon which could be utilized by the Gaullists and their allies as a scaremongering tactic, as in the June 1968 general election held in the wake of the infamous 'events'.

The Gaullists claimed that in addition to party political opposition, much of the press was also opposed to their rule. For example, Alain Peyrefitte, the most influential of many Ministers of Information during the de Gaulle presidency, sought to justify the pro-government stance of the regional news programmes on state television by pointing out its balancing effect in areas where the press reflected the views of the opposition.[13] Anderson writes that 'the absence of a serious large-circulation newspaper or weekly supporting the government convinced the Gaullist leadership early in the Fifth Republic that it was faced by a predominantly hostile press'.[14] If Anderson is correct, then the Gaullists perceived their regime to be under attack from a very powerful sector of the media. They could then claim that, far from infringing the rules of pluralist coverage, one-sided control of television was actually designed to achieve this goal across the press and audiovisual media combined.

The third and final feature of Gaullist rule which shaped the relationship between the state and television during the 1960s was the combination of de Gaulle's domination of the political system and his own personal skills in exploiting the audiovisual media to good effect. De Gaulle had a strictly presidentialist interpretation of the Fifth Republic's ambiguous constitutional provisions. Though he was prepared to allow his Prime Minister responsibility for the day-to-day implementation of domestic policy, there was never any doubt as to who was the chief executive during his presidency. De Gaulle formed the presidency into the key decision-making office, particularly in the realms of foreign and defence policy.

At the same time the President presented himself in both the domestic and international political environments as the incarnation of a revivified French greatness. His tenure of the presidential office did not just have a substantive impact on the formulation of policy and the functioning of the institutions. It was also heavily laden with symbolism. De Gaulle used television to help propagate the myth of his self-ascribed destiny to rule France. His television appearances were as much a part of his own conscious fashioning of his place in history as immediate responses to the exigencies of the political situation. This is not to deny or even to minimize de Gaulle's contribution to the creation of a stable and effective political system. His occupation of the presidency and the maintenance of the regime seemed, and perhaps were, inextricably bound up with each other. During the 1960s it certainly appeared that de Gaulle *was* the Fifth Republic. The point to note here is that de Gaulle never sought to play down this link. On the contrary, he emphasized it at times of political crisis and used television to drive the unambiguous message home – without de Gaulle, there was only chaos. Television did not just help implant the regime or project an image of de Gaulle's presidential authority. In fusing the two, it sought to disseminate de Gaulle's own view that he and the regime were inseparable.

De Gaulle's previous experience of using the broadcasting media helped form his appreciation of their potential as a means of political communication and propaganda. Well before his accession to the presidency, the success of his wartime radio broadcasts had led de Gaulle to invest the broadcasting media with a special power to influence the French people – a power which he was determined to exploit to the full. From the very start of his political career, therefore, de Gaulle was aware of the political significance of broadcasting and he maintained this sense of awareness throughout his presidency.

The role played by radio during the war also allowed de Gaulle to familiarize himself with the necessary media skills which he was later to employ with such remarkable effect as President. His expertise in the use of radio and television was naturally of paramount importance during periods of political crisis. For example, during the Algerian war de Gaulle asserted his authority via the broadcasting media on two important occasions: first, during the week of the Algiers barricades in January 1960 when he appeared on television in army uniform to condemn the insurgents and to call for the strictest discipline from the army;[15] and second, during the attempted putsch by the generals in April 1961. During the early crisis years of the regime de Gaulle had frequent recourse to television: between the start of 1960 and October 1962 he addressed the French people directly 21 times on screen.[16] In similar fashion, de Gaulle's frequent interventions on television in election and referendum campaigns were considered by the Gaullists and their opponents to be crucial in rallying support to the Gaullist camp. In the 1961 referendum campaign on Algerian self-determination, for example, de Gaulle opened the campaign, made two broadcasts in the week before the poll and had almost as much time on the air as all the parties put together.[17]

The finest examples of de Gaulle's use of the broadcasting media were the presidential press conferences which received saturation coverage on radio and television. Since many of the major policy decisions of the President were announced at these conferences, these occasions would have been significant from the point of view of content alone. What made them such impressive events, however, was de Gaulle's style. Presidential policy decisions were revealed on television not only to the viewers but also to government ministers who up until the start of the conference were often themselves unaware of what policy initiative de Gaulle was going to announce. The President used an element of suspense to dramatize his utterances for maximum impact. By dint of careful stage management de Gaulle not only enhanced the prestige and dignity of the presidential office and its incumbent, but also demonstrated the force of television as a political instrument.[18]

De Gaulle spared no pains to ensure that he performed well on television. He took

> all the trouble to write out his text, to learn it off by heart . . . to make the most of his mannerisms which, in the end move rather than irritate people. He rehearses his TV speeches in front of a mirror and with the help of a tape-recorder. . . . He even took lessons in diction from an eminent actor of the *Comédie Française*, and knows all the right cadences, and is aware of the gestures and intonations to avoid.[19]

De Gaulle was thus perfectly prepared to adjust to the demands of the medium in the television age. Television did not just expand its audience during the 1960s; it also helped bring about a fundamental change in the nature of political communication. Combined with the introduction of popular elections to the presidency, television personalized political conflict by focusing public attention on *national* political figures such as the party leaders and, most importantly, the President himself. Television provided de Gaulle with a readily available means of nationwide coverage.[20] A president who could control television could to a significant extent hope to control the agenda of French politics. The temptation for a skilful media performer like de Gaulle was irresistible. In fact, throughout his presidency, de Gaulle exploited the power of television to such an extent that the regime was described by one commentator as a 'telecracy' – government by television.[21]

THE ESTABLISHMENT OF GAULLIST CONTROL OF TELEVISION

Within this context of de Gaulle's Fifth Republic as a contested regime, the Gaullist state manipulated and controlled television in pursuit of its short-term electoral and long-term ideological objectives. With the increased stability of governments after 1958 and the simultaneous expansion of television, partisan politicization of broadcasting became a hallmark of the de Gaulle presidency. Government control of the medium, especially news content, was institutionalized. While at one level this Gaullist practice merely continued a tradition established in previous regimes, the impact in the 1960s was significantly different for two reasons. First, as an excitingly new visual medium, television exerted greater influence on popular perceptions of politics than radio had done previously. Second, compared to the transient governments of the Fourth Republic, executive stability meant that government control of broadcasting could be used to greater effect to shape the political agenda over a protracted period of time.

The relationship between television and the state during the de Gaulle presidency was not one of equals. The needs of the regime always took precedence, with the result that television was never allowed to develop anything approximating to an autonomous sphere of activity in its links with the state. It did not achieve even the freedom of manoeuvre enjoyed by broadcasters in the British public service model.[22] Rather, in its key formative years, television was strictly subordinated to state control. The role played by television in the 1960s was to a large extent determined by this organic relationship with the state. Important though it may have been, it was not de Gaulle's *personal* expertise in using television for his own political ends which left such an indelible mark on the historical development of the medium during his presidency. It was rather the way in which the regime quickly established close *structural* links with the broadcasting services, which in turn produced a web in which television was systematically enmeshed by the Gaullist state.

One facet of this relationship between the state and television during the de Gaulle presidency was the practice of partisan appointments to key decision-making posts. On coming to power in 1958, the Gaullists began to install their own men at the Ministry of Information and in the top posts of the French state broadcasting organization, the Radiodiffusion-Télévision Française (RTF). In July Jacques Soustelle, a historic Gaullist who had joined de Gaulle in London in the summer of 1940, was appointed Minister of Information, a post he had already occupied after the Liberation. Within a month of his appointment Soustelle had 'changed the holders of a dozen key posts in the RTF (director general, president of the higher council, director of news, editor of television news, head of the politics desk, general secretary, etc.), appointing to all these levels, except one, Gaullist loyalists'.[23] For example, Christian Chavanon, a Gaullist *conseiller d'Etat*, was appointed director general of the RTF, while Louis Terrenoire, a former general secretary of the Gaullist movement, was given the post of director of news before becoming Minister of Information in 1960.[24] Albert Ollivier, former director of the Gaullist newspaper *Le Rassemblement*, was appointed director of television news and then moved on to establish his reputation as head of programmes. By the end of 1959 the key decision-making posts at the RTF on both the news and general programming side were almost without exception occupied by Gaullist sympathizers. This trend was not to alter significantly during the 1960s.[25]

A notable feature of those appointed to top posts in state broadcasting in the early years of Gaullist rule was their lack of familiarity with television and, indeed, with the media in general. For example, Jacques-Bernard Dupont, deputy director general of the RTF from late 1963 to mid-1964 and then director general of the ORTF until July 1968, had had no experience in television on taking up his post in the state broadcasting corporation. Raymond Janot, director general from March 1960 to February 1962, did not even have a television set at home![26] Whereas television management during the Fourth Republic had generally come from the milieu of the press, the directors general and their chief assistants between 1958 and 1964 were all top civil servants. Some were parachuted in from other administrative posts, while others slightly lower down the hierarchy had worked for a considerable time in state broadcasting. Imbued with the technocratic ethos of the prestigious Ecole Nationale d'Administration (ENA), with its emphasis on the public interest harnessed to a desire for administrative efficiency, the *énarques* were to have a profound influence on the management of state television in the 1960s and beyond.

The consequences of this Gaullist colonization of the state broadcasting organization were quickly in evidence. In the crisis-ridden environment of the early years of the Fifth Republic, the new regime had to be defended at all costs. This meant keeping political opponents off the air, while government ministers were constantly being paraded on radio and television celebrating the success of Gaullist policy initiatives.[27] This partisan domination of state television was particularly evident during election and referendum campaigns. Gaullist politicians were given a vastly disproportionate amount of time in which to outline their policies, while opposition spokesmen were either denied the opportunity of replying or their replies were deliberately distorted by skilful editing. During the 1958 referendum campaign on the new Constitution, for example, de Gaulle's 'yes' campaign was enthusiastically reported and Soustelle was allowed most of a news programme in which to refute the arguments of the opposition.[28] Commenting on the use of the state broadcasting services during the 1958 campaign, Viansson-Ponté wrote:

Never since the Second Empire, with the possible exception of the 1877 elections, had one witnessed in France under a Republican constitution such an unleashing of propaganda. Never had the hold over the RTF, the deliberate distortion of radio and television news, attained such a degree. Never had simple equity in an electoral contest been so flagrantly pushed aside. [29]

In similar vein, in the 1962 referendum campaign on the proposed constitutional amendment and in the parliamentary elections one month later, 'radio and television were thoroughly exploited' and 'the supreme governmental weapon was, as always, de Gaulle's own broadcast'.[30]

The Ministry of Information was the key governmental instrument in securing the support of state broadcasting for the Gaullist regime and especially in setting the agenda for the main evening television news bulletin. Though not an innovation of the Fifth Republic, the Ministry of Information in the 1960s came to be associated in the eyes of broadcast journalists, opposition politicians and the general public with the authoritarian face of Gaullism. The lack of separation between the ministry and the state broadcasting services was manifest. In the early years of the regime the ministry even shared the same premises with top broadcasting management. A small, but characteristic, indication of the lack of distinction between government and broadcasting took place in 1963: when the RTF introduced a new formula for their main evening news bulletin, it was announced 'live' on screen not by the director of news or the RTF's director general but by the Minister of Information.[31]

The Gaullist authorities were particularly careful about the content of television news programmes, especially the main evening bulletin. Close control of television news content is frequently contrasted with a more liberal, hands-off attitude towards current affairs and magazine programmes. To some extent this view is justified. Under the triumvirate of Pierre Lazareff, Pierre Desgraupes and Pierre Dumayet, the best-known magazine programme of the early 1960s, *Cinq colonnes à la Une*, did deal with topics which news bulletins shunned. In particular, *Cinq colonnes* covered the thorny question of France's involvement in the bloody war in Algeria. Yet real as it was, this contrast between a controlled news service and a liberated documentary output should not be exaggerated. In the specific case of its Algerian coverage, Bourdon argues that the government allowed *Cinq colonnes* greater leeway because, in highlighting the military difficulties and the disenchantment of the *pieds noirs*, the programme was 'a perfect counterpoint to the policy of General de Gaulle. It was a pedagogic tool for decolonization'.[32] In any case, a study of the topics featured on *Cinq colonnes* shows that the programme was predominantly geared towards coverage of foreign themes. In general, domestic political issues did not figure prominently, as if the programme makers themselves were well aware of the all too finite limits on their freedom of manoeuvre.

THE ORTF

From the very beginning of its public transmissions after the Liberation, French television was organized within the framework of the state broadcasting monopoly. France was by no means unique in adopting such an organizational principle for its nascent television service. This legal framework for the management of television was common practice in several western European countries in the immediate postwar period. In Britain, for example, the BBC enjoyed a monopoly of television programming until 1955, while in Italy the RAI benefited from a similar privileged status.

Yet there were also specific domestic factors which worked in favour of the application of the state monopoly model to television in postwar France. In his cross-national study of television, Smith lists the following:

> Firstly, there was the tradition of government control of the telegraph initiated in the middle of the nineteenth century because of fear of its use by enemies of the regime.
>
> Secondly, there was no real debate within France over who was to control broadcasting. . . . State control was a convenience rather than the result of a firm policy.
>
> Thirdly, the newspapers seeing that radio elsewhere, and later of course television, was potentially a usurper of advertising revenue became staunch supporters of a system by which the state would guarantee the financial viability of a French system of broadcasting.
>
> Fourthly, broadcasting was seen as a primary instrument of the traditional French policy of cultural diffusion. In private hands, as in the United States, broadcasting automatically became an instrument of low culture; the French . . . saw that centralised control of broadcasting was the only guarantee that the instrument would be employed to ensure that high culture would prevail.
>
> Finally, there had been throughout the century an anxiety in many sections of French society that their state lacked coherence and a centre of gravity; there were fears constantly that French society might crack up altogether and the knowledge that broadcasting was centralised and in public hands made society as a whole that much more secure.[33]

Some of these explanatory variables are more persuasive than others. The opposition of the press to commercial television and the prime role of the state in cultural diffusion are uncontentious. Conversely, the tradition of government control of the telegraph, though an important historical antecedent, had not prevented the flourishing of private radio stations in the inter-war period. Moreover, the arguments that the broadcasting monopoly came about because 'state control was a convenience rather than the result of a firm policy' and that 'the state lacked coherence and a centre of gravity' are not convincing.

The monopoly may well have been a convenient policy response, but it was also a deliberate policy output which could mobilize a wide cross-section of political and social groups in its support. There was a large degree of consensus among the political elites in the immediate postwar period in favour of the monopoly solution to the organization of broadcasting. In the postwar climate of antipathy to capitalist forces and enthusiasm for collectivist solutions to problems of economic management, it was not difficult to defend the state's appropriation of the main means of mass communication. Adherence to the principle of the state monopoly found favour among Gaullists, Christian Democrats, Socialists, Communists and the main trade union confederations among others. The incorporation of radio and television into the enlarged sector of state activities testified more to the growing power of the state after the Liberation than to its incoherence and rootlessness.

When they came to power in 1958, the Gaullists did not lose their support for the framework of the state monopoly, which had survived untouched throughout the Fourth Republic. In part this was because as the party of government, the Gaullists now benefited from partisan control of state broadcasting. However, it is also fair to say that defence of the monopoly was an issue of principle for de Gaulle and many Gaullists. The Gaullist movement in the 1960s was in no sense a simple right-wing party wedded to the ideals of the free market. It was quite prepared to uphold the merits of a strong and active role for the state. While Gaullist attachment to the concept of a powerful state manifested itself most clearly in foreign and defence policy on issues such as the defence of French interests within the EEC, withdrawal from the integrated command structure of NATO and commitment to an independent nuclear deterrent, it was by no means confined to these policy areas. In economic policy the Gaullists supported indicative planning, maintained the nationalized status of the key public utilities and extended the role of the state in industrial policy. Gaullist support of the state monopoly in broadcasting was only part of the party's commitment to a strong state as a powerful unifying force in a fragmented French society.

The 1964 statute, the major legislative text on broadcasting during de Gaulle's presidency, renamed the state broadcasting organization the Office de Radiodiffusion-Télévision Française (ORTF) – a set of initials which, for the opponents of the regime, quickly became one of the hated symbols of the repressive Gaullist state.[34] There was no change, however, to state television's monopoly status. Moreover, there was little party political opposition to this aspect of the new legislation. The Socialist and Communist parties were stout defenders of the regulated, centralized state monopoly system, even if they were the prime victims of its highly manipulated political output and condemned its subordination to the interests of the Gaullist government.

Under the provisions of the 1964 legislation, the public service ethos of state broadcasting was reaffirmed, with the ORTF being given the task of satisfying the needs of the public in information, culture, education and entertainment. There was no agreement, however, about what the ethos of public service entailed in practice. As a result, the concept was given different interpretations by the various players involved in the implementation of the state's broadcasting policy. For ORTF engineers, for example, public service was equatable with the universal provision of the service via an integrated transmission network: a purely technical, though by no means insignificant, interpretation of the concept.[35] For many television professionals and a few government ministers, public service was synonymous with programmes of a high cultural content. This interpretation stressed television's role as a privileged means of disseminating high culture to a mass audience. For some television managers the idea of public service meant running the state corporation as efficiently as possible: a managerialist interpretation which did not distinguish between television and other public services such as gas or electricity. For broadcasting journalists the tenets of public service meant a balanced and impartial treatment of political information. For many Gaullists, however, the concept of public service was a convenient cloak behind which they could control television for their own purposes. If the President and his government represented the popular will, then the interests of the nation and those of the government were one. It was for the government to decide what was in the public interest and to control television accordingly. Such was the sophistry by which the circle of public service was squared with the practice of government control.

At the head of the ORTF was the director general, who was appointed by the government and was responsible for the day-to-day management of the corporation. Proposals that the director general be chosen by the board of governors were rejected by the Gaullist authorities, who wanted to ensure that the post remained in their gift. In an innovatory move, a board of governors was established with a range of supervisory powers, including a general responsibility for the objectivity and accuracy of news programmes. However, in a classic illustration of taking back with one hand what was proffered with the other, the government directly appointed half the members of the board. There was to be no question of an anti-government majority forming at board level. Those appointed by the Gaullists were there to serve the interests of the government, not to defend some vague and fluid concept of the public interest – or, perhaps more accurately, they were selected to promote the partisan Gaullist interpretation of what was in the public interest.

The government argued that the 1964 statute represented a major step towards greater autonomy for the state broadcasting organization. It was argued by Gaullist proponents of the reform that the ORTF would operate as a French BBC. This was both a compliment to the independence which the French authorities believed the BBC enjoyed in its day-to-day decision making and an evocation of the role played by the BBC during the Nazi occupation of France. As Minister of Information between 1962 and 1966, Peyrefitte controlled the key government ministry on broadcasting and was responsible for piloting the proposed legislation through Parliament. Introducing the bill in the National Assembly, he stated that 'the fundamental defect which we intend to remedy by the present statute is the permanent confusion which has taken root in the minds of the public between the RTF and the government'.[36] In his book, *Le mal français*, Peyrefitte later sought to present his term in office as one characterized by the liberalization of the links between the government and state broadcasting, symbolized by the 1964 statute.[37]

Despite these claims, several members of Peyrefitte's advisory staff were appointed to key positions in the ORTF during the late 1960s. These included: Jean-Jacques de Bresson, director of Peyrefitte's *cabinet* at the Ministry of Information before becoming director general of the ORTF (1968–72); Claude Contamine, also a former director of Peyrefitte's cabinet prior to becoming director of television (1964–67); and Georges Riou, who became director of the general administration of the ORTF in July 1964. At the same time the dominance of *énarques* in the top administrative posts at the ORTF was reinforced. Imposing their managerialist style on the running of the corporation, their *énarque* views inevitably clashed with alternative technological, artistic and information-oriented perspectives held by engineers, programme directors and journalists respectively.[38]

The 1964 reform did not herald the beginning of a new era in the relationship between television and the Gaullist state. The board of governors proved to be powerless as a decision-making body and failed to act as a protective barrier between the government and the professional broadcasters. In fact, even as a talking shop the board did not always serve a particularly useful function. It was largely kept in the dark, for example, over the decision to introduce advertising on the ORTF television channels in 1968.[39] The director general was selected for his political acceptability as much as for his administrative competence. Frequently he was not the initiator of policy but rather the transmission belt for decisions made at ministerial level, either at the Ministry of Information or the Ministry of Finance.[40] Through the director general the government was prepared to exact political retribution against journalists, producers and trade union officials (especially those with suspected Communist sympathies) who transgressed the frequently narrow limits of Gaullist tolerance. Paradoxically, the transparent subservience of the director general to his political masters meant that sometimes the ORTF management welcomed industrial action by staff as a way of bringing government attention to a problem and inducing a solution. A skilful director general could use staff discontent to resolve a conflict between himself and the relevant ministry. In the main, however, the role of the director general was to manage the corporation efficiently and to ensure that it performed the political functions asked of it by the government.

The Peyrefitte legislation did nothing to stop the one-sided presentation of news and government policy on state television. A government agency, ostensibly set up by the Ministry of Information with the perfectly laudable aim of coordinating the information functions of the different government ministries in their relations with the media, also carried out the far less worthy task of trying to define the parameters of state television's news coverage. Established by Peyrefitte, the Service des liaisons interministérielles pour l'information (SLII) was to acquire a reputation as the body through which much of the government's agenda-structuring activity for television news was channelled. Its meetings were attended by representatives of the Ministry of Information and the heads of the broadcasting news departments among others. However, while the importance of the SLII as an agenda-setting mechanism should not be underestimated, much government manipulation and censorship of television news were performed on a more direct basis between different government ministries and the heads of the broadcasting news departments either by telephone or through personal contact.[41]

The 1965 presidential election showed that this strict control of broadcast output through partisan appointments and direct supervision of news content could be counter-productive. The allocation of broadcasting time among the candidates during the official campaign period (but not before) was supervised by a special *ad hoc* committee appointed by the government for this purpose. For the few weeks of the official campaign, opposition candidates, including François Mitterrand and Jean Lecanuet, appeared on television to present their case. Long accustomed to the bombardment of Gaullist propaganda, the electorate was for the first time exposed to critics of the regime who used their screen time to put forward anti-Gaullist policies. The effect was shattering:

> Television which for seven years had tirelessly offered the same faces, the same pictures, the same satisfied and soporific statements, seemed suddenly shaken by a fit of madness. Unknown faces appeared on the screen to tell millions of stupefied Frenchmen that everything was not for the best, that de Gaulle was not always right, that the government was not the best one possible. People felt shocked as if the ORTF had fallen into the hands of dangerous rebels.[42]

While prior to the first ballot de Gaulle had scarcely used his allocation of television time, the necessity of a second ballot convinced him that he could not remain above the battle in the face of his opposition critics. He had to descend into the electoral arena, which he did in typical style in a televised interview with the Gaullist journalist, Michel Droit. The political impact of television on electoral attitudes and behaviour was demonstrated in the 1965 campaign, with opinion polls showing de Gaulle losing more ground among viewers than non-viewers.[43]

Though de Gaulle won the election, the fact that he was forced to a run-off against Mitterrand alerted the authorities to the dangers of crude partisanship in political information on television. There quickly followed a limited relaxation of government control over political output. New current affairs and documentary programmes (such as *Face à Face*, *Zoom* and

Caméra III) were introduced, usually on the less widely viewed second channel. These featured opposition politicians and dealt with controversial topics such as racism and sexual relations. Such programmes strove to be more politically balanced and to widen the range of social and political topics covered on television. Even the main evening news programmes gave more screen time than before to speeches by opposition leaders. Ardagh writes that

> This was because the ORTF had come under such criticism that it now employed a certain subtlety and avoided needling the opposition unnecessarily – when I myself took part in a French TV programme in 1967, I was *not allowed* by my producer to criticize the Communists![44]

None the less, the television news agenda continued to be controlled by the Minister of Information through a combination of appointments of sympathizers to key posts and ministerial directives. Self-censorship by journalists and news staff also remained in evidence, both in Paris and in the regional news stations set up by Peyrefitte to counter the alleged anti-Gaullist bias in the provincial press.[45]

THE INTRODUCTION OF ADVERTISING ON STATE TELEVISION

The state was concerned not only with the fine details of television's news agenda. The ORTF was also a large public sector institution whose efficient management was of prime interest to the Gaullist authorities. Control of television news output by the Ministry of Information was supplemented, therefore, with close budgetary supervision from the Ministry of Finance. Under the provisions of the 1964 statute the internal budgetary management of the corporation was meant to be the responsibility of the director general, while the newly created board of governors had a supervisory role with regard to the long-term financial position of the Office. In theory, the 1964 statute introduced a system of *a posteriori* monitoring to replace the *a priori* financial controls which until then had been the traditional means of governmental supervision of the broadcasting corporation's budget. In 1962, for example, out of 6,505 items of expenditure, only 1,904 had escaped *a priori* control by the relevant ministry.[46]

The *a priori* system of financial control was particularly ill-suited to the needs of a mass communication organization, as it stifled the managerial flexibility required for the institution to function effectively. In September 1961, for example, at the time of an earthquake in Chile, the RTF news team left fully eight days after the event had taken place. Yet counter to the provisions of the Peyrefitte legislation, in practice the financial arrangements of the ORTF continued to be closely controlled by the Ministry of Finance right up to the end of the de Gaulle presidency.[47] Many key expenditure decisions still remained outside the control of the corporation's management and in the aftermath of the 1968 strike it was clear that the 1964 legislation had not provided the ORTF with the financial room for manoeuvre it required.[48]

Constrained on the expenditure front, the ORTF had virtually no control over the size of its income either. For most of the 1960s the state television service was financed overwhelmingly from licence revenue. The government fixed the cost of the individual licence fee subject to approval by Parliament.[49] With sales of television sets expanding rapidly during the 1960s, total licence revenue rose proportionately and in general adequately covered the corporation's running costs. As the prospect of a slowdown in the sale of sets began to loom, however, it became clear that any substantial growth in licence revenue would in future depend on increases in the annual fee. As a result, the possibility of introducing advertising on television became a controversial topic on the political agenda.[50]

The debate on this issue had been rumbling beneath the surface for some time. In the early 1960s there had been talk of a commercial network or, if that proved politically unpalatable, of advertisements being shown on the new ORTF second channel. Later in the decade a lobby group was formed with the objective of securing the creation of a third television channel to be financed wholly from advertising. Pro-TV received support from major advertising agencies, who wanted access to a powerful nation-wide medium, and from the domestic electronics industry, which was keen to boost the sale of colour television sets.[51] However, the option of a fully fledged commercial channel was a non-starter in the 1960s, since President de Gaulle was a firm believer in the desirability of the 'brute force of monopoly'.[52]

The possibility of introducing advertising on the ORTF was another matter. The government's decision to allow commercials on state television in 1968 killed two birds with one stone. The primary objective was to supplement the ORTF's income at no extra cost to the licence payer. At the same time the initiative defused the pressure for the establishment of a commercial channel. Advertising was introduced on the ORTF's channel one in October 1968 and on the second channel in January 1971. Compared to its main European neighbours, France was a relative latecomer to advertising-funded television. In Great Britain advertising had been introduced into the television system through the creation of ITV in 1955. During the same decade it had also found a place in the Italian (1957) and West German (1959) television systems, where, as in France, it was introduced on to the existing public sector channels.

Strict regulations were initially put in place to contain the impact of commercial advertising on state television and to placate those groups, particularly the press, who feared that their interests would be harmed by the new policy. Advertising time was to be strictly limited so as not to dominate programme schedules. Only three product categories were originally authorized: food, household electrical appliances, and textiles and clothing. Programmes were not to be interrupted to make way for commercial breaks. The government also decided that advertisers would not be allowed to sponsor programmes (though this was not strictly enforced) or to interfere in programme scheduling or content. A new body was set up to enforce these and other advertising-related regulations. The creation of the Régie Française de Publicité, independent of the ORTF, was designed to minimize the possibility of interference by advertising agencies in the management of the corporation.

The early financial impact of advertising was very small. In the last three months of 1968 it amounted to 26 million francs, which represented only 1.9 per cent of the ORTF's total revenue. Once the principle of advertising-funded television had been accepted, however, there was no going back and soon advertising income was approaching 25 per cent of ORTF revenue. Its presence on the screen also became more noticeable. Total advertising breaks grew from a mere 2 minutes per day in late 1968 to 4 and then 6 minutes in 1969, 8 minutes in 1970 and then 12 minutes in 1971. The list of authorized products became more all-encompassing, to the point that 20 years after the introduction of television advertising only a few products, notably tobacco and alcohol, could not be advertised on French television. Moreover, as advertising gradually came to be perceived as a normal part of the broadcasting environment, it began to play an increasingly important role in the financial arrangements of French television (see table 4.6).

TELEVISION AND STATE CULTURAL POLICY

The state monopoly in broadcasting formed part of the increasing role of the state in the cultural domain during the de Gaulle presidency. One of the functions of state television in the 1960s was the dissemination of French high culture to the mass audience, as part of a wider governmental initiative to 'democratize culture'.[53] Like the *maisons de la culture* which, under the stewardship of the Gaullist Minister of Cultural Affairs André Malraux, were springing up across France at this time, the ORTF was an instrument of the government's policy of exposing the French people to the civilizing benefits of the nation's cultural heritage.[54] In a French version of the Reithian BBC ethos, television was expected not just to reflect popular taste or to pander to the lowest common denominator. Instead, part of its public service mission was to expose viewers to a range of programmes which in a competitive system they might not choose to watch. If the news output of French television in the 1960s was not an accurate reflection of the country's political diversity, its general programming content scarcely mirrored the tastes and preferences of the mass audience either.

This self-conscious cultural mission was particularly noticeable in the

Table 4.6 Advertising revenue on state television 1968–86

Year	Amount in million francs	% of total resources
1968	26	1.9
1969	195	14.8
1970	348	21.0
1971	387.6	20.9
1972	435.1	21.4
1973	497.5	22.6
1974	569	24.0
1975	690	24.6
1976	820	25.0
1977	940.3	25.0
1978	1,065.2	25.0
1979	1,255	25.0
1980	1,434	25.0
1981	1,613	25.0
1982	2,025	25.0
1983	2,438	25.0
1984	2,612	25.0
1985	2,967	26.5
1986	3,302	25.0

Source: J.-J. Ledos, J.-P. Jézéquel and P. Régnier, *Le gâchis audiovisuel*, Paris, Editions ouvrières,1986, p.185.

early years of state television when it was under the guidance of figures such as Jean d'Arcy and Albert Ollivier.[55] Drama, for example, was an important feature of the schedules in the early 1960s. Plays were not usually written specifically for television, but tended to be adaptations of theatrical or literary works from the canon of high culture.[56] Classical French theatre and the nineteenth-century novel formed a large part of the staple diet of television drama productions. Such adaptations were encouraged by Ollivier as director of programmes and apparently appreciated by the viewers. Many television directors, often with left-wing political sympathies, also had a firm commitment to television's cultural mission as part of their interpretation of the public service ethos. They played a key role in shaping the output of the French television system up until 1968.[57]

This policy of celebrating the output from the national pantheon of literary and dramatic greats was perfectly in tune with the government's general cultural policy. It also complemented the foreign and defence policies of the de Gaulle presidency with their emphasis on French grandeur and national independence, driven by a general mistrust of and even hostility towards the United States. In celebrating the glories of French civilization, state television reinforced this emphasis on national greatness. While programme imports, including feature films and series from the United States, were not absent from the schedules of state television in the 1960s, much of the output was produced in France as a celebration of the superiority of French tastes and sensibilities. For employees of the ORTF this policy had the added advantage that a large proportion of programming was made by the corporation's internal production services. During the 1960s state television had the capacity to produce much of its programming in-house and the ORTF exercised a monopoly on programme production until 1964. While the establishment of the second channel made the reliance on in-house production increasingly unrealistic, the use of external private production services in the mid- to late 1960s still remained restrained by contemporary standards.[58]

Such a programming and production policy could be sustained only because of the way in which television was organized in the late 1950s and 1960s. Television was a severely rationed product. Until 1964 there was only one channel and for the rest of the decade a mere two. Transmissions were largely confined to the evening. Though the total number of programme hours steadily increased throughout the 1960s, they remained very limited when compared to today's output. Multi-channel television and round-the-clock programming were a dream – or nightmare – still a long way off. Moreover, in the absence of any commercial competition, state television had a totally captive audience. Benefiting from its monopoly status, the ORTF could dictate the viewing content of the audience nationwide. The two state channels did not even compete against each other for viewers until 1967. For most of the 1960s a policy of complementarity was followed in their scheduling, with the first channel being by far the more popular in terms of ratings.[59]

The propensity of French television in the 1960s to transmit an output of peak-time programmes with a high cultural content should neither be exaggerated nor seen in isolation from other aspects of scheduling. Not all the management at the ORTF was imbued with the same sense of cultural mission as d'Arcy and Ollivier. In any case, as television developed as a mass medium, an inevitable tension arose between those managers and creative staff who wanted to use the ORTF to raise popular tastes by showing demanding programmes and those who wanted the corporation's output to cater for the preferences of the mass of viewers. Serving a nationwide audience from all social classes and of different educational backgrounds, television could not simply confine itself to the cultural high ground. As a state monopoly financed overwhelmingly from licence revenue, the medium had to cater for a spectrum of tastes and interests. Moreover, as audience measurement techniques became more sophisticated, programme ratings began to have more of an impact on scheduling decisions.

Inevitably, therefore, television also became a major producer and disseminator of *mass* culture during the 1960s. Fiction and light entertainment, for instance, were an integral part of the ORTF's programme output.

In fact, while many serious programmes were pushed to the outer fringes of the schedules, series and serials aimed at the mass market were on the increase during the 1960s.[60] French television also had its fair share of variety programmes and game shows. Indeed, the popularity of one game show – *Intervilles* – which pitted teams from different French towns against each other was later to inspire a Eurovision version, *Jeux sans frontières*. In short, French television provided a broad range of programmes in the 1960s, as it sought to serve its growing mass audience and at the same time reflect a rather elitist interpretation by many of its practitioners of the concept of public service. Programme quality was mixed, with some outstanding productions but also much that was mundane and mediocre.

TELEVISION AND STATE INDUSTRIAL POLICY

A resource for the exercise of government patronage, a news weapon in the political battle, an organization to be managed effectively and a medium of cultural dissemination – television represented all of these for the Gaullist authorities. It was also a technology whose development could be directed so that it conformed with the wider goals of state industrial policy. In this respect the role of the Gaullist state prefigured the heavily interventionist stance adopted by many French governments in the 1970s and 1980s in the formulation and implementation of their policy on the new media of cable and satellite. Using its monopoly control of the medium, the state could set technical standards and if necessary put pressure on television manufacturers to abide by them. Ministers hoped that the establishment of high-quality technical norms within the domestic market would provide the French television manufacturing industry with a sound base from which to launch a successful export drive. In this way French television would become an international symbol of the nation's technological prowess. At the same time, if the relevant state agencies could be 'captured' by the manufacturers, then the state's monopoly control might be harnessed to provide a protected market for French goods against foreign competition. The Gaullist state usually wanted the best of both worlds: to pursue a policy based on technological excellence *and* economic nationalism.

State policy in this field was formulated against the background of a changing technological environment and an expanding television system, which together had important consequences for both programme production and transmission. On the production side, television was becoming industrialized as mass production techniques replaced the artisanal approach to programme making of the 1950s. 'Live' transmission of many programme genres was replaced by the use of film and video, with the share of direct transmission falling from 41 per cent in 1960 to 24 per cent in 1964 and then to 20 per cent in 1968.[61] On the transmission side, an important policy choice had to be made concerning the line system for the second channel. In 1948 the 819 standard for channel one had been chosen by François Mitterrand, Minister of Information, in what represented a victory for the television engineers.[62] In the early 1960s the authorities were under pressure from French television set manufacturers to retain the high definition 819 line system for the new channel. In effect, this meant that this section of French industry was looking to the state for the formulation of a protectionist policy which would isolate the domestic market from foreign competition. On this occasion, however, the government plumped for 625 lines to bring France into line with most other European countries, though the state compromised by taking technical steps to protect French manufacturers.[63]

By far the most notable case of state intervention in television technology during the de Gaulle presidency was the choice of the colour television process SECAM. In a classic example of Gaullist technological nationalism, the state wanted to ensure a French presence in what it regarded as a key industrial field. Under pressure from industrialists in the television manufacturing sector, de Gaulle was particularly keen that France should establish its own presence in the colour television industry to compete against German and American systems. The result was SECAM, which was not only established as the norm in France, but was adopted by francophone Africa, Iran and Saudi Arabia. De Gaulle even negotiated a deal with the Soviet Union that it should use SECAM, which was then taken up by the Warsaw Pact countries.[64] Most west European countries, however, chose to use the German system, PAL.

The SECAM initiative was an example of French industrialists working through the state both to protect their own profitable domestic manufacturing market and to put the French system into the keenly sought-after export market. It was not, however, a decision welcomed at the ORTF, especially by the engineers who believed that political criteria had won out over technical arguments. According to Bourdon, they would have preferred a choice which would have gained acceptance at a pan-European level. In their view, the state had imposed a decision on the corporation and deliberately chosen the solution of French isolation under pressure from short-term private sector interests.[65]

TELEVISION AND THE 1968 'EVENTS'

French television was profoundly affected by the 'events' of 1968, both as a news medium and as a state institution. As a news medium, it had to take a stance on reporting such a major regime crisis. Here was an issue made for saturation television coverage: a highly visual protest, characterized by strikes, occupations and street demonstrations; barricades in the streets of the capital; scenes of police violence; a government in disarray; a President who seemed to have lost the will to rule; an opposition ready to seize

power; and a society apparently in revolt against the authoritarian pater-
nalism of Gaullist rule.[66] With a vacuum of authority at the very heart of
the state, for several days France gave the impression of being ungoverned
and ungovernable. To ignore or downplay the student and worker protest
would have been a denial of television's information function. Yet at
the same time, the broadcasting corporation was part of an institutional
infrastructure which was popularly identified with the Gaullist state. As
other state institutions like the higher educational system came under
attack, so the legitimacy of the ORTF was inevitably called into question.
The ORTF could not just report the 'events' as a detached outside
observer. As a state organization it was directly implicated in the challenge
to the Gaullist political system.

Television's dilemma in 1968 affected the main players in different ways.
First, the ORTF management had to decide the amount of coverage to give
the protestors and how to reconcile the newsworthiness of the 'events'
with the need not to upset their political masters. While the decision to
minimize the impact of the protest was predictable, the lack of coverage
given to the 'events' in their initial phase clearly revealed the extent to which
state television functioned as a *de facto* part of the executive branch of
government. Second, at a time of acute polarization between the authorities
and the protestors, the ORTF journalists found the contradictions of their
situation fully and cruelly exposed. Notions of balance and impartiality
seemed inappropriate as the Gaullist state and its television service came
under attack. With French society appearing to divide into warring camps,
television journalists were obliged to take sides. Some of them supported the
management. Others gave up trying to report the protest and instead
became participants in it, belatedly joining the strike of ORTF technical,
administrative and artistic staff. Third, the Gaullist authorities were forced
to recognize the limitations of their model of state control of the medium
and yet were unable, and for the most part unwilling, to conceive of a new
type of relationship between the state, broadcasting and society. Recourse
to another bout of repression in late summer looked a tired and wholly
inadequate response to a problem which could not be reduced to one of
individual striking journalists. In the immediate aftermath of the ORTF
strike, however, the question of the structural links between the state and
broadcasting did not surface on the government's reform agenda.

For the first half of May state television tended to ignore the protest
movement, even though the press, the peripheral radio stations and state
radio were full of little else.[67] As student and worker dissent spread and the
reaction of the authorities became more repressive, the personnel of
the ORTF were drawn directly into the conflict. During May, first the
corporation's general staff and later its journalists came out on strike. They
condemned the government's directives regarding the coverage of the
'events' and the ORTF management's ready compliance. Their action

represented the release of the pent-up frustration they felt at the way in which the government had manipulated the state broadcasting services for the previous ten years. The headquarters of the ORTF were occupied by the strikers, a move which so infuriated de Gaulle that he ordered the Minister of Information, Georges Gorse, to restore order by getting rid of the troublemakers.[68] The strikers called for a new ORTF statute to guarantee the autonomy of the broadcasting services, freedom from ministerial pressures and an impartial news service. More specifically, they insisted that the ORTF board of governors should no longer contain a *de facto* government majority, that the director general should be elected by the board of governors and not appointed by the government and that a 'committee of wise men' independent of the board of governors be set up to ensure objectivity in news content. Clearly the Gaullist authorities could not accept these demands.[69]

The government's response to the ORTF strikers was determined by the changing social and political climate. This had begun to turn in its favour by the end of May, following de Gaulle's radio broadcast and the huge demonstration in support of Gaullist order. As France returned to work, the strike at the ORTF petered out, with the journalists last to go back. Benefiting from the climate of popular reaction, the Gaullists won a huge parliamentary majority at the general election held at the end of June. Buttressed by this overwhelming victory, the government proceeded to settle accounts at the ORTF. Some minor conciliatory moves were made, including an increase in the number of staff representatives on the board of governors (which, none the less, still remained dominated by government supporters), a relaxation in governmental control over ORTF expenditure and the abolition of the SLII. However, with de Gaulle's backing, more significant steps were taken to punish the strikers and to set an example *pour encourager les autres*. In August 34 journalists were dismissed, 16 'exiled' from Paris to posts in the provinces, several were forced to accept early retirement and many freelancers were informed that their services were no longer required.[70] The repressive measures were particularly directed at active trade unionists. De Gaulle informed his ministers that as far as television news was concerned, its only commitment should be to support government policy. Yves Guéna, the hardline Minister of Information in June 1968, wrote that de Gaulle regarded French television as *his* television.[71]

> Later there was a purge at the ORTF, a purge which of course came from the state authorities. It was the only state service in which there was one. . . . General de Gaulle could not tolerate a situation in which television was not at the service of his policies. Television had betrayed him in May and it was necessary to punish the journalists. Georges Pompidou, Michel Jobert and General de Gaulle's entourage thought: 'They posed us problems for two months; we won't see them again on screen.'[72]

This view is also reiterated by Bourdon, who comments that the authorities expected television journalists to support the state, at a time when the President identified loyalty to the regime and to the nation with loyalty to himself personally.[73]

Television news bulletins over the next few months passed over certain events and personalities in stunning silence. The reform of higher education undertaken by Edgar Faure, for example, was hardly covered, while Pompidou was 'practically forbidden' from being shown on television after his dismissal from the premiership in July by an ungrateful de Gaulle.[74] Documentary and current affairs programmes were axed and replaced by others less outspoken. In short, apart from a few largely cosmetic concessions, the government proceeded to reassert its authority over the ORTF and in particular to re-establish its control of political information.[75]

The strike at the ORTF in 1968 and the government backlash proved, if further proof were necessary, that the 1964 statute had failed to remedy the 'fundamental defect' to which Peyrefitte had referred: the permanent confusion between the state broadcasting services and the government. The historic faultlines in the relationship between the state and broadcasting were scarcely ameliorated by the 1964 reform. In April 1968, only a few weeks before the ORTF strike, a Senate report concluded that 'the depoliticization promised by the government was to say the least scarcely evident and the instructions of the authorities, far from diminishing, appeared rather to be increasing. . . . Political personalities close to the government benefited from favourable treatment: they were systematically shown to advantage'.[76] Or as Viansson-Ponté put it more succinctly, 'television is the absolute weapon of the regime'.[77]

The role played by television as a medium of political information during the 1968 'events' was a perfect illustration of its institutional subordination to the state under de Gaulle. Yet, at the same time 1968 marked the end of the era of naked government manipulation and control. Not only had the broadcasting workforce forcibly and publicly expressed its discontent. More importantly, television viewers were becoming more sophisticated and less willing to accept at face value messages at odds with their own personal experience. With its output being received by a more sceptical public, television could no longer be used as a crude propaganda weapon by the government. In these circumstances, the Gaullist authorities could not just return to the *status quo ante*, despite the immediate aftermath of government repression. The lesson of 1968 was that the state would have to modify its relationship with television if the medium were successfully to perform its function of regime legitimation with the audience.

Chapter 5

Television: the decline and fall of the ORTF

In several important respects the 1970s was a decade characterized more by continuity than change in French television. Ownership of sets increased throughout the decade, but the pace of growth was far less striking than in the 1960s (see table 5.1). By 1969 under 70 per cent of French households already possessed a television set. While ten years later this figure had climbed to 92.7 per cent – a not insignificant statistical progression as France sought to catch up with its main European neighbours – this represented a continuation of the trend established in the previous decade rather than an innovative breakthrough.[1] Nor was there any major modification in the 1970s in the daily amount of time spent watching television by French viewers. The average French adult watched television for 128 minutes per day in 1979 compared with 107 minutes at the end of the 1960s. Moreover, even this small increase was more a result of the medium's growing market penetration than of alterations in individual viewing habits.[2] In terms of both television ownership and audience usage, therefore, it is clear that by the end of the de Gaulle presidency, the medium was no longer a new social phenomenon. The possession of a television set had become an integral part of a consumption pattern which embraced all socio-economic groups, while television viewing had fully metamorphosed into a routinized leisure activity.

Key aspects of the state's relationship with television in the 1970s also showed strong elements of continuity with the previous decade. Both Presidents Pompidou and Giscard d'Estaing sought to stamp their mark on broadcasting through a major piece of legislation, just as President de Gaulle had done in 1964. A central feature of both the 1972 and 1974 statutes was the reaffirmation of the principle of the state monopoly which had been defended throughout the de Gaulle presidency. Even the establishment of a third television channel in 1973 did not fundamentally alter the functioning of the state system. It represented an incremental addition which complemented the output of the existing two channels rather than a competitive threat to their market dominance. The government continued to fix the level of the annual licence fee which remained by far the single

Table 5.1 Television ownership 1970–79

1970	9,900,000
1971	10,600,000
1972	11,500,600
1973	12,200,000
1974	12,900,000
1975	13,700,000
1976	14,400,000
1977	14,800,000
1978	15,000,000
1979	17,500,000

Source: *Le Matin*, September 6 1979.

most important source of broadcast income overall. The practice of partisan political appointments to key decision-making posts within state broadcasting was also largely preserved under the two right-wing successors to de Gaulle, as their governments tried to ensure favourable coverage of the policy agenda in a predominantly unfavourable economic climate. In many ways, therefore, the French state during the Pompidou and Giscard d'Estaing presidencies continued to regard television as both its own privileged instrument of political information and a primary arena for the exercise of political patronage.

Yet it would be a mistake to suggest that the 1970s was a decade marked only by consolidation and continuity in the broadcasting field. For instance, crude censorship of political information and overt governmental directives on television news content were far less in evidence than before. Major changes also took place in the organization of French television, most notably and controversially the 1974 reform which abolished the ORTF. By splitting up the system into its constituent parts, this reform facilitated many of the more radical changes which were to occur during the 1980s. It encouraged greater competition between the television channels – now managed as separate companies – and made advertising a more important source of television revenue. At the same time the question of whether the state monopoly was the optimal framework for the organization of radio and television became a more dominant theme in political debates on broadcasting. In retrospect, by preparing the ground for the sweeping innovations of the Mitterrand presidency, the 1974 reform represented a transition from the Gaullist model of state television of the 1960s to the market-oriented commercial model of the 1980s.

Another important difference between the de Gaulle presidency on the one hand and the Pompidou and Giscard d'Estaing administrations on the other was the emergence of clear divisions at the very heart of the executive on the question of the optimal relationship between the state, television and society. During the Pompidou presidency (1969–74), for example, a conflict of opinion quickly became manifest between the President and the Prime Minister, Jacques Chaban-Delmas, on this issue. Both were Gaullists, but they represented different tendencies (and generational cohorts) within the broad movement of Gaullism. The power struggle between them was certainly a personal battle for control of the party and government. However, it was also a conflict about the direction Gaullism should take in response to the social upheaval of 1968. Pompidou was not opposed to the introduction of reforms. Yet he was essentially a conservative, who believed that increased economic growth and higher living standards would largely satisfy the demands of the 1968 protestors.[3] In contrast, Chaban-Delmas argued that structural reform of key areas of the French state and society were essential. Their disagreement on the role of state television in the vital area of political information was a powerful symbol of the fracturing of the Gaullist movement in the early 1970s and a symptom of the wider tensions within the upper echelons of the state on the nature of post-Gaullian Gaullism.

After Pompidou had been replaced by Valéry Giscard d'Estaing at the Elysée in 1974, control of television was one of the many issues of contention between the two components of the governing right-wing coalition. During the Giscard d'Estaing presidency (1974–81) the main cleavage within the Right was between supporters of the President on the one hand and the followers of Chirac, leader of the Gaullist party, on the other. Initially, the reliance of the President on a parliamentary coalition dominated by the Gaullists influenced his decision to retain the state monopoly in broadcasting. Later, when Chirac presented himself as a rival for the presidency, state television was mobilized against him. As the hold of the divided Right on the institutions of the state weakened in the late 1970s, the content of television news programmes reflected the conflict between Gaullists and Giscardians for the conservative electorate, though not in an impartial fashion. Simultaneously, battle for control of television's top posts between the two rival camps intensified, with the Giscardians holding the upper hand.

The aim of this chapter is to situate the relationship between the state and television during the two post-de Gaulle presidencies within the political context of a fragmented Right. The French state remained a powerful actor in the broadcasting field during the 1970s. Many of its formal and informal powers were unchanged from the previous decade. None the less, during the Pompidou and Giscard d'Estaing presidencies, the state was unable to control television news output or impose its agenda on television coverage in as effective a fashion as before. The paradox of this era is that while both Pompidou and Giscard d'Estaing were more interventionist Presidents in domestic policy than de Gaulle had been, television was a less effective government weapon than in the 1960s. One reason for this was the diffi-culties the authorities experienced after 1968 in adjusting to the failures of the Gaullist model as a means of message transmission and audience persuasion. A tension between those advocating a more liberal approach to political information on television and those who still championed strict control permeated decision making and prevented the pursuit of a coherent approach. Growing party political divisions within the Right during the second half of the decade weakened the power of the President to impose his view of events, despite a strong effort from the Elysée to use the power of patronage to achieve this end. Meanwhile, the Right were also divided on the question of the state monopoly, which, though maintained under both Pompidou and Giscard d'Estaing, was clearly under threat by the end of the decade.

THE STATE AND TELEVISION DURING THE POMPIDOU PRESIDENCY

The broadcasting issue was an important one during the Pompidou presidency, first because of television's primacy as a means of political communication and second because the ORTF was becoming a much more difficult public sector organization to manage effectively. Within the overall context of the state's response to the demands of the 1968 protest, the question of the government's control of television's information function remained a stolid fixture on the political agenda. In addition, with the electoral decline of Gaullism and the emergence of the mainstream Left as a major opposition force in the early 1970s, the capacity of the government to manipulate television's political output became crucial for its political survival.[4] Simultaneously, the institutional expansion of the ORTF and its public reputation for inefficiency and mismanagement ensured that the running of the corporation was a regular feature of hostile press coverage and parliamentary debate. The ORTF was the victim of much adverse criticism in the public realm, which ensured that the government paid close attention to its operations. If the government craved favourable news coverage from state television, it also wanted the corporation to be a model of financial and administrative good practice.

Though the 1968 protest had failed to bring down the Gaullist government, far less the regime of the Fifth Republic, it did lead indirectly to de Gaulle's resignation from the presidency in the spring of 1969. The overwhelming victory of the Gaullist party in the previous year's general election could not be equated with a vote of confidence in the General personally. Consequently, in an attempt to reassert his authority, de Gaulle had recourse to the constitutional tactic which he had been able to exploit so successfully in the early years of the regime – the referendum.[5] However, on this occasion television showed a leader who was out of touch with the mood of the country. As a result he was unable to exploit the medium to mobilize the electorate in his favour. The combination of television and plebiscite which had served him so well on the issues of Algerian self-determination and constitutional reform now failed him, and his presidency was brought to an ignominious conclusion.

In the ensuing presidential election, the contest was dominated by Pompidou and the Centrist candidate, Alain Poher. It was largely due to the latter that the relationship between the state and the ORTF became an election issue.[6] On numerous occasions Poher attacked the ORTF's lack of objectivity in its presentation of the campaign and put forward plans for a reform of the 1964 statute. These proposals, similar in many respects to the demands of the 1968 strikers, favoured greater independence for the ORTF from government interference and, in particular, the abolition of the detested symbol of Gaullist control of the broadcasting media – the Ministry of Information.[7] In reply to these proposals Pompidou was obliged to outline his own views on the ORTF. He too pledged support for a more liberal statute which would guarantee the state broadcasting services 'real autonomy'.[8] Echoing the declarations of his rival for the presidential office, Pompidou advocated the abolition of the Ministry of Information as well as the establishment of competition between the two ORTF channels. There was no question, however, of any commercialization of broadcasting or indeed of any modification of the state monopoly.

After becoming President, Pompidou always showed himself very conscious of the national vocation of the ORTF and its distinctiveness from other mass media such as the press. From this perspective any liberalization of state broadcasting could not be allowed to detract from the quintessential role of the ORTF as 'the voice of France'. During the 1969 campaign, for example, Pompidou argued that 'because we have a national radio and television service . . . they are in a sense the official voice of France, and there is a certain tone to be maintained which must be the tone of France'.[9] This view of the ORTF as the mouthpiece of the state was much more representative of the new President's thinking on the subject of broadcasting than his expedient advocacy of any liberal, reformist measures during the election campaign.

After the formation of the new government in June 1969, responsibility for government policy on broadcasting was given to the Prime Minister, Chaban-Delmas. In the government's declaration of policy before the National Assembly in September, the Prime Minister launched his project to transform France's 'stagnant society'. Included in his proposals to construct 'the new society' was a reorganization of the ORTF. This reform included proposals for greater financial independence for the state broadcasting corporation, more competition between its two television channels and the allocation of screen time to political groups and socio-professional organizations. In a move heavily laden with symbolism the Ministry of Information was swept away. The 1969 proposals did not call into question the state monopoly or the unitary structure of the ORTF; nor was a new statute required for their introduction. The Prime Minister wanted to establish his reformist credentials quickly and not allow his initiative to become bogged down in a parliamentary debate which might bring him into conflict with the conservative wing of the Gaullist party.

The most controversial measure sought to hive off the news departments on each of the two channels to form independent units whose directors would enjoy a hitherto unparalleled degree of political and institutional autonomy. The directors of these news departments were able to choose journalists for their respective teams without any interference from either the government or the channel directors. As a guarantee of their independence they were not required to submit their material in advance for higher approval, thereby reducing the need for self-censorship. In addition, the news directors were appointed for a fixed period of three years and could be dismissed only in the event of serious professional misconduct.

The director subsequently placed in charge of the news department on the second channel was a dedicated Gaullist supporter, Jacqueline Baudrier. For the more widely viewed first channel the Prime Minister chose a television journalist known for his independent views, Pierre Desgraupes. Desgraupes had been among those who had signed a communiqué protesting against government interference in the television coverage of the 1968 'events' and had taken part in the subsequent strike by ORTF staff. Though a person of undoubted professional ability with a proven track record in media journalism, Desgraupes was also a political maverick who showed no allegiance to the Gaullist party or the new President.

Welcomed by broadcasting staff and independent commentators as the sign of a fresh approach to news broadcasting, the appointment of Desgraupes resulted in important changes in the performance of state television's political information function. The news programmes on channel one were openly critical of government policy in social and economic affairs and opposition leaders appeared almost as often on television as government spokesmen. Ministerial interference in news programming declined.[10] The 1969 reform, however, ushered in a period of tension between many Gaullist parliamentarians and the President on the one hand and the Prime Minister's office and the channel one news department on the other. It was obvious that President Pompidou did not fully associate himself with his Prime Minister's 'new society' policy in general or his reform of the ORTF in particular. At the end of 1969, for example, Pompidou stated that he had *accepted* the reform of the ORTF and implied that he disapproved of the way in which events were being presented by the news department of channel one. Pompidou's scarcely veiled criticisms of his Prime Minister's broadcasting reform echoed those of a large phalanx of Gaullist deputies, who harked back to their partisan control of the broadcasting services during de Gaulle's presidency.[11]

Whatever the merits of the 1969 reform, therefore, it did not fundamentally alter the underlying attitudes which the President and certain sectors of the Gaullist party manifested towards broadcasting.[12] The reorganization of the news departments was largely a reflection of the personal convictions of the Prime Minister and his immediate entourage. Desgraupes in particular owed his appointment to Chaban-Delmas personally and as a result his fate became inextricably linked with that of the Prime Minister. When Chaban-Delmas was dismissed from the premiership by Pompidou in July 1972, Desgraupes left the ORTF soon after, one of the first victims of the abandonment of the spirit of the 1969 reform.[13]

The publication in 1972 of two critical parliamentary reports on the ORTF brought the issue of state broadcasting once again to the top of the political agenda and provided Pompidou with the pretext to introduce a new reform of broadcasting.[14] Both reports emphasized elements of maladministration and even corruption at the ORTF, building up a picture of a large organization which was out of control. A government-commissioned report published in 1970 had also criticized the organizational structure of the ORTF, arguing that the corporation was too centralized and proposing a decentralization of management structures without going so far as to suggest that the corporation itself needed to be broken up.[15] The organizational defects of the ORTF and the public scandal which greeted revelations of corruption within state television in 1971–72 afforded Pompidou sufficient pretext for a full-scale reform of the broadcasting services. The task of drafting a new statute was given to Philippe Malaud, a conservative hardliner, whose political philosophy was about as far removed from that of Chaban-Delmas as was possible within the confines of the same governing coalition.[16]

Organizational factors played an important part, therefore, in persuading the President that a new broadcasting statute was necessary. As always in France, however, developments in the wider political context played a crucial role in shaping the attitudes of the authorities on the relationship between the state and television, especially in the area of political information. By 1972 the parties of the Left, now fighting together on a joint manifesto (*le programme commun*), were posing a strong challenge to Gaullist control of the institutions of the Fifth Republic. With a general election due in the spring of 1973, Pompidou realized that a well-orchestrated campaign would be required by the Gaullists and their allies to combat the Union of the Left alliance of Socialists and Communists. Clearly it was in the interest of Gaullist deputies, last elected in the unusual circumstances of the law and order election of June 1968, that the news programmes of the ORTF should publicize government policy in a more favourable light than had been the case since 1969. While many Gaullists could not reasonably hope to retain their parliamentary seats in the changed economic and political climate of 1973, Pompidou and the party leadership naturally wanted to limit electoral damage, so that the government would retain as sizeable a parliamentary majority as possible.

The effect of the loss of government control of news at the ORTF had been well illustrated in the eyes of many Gaullists by television coverage of the 1972 referendum campaign on the enlargement of the EEC. Like de Gaulle before him, Pompidou tried to use the device of the referendum to boost his own popularity and mobilize in support of his presidency a popular majority extending beyond the limits of party Gaullism. In particular, the President sought to use the referendum to embarrass the Left, by focusing on the clear divisions between Socialists and Communists on the issue of European union. However, the referendum backfired on the President owing to a very high rate of abstention at the polls. Pompidou attributed the mediocre success of the 'Yes' vote to the inadequate presentation of the campaign by the ORTF. In particular, he was incensed at the scarcely concealed preference for abstention which many of the television journalists had apparently shown.[17] Instead of mobilizing the electorate, the coverage of state television had in Pompidou's eyes helped to demobilize them. This was a situation which Gaullists could easily contrast with the positive impact of television campaigns before the referenda on the Constitution and Algeria in the early 1960s.

The 1972 statute confirmed the state monopoly in broadcasting.[18] The directors of the news departments lost the independence which had been accorded them in 1969. Responsible solely to the board of governors after 1969, which meant a high degree of *de facto* independence on a daily basis, the news directors now became subject to the authority of the channel heads. This reintegration of the news departments within their respective channels was a complete volte-face on the policy initiated by Chaban-Delmas. Desgraupes resigned as news director on channel one, while some members of his team were sacked and the rest were transferred to the much less widely viewed second channel.

The posts of director general and chairman of the board of governors were fused to centralize responsibility at the top of the ORTF and remove any potential countervailing force. The new post was given to Arthur Conte, one of the leading critics of the 1969 reform within the Gaullist party. Other Gaullist sympathizers were given key posts, including the hardliner Jean-Louis Guillaud as director of the new third channel. The declaration of the ORTF director general that his objective was to ensure a 'loyal' news coverage did nothing to stem the criticisms which greeted the integration of the news departments within the structures of their respective channels. At the same time, a revamped version of the Ministry of Information was reconstituted and Malaud became the minister in charge.

The 1972 statute was not a success. The ORTF's system of financial control was in a mess and the organization appeared to be suffering from a structural bureaucratic malaise. The establishment of the third channel in 1973, ostensibly to provide a service for the regions, exacerbated the management difficulties of the corporation. The decentralizing provisions of the legislation were not properly implemented. Finally, Malaud and Conte fell out in late 1973, leading to both of them being replaced.[19] Attempts to remedy the situation in early 1974 under a new director general were halted by Pompidou's death. Even this sombre event afforded an insight into the nature of the links between the ORTF and the state, since the television news department had been 'forbidden to make an obituary programme in advance . . . for fear of disturbing the delicate political situation which would ensue upon his demise'.[20] At virtually the same time as two American newspaper journalists were bringing down President Nixon in the Watergate affair, French television was undecided how to cover the death from natural causes of the President of the Fifth Republic.

PRESIDENT GISCARD D'ESTAING AND THE ABOLITION OF THE ORTF

Pompidou's death brought an end to the Gaullist domination of French politics. With the Gaullist party deeply divided on the succession and in any case clearly in electoral decline, the Right were represented in the second ballot of the 1974 presidential election by the leader of the Independent Republican party, Valéry Giscard d'Estaing.[21] Elected to the presidency by a narrow popular majority on a platform of 'change without risk', Giscard d'Estaing immediately sought to present a different brand image from his two Gaullist predecessors.[22]

In particular, the election of a new President brought the long-running debate on ORTF reform to a speedy close. Rather than tinker with the existing structure, Giscard d'Estaing decided to implement a radical reorganization of broadcasting which heralded the end of the ORTF's stormy ten-year existence. The 1974 statute, the third major piece of legislation on broadcasting in a decade, was presented as marking both a symbolic and a substantive break with the Gaullist era. The break-up of the state broadcasting corporation, an institution closely associated with one of the more unattractive features of Gaullism, was intended to show the new President's liberalism in the media field. Yet in spite of this reform, the relationship between the state and the audiovisual media remained a controversial issue during the whole of Giscard d'Estaing's term of office.

A reform of broadcasting was particularly opportune at the very start of the new presidency. The ORTF was going through yet another corporate crisis, which on this occasion would soon prove to be terminal. The corporation's recent history of scandals; its reputation for excessive bureaucracy and mismanagement; a succession of critical parliamentary reports in the early 1970s, including a damning one published in early 1974;[23] the reputedly disruptive broadcasting trade unions, some of whom obligingly came out on strike in the spring of 1974; an alleged financial deficit the previous year; and a loss of public confidence in the capacity of the institution to deliver popular programming – all made the ORTF a suitable case for treatment in the early months of the Giscard d'Estaing presidency.

More overtly political factors also help explain the new President's desire to concentrate his reforming zeal on the television issue. A reform of broadcasting neatly fitted in with Giscard d'Estaing's electoral campaign in favour of change. In fulfilment of his electoral pledge the President wanted to settle the broadcasting problem with an impressive flourish so that the new companies could be in operation by the start of 1975. The speed with which the reform proposals on broadcasting were drawn up and then steamrollered through Parliament in a special legislative session reflected Giscard d'Estaing's desire to prove to the electorate that his espousal of a policy of change was not simply empty rhetoric.

In addition, the reorganization of the state broadcasting services was one of several measures intended to aid the implantation of the Giscardian state, forestall the criticisms of the left-wing opposition and, most importantly, mark the end of the Gaullist domination of ministerial and administrative posts which had lasted since 1958. In abolishing the ORTF, Giscard d'Estaing was dismantling one of the major edifices of the Gaullist state. At the same time, the fact that the reorganization of state broadcasting was the first major substantive reform of the Giscardian presidency was further testimony to the importance of television as a political weapon for disseminating information and structuring the political agenda. The presentation, explanation and justification of government decisions across a wide variety of policy areas would be affected by the way in which the broadcasting media were structured and in particular by the relationship established between the state and the television news departments.

At the time of Giscard d'Estaing's election there was no shortage of policy proposals on the broadcasting issue. The director general of the ORTF had already drawn up plans for a wide-sweeping internal reorganization of decision-making structures within the corporation. Meanwhile, private interests were exploiting the ORTF's crisis and the change of presidency to launch another bid for the establishment of a commercial television channel. The new President's own views on broadcasting policy would clearly be crucial in establishing the main axes of the reform. However, somewhat surprisingly, Giscard d'Estaing was not obliged to show his hand on this matter during the election campaign.

Paradoxically, despite the adverse publicity surrounding the ORTF, the broadcasting issue did not assume nearly the same degree of importance during the 1974 campaign as it had done five years previously. Moreover, though as Minister of Finance Giscard d'Estaing had been closely involved in the financial supervision of the ORTF, he had never publicly outlined his views on the optimal framework for the organization of the broadcast media. During the campaign he had set out his position on this issue only to the extent of explicitly rejecting Pompidou's view that the ORTF was the voice of France:

> The ORTF is a public body. It exercises a function of information, but – and this is my profound conviction – France is something too valuable and too important to be identified with anything else. The voice of France can be heard in the presidential election and not through an instrument or a sector of information. . . . I do not think that the ORTF has the task of being the voice of France. The voice of France is the President of the Republic or the French people.[24]

Only after the election was Giscard d'Estaing compelled to spell out his policy goals, which ultimately involved steering a path between those advocating the establishment of a privately owned television channel and those supporting the principle of the state monopoly. The President was widely thought to be in favour of the establishment of commercial competition for the state television service since the bulk of the Independent Republican party, his closest party adviser Michel Poniatowski, and his brother Olivier, had all come out in favour of this option in the recent past.[25] Given the financial and administrative crisis of the ORTF, the pressure exerted by different groups campaigning in favour of a commercial alternative to the state networks and Giscard d'Estaing's own liberal economic outlook, there was a reasonable chance that the President would open up broadcasting to private competition. Yet though many of his supporters were ideologically predisposed towards the introduction of a commercial channel, the President himself was very circumspect about abandoning the state monopoly.

In part this might have been a product of his strong technocratic training with its emphasis on the primary role of the state. It might also have reflected his personal conservatism and innate political caution. Moreover, the President was well aware that government control of news output would be facilitated in a system where the state had a monopoly of ownership. He also had to take account of the strong support for the state monopoly shown by the regional press, which vociferously articulated its fears of losing a large amount of advertising revenue if a commercial channel were established. A commercial channel might also destabilize the ORTF's finances, since the state corporation was now heavily dependent on advertising as an additional source of income to the licence fee.

Perhaps most crucially, the President's freedom of manoeuvre was restricted by his dependence on the Gaullist party in Parliament to support his legislative proposals. There was no large Giscardian party in the National Assembly to vote through the President's initiatives on this (or any other) policy. Therefore, the first non-Gaullist President of the Fifth Republic was forced to rely on the Gaullist party to provide his parliamentary majority on the broadcasting reform bill. In contrast to the Giscardians, many Gaullists remained committed to the principle of the state monopoly. The President would have been running an unacceptably high risk if he had sought to adopt a policy which appeared to undermine one of the central tenets of Gaullist faith. Moreover, there was no possibility on this issue of trying to form an *ad hoc* coalition with the parliamentary Left, as the President was successfully able to do on his abortion reform in late 1974. The Socialists and Communists were opposed on principle to the abolition of the monopoly and the introduction of private interests into the broadcasting media. Whatever their complaints against government abuse of state broadcasting under the Gaullists, there was no question at the start of the Giscard d'Estaing presidency of their supporting a bill to introduce a commercial television channel. In the light of the parliamentary arithmetic, therefore, the option of a commercial channel would have been a highly speculative venture for the new President.

In the event the President and his advisers settled on a hybrid solution: the state monopoly was retained, but the ORTF was broken up and replaced by a system of regulated competition between separate companies with their own distinctive institutional identities. Yet though the monopoly in programming and transmission was preserved, supporters of commercial television were not wholly displeased with the 1974 reform. They regarded the new statute as a first step towards the abolition of the monopoly, believing that the break-up of the ORTF's unitary structure would facilitate the future hiving off of one or more television channels to private interests when circumstances proved more propitious. Their belief was that the Giscardian government was preparing the terrain for such an eventuality, which would come to pass either once the Gaullist parliamentarians could be persuaded to renounce their commitment to the state monopoly or if the Gaullist deputies could be replaced by more economically liberal Giscardians. In this respect they were eventually proved correct, though it was not until 1986 that a bill to privatize one of the state television companies was passed in the French Parliament. The privatization of TF1 under the premiership of the Gaullist Chirac could be seen therefore as the logical end-point of the Giscardian reform of more than a decade previously.[26]

Yet throughout the Giscard d'Estaing presidency itself, the monopoly was stoutly defended, particularly when it came under attack from pirate radio stations.[27] As a result, when in 1981 the President lost his bid to secure a second term of office, there was still no commercial television channel operating in France. This meant that, during the 1970s, only a minority of French viewers living in certain frontier regions could receive programmes from channels other than the three state networks. Meanwhile, cable television, the only other potential threat to the predominance of the state television companies in this pre-satellite era, was successfully blocked by the Giscardian government.[28]

Under the terms of the 1974 statute the ORTF was abolished.[29] It was replaced by a new broadcasting system made up of seven companies organizationally independent of one another: a transmission company – Télédiffusion de France (TDF); a production company – Société Française de Production (SFP); an archive and research institute – Institut National de l'Audiovisuel (INA); a national radio company – Radio France; and three television companies – Télévision Française 1 (TF1), Antenne 2 and France Régions 3 (FR3). FR3 assumed responsibility for regional radio and television. The ORTF was thus broken up into its constituent parts with no central body to coordinate the running of the seven different companies. These would either contract with each other for the provision of certain services (for example, the television companies paid TDF for the transmission of their programmes) or compete against each other subject to certain statutory regulations. The two major national television companies, TF1 and Antenne 2, were placed in direct competition with each other for both finance, especially commercial advertising revenue, and audiences. It was hoped by the government that these smaller, slimmer units would operate more efficiently than the previous unitary structure which had recently come in for so much adverse criticism. The dissolution of the ORTF was also defended in the President's slim, pretentious and vacuous volume on French democracy as a step towards greater pluralism in the media and improved programme quality:

> The break-up of the former ORTF into several national companies, completely independent of each other, contributes to the preservation of our liberties. The rule of independence and of competition must be developed in all its aspects, including the objective of the cultural quality of the programmes.[30]

The abolition of the ORTF had other objectives as well. A single state broadcasting organization was considered not just to be too large and unmanageable. After the Conte–Malaud conflict, it was also feared that it might provide a potential power base for a politically ambitious director general. Such a possibility would not be present in the new smaller companies. At the same time, the reform was designed to weaken the power of the broadcasting unions, who had been used as a convenient scapegoat for many of the problems of the ORTF. Their capacity to act collectively in the future, and in particular their ability to shut down the whole system, would be significantly reduced by the establishment of separate companies. The break-up of trade union power in broadcasting was a major part of the government's thinking when it drew up the 1974 reform.[31]

Whatever the specific reasons behind the break-up of the ORTF, the demise of the unitary corporation brought an era of French broadcasting to a close. The 1974 reorganization was the equivalent of a British government abolishing the BBC and splitting up the corporation into separate transmission, production, radio and television companies. Inevitably, such a radical transformation had massive consequences for the French broadcasting system, many of which had scarcely been foreseen by the proponents of the reform. In the short term the dislocating impact for many broadcasting services and staff was severe, as certain centralized ORTF facilities were divided up in an *ad hoc* and frequently chaotic fashion. The transition gave some managers the opportunity to settle old scores with their employees, while short-term contract and freelance staff remained uncertain about their future employment prospects.

One aspect of the reform which was much trumpeted by government spokespersons during the transitional period of late 1974 was that it represented a clean break with the Gaullist view of the broadcasting media as an integral part of the state apparatus. President Giscard d'Estaing argued that the abolition of the ORTF would involve severing the close links of political control which had previously existed between the government and broadcasting. In particular, in a letter to the heads of the new companies, he declared that the professional broadcasters would henceforth assume full responsibility for news production and content.[32] The abolition of the Ministry of Information was explicitly designed to draw attention to the beginning of a supposed new era in the relationship between the state and broadcasting.

In this context both the method of appointment to the director generalship of the new companies and the first incumbents of these posts came as a disappointment to those expecting change. First, the 1974 reform maintained the procedure whereby the government, rather than a separate regulatory authority, appointed the director generals of the radio and television companies.[33] Second, the reform did nothing to alter the established practice of using largely political criteria in the selection of candidates. When the first appointments were announced at the end of 1974, there was nobody who had any connections, however tenuous, with the ranks of the left-wing opposition. Indeed, many of those appointed to upper-level management posts, such as Jacqueline Baudrier at the head of Radio France and Claude Contamine at the head of FR3, had well-known sympathies for the Gaullist party. Moreover, most of the top management in the four new programme companies had worked in some capacity at the defunct ORTF and had simply moved across to occupy similar positions in the new system. Finally, the different boards of governors continued to have a *de facto* pro-government majority among their members.[34]

Only the appointment of Marcel Jullian as director general of Antenne 2 seemed a concrete manifestation of the trumpeted desire for a fresh start. However, after a series of disputes within the company, and in particular a succession of directors of news and news editors, government confidence in Jullian's ability to manage Antenne 2 quickly evaporated.[35] It was no surprise, therefore, when Jullian's contract was not renewed at the end of 1977. His replacement by a former civil servant, Maurice Ulrich, marked the return to prominence of high-ranking civil servants in the top management posts in state broadcasting. While in 1975 only two of the seven broadcasting companies were headed by former civil servants, by the end of 1979 this total had climbed to five.

In addition, and in breach of both the letter and the spirit of the 1974 statute, the government intervened where it thought necessary to ensure the appointment to other key posts of partisan supporters or politically reliable careerists. Such intervention was particularly evident in the news departments of the television companies. During late 1974, the Prime Minister Jacques Chirac and the Minister of the Interior Michel Poniatowski exercised a *de facto* veto power over appointments to the top news posts.[36] At Antenne 2, various candidates for the post of editor-in-chief were vetoed by the government on political grounds.

Even before the new broadcasting companies were operational, Antenne 2 gave the government the greatest cause for anxiety in this key area. In large part this was due to the more independent stance adopted by Jullian, a newcomer to broadcasting management, who appeared to believe the government's own propaganda regarding the independence of the companies from governmental interference. His naïveté in this respect was to be short-lived. After Jullian had read out on television a letter from the President assuring him that he would enjoy managerial and editorial independence at Antenne 2, a leading government official upbraided him the next day, telling Jullian that he should know that such a letter is destined not to be put into effect.[37]

Political interference in news production was not confined to the upper echelons of the news teams. The reallocation of ORTF journalists among the new companies in late 1974 was open to political abuse. Not only were several ORTF journalists not re-employed in the new companies. More significantly, there is evidence that the government availed itself of the opportunity presented by the dismantling of the ORTF to remove from the broadcasting services a number of trade union activists and suspected political opponents of the Giscard d'Estaing presidency, both on the Left and among the Gaullists. Even before the companies began their transmissions, therefore, the dice were loaded against the achievement of balance and impartiality in political information on the state broadcasting media.

FINANCE AND PROGRAMMING

Once the new system had bedded down during 1975, attention turned to the central features of its operation. If the authorities had hoped that by killing off the ORTF they would somehow remove the broadcasting issue from the realm of political controversy, they were quickly disabused of this fantasy. Critics argued that since services previously centralized at the ORTF now had to be duplicated within each of the four programme companies, this undermined the government's claim that the new system was less bureaucratic than its predecessor. They also pointed out that whatever its public reputation for wastage and inefficiency, the ORTF had not been as badly managed as the government had maintained. In fact, in its final operating year, the state corporation had actually made a small profit.[38]

As the impact of the 1974 reform began to make itself fully felt, two aspects of the running of the new television companies came in for particularly sharp criticism: the financial arrangements and programme output. With regard to the former, revenue from the licence fee, whose annual level continued to be fixed by the state, remained the major single source of finance for the broadcasting system as a whole. The financial input from commercial advertising was still limited to 25 per cent of total broadcasting income. However, this proportion of three parts licence revenue to one part commercial advertising across the whole system is profoundly misleading. The national radio company, Radio France, and the regional programme company, FR3, obtained no revenue from advertising at all, since the government wanted to protect the market position of the peripheral stations and the regional press respectively. Advertising income was concentrated in the two national television companies, TF1 and Antenne 2, both of which came to depend on this source of revenue for over 50 per cent of their respective turnovers. For the two main state television channels, therefore, advertising was not a supplement to licence revenue; it represented the single largest source of income (see table 5.2).

In practice, this meant that the statutory maximum quota on advertising revenue across the state broadcasting system as a whole became a target for TF1 and Antenne 2 to achieve if they were to balance their books. In purely financial terms, this was not too difficult a task in normal circumstances, since between them the two companies still had a monopoly hold over television

Table 5.2 Advertising revenue for TF1 and Antenne 2 1976–80 (expressed as a % of total company income)

Year	TF1	Antenne 2
1976	60	46
1977	61.5	51
1978	57	50
1979	61	52
1980	61	53

Source: Annual budgetary reports on broadcasting by the National Assembly finance committee.

advertising supply. However, the consequences for programme scheduling and output were clear. The growing importance of advertising as a means of finance tended to push the television system in a more market-oriented direction. A qualitative change in the functioning of the system had been brought about by the break-up of the previous unitary structure combined with the increased role of advertising as a source of revenue for the two national television companies.

Competition for advertising income between TF1 and Antenne 2 was naturally accompanied by competition for viewers, as both networks sought to maximize their audience ratings. The head-to-head battle for audiences between the two channels was not itself new, since it had existed at the ORTF between 1969 and 1972. However, within the unitary structure of the corporation, this competition had not had major financial consequences and so its impact on programming could to a large extent be contained. This was much less true after the 1974 reform, which exposed the two main networks to direct competition for advertisers and so inevitably had an important effect on their programming policies.

To mitigate the undesirable effects of market competition after 1974, the government tried to ensure that the networks would comply with their public service obligations by imposing fairly detailed programming norms through a framework of statutory regulations. These included a minimum quota of French-produced programmes and a ceiling on the number of feature films shown on television, as well as the usual public service requirements of balanced scheduling (education, information and entertainment) and impartial news output. The companies' compliance with these programme obligations was monitored by a state agency.

Depending on one's perspective, the result was either an acceptable compromise or an ill-thought-out fudge between two essentially distinct and contradictory approaches to the organization of broadcasting.[39] The Giscardian system tried to combine a commercial and a public service logic in the running of the state's two national television networks. In theory it was hoped that the result would provide the best of both worlds, providing quality programmes across a range of genres within an efficiently managed and tightly regulated competitive system.

In reality, however, this particular mix of public service and commercial approaches satisfied few people.[40] For some, the system stopped critically short of promoting commercial competition. The statutory ceiling on advertising revenue gave the companies insufficient incentive to pursue the mass audience at all costs. It also inhibited their capacity to generate additional revenue for programme making by exploiting an untapped reservoir of advertising income. For many others, the system placed too much emphasis on competition and the pursuit of high ratings at the expense of quality productions and programmes for minority audiences. The dependence of TF1 and Antenne 2 on income from commercial advertising meant that their willingness to adhere to public service norms was constantly being put to the test. The length of programme schedules increased inexorably, with the annual number of hours of television transmission breaking the 10,000 barrier in the late 1970s (see table 5.3). The result was that both networks became reluctant to commit scarce resources to high-cost dramas and fictional programmes. Cheap game shows, 'talking heads' programmes, imported material and feature films became the staple diet of the programme schedules.[41]

This programme policy had important ramifications for the former production services of the ORTF. The dismantling of the corporation had exposed the weakness of the production company with its heavy fixed costs and relatively inflexible working practices. Now organized as a separate company, the SFP was no longer protected by being part of a large, unitary, multifunctional broadcasting corporation. Conscious that in an unregulated competitive environment the state production company would encounter severe financial problems, the government tried to support it in the short term by imposing on the television networks the contractual obligation to order a certain quota of programmes from the SFP. This was a clear – if arguably justifiable – interference in the managerial independence of the programme companies to prevent the SFP from going under. However, it was never intended to be a long-term solution to problems caused by what was essentially a new structural relationship between television programming and production. The more the system moved away from the practices of the ORTF, the more the state production company came to assume the status of an anachronistic relic from a previous broadcasting era.[42]

Not surprisingly, the Giscardian government came under pressure from various sources to boost domestic television production. The issue was particularly highlighted in a much publicized meeting between the well-known television director, Jean-Christophe Averty, and President Giscard

Table 5.3 Annual number of hours of television transmission 1975–81

Year	TF1	Antenne 2	FR3*	Total state networks
1975	3,392	3,373	1,333	8,098
1976	4,157	3,902	1,570	9,629
1977	4,080	3,828	1,750	9,658
1978	4,033	3,857	1,855	9,745
1979	3,972	4,199	1,834	10,005
1980	4,235	4,455	1,930	10,620
1981	4,339	4,516	2,028	10,883

* national programme output only

Source: Commission nationale de la communication et des libertés, *Douze ans de télévision 1974–1986*, Paris, La documentation française, 1987, p.91.

d'Estaing in 1976.[43] Barely a week later, the President confessed that he was concerned about the decline in programme quality since the break-up of the ORTF.[44] As a result, some measures were introduced to encourage French programme production. However, little additional money was made available by the government. More importantly, there was no attempt to introduce any structural changes to the 1974 reorganization, with the result that criticism of the impact of the break-up of the ORTF on programming continued unabated throughout the remainder of the Giscardian presidency.

TELEVISION'S POLITICAL COVERAGE

The Gaullist model of state control which had placed considerable emphasis on direct ministerial intervention in news programming was largely abandoned after 1974. However, this did not mean that the principles regarding impartiality and balance in news output enshrined in the charters of the programme companies were put into practice. During the Giscard d'Estaing presidency, the state authorities preferred to work through politically sympathetic management and news directors, with government manipulation becoming more indirect and generally more subtle than in the Peyrefitte era of the 1960s. The system of partisan appointments to top posts in broadcasting assumed crucial importance.

Prior to 1976, a certain balance in top broadcasting appointments was maintained between Gaullist and Giscardian supporters, reflecting the coalition nature of the right-wing government. However, after the resignation of Chirac from the premiership in August and the dilution of the Gaullist component within the ranks of government ministers, this balance tilted sharply in favour of those who were either personally faithful to President Giscard d'Estaing or for career reasons supportive of his presidency. Using their power of patronage to place sympathizers in key managerial and editorial posts in state broadcasting, the Giscardian authorities had by the late 1970s established a system of control via presidential appointments.

The President denied that these appointments represented a conscious political strategy on his part, arguing that they were made on the professional ground of merit alone. However, his parliamentary supporters were less equivocal. Replying to criticisms made by the Gaullist members of a parliamentary committee of inquiry on the media, the Giscardian members affirmed that since the state was the sole shareholder in the national broadcasting companies, it was logical that it should be the state which should have the role of appointing the management of these companies according to its own criteria. Referring to the Gaullist colonization of the state broadcasting services between 1958 and 1974, the Giscardian parliamentarians continued:

Therefore, one has to be very naive or suffer from a curiously selective amnesia to find in the present situation a worrying innovation. For what reasons should something which was natural twenty-five or ten years ago suddenly become scandalous? Other systems of appointment would undoubtedly be possible and perhaps better, in the tradition of the Anglo-Saxon democracies. One must, however, understand that they have never been adopted in our country where the weight of tradition is quite different.[45]

One of the more infamous Giscardian appointments was that of Jean-Pierre Elkabbach to the post of director of news at Antenne 2 in early 1977. During the previous two years the Antenne 2 news team had been led by no less than three different directors, a situation which had done much to contribute to the company's public image of chronic instability. The administrative problems of Antenne 2 under Jullian's stewardship had been a constant source of concern to the government. More worryingly for the Giscardians, in the changed political context of a divided Right, they now faced the alarming prospect of an electoral squeeze between the Gaullists on the one hand and the Union of the Left on the other. With important municipal elections just a couple of months away and a crucial general election scheduled for the spring of 1978 at the latest, the Giscardians were in an electoral double bind. The newly created mayorship of Paris – a presidential initiative which guaranteed the victor a strong power base and a high media profile – could well be captured by Chirac, while the Socialist–Communist opposition were widely tipped to win the general election a year later. In these circumstances the Giscardians considered it imperative that they had a man they could trust running the news operation at Antenne 2. Elkabbach was an inspired choice.

Elkabbach's appointment demonstrated the very real limits on the freedom of manoeuvre of the management of the broadcasting companies in the politically sensitive field of news programming. In some cases these limits were readily accepted by the director general and management team, with the result that overt interference by the government was unnecessary. The other company heads were usually more willing than Jullian to accept ministerial suggestions regarding politically acceptable candidates or, more normally, they made the appointments themselves with full knowledge gained from long professional experience in the field as to who were 'one of us'. In other cases, constraints were imposed by the government either in the form of ministerial veto or positive recommendation. Whether overt or covert, willingly accepted or resisted, the existence of these constraints belied the government's guarantees regarding the independence of the television companies.

A variety of factors militated against a balanced and impartial political output. For example, within the different news departments the organization was of a strongly hierarchical nature, with any controversial decisions being made at the top by the director of news or editor-in-chief. The daily meeting within each news department at which the structure and content of the news bulletins were decided did not reflect a democratic decision-making procedure, since the final decision always lay with the director of news and his immediate subordinates. For political and/or career reasons, the holders of these key posts were unlikely to want to embarrass the President or his government. Though not all the journalists in the television news departments were by any means favourable to Giscard d'Estaing or to the parties of the governing coalition, they had very limited possibilities of making their voice heard. The decision-making structure, the level of unemployment in their profession, the experience of journalists sacked or marginalized on previous occasions (such as 1968 and 1974) and the tradition of governmental interference in broadcasting – all tended to reduce the likelihood of journalists contesting the decisions of their superiors within the news departments or, *a fortiori*, of successfully opposing them.

This did not mean that, having drawn up the rules of the game and chosen the key players, the Giscardian government was content always to remain on the sidelines. Certainly, the excesses of the Gaullist period were now out of fashion. After 1974, cases of overt ministerial censorship became the exception rather than the rule. The successor to the Ministry of Information, the Ministry of Culture and Communication established in 1978, exercised no influence on news programming. Many journalists with Gaullist and Socialist sympathies, though few with Communist leanings, were employed in the state programme companies, some in fairly senior posts. Representatives of the Socialist and Communist parties appeared frequently on television. For example, Michel Rocard's standing with the electorate was measurably improved by his television appearances. The Communist party leader, Georges Marchais, became a television personality in his own right through appearances on the lively political discussion programme, *Cartes sur table*.

Though there was an imbalance in the allocation of time between supporters of Right and Left, television news coverage was no longer amenable to a crude stopwatch approach. In fact, sometimes the Left might have thought that it was being given too much television news coverage. For example, in September 1977 when the Union of the Left was dissolved, Socialist and Communist spokespersons seemed to be in permanent occupation of the television screen. While this very public media breakdown in the relationship between the Socialist and Communist parties could be explained by the pro-Giscardian political sympathies of television news chiefs, it could also be satisfactorily accounted for in terms of professional news values. After all, the split in the Union of the Left was the major political news story of the year in France.[46]

Other improvements were also made after 1974. A right of reply for the opposition parties was established, albeit within a very limited framework. Party political broadcasts were programmed on the basis of strict equality of time between the governing parties and the opposition. A daily access programme, *Tribune libre*, was established on FR3, giving some opportunity to minority groups to express their point of view. Antenne 2's *Cartes sur table*, during which a politician was interviewed at length about policies and topics of current controversy, made a positive contribution to the discussion of politics on television. Furthermore, if one excluded the coverage given the President, there was not a great disparity between the length of time allocated to government ministers and spokespersons of the governing parties on the one hand and that accorded representatives of the opposition on the other. In these circumstances, it was understandable that many viewers considered that television news programmes after 1974 were more objective than in the years prior to the reform.

However, the political coverage of the state programme companies was neither balanced nor impartial. Nor, given the systemic links which existed between the government and the companies, could it reasonably have been expected to be so. One aspect of this imbalance was the unduly favourable coverage given to President Giscard d'Estaing. The disproportionate amount of time accorded the President could not be wholly explained by the importance of his position, nor could the generally obsequious stance adopted by journalists when questioning the President be totally attributable to the alleged reticence of all French politicians on television to indulge in spontaneous dialogue.[47] The uncritical roles performed by such leading television commentators as Patrice Duhamel (TF1), Yves Mourousi (TF1) and Jean-Pierre Elkabbach (Antenne 2) were particularly evident in television interviews with the President.

The refusal to deal in any significant detail with controversial topics such as France's commitment to nuclear power and the Bokassa diamonds scandal demonstrated the stifling nature of the relationship between the television news departments and the Giscardian presidency, as did the ceaseless reiteration on television news that the quasi-totality of France's economic problems were attributable to the world oil crisis.[48] Alternative explanations, such as those put forward by the opposition, received short shrift in comparison. A defence of Giscardian policies was proposed by several commentators as though this was in the natural order of things.

In contrast with the Gaullist period, controls were largely internalized within the television companies, with self-censorship making censorship quasi-redundant. The directors of news and their immediate colleagues replaced the Minister of Information as the key figures in the news production process. A major part of their role was to act as dishonest brokers between the government and the news departments, converting political pressures into professional directives. The consequence of this was the partisan political coverage, more qualitative than quantitative, which operated in favour of the President, his supporters and their policies.

This partisan coverage became more noticeable after the 1976 local elections, which were disappointing for the governing coalition, and intensified after Chirac's resignation from the premiership later the same year. During politically sensitive periods, such as election campaigns, there remained a tendency to resort to direct pressure on broadcasters rather than rely solely on the political correctness of the sympathetic management within the news departments. Direct Elysée and ministerial pressure was exerted on the news departments, usually at the level of the company heads and news directors rather than on the journalists themselves. In television coverage of the 1977 municipal, 1978 parliamentary and 1979 European elections, Giscardian candidates were favourably treated, particularly in the period preceding the official campaign. During the election campaigns of 1977 and 1978, there were complaints from broadcasting journalists of pressure from ministers and from their news directors aimed against both the Socialist–Communist Left and the Chirac-led Gaullist party. During the 1979 European election campaign the Giscardian list, headed by Simone Veil, benefited from more favourable coverage than the other three major rival lists (Gaullist, Socialist and Communist).

Television coverage of the 1981 presidential campaign offers a useful illustration of the nature of the relationship between the Giscard d'Estaing presidency and state television. As it had done at every national election since 1965, television constituted a primary source of information for the electorate in 1981. During the official campaign period, which began two weeks before the first ballot, an electoral control committee composed of top civil servants supervised the coverage of the different candidates by state television. Strict equality of time allocation was maintained between the candidates during the official campaign broadcasts, which were shown simultaneously at peak viewing times on both TF1 and Antenne 2. Little can be said about the official campaign broadcasts, except that they represented a limited and very ostentatious attempt at balance in political coverage.

Political balance in the official campaign broadcasts did not extend, however, to coverage of the election in the immediate pre-campaign period or on television news bulletins during the campaign. Alleged discrepancies in time allocation and quality of treatment in favour of presidential candidate Giscard d'Estaing were condemned by all his rivals. Gaullist, Socialist and Communist parties regularly published accounts of the amount of time accorded to their candidates in comparison with Giscard d'Estaing, with the latter always the beneficiary. Sections of the French press were also quick to point out the unequal treatment of the different candidates, as were the more disinterested Paris correspondents of quality British newspapers. All pointed to the difference in tone and style of questioning between interviews with Giscard d'Estaing on the one hand and those with his rivals on the other.

The television highlight of the campaign was the face-to-face confrontation between Giscard d'Estaing and Mitterrand before the second ballot, which attracted an audience of over 25 million.[49] Whilst the content of the debate was fairly predictable, the controversy surrounding the staging of the televised duel was quite remarkable. Remembering the débâcle of 1974 when supporters of Giscard d'Estaing had vastly outnumbered those of Mitterrand in the studio audience, Mitterrand and his advisers posed a series of extremely detailed preconditions to the debate's taking place at all. For example, the interviewers were to be chosen among journalists not employed in the state television companies. There was to be no cutting away from the candidate who was speaking to show the reaction of his opponent. Even the distance between the two candidates was specified by the Mitterrand camp. From the viewpoint of the professional broadcaster such conditions may have made for a sterile programme. However, Mitterrand obviously considered it necessary to pose such conditions not just because he was generally reckoned to be a poorer television performer than Giscard d'Estaing, but more importantly because he considered he could not trust the state television companies to maintain equity. For Giscard d'Estaing's presidential rival in 1981, the state television studio was not a neutral venue but enemy-occupied territory.

THE 1974 REFORM IN RETROSPECT

The break-up of the ORTF represented a major reorganization of French television, the impact of which continued to resonate throughout the broadcasting system during the 1980s. At one level the Giscardian reform was a quick fix technocratic solution to an organizational problem which the new President inherited on coming to office. The ORTF was perceived to be out of control: too large, unwieldy and bureaucratic to be capable of efficient management. The state corporation also appeared ill prepared to cope with potential expansion into new fields such as local radio, too inflexible to respond to new developments in television technology such as satellite television and over-complacent in the face of the financial problems resulting from the market saturation of television ownership and its implications for licence fee funding. Buffeted by scandals, prone to industrial action by demoralized staff and, most crucially of all, abused by the authorities as both a political tool and a convenient scapegoat for the latter's own policy failures, the ORTF was an organization which by 1974 had lost its sense of direction.

However, it would be misleading to represent the abolition of the ORTF as just a short-term response to an immediate problem of corporate management. The Giscardian broadcasting reform was also an attempt to prepare the ground for the future. In its institutional separation of the different functions of the broadcasting process (transmission, programming and production), the 1974 statute set out a blueprint for the organization of television in a more highly competitive environment. There was a clear economic rationale underpinning the reform. At a time of anticipated technological expansion and a growing desire among the audience for greater choice in programming, government policy was designed to produce a leaner and fitter television industry which would be capable of responding quickly to multifarious pressures for change. The creation of smaller television companies and the measures taken to weaken the power of the broadcasting unions were designed to facilitate this process. The abolition of the giant monolith of the ORTF thus prepared the way for a more flexible market-style relationship between transmission, programming and production. In effect, the television companies after 1974 became like publishing houses. They were directly responsible for some of their smaller-scale productions, but bought in much of their product from the SFP or from abroad. In this respect there are strong parallels between the Giscardian reorganization of French television in the 1970s and the Conservative government's reform of the British ITV system in the early 1990s.

Though the ORTF had its defenders, especially among the broadcasting unions and sections of the mainstream Left, there was no widespread elite or popular groundswell of support for its maintenance as there would have been, say, for the BBC in Britain in similar circumstances. In part this was because the ORTF's institutional existence was that much shorter. It had been functioning for only ten years, whereas the BBC can trace its origins back to the beginning of broadcasting in the early 1920s. The French state broadcasting corporation had simply not benefited from sufficient time to implant itself in the popular consciousness as a broadcaster whose integrity was worth defending. This meant that, unlike the BBC, the ORTF had not participated in the great moments of the nation's history or commemorated the ritual celebrations of national unity. It had not made the symbolic and substantive contributions to the national way of life which its cross-Channel counterpart had done, for example during the Second World War or in covering events such as the Coronation.

Most crucially, the structural linkages between the broadcasting corporation and the regime meant that the ORTF was widely regarded as a branch of the Gaullist state rather than a mirror of French society or a public sphere for the interchange of views among the political elites. While in reality no broadcaster reflects a nation in all its diversity or covers opinions impartially across the whole of the ideological spectrum, a state monopoly must at least appear to represent a wide cross-section of social tastes and political opinion if it is to enjoy legitimacy among the population and elite groups. This the ORTF manifestly failed to accomplish. As a result, its fate was inextricably bound up with that of its founders – the Gaullists. As long as they were in power, the ORTF could be exploited to serve their partisan interests. However, when the Gaullists lost control of the Fifth Republic's key political office in 1974, the existence of the ORTF was bound to be imperilled.

The break-up of the ORTF, therefore, was not just the latest in a series of administrative reforms of French broadcasting. It was both a symbol and a product of the transfer of political power, marking the end of the 16-year domination of the Fifth Republic by the Gaullists. Yet after his own election victory in 1974, President Giscard d'Estaing never succeeded in marginaliz-ing the Gaullists as an electoral force or significantly undermining their parliamentary importance. As a result, he was unable to impose his authority on the whole of the French Right. Against the background of growing disharmony between Giscardians and Gaullists as Chirac prepared his own presidential candidacy for 1981, the President tried to reinforce his control of television.[50]Appointments to top broadcasting posts in the late 1970s were part of an exercise of presidential patronage in an attempt to place Giscardian supporters in key positions within state and para-state bodies. At the same time, the President appeared frequently on television in a vain attempt to set the political agenda and defend his policies.

As the 1981 presidential election loomed ever closer on the horizon, the tensions and contradictions in the Giscardian approach to broadcasting reform became manifest. The early commitment to the *political* liberal-ization of information conflicted with the electoral needs of the incumbent President in an increasingly difficult economic and political climate. Mean-while, the push towards the *economic* liberalization of the broadcasting system was severely compromised, first by the President's dependence on the Gaullist party in Parliament to support reform, and later by the belief that the state monopoly was desirable if the Giscardian regime were to maintain some form of control of the audiovisual media.

When Giscard d'Estaing left office in 1981, various problems concerning the relationship between the state and the broadcasting media had not been resolved. Alleged government attempts to set the news agenda and manipulate television coverage in its favour were routinely condemned by opponents. Such criticisms had become part of the ritual of political discourse in the Fifth Republic. Yet despite this appearance of continuity, the terms of the debate on broadcasting policy were clearly changing by the end of the 1970s. There was a distinct shift of emphasis away from a narrow concern with news bias towards a wider consideration of the balance between public and private control in the broadcasting system. In particu-lar, the postwar elite consensus supporting the framework of the state monopoly had totally disintegrated. The fundamental issue dominating the policy agenda on the media by the time of Giscard d'Estaing's electoral defeat was not how political information on the state broadcasting networks could be made more balanced and impartial. Instead, the central concern of policy makers was what kind of broadcasting system should replace the traditional centralized state monopoly which had been in place since the Liberation. Providing a response to this question was one of the early tasks to be accomplished by the new Socialist administration under the first left-wing President of the Fifth Republic, François Mitterrand.

Chapter 6

Television: the end of the state monopoly

During the first five years of the Mitterrand presidency (1981–86) the French broadcasting system underwent a near-revolutionary upheaval. The 1982 broadcasting statute echoed the 1881 press law in proclaiming that audio-visual communication was free. The substantive application of this principle saw the traditional postwar framework of the state monopoly being swept away, first in radio and then in television.[1] In addition, a new regulatory agency, the High Authority for Audiovisual Communication, was set up in an attempt to distance the state from day-to-day control of broadcast output and to remove its power of appointment to top broadcasting posts. Two years later Europe's first terrestrially transmitted pay-television channel, Canal Plus, began transmissions. While initially received with considerable public scepticism, Canal Plus quickly became a major force for innovation within French television and, by the end of the decade, was a key media player at both the national and supranational levels. Finally, at the start of 1986, two commercial television channels were established, financed from advertising revenue and free to the viewer at the point of reception. The sum of these changes was of such magnitude that by the time the Socialist government fell in the 1986 general election, key features of the French broadcasting system of the pre-Mitterrand era were little more than a distant memory.

The primary cause of these innovations in the broadcasting environment can be traced to the momentous political change of 1981. The election that year of the Socialist party leader François Mitterrand as President marked the end of the domination of the Fifth Republic by the Gaullist–Giscardian Right. For the first time since the establishment of the regime in 1958, the Left had succeeded in winning national political office. Capitalizing on his personal success in the presidential contest, Mitterrand called a general election a few weeks later, at which the Socialist party gained an absolute majority of parliamentary seats – only the second time that a single party had performed such a feat during the Fifth Republic. By the autumn of 1981, the Socialists had a firm grip on the offices of the presidency and premiership, occupied the most important posts in the

Council of Ministers, had a secure majority in Parliament and were placing supporters in selected key decision-making posts in the administrative and para-administrative sectors of the French polity. Given the tradition of politicization of French broadcasting during the Fifth Republic, this historic change in the holders of political power was bound to have profound repercussions for relations between the state and the audiovisual media.

The new President was himself very well aware of the deficiencies of the broadcasting system bequeathed to him by his right-wing predecessors. In his role as *de facto* leader of the opposition during the Giscard d'Estaing presidency, Mitterrand had been at the forefront of those who had criticized the control exercised by the authorities over radio and television. Indeed, a large section of the chapter on the Giscardian state in his book *Ici et maintenant* was devoted to a fierce attack on Giscard d'Estaing on the media issue.[2] Mitterrand had also taken more practical action against the Giscardian government's interference in broadcasting by participating in the illegal broadcasts of the Socialist party's pirate radio, Radio Riposte, in the summer of 1979 – an action which had led to his appearance in court on the charge of infringing the state's broadcasting monopoly. A victim throughout the Fifth Republic of the partiality of the government's hold over broadcasting, Mitterrand was now in a position as President to reform state–broadcasting relations more or less as he wished.

Yet it would be misleading to analyse the broadcasting initiatives of the new Socialist government solely within the political context of presidential and governmental change. Other factors underpinned the radical thrust of government policy in this field. One was the realization among policy makers that the technological straitjacket in which radio and television transmissions had been constrained for so long was now outmoded. Advances in new communications technologies, such as cable and satellite, opened up the way to a multi-channel television system in the not too distant future and called into question the rationale for monopoly in a field which was no longer a scarce public resource. By the early 1980s the technical arguments supporting the state monopoly case had quite simply lost their persuasive force.

The authorities were also under pressure to open up broadcasting to certain social and professional groups, who felt that they had been excluded from, marginalized by or undervalued in the system prior to 1981. Generally sympathetic to the Left, these groups included new social movements, the trade union confederations, radio and television journalists and artistic personnel. Some wanted more sympathetic coverage of their case on radio and television; others wished to enhance their professional status within the broadcast media. All hoped to make an input into the policy-making process on broadcasting and to benefit from any structural reform of radio and television introduced by the Socialists.

There were also powerful economic arguments in favour of an expansion of the broadcasting system and the entry of new non-state actors as financial contributors and programme providers. Domestic manufacturers of audiovisual hardware, such as television sets, decoders and programme transmission/reception equipment, stood to gain. Advertisers too were looking for new and cheaper outlets in a more competitive market where the supply and cost of television advertising would in their view be more responsive to demand. Opening up the television advertising market would allow more commercial resources to flow into the system as a whole, providing additional funds for programming. At the same time, television channels functioning outside the state sector would make no demands on the already overburdened licence fee. Finally, French programme production industries hoped to benefit from an increase in their customer base, the television channels, which, because of the continuation of state regulations and quotas, would need to use home-produced programming for a significant part of their output.

Audience dissatisfaction with the programme output of the state mono-poly also fed the impetus for reform. Opinion polls in the 1970s had generally shown that many viewers found the output of the state monopoly channels stultifying and unimaginative. The tastes and interests of different groups in French society were not being adequately catered for by the status quo, with the result that there was a widespread demand by viewers for greater diversity, increased choice and a more pluralistic output. While the govern-ment's desire to court public opinion was probably not a major motivating factor behind the 1982 reform, it did play a part in President Mitterrand's decision in 1985 to introduce new commercial television channels. Even in 1982, however, the Socialists recognized that so inextricably confused had the concept of state monopoly and the practice of partisan political control become that merely to tinker with the inherited system would be an insufficient public affirmation of the electoral commitment to change.

Though mindful of these different pressures for change, the Socialists were also aware of the risks involved in moving too rapidly along the paths of economic and political liberalization. First, there was the cultural danger that new television channels might become mere distribution outlets for foreign, especially American, programming. In the early 1980s the potential threat posed by the media artefacts of American cultural imperialism was emphasized by various Socialist spokespersons, most notably the Minister of Culture, Jack Lang. In part such dire pronouncements could be interpreted as nothing more than chauvinistic rhetorical posturing. Yet there did also appear to be a concern on the part of the authorities that the nation's cultural identity might be overwhelmed if the television system were to expand too quickly and insufficient French product were available to fill the schedules.

Second, there was the undesirable impact on the balance of the media system which might accompany rapid and uncontrolled change. The example of Italy, where a wholly unregulated private sector had been established in the late 1970s, was a model constantly cited by the Socialists as one to be avoided at all costs.[3] For the French authorities the new Italian model combined a variety of disadvantages. It had led to a huge increase in foreign programme imports; it had destabilized the Italian film industry, the press and the public sector broadcasting organization, the RAI; it had lowered programme quality; it had not been associated with any technological improvements in the communications infrastructure; and it had resulted in anarchy over the airwaves from which the strongest economic forces, notably the Berlusconi empire, had emerged to impose their own dominance on the private broadcasting sector. The antipathy towards the Italian experience exhibited in the upper echelons of the French state was translated into a strong policy preference that any expansion and liberalization of the broadcasting system should be closely managed from the top down by the authorities.

Finally, there was the ideological risk of allowing the enemies of Socialism access to ownership and control of the broadcasting media. This fear manifested itself in different ways. For example, in 1981 the desire for revenge against media professionals too closely associated with the Right was strong in certain Socialist circles, as was the temptation to replace them with supporters of the new Mitterrand presidency. More generally, there were many in the Socialist party who wanted to exploit television as a vehicle for the mobilization of popular support behind the Left's programme of economic, political and social reform. Having waited so long to assume power in the Fifth Republic, many Socialists were reluctant to see the state abandon its hold over such a powerful mass medium as television. During the premiership of Pierre Mauroy (1981–84) in particular, the authorities feared the incursion of powerful private interests in the audiovisual sector.

The objective of Socialist government policy on broadcasting between 1981 and 1986 was to achieve an optimal balance between these different and often conflicting policy pressures. 'Controlled deregulation' was the phrase often used by Socialist policy makers during this period to describe the new role assumed by the state during this period of broadcast media expansion.[4] While the state was relinquishing its monopoly of ownership in radio and television, it still wanted to use its regulatory powers to achieve specific policy goals (for example, technological development and cultural protectionism) and in particular protect the public sector media from some of the more adverse consequences of untrammelled competition. Yet while the Socialists dominated the French state during this period, they were by no means in total control of the policy-making environment in the audiovisual field. Not only did certain policy objectives prove mutually incompatible. In addition, the difficulties of mastering technological change, the problems of regulatory enforcement in the media field, the general downturn in economic performance and the government's need to court short-term electoral popularity, all undermined the apparent coherence of broadcasting policy in the early 1980s. As a result, though some notable successes were registered, many of the government's policy goals proved elusive.

THE SOCIALIST TRANSITION

The election of a Socialist President immediately called into question the status of those holding key positions in the state broadcasting companies. The first problem the Mitterrand presidency faced was how to rid state radio and television of those appointed to top managerial and editorial posts under the previous Giscardian administration. In the eyes of the Socialists, the director generals and editors-in-chief in post in the summer of 1981 were too closely associated with the Giscard d'Estaing presidency to retain their positions once the Left had come to power. Understandably, the new authorities regarded the incumbents as 'yesterday's men', who were clinging to their posts despite the electoral rejection of their patron. They had to be removed – and quickly, as the crowd who celebrated Mitterrand's victory in the place de la Bastille knew only too well. In this respect the Socialists were merely continuing a tradition of the Fifth Republic whereby new administrations appoint their own supporters to key posts in state broadcasting – a fact of political life which was apparently accepted by a majority of the French electorate as 'normal'.

In the case of the director generals of the state broadcasting companies, however, the dilemma facing the Socialists was that the contracts of many of these courtiers of the *ancien régime* had been quite legitimately renewed for another three-year term towards the end of the Giscard d'Estaing presidency. A new broadcasting statute introduced quickly at the start of Mitterrand's presidency, as Giscard d'Estaing had done in 1974, would have resolved this problem. However, Socialist reform proposals in the broadcasting field were not yet complete and a variety of interested parties, including the broadcasting unions, were insisting on their right to make their own contribution to the debate. Since they had severely criticized Giscard d'Estaing for steamrollering his own broadcasting bill through Parliament in 1974 without adequate consultation of those affected, the Socialists were reluctant to lay themselves open to similar charges. In any case, other legislative proposals concerning the decentralization of power to the regions and *départements* and the early nationalization measures took precedence over a structural reorganization of broadcasting. Thus, the new Socialist administration had somehow to remove the old Giscardian guard in broadcasting without at the same time being seen to indulge too overtly in a political witch-hunt, a practice they themselves had condemned in 1968 and 1974.

The Socialist response to this problem was to apply pressure on certain directors of news and company heads to resign 'voluntarily', either directly through ministerial meetings with those concerned or indirectly by urging the broadcasting staff, particularly the journalists, to force the issue within the companies. The new minister in charge of media policy, Georges Fillioud, a former broadcasting journalist who himself had been a victim of a previous Gaullist purge, was especially vitriolic in his condemnation of those pro-Giscardian elements who still sought to retain their posts after the change of presidency. So too was Claude Estier, a leading member of the Socialist party, who at the party's victory conference in Valence asked: 'How do you expect economic journalists trained in the school of liberalism . . . to explain truthfully the meaning of the nationalizations or the industrial reforms?'[5]

Yet while the heavy-handed means employed by the new government left many commentators and broadcasting staff with an uncomfortable frisson of *déjà vu*, they did gradually succeed in attaining their goal of easing out Giscardian and Gaullist loyalists from their posts. By early 1982 all the heads of the broadcasting companies, with one minor exception, had been replaced. So too had all the directors of news, including the well-known Socialist *bêtes noires* Jean-Pierre Elkabbach, director of news at Antenne 2, and Patrice Duhamel, news editor at TF1.[6] Widespread changes of top personnel also took place among the management of the peripheral radio stations. At the same time, several journalists removed from their posts in previous Gaullist and Giscardian purges were reinstated, with some being given quite senior posts by the Socialist government.[7]

Not all those appointed could be regarded as Socialist loyalists. In fact, some possessed an impressive record of professional competence and political independence. None the less, the manner in which the changeover at the top of the broadcasting companies was handled by the government raised doubts about the extent to which a commitment in principle to public service norms regarding impartiality and independence could be reconciled with the well-established practice of partisan political appointments. The Socialists might well argue that they were merely clearing out the Giscardian legacy prior to making a fresh start. However, fears that the Socialists would be unable to resist the temptation to appoint their own political sympathizers were scarcely allayed by statements such as that made by President Mitterrand in the autumn of 1981:

> We do not want a purge, but nonetheless a certain number of command controls have to be held by men and women whose views correspond with those of the majority of the country. We must ensure that the policies desired by the majority, which we are putting into practice, are really implemented.[8]

Applied to the realm of broadcasting, Mitterrand's statement had a hauntingly Gaullist ring about it. The President had a direct hand in the appointment of the new heads of the state broadcasting companies, though he had to be persuaded by his Prime Minister, Pierre Mauroy, regarding the desirability of the appointment of Pierre Desgraupes at Antenne 2.[9]

None the less, complaints by right-wing commentators and opposition politicians of a leftist takeover of the state broadcasting media via the new appointments were exaggerated.[10] Communist sympathizers were few and far between in the top managerial and editorial posts, as the Communist party leadership took great pains to point out. Journalists with Communist sympathies were also under-represented in the news teams, particularly at the upper levels. While persons with Socialist sympathies were more numerous, the political colonization of broadcasting in 1981–82 was no more extensive, and arguably much less so, than had occurred during the Peyrefitte era in the 1960s or the Giscard d'Estaing presidency in the mid-1970s.

Apart from these changes in top personnel, the first year of television during the Mitterrand presidency scarcely lived up to the expectations of radical change which had followed his election victory. Some improvements were noticeable in the early months. Programmes critical of the French people in times of crisis, such as *Le chagrin et la pitié*, were shown for the first time on French television after having been kept off the screen during previous presidencies. In the main, however, change was either lacking or had a negative impact. The broadcasting unions held a general strike in protest against the alleged lack of consultation by the Ministry of Communication in the drafting of the new broadcasting bill, a complaint similar in substance to that made by the same unions at the time of the Giscardian reorganization in 1974. The Minister of Communication tried in vain to prevent the screening of a documentary programme, an intervention worthy of Gaullist Ministers of Information in the past. As in previous presidencies, the opposition parties alleged one-sided presentation of news and political coverage.[11] Certainly in the early honeymoon period of the Mitterrand presidency, when the Right were politically weak and in organizational disarray, the policies of the new government were favour-ably presented on television. Socialist spokespersons and government ministers, clearly enjoying the fruits of power, seemed never to be off the screen. Perhaps this goes some way to explaining one change which was noticeable during the first year of the Mitterrand term: television viewers, annoyed at the patronizingly didactic style and content of programmes, switched off in increasingly large numbers.

Perhaps most worryingly, Socialist spokespersons attacked the lack of objectivity of television journalists, while at the same time arguing that broadcasting was not doing enough to explain and defend the government's policies. This was reminiscent of those Gaullist representatives in the early 1970s who had criticized the Chaban-Delmas broadcasting experi-ment both for lacking balance and for being inimical to the interests of the Gaullist regime. Following the 1982 local council elections, which were disappointing for the Left as the Right made substantial electoral gains, certain Socialist spokespersons argued that if the electorate were becoming disillusioned with the Mitterrand presidency this was because Socialist policies were not being satisfactorily presented to the viewers by the state broadcasting networks. The President of the National Assembly, the Socialist Louis Mermaz, argued that the Socialists did not yet have 'the television of change'.

In one sense Mermaz was quite correct. For the first year of the Mitterrand presidency the Socialists were negotiating a transitional phase, which was largely confined to papering over the most obvious cracks in the system inherited from the Giscardians. The 1982 broadcasting statute, the key to any fundamental change in the organization of broadcasting, was not to become fully operational until the beginning of 1983. Only after the implementation of new legislation would it be possible to ascertain how far the Socialists were prepared to go down the paths of economic and political liberalization.

THE END OF THE STATE MONOPOLY

As part of their preparations for the introduction of a new broadcasting statute, the Socialist government set up an official advisory committee made up of persons with undoubted professional competence in the cultural and media fields, many (though not all) of whom were politically sympathetic to the Mitterrand presidency. Chaired by Pierre Moinot, a top civil servant and former governor of the ORTF, the committee produced its report in October 1981, after only a few weeks of deliberation.[12] The main thrust of the report's recommendations was accepted by the Socialist government as the basis of its broadcasting bill which was introduced in Parliament in early summer 1982.

In terms of structural reform, the broadcasting system which emerged from the 1982 statute consisted of an apparently bewildering complexity of organizations. There were to be two Paris-based television companies (TF1 and Antenne 2), screening programmes nationwide; a third television company (France Régions 3), which was given responsibility for coordinating the running of the 12 regional television companies envisaged by the reform; a national radio company (Radio France), which was not only to run all public service radio at the national level, but also to finance regional radio companies; an unspecified number of regional radio companies to manage those local radio stations in the public sector; a public corporation (the former TDF), which would be responsible for the maintenance of the technical infrastructure and for transmitting the programmes of the programme companies; another public corporation (Institut National de la Communication Audiovisuelle), which would be responsible for broadcasting research, archive conservation and staff training; a national company (Société Française de Production et de Création Audiovisuelles), which would make programmes for the television companies; a national programme company to coordinate the operations of the broadcasting services in the overseas regions and territories; a national company responsible for radio programmes broadcast abroad (Radio France Internationale); and, finally, a separate company with the task of publicizing and selling French radio and television programmes to foreign broadcasting services.

All of these different companies together formed the state broadcasting sector. The 1982 reform eschewed the possibility of returning to the unitary structure of the ORTF. In fact, the seven separate companies set up by the 1974 Giscardian reform remained in existence and were even joined by some new ones. In one sense, therefore, there was greater fragmentation in the post-1982 broadcasting system than had resulted from the much criticized Giscardian reorganization. However, the Socialists hoped that the centrifugal excesses of the 1974 reform would to some extent be offset by the creation of a central regulatory authority to supervise the operations of the different companies.

Under the terms of the 1982 legislation French broadcasting retained its status as a public service. State radio and television were required, *inter alia*, to ensure 'honesty, independence and pluralism in news coverage', to give access to cultural, social, professional, spiritual and philosophical groups, to protect the French language and promote regional languages, to help spread French culture and to increase the knowledge and develop the initiative of the citizenry. Detailed public service obligations were laid down in the operating conditions of the different companies.

The three state television networks would continue to be financed from a mixture of licence revenue and commercial advertising. While in the original joint manifesto of 1972 the Socialists and Communists had pledged to abolish advertising in state television, spiralling costs ensured that advertising remained a major source of income. The 1982 reform even allowed for advertising by the regional television companies, whereas under previous right-wing governments advertising had been allowed only on the two national television channels. The acceptance of advertising as a source of finance for state television showed how far the Left had moved in its policy on broadcasting during the 1970s. Advertising was no longer regarded as a capitalist Trojan horse inside state broadcasting, but as an essential means of funding in a system where the market for television ownership was saturated and licence fee revenue could not hope to cover costs on its own.[13]

The single most important innovation of the 1982 reform was undoubtedly the abandonment of the state monopoly in radio and television programming. The existence of the state monopoly since the end of the Second World

War meant that within France there had been no competition from commercial television, not even of the regulated, public service variety which breached the BBC's monopoly in Britain in the 1950s. At the same time, the limitations of terrestrial transmission technology had ensured that most of France remained hermetically sealed off from the programme output of the television systems of neighbouring countries. The result of these mutually reinforcing legal and technological constraints was that French viewers were a captive market for the programme output of the state television networks. The 1982 statute brought this era of state domination of the airwaves to an end. Though the state continued to have overall charge of frequency allocation and of national transmission facilities, it gave up its jealously guarded exclusive rights to controlling all sources of broadcast output.

The abolition of the monopoly marked a sea change in political elite attitudes towards the organization of television in France. During the 1960s there had been a general acceptance of the framework of the state monopoly by the political parties of both Right and Left. The Left may have challenged what it regarded as the Right's abuse of the monopoly for its own political ends, but it defended the principle of the monopoly itself. By the early 1980s this elite consensus had disintegrated. The postwar belief in the organizational principle of the state monopoly as the best guarantee of a public service broadcasting system had irreparably broken down.

The 1982 legislation was passed in the National Assembly with the Socialist deputies voting in favour and the Gaullists and Giscardians against. The Communists abstained. The opposition of the Right was to be expected. Many right-wing deputies wanted the reform to go much further in opening up broadcasting to private interests through the immediate introduction of a commercial television channel. They also wanted to express their displeasure at the alleged Socialist takeover of state broadcasting during the months prior to the introduction of the reform bill. The abstention of the Communists reflected their fear that the new legislation went too far in weakening the state's overall control of broadcasting and prepared the ground for the incursion of private interests. They also wanted to censure the government for not proceeding quickly enough in increasing the number of journalists with Communist sympathies in the state radio and television companies. Outside Parliament the reform was criticized by the broadcasting unions, notably regarding the anti-strike provisions of the new statute, and by the regional press, which condemned the government's decision to allow advertising on regional television as a direct attack on their industry.

THE HIGH AUTHORITY

Following the abolition of the state monopoly, the second major innovation of the 1982 statute was the establishment of a completely new regulatory body – the High Authority for Audiovisual Communication – to act as a buffer between the state and the public service broadcasting companies. The decision to set up the High Authority represented an attempt by the Socialists to remedy what was widely perceived as a defect of the postwar statist model: excessive governmental interference in key appointments and in political information. Criticism of right-wing interference in these areas made by the Socialists during their long period in opposition guaranteed a structural response in the 1982 legislation.

The Socialists recognized that French television suffered from a legacy of political control, whereby governments had pursued their own interests to the detriment of the implementation of the public service ethos. The Gaullist and Giscardian authorities had been conscious, perhaps too conscious, of the power of broadcasting as an ideological weapon. In their different ways they had sought to manipulate broadcasting for their own partisan purposes and to use it as an area for the exercise of political patronage. Control of broadcasting had become an ingrained facet of elite political culture, with state radio and television being perceived as legitimate spoils of electoral victory. As a result, television had come to be widely regarded as an integral part of the state apparatus: not just a legal monopoly, but a political one as well. One objective of the reorganization of broadcasting in 1982 was to break with this legacy. While the state would continue to determine the regulatory framework for broadcasting, it would not intervene in the day-to-day management of the companies.

The High Authority was set up to help achieve this objective, as well as to protect broadcasters from political interference from whatever source. In addition, the new body was given the task of ensuring that the broadcasting companies respected the public service norms contained in their operating conditions, for example with regard to news coverage. The High Authority was also responsible for granting licences to broadcast at the local level, for harmonizing the programme schedules of the state television companies and for representing French broadcasting in the relevant international agencies. Finally, the new body took over responsibility from the government for appointing the director generals in the state radio and television companies and also for the selection of a minority of the governors on the different boards. This power of appointment was a crucial break with the former practice of government patronage. Clearly, the High Authority represented a vital part of the new broadcasting arrangements and its role was considered central to their success.

The appointments procedure and composition of the High Authority were naturally subjects of fierce political controversy. The Moinot committee had recommended that the Authority should have nine members, only three of whom would be political appointments to be made by the President.[14] However, just as he had intervened in the selection of candidates to top broadcasting posts in the summer of 1981, Mitterrand took it upon himself to decide that the source of appointment of all nine members should be political: the President of the Republic would nominate three members including the chairperson, three would be chosen by the President of the National Assembly and the final three would be selected by the President of the Senate.[15] Since the President of the National Assembly was also a Socialist, fears were expressed that the authorities might pack the new body with their supporters, just as previous right-wing governments had packed the governing boards of first the ORTF (1964–74), and then the separate state companies (1974–81).

In fact the Socialists did not succumb to this temptation – at least, not in as crude a fashion as their predecessors. Of the nine members appointed to the High Authority in the summer of 1982, two (both of whom had been heads of broadcasting companies during the Giscard d'Estaing presidency) could be regarded as representing the Right or Centre–Right; another two had no clearly defined political leanings; of the others, one had sympathies for the Communist party and three for the Socialists. The chairperson of the new body, Michèle Cotta, who had been appointed head of Radio France in August 1981, was an experienced journalist whose professional reputation had been enhanced by her role as one of the two interviewers in the Giscard d'Estaing–Mitterrand television duel during the 1981 presidential election campaign. Her political sympathies were left of centre, but she was not politically tainted. Overall, the High Authority had a centre–left complexion in terms of the background of its members, but it was not markedly committed to the Mitterrand presidency.

Between 1982 and 1986 the High Authority managed with considerable success to establish itself as an independent agency in the broadcasting system. Unlike the board of governors at the ORTF, for example, it did not automatically assume a pro-governmental stance in political disputes. It upheld complaints of partial treatment from opposition politicians, most notably by the Gaullist party leader Jacques Chirac. In addition, during the municipal election campaign of 1983 the High Authority ensured that the television and radio companies maintained a party political balance in their output, while in the allocation of local radio frequencies the Authority's decisions were not determined by party political considerations.

One advantage of the High Authority for the broadcasters was that it became the focal point for complaints from political parties, interest groups and individuals, which in turn relieved the pressure on the managements and staffs of the individual broadcasting companies. Conversely, the interventions of the Authority were themselves not always welcomed by the channels, especially the journalists who sometimes voiced their resentment at what they regarded as illicit trespassing on their professional territory. Overall, however, the institution was a relative success. The Socialists had managed to create a body which supervised broadcasting without at the same time enjoying close or subordinate links with the authorities, a feat which had defied previous right-wing presidencies.

This did not mean that the existence of the High Authority led to the emergence in France of anything approaching a consensus regarding the political independence of the channels or the balance of their political output. The right-wing opposition contended that the High Authority was largely content to confirm the appointments to the top broadcasting posts made by the government prior to the enactment of the 1982 reform. Moreover, the Right argued that appointments made after the establishment of the High Authority, such as that of Hervé Bourges as director general of TF1 and in particular of Jean-Claude Héberlé as head of Antenne 2, were politically motivated. This last charge appears well founded. According to Cotta, the replacement of Pierre Desgraupes by Héberlé in 1984 was solicited by the Prime Minister, Laurent Fabius, whom she accuses of being hostile to the creation of the High Authority and of wishing to dominate, even tame, broadcasting.[16] Nor were criticisms of the Authority confined to the Right. The Communist party voiced complaints in 1982 that no Communist supporter had been nominated to the post of director general in any of the programme companies.[17] Members of the Socialist government and party also frequently expressed disapproval of the decisions of the High Authority.

Even allowing for the natural hyperbole of French opposition parties in condemning their alleged mistreatment at the hands of state radio and television, the Right did have a prima facie case. Despite the good offices of the High Authority, political output on the state television channels was not impeccably balanced or impartial. As in the past, the amount of coverage given the President, the government and the parties of the governing coalition far outweighed that accorded to the opposition. It proved very difficult for the Socialists to make a clean break with the tradition of political interference, since their support in principle for the application of public service ideals to political output clashed in practice with their desire to have their policies presented in a favourable light, particularly at times of economic crisis and electoral decline. Moreover, many journalists working in the television news departments were Socialist supporters. Yet at the same time political output was not nearly so crudely one-sided as it had been in the 1960s under the Gaullists. Also, most of the French press was sympathetic to the Right, an advantage which the Left had not enjoyed when in opposition.

Ultimately the main drawback of the High Authority was not so much that it was politically partisan, but rather that many of the most important developments in French television fell outside its jurisdiction. For example, the activities of the commercial channels were outside its remit. Indeed, the High Authority was not even consulted before the decision was taken in 1985 to set up two commercial television channels, a manoeuvre which

Cotta describes as marginalizing and even ridiculing the High Authority.[18] This may have been an indication of President Mitterrand's displeasure at the way in which Cotta had stood up against government interference in the appointment of company heads. Nor was the Authority consulted in advance on the drafting of the operating conditions of the new channel five. Whatever the explanation for this marginalization, the result was that the High Authority was never a major player in the key policy decisions which determined the configuration of the television system in the mid-1980s. Its abolition by the incoming right-wing government in 1986 was more a symbolic revanchist measure than an acknowledgement of the High Authority's power or its partisan behaviour.

THE LAUNCH OF CANAL PLUS

In the arena of television the abandonment of the state's programming monopoly first made its impact on the French public in November 1984 when a fourth channel, christened Canal Plus, was launched. This was the first new television channel in France for 12 years. In contrast to the three existing channels, Canal Plus was not integrated within the state broadcasting system; rather it was run by the multimedia conglomerate Havas.[19] Yet though Havas with its advertising, media and tourism interests operated in a commercial environment, the company enjoyed close links with the authorities. The state owned just over half of its shares and could steer company policy through its control of appointments to top management.

The crossover of personnel between the state and the Havas board provided a particularly important link for the authorities.[20] The chairman of Havas in 1984 was André Rousselet, who had been director of Mitterrand's presidential *cabinet* until the summer of 1982 and was known to be a close associate of the President.[21] While at the Elysée, Rousselet had been actively involved in drafting the 1982 broadcasting reform and had helped supervise the top appointments in state radio and television made by the Socialists in the aftermath of their 1981 election victory. A key figure in shaping Socialist government attitudes towards the broadcast media, Rousselet was given responsibility for the establishment of Canal Plus and later became the television company's first chairman.[22]

It was apparent, therefore, that the state authorities had a vested interest in doing everything they could to facilitate the entry of the new channel into the market. Though Canal Plus was not part of the state monopoly, the Mitterrand presidency did not want this major new broadcasting initiative to be stillborn. On the contrary, the state wanted to stack the odds to ensure the channel's success. It is scarcely surprising, then, that for one commentator Canal Plus represented 'a new, more indirect mode of state intervention rather than a real disengagement',[23] while others have argued that 'rather than liberalization, Canal Plus revealed the desire of the authorities to pursue a gentle deregulation of the audiovisual sector'.[24]

One advantage that Canal Plus enjoyed from the beginning was the existence of a vacant terrestrial transmission network, the use of which reduced capital investment costs and guaranteed the channel coverage of virtually the whole of the national territory within a year of start-up.[25] The question Rousselet and Mitterrand's media policy advisers had to resolve was what sort of channel would prove viable in competition with the output of the three state networks. Possible options of a cultural, educational or 'alternative' channel were explored in the early 1980s and then rejected because of the difficulty of resolving the problem of funding.[26] The novel option decided on was a pay-television channel which would market itself on providing the viewer with a different programme schedule from the mixed diet of the three public service networks. In return for a monthly subscription on top of the annual television licence fee, subscribers would be able to watch programmes, especially films, not available to the mass audiences of TF1, Antenne 2 and FR3.

The Canal Plus venture was by no means assured of success and for a while it looked as if its initial 12-year franchise was wildly optimistic. In the early months after its launch, the channel encountered various problems. The first was attracting subscribers. Concentrating on major urban areas in the first instance, Havas hoped that a sufficient number of subscribers would be quickly found to make the new service commercially viable. However, this proved far from easy as consumers showed a marked reluctance to take out subscriptions for an unfamiliar product. In fact, for some months the continued existence of the channel was very much in doubt. In the summer of 1985, for instance, Prime Minister Laurent Fabius argued that the pay channel should be abandoned and Rousselet had to seek President Mitterrand's support to continue with the venture.[27]

The slow subscription take-up gave rise to financial difficulties as income fell below projected estimates. Initially it had been intended that Canal Plus would be funded through a combination of viewer subscription and programme sponsorship by commercial companies. The advantage of these financial arrangements for the state was that since Canal Plus would be self-financing, no extra strain would be placed on the already overloaded licence fee system. It was also originally envisaged that the channel would make no demands on the commercial advertising sector, which was so important for the budgets of the state television networks. However, in March 1985, in an attempt to boost income, Canal Plus was permitted to show advertising. The programme schedule of the new channel was also amended towards a greater emphasis on feature films to boost subscriptions. A two-track service was established. The encrypted part of the programme output remained without advertising breaks and concentrated on feature films and sport. The non-encrypted element of the schedule showed advertising and tended towards game shows and variety programmes.[28]

The programming of feature films by Canal Plus aroused the greatest controversy. The total number of feature films to be screened, the interval between general release in the cinema and their transmission by Canal Plus, and the quota of French productions, were all subjects of fierce debate between the channel and the French film industry. The fears expressed by the film industry on these issues were perfectly understandable, given that the implantation of television had coincided with a decline in cinema attendance in France. A new channel using feature films for much of its output might mark the death knell of French cinema. The agreement finally hammered out between Canal Plus and the cinema industry covered four essential points: first, the number of films shown could be as many as 320 per annum, almost one new film a day; second, films could be shown six to 18 months after general release compared with two to three years for the state channels; third, they could be shown on every day of the week, whereas the state channels were restricted to certain days only; and, finally, in return for these concessions, Canal Plus would spend 25 per cent of its operating budget on feature films.[29] Overall, these arrangements were to prove particularly beneficial for the pay channel.

In contrast to the three state channels, Canal Plus was bound by very few public service obligations. Its operating conditions published in 1986, for example, contained only 26 provisions compared with 155 for Antenne 2.[30] Canal Plus was not specifically obliged to have news programmes, cultural programmes or a balanced schedule. As a result, it was much less constrained than the three state networks with regard to its programme policy. Canal Plus was free to concentrate on carving out a market niche for itself. This it did by focusing its output on films and sport, including 'live' coverage of major sporting events such as French league football. To maximize its film audience, Canal Plus introduced the system of 'multi-diffusion', whereby a film was shown three to six times over a two-week period at different times of the day. It also transmitted for 20 hours a day during the week and 24 hours a day at weekends.

As with the development of cable, the establishment of Canal Plus formed an integral part of the government's policy to build up the national electronics industry as a principal growth sector in the economy.[31] The decoders which subscribers had to rent to descramble the transmission signal were manufactured in France. In addition, as many older television sets were unable to receive Canal Plus even with a decoder, the government expected an increase in the sale of television sets, most of which it hoped would be French made. The launching of Canal Plus, therefore, conformed to a long-standing governmental objective, which pre-dated the Mitterrand presidency: the protection and encouragement of the domestic television manufacturing industry.

The new fourth channel was also part and parcel of an attempt by the French government to minimize the penetration of foreign video cassette recorders into France. This included the decision in 1982 to impose *de facto* import controls on the importation of video recorders from Japan by channelling them through one small customs post at Poitiers. The short-lived annual tax on video ownership complemented this strategy of dampening down demand for a foreign import. Canal Plus was intended to soak up the demand for video recorders and keep French viewers watching a French medium and, if possible, a French product.

Once its teething problems had been successfully overcome, Canal Plus went on to demonstrate that French viewers were willing to pay a sub-scription in addition to the licence fee for a different type of television programming. After nine months in operation the pay channel had 400,000 subscribers and by the beginning of 1986 it reached break-even point at 700,000. As well as providing a financial cushion for the company in the years ahead, this statistical breakthrough showed that there was room for expanding the sources of television supply in France. The Socialist government, however, had not required this evidence before proceeding to open up the market further. As Canal Plus was still struggling to find its feet, President Mitterrand announced the creation of new commercial channels.

THE INTRODUCTION OF COMMERCIAL TELEVISION

The difficulties Canal Plus experienced in attracting subscribers in the early months of 1985 were not just attributable to problems with the decoding equipment or to the initial reluctance of consumers to embrace a new and untested product. The launch of the pay channel was undermined by other initiatives taken by the French state in the audiovisual policy field. Barely a few weeks after Canal Plus began transmissions, President Mitterrand unexpectedly gave his support for the establishment of two commercial television channels funded from advertising revenue. With impeccable Cartesian logic many French viewers preferred to wait for these new 'free' channels to come on stream rather than impose on themselves the extra burden of taking out a subscription to Canal Plus.

Once the President had made his wishes known, the apparatus of the state was mobilized to convert the presidential will into a coherent set of policy proposals. A committee under the chairmanship of Jean-Denis Bredin was set up to examine the possibility of 'rapidly increasing the different means of transmitting television programmes'.[32] It was asked to present its report within the short time span of three months. Among its many recommendations, the Bredin committee proposed the creation of two new national channels, which, because of technical constraints, would initially be available to about one-third of French households.[33] Following the report's publication, the government rushed to make the necessary technical and administrative arrangements so that two privately owned channels could be in operation by early 1986. The best efforts of the opposition leader and Mayor of Paris, Jacques Chirac, to frustrate the government's plans by trying to block the use of the Eiffel Tower as a transmission point were to no avail, though he bowed to the inevitable only when the 'forces of order' were called in to ensure access to the engineers! The whole policy process – from the presidential announcement to the first programmes of the new channels – took almost exactly a year to complete, an astonishingly short length of time by the standards of British government policy making in the broadcasting sector.

The Socialist government awarded the franchise for channel five (La Cinq) to the Italian media magnate Silvio Berlusconi, and to two French businessmen whose political sympathies for Mitterrand were common knowledge. Berlusconi's Fininvest company already controlled a huge slice of private television in Italy.[34] His friendship with the Italian Socialist party leader Bettino Craxi, and his success in the private sector of Italian television programming, were enough to persuade Mitterrand of the suitability of his political and commercial credentials.

Financed from commercial advertising, La Cinq was a general entertainment channel whose schedule in these early months was a none too subtle mix of game shows, cheap programmes from western Europe, even cheaper programmes from the United States and old feature films. Its statutory obligations with regard to programming were considerably less onerous than those applied to the state channels. In fact, initially they were virtually non-existent, such was the Socialist government's desire to see La Cinq in operation as quickly as possible. The new fifth channel was soon followed by a sixth, TV6, whose main shareholders were the advertising group Publicis and the film distribution company Gaumont. Also financed from advertising, TV6 was primarily a music channel aimed specifically at the youth market. One of its primary sources of programming was video-clips produced by the music industry.

Unlike the state's promotion of the new media of cable and satellite, the establishment of two new terrestrial channels was not technologically driven. Nor did the policy form part of a coherent plan to build up a new information and communications infrastructure. Instead, the motivation behind this initiative was political rather than technocratic, with the whole policy-making process smacking of short-term opportunism on the part of the government. The dominant framework within which this policy output must be placed is the electoral context of a Socialist party facing annihilation at the polls in the 1986 general election, the first since the Left's *annus mirabilis* of 1981. In an attempt to limit the damage to his party, President Mitterrand had already engineered a change in the electoral system to one based on proportional representation. Despite this manoeuvre, however, the Right were still widely expected to win an overall parliamentary majority. If so, Gaullists and Giscardians would then be in a position to introduce commercial television, allocate the franchises to their supporters and claim the credit for extending viewer choice. Broadcasting was an obvious area in which the liberal rhetoric with its emphasis on free enterprise and market forces could be given practical embodiment.

Mitterrand, secure in his own position at the Elysée until 1988, could not accept this scenario with equanimity. Intent on frustrating the Right and, if possible, boosting the electoral fortunes of the Socialists, he determined to launch his own pre-emptive strike. As his government performed its economic U-turn after 1982 and moved ideologically away from the left towards the centre ground of French politics, it had sought to project a new electoral image. Socialism was brusquely jettisoned and modernization became the vogue term of Laurent Fabius's premiership. The creation of private television channels perfectly encapsulated this ideological shift. It was a clear signal to the electorate that the Socialist party of the mid-1980s was a forward-looking, pragmatic force which could give realization to consumer demands for greater choice.

At the same time, Mitterrand hoped to boost his own flagging popularity. The President seized the opportunity to open up television to private entre-preneurs, just as he had legalized local radio at the start of his presidency, grabbing whatever kudos he could from the initiative at a time when his presidency was going through a sticky patch. Mitterrand also hoped to limit the freedom of manoeuvre of any incoming right-wing government by allocating the commercial television franchises in advance of the electoral contest. By the time the Right did win the election, albeit not as convincingly as the Left had feared, the two commercial channels were already in operation, transmitting programmes through the final days of the Socialist government.

THE SOCIALIST BROADCASTING REFORM IN RETROSPECT

The period of Socialist government between 1981 and 1986 marked a crucial turning-point in the French television system. The creation of Canal Plus and the introduction of commercial television finally buried the concept of the state monopoly. While the 1974 Giscardian reform had confined itself to a reorganization of state broadcasting, the 1982 Socialist statute introduced competition between the public and private sectors. Moreover, whereas in the past the television system had grown very slowly, with one channel being added every ten years or so, the Socialists had doubled the number of channels in less than five years. As the market was opened up to new players, the penury of the Gaullist–Giscardian era was replaced by a relative *embarras de richesses*, scarcely conceivable a few years previously.

Meanwhile, the creation of the High Authority represented an important, if limited, step in the direction of the political liberalization of broadcasting.

Of course, such a structural innovation could not change habits overnight. Long-established elite attitudes and patterns of behaviour remained, as traditional concerns regarding access, patronage and control of content continued to be raised. Appointments to key posts in broadcasting were still scrutinized by politicians and commentators for their political significance, while television's political output remained a contested arena, closely monitored by politicians of all parties for indications of bias. In short, the 1982 reform did not depoliticize the broadcasting issue in France.

Nor was the introduction of a more competitive system without its problems and contradictions. In particular the creation of La Cinq and TV6 did not fit into the coherent audiovisual communications policy announced by the Socialists in the early 1980s. The two commercial channels, introduced with such haste in 1985–86, soaked up some of the consumer demand for more television without contributing to the development of new technology, one of the prime goals of Socialist media policy. Nor did they use much indigenous production, thereby contributing very little to the stimulation of the domestic programme production sector. Their use of foreign programming also undermined the policy goal of using television to promote French culture. By 1986 it was legitimate to wonder why the Socialist authorities had made so much fuss about the undesirability of 'Coca-Cola satellites' transmitting into France, when only a few months later they were giving the go-ahead to channels which used so much non-French product. Finally, while the much criticized excesses of the Italian model were not replicated in France, the ultimate irony of Socialist policy in the mid-1980s was that it allowed the entry into the French television system of the media entrepreneur who had profited so much from Italian deregulation, Silvio Berlusconi. The attempt by the Socialists to open up competition in television in a controlled fashion had been sacrificed by Mitterrand on the altar of political expediency.

Chapter 7

Television: privatization and liberalization

One of the early reforms of the new conservative administration which governed France between 1986 and 1988 was a reorganization of broadcasting, the fifth major piece of legislation on this topic since the 1964 statute which established the ORTF. In line with the tradition of Fifth Republic politics in the field of audiovisual policy, the re-election of a government of the Right immediately called into question the Socialist administration's 1982 reform of radio and television. Indeed, if on returning to power in 1986 the Right had *not* introduced a new broadcasting statute, this would have been evidence of a huge change in the culture and behaviour of the political elites in France.

The 1986 statute on freedom of communication did not, however, involve a return to the *status quo ante* 1982. Too many changes had taken place in the intervening years for the Right to pretend that the Socialist media legacy could be dismantled *in toto*. In any case, there were some aspects of the Socialist reorganization which the conservative government could happily accept. The abolition of the state monopoly and the economic liberalization of the television system were welcomed. Conversely, the role and composition of the High Authority were anathema to the new administration and the establishment of a new regulatory authority was a priority. In some cases the government wanted to change the rules of the game by introducing structural changes to the system, such as the privatization of TF1. Elsewhere they were willing to accept the rules, but wanted to change the key players, as in the reallocation of the franchises for channels five and six. Overall, the policy followed between 1986 and 1988 accepted the commercializing thrust of the Socialist reform, extended it to embrace the concept of privatization and sought to ensure that persons and interests sympathetic to the Right dominated the new regulatory body and television company management.[1]

The 1986 reform has to be situated in the context of the political change which followed the general election result earlier that year. The widely predicted defeat of the Socialists led to the formation of a right-wing government, which commanded a small overall majority in Parliament.

Since this was the first time in the history of the Fifth Republic that the presidential and parliamentary majorities did not coincide, the potential for a major institutional crisis was evident. Even the possibility of a total breakdown in the functioning of the political system could not be ruled out. However, this latest test of the legitimacy of the regime was successfully negotiated by the political elites of Right and Left, both anxious to avoid a confrontational war of attrition which might damage their electoral appeal in the run-up to the 1988 presidential contest. Rather than leading to stalemate and political immobility, therefore, the 1986 election result opened the way for the constitutional experiment known as *cohabitation* between the presidency, still held by Mitterrand, and the government, now headed by the Gaullist Prime Minister Jacques Chirac. As a result, in the following two years it was the government which assumed responsibility for the formulation and implementation of policy, especially on domestic matters, while the President withdrew to a role more in keeping with the formal powers laid down in the 1958 constitution.[2] It was the conservative government, therefore, rather than the President, which piloted the 1986 broadcasting bill through Parliament.

The substance of this legislation formed part of a radical New Right agenda which had been adopted by many leading French conservatives in the 1980s. The main provisions of the 1986 broadcasting statute have to be understood, therefore, with reference to this new ideological climate, which during the short-lived government of the Right was to have a profound effect in various policy areas. The views of the conservative coalition on the respective roles of the state and the market in the provision of goods and services had been strongly influenced by the spread of New Right ideas from across the Atlantic. These had flourished in academic circles in the United States and provided the theoretical underpinning for policy formulation in various fields there, including broadcasting and telecommunications.[3]

In the French political context of the early 1980s, the intellectual ascendancy of these radical views within the ranks of the French Right allowed the Gaullist–Giscardian opposition to differentiate themselves from the Socialist government in terms of their electoral discourse on public policy issues. The Right's commitment to rolling back the frontiers of the state and their emphasis on the primacy of private enterprise and market forces contrasted with the statist approach adopted by the Left in the period immediately following the 1981 presidential and parliamentary victories. The championing of the goals of privatization and deregulation was used by the Right as a battle cry against the Socialist government.

Yet Socialist thinking on the appropriate role of the state in the economy also evolved during the 1980s. The 1982 nationalization measures represented the high-water mark of state ownership in the French economy. In retrospect, however, they seem to have signified more of a symbolic than a substantive extension of state control. They were part of a self-conscious attempt by the first government of the Left in the Fifth Republic to link itself with previous left-wing administrations, such as the Popular Front government of the 1930s and the postwar Tripartite coalition, both of which had nationalized important utilities. Once the state sector had been extended in 1982, however, the Socialists allowed the heads of the nationalized industries to run their firms on commercial lines. During their five years in government, therefore, the Socialists proved themselves to be very pragmatic when it came to the economic management of the state sector, in contrast to the more ideological rhetoric which they had espoused in the 1981 election campaigns.

The 1982 nationalization measures had also grown out of the postwar approach to economic management and welfare provision which had emphasized the positive features of state intervention. This approach had to a large extent cut across traditional ideological divisions in the party spectrum. As we saw in chapter 4, a belief in a powerful state, not just in defence and foreign affairs but also in economic management, had been a central plank of the Gaullist party during the de Gaulle presidency. The 1980s, however, witnessed a move away from this support for state intervention in the economy, an important ideological shift in the attitudes and beliefs of the Gaullists.[4] As a result of the impact of new ideas on policy makers in both government and opposition, the ideological climate in the mid-1980s was less favourable to state ownership and control of industrial firms and financial companies than it had generally been throughout the postwar period.

The new government of the Right provided concrete evidence of this change in the elite *Zeitgeist* with the announcement of an ambitious set of privatization proposals. Covering groups in the industrial, banking and media sectors of the economy, including the powerful advertising and media company Havas, this programme was designed to highlight the radical credentials of the new administration.[5] According to Bauer, the objective of the privatization programme was twofold: 'to make the French a nation of shareholders in the name of participation . . . and to restrict the economic role of the State'.[6] Privatization was not confined to the denationalization of companies and firms taken into the public sector in 1982. It also included companies originally nationalized by de Gaulle after the Second World War – a legacy of the Resistance which governments of Left and Right had not dared tamper with during the following four decades.

Though controversial, the programme was implemented with breathtaking speed:

Within a year the Chirac government, with its policy of privatisation, pulled off a remarkable political and economic success. With eleven flotations it privatised eight large groups [including Havas and TF1] and three medium-sized banks . . . the government carried out within one year a third of its five year programme.[7]

By February 1988 nearly half of the planned programme had been completed. Of the 65 companies on the government's list, 29 had been returned to the private sector, affecting around 500,000 workers, and the sales had produced an income of approximately 120 billion francs.[8] The number of shareholders in France had increased from 1.5 million in 1981 to 8 million by the end of 1987.[9]

THE 1986 STATUTE ON FREEDOM OF COMMUNICATION

The three main objectives of the 1986 broadcasting legislation were, first, to reduce the level of state ownership in the French media, primarily through the privatization of TF1; second, to make the system more competitive and less hidebound by regulation; and finally, to replace the Socialist regulatory authority with a new body more sympathetic to the Right. While the realization of these objectives signalled a change in the nature of the relationship between the state and the broadcast media, it certainly did not indicate a complete withdrawal by the former from this area of activity. After 1986 the state's ownership role declined, continuing a trend established by the Socialists. However, the state continued to play a major regulatory role, not just in setting out the different normative frameworks for public and private sector television, but also in controlling appointments to the new regulatory body which replaced the High Authority. The state's pursuit of privatization and lighter regulation had to be offset, therefore, by activity which sought to maintain a highly interventionist and partisan role for the authorities.

An early manifestation of this interventionist tendency concerned the franchise allocations for channels five and six. As we saw in the previous chapter, the channels had been set up in early 1986 in a classic spoiling operation intended to confront the incoming right-wing government with a *fait accompli* which could not easily be overturned. None the less, the new conservative administration was more than willing to rise to the challenge. In August 1986 the channel five franchise, which had originally been awarded to the Berlusconi–Seydoux–Riboud consortium, was revoked. Predictably, the consortium claimed damages in the law courts.

After the passing of the 1986 statute in September a compromise solution was arranged. At the beginning of 1987 the new regulatory authority, the National Commission for Communication and Liberties (CNCL), awarded the channel five franchise to a consortium led by Hersant (25 per cent) and Berlusconi (25 per cent) in preference to a rival bid from a group headed by Sir James Goldsmith. Seydoux, the left-wing industrialist, saw his share in La Cinq fall from 62 per cent to 10 per cent. According to Palmer and Tunstall, the Chirac government had previously urged the Havas conglomerate not to bid for the channel five franchise, after Hersant had chosen to bid for La Cinq in preference to the more expensive TF1.[10] The result of these political and economic manoeuvres was that while Berlusconi remained a key figure in La Cinq, Hersant became the main driving force. The leading press baron in France had succeeded in adding television to his other media interests in newspapers and radio. At the same time the channel six franchise was taken from TV6, despite the fact that the predominantly pop music and video-clip channel had built up a mainly young audience of a very respectable 1.5 million by February 1987.[11] The CNCL awarded the new franchise to a consortium led by La Lyonnaise des Eaux (whose chairman, Jérôme Monod, was a former general secretary of the Gaullist party) and the Luxembourg audiovisual group, CLT.

The reallocation of the channel five and six franchises was a sideshow, however, to the main elements of the 1986 reform: the privatization of TF1 and the creation of a new regulatory body to replace the High Authority. Indeed, the privatization of TF1, the equivalent of privatizing BBC1 in Britain, was in many ways the centre-piece of the 1986 statute – the jewel in the crown of the Right's audiovisual reform package. Not only was it a symbolic and substantive embodiment of the principle of private ownership in television; it was also a rebuff to Mitterrand, showing that the Right's freedom of manoeuvre to innovate had not been as constricted as the President had intended. Yet at the same time, by introducing a powerful and aggressive competitor into the fragile commercial television sector, the conservative government's faith in the primacy of private ownership was to have crucial destabilizing consequences for French television. Paradoxically, and to the chagrin of champions of the free market, it was to lead to the collapse of a privately owned, commercially funded channel barely five years later.

By 1985 TF1 had established itself as the most popular television channel in France, overtaking its traditional rival Antenne 2, which had prospered in the early 1980s under Desgraupes. Under the management of Hervé Bourges, the channel had climbed its way back up the ratings with a mix of entertainment and information programming subject to public service regulations.[12] Though funded in large part from advertising, TF1 also received revenue from the licence fee. Consequently, one electoral advantage of the privatization of TF1 was that the government could promise viewers a reduction in the level of the television licence, since the company would cease to receive any funds from the public purse.

Despite this electoral carrot, the privatization of TF1 was very controversial. It was regarded with hostility by the opposition in Parliament, who argued that it would have a massive dislocating impact on the television system as a whole. Many media professionals were also critical of the change of status, while opinion polls showed a majority of the French public opposed to the privatization.[13] The government's credibility was not enhanced by the open disagreement on which channel to privatize between

François Léotard, the Giscardian Minister of Communication responsible for piloting the reform through Parliament, and the Gaullist Prime Minister Chirac. Bourges argues that Léotard wanted to privatize Antenne 2, while Chirac preferred FR3. In the end, TF1 was a compromise solution.[14]

The conflict to win the TF1 franchise was keenly fought. Edouard Balladur, the minister responsible for the privatization programme, valued the company at 4.5 billion francs. Fifty per cent of the shares were to be allocated to the winning consortium, with 10 per cent reserved for TF1 employees and 40 per cent for the general public. Though the company had an established track record, the purchase price was generally considered to be high. Moreover, to gain its 50 per cent stake, the successful consortium had to pay 3 billion francs, a sum defended by the government on the basis of TF1's potential earning capacity over the ten-year life of the franchise.[15]

After the surprise withdrawal of Havas from the consortium led by Hachette, the battle lines were drawn between a regrouped Hachette consortium (which included among its members *Le Monde*, the British television company TV South, the Spanish newspaper *El Pais* and various French banks) and a consortium dominated by the Bouygues construction group. The Bouygues consortium, led by the company chairman Francis Bouygues, included the Robert Maxwell empire and some French publishing houses among its ranks.

Maxwell's participation in the Bouygues consortium was part of a wider diversification strategy by his own communications group into the French media in the mid-1980s. He had already been enticed in 1985 into buying a stake in the French satellite broadcasting project, TDF1, though the deal had eventually fallen through because of the change of government in 1986.

> 'Mitterrand', recalls one of the aides, 'sensed that there could be some benefits from Maxwell. By then we feared annihilation at the polls. The political climate was against us. We were friendless, especially among the media barons and here was a Francophile press magnate, a man who gave the impression that he was the biggest in the world, offering us, the socialists, his friendship. The opportunity was too good to miss.'[16]

To curry favour with the then Socialist government Maxwell also purchased the ailing press agency, Agence Centrale de Presse, which had been set up by the prominent Socialist politician Gaston Defferre after the war. In addition, he made an abortive bid for the Provençal newspaper group (another Defferre legacy in trouble), failed in an attempt to secure a stake in Havas and announced plans to launch a popular French daily newspaper, which in the end came to nothing.[17]

Maxwell's main sortie into France, however, was his participation in the Bouygues consortium for a controlling interest in TF1. According to Bower, his support had been sought after by the Bouygues company who were looking to foreign backers to give their bid international weight:

Bouygues's unsolicited invitation was motivated not only by the Frenchman's need for extra cash but also because no one else in his consortium had any connection with either television or daily newspapers. Bouygues's application needed credibility and without Maxwell the prospects of success were reduced, not least because Bouygues's foremost rival was a consortium including the Hachette publishing company and *Le Monde*. At that moment, the Hachette consortium . . . was the favourite.[18]

In an early test of the political independence of the CNCL, the new authority awarded the TF1 franchise to the Bouygues consortium. The Bouygues group itself gained a 25 per cent share of the television company, while Maxwell obtained a 12.5 per cent stake. Lacan argues that in rejecting what appeared to be the government-backed front-runner bid from Hachette, the CNCL recognized the force of opinion expressed by different players in the lobbying process, many of which converged to block Hachette. These views included:

> those of the Hersant group, which feared to see its principal competitor in the press become its main rival in television. Those of television writers and producers, who have judged the promises by Hachette inadequate and have made this known loud and clear. Those of the Socialists, who have clearly campaigned against 'the candidate of the Prime Minister's office'. . . . How could the CNCL remain insensitive to such a convergence of views when in the past few days the government itself seemed to abandon Hachette after having supported it in too clumsy a fashion?[19]

For Palmer and Tunstall, the victory of the Bouygues consortium symbolized a new order in French broadcasting:

> the success of France's leading public works construction group in 'acquiring' TF1 signified even more clearly how new groups were entering the communications industry; and how the politico-cultural preoccupations that had marked French broadcasting for generations were no longer relevant.[20]

In the wake of their victory, Bouygues became chairman of TF1, Patrick Le Lay was appointed vice-chairman and Maxwell formally took the title of director general. However, relations between Bouygues and Maxwell were never cordial. Bouygues wanted to manage his new asset directly and became increasingly hostile to what he regarded as undesirable interference by Maxwell. By the summer of 1988 Maxwell lacked any direct influence over TF1's management, having been outwitted by Bouygues and Le Lay.[21] Announcing his intention to pull out of TF1 in February 1991, he sold his stake in the French channel a few months later.[22]

The second main feature of the 1986 statute was the transfer of the regulatory function to a new body, the CNCL. This had substantially greater powers and resources than those enjoyed by its predecessor, the High Authority, including some the Socialist government had continued to exercise between 1982 and 1986. The CNCL acquired the authority to regulate telecommunications as well as broadcasting. Within the audio-visual sphere, its regulatory scope included the private sector as well as public service radio stations and television channels. For example, the CNCL was responsible for the franchise allocations of TF1, La Cinq and M6 (the successor to TV6) in 1987. Like its predecessor, it also had formal authority to appoint the heads of the public service broadcasting companies and to allocate private local radio franchises.

However, despite the increased role for the CNCL, the state continued to retain important powers in the audiovisual field. With the support of a sympathetic parliamentary majority, the government managed the legislative process and so could define the structural and operational parameters of the broadcasting system. It was the government, for instance, which decided that TF1 should be privatized. The government also continued to fix the level of the licence fee and in effect thereby controlled the total amount of public resources devoted to the public sector component of the broadcasting system. Through its power to draw up regulatory provisions, the state was also able to impose programming and production requirements on Antenne 2, FR3 and even the privatized TF1 (such as the number of feature-length films to be shown and regulations concerning advertising).[23]

The final major feature of the 1986 legislation consisted of a detailed set of provisions to tackle the thorny issue of concentration of media ownership. Under the traditional state monopoly system before 1982, cross-media ownership had not been an issue: French radio and television belonged to the state. Private commercial interests, whether French or foreign, had no say in the management of this jealously guarded asset. However, the legalization of private local radio, the official go-ahead for cable television networks, the introduction of Canal Plus, the establishment of channels five and six and the privatization of state media assets including TF1 opened up ownership of French broadcasting to domestic and foreign companies. Many French media firms, including press groups and publishing houses, had sought to diversify into the burgeoning radio and television sectors. Meanwhile, leading European media entrepreneurs, such as Berlusconi and Maxwell had also rushed to grab a stake in this fast-expanding audiovisual market with their holdings in La Cinq and TF1 respectively.

Concentration of media ownership in the hands of a few companies was a worrying development in the eyes of many. In the case of foreign companies, there was a clear risk that national cultural values would not be respected. Yet even if the firms were French-owned, there was still the danger of an unacceptable narrowing of the range of views expressed in the media: a diminution in the capacity of the media to reflect the diversity of opinion in society. Moreover, as the example of the Murdoch empire in the UK demonstrates, cross-media ownership tends to lead to the output of one media sector in the group being given unduly favourable coverage by other media outlets of the same group. One graphic illustration of this negative synergy of media diversification was revealed by a study which undertook a comparative analysis of the views of *Le Figaro* and *France-Soir* on the programme output of La Cinq. This demonstrated the extent to which the views of the newspapers changed from negative to positive after the Hersant group, which happened to own both newspapers, was allocated the franchise for the fifth television channel.[24]

Conversely, the conservative government was conscious that by European and global standards, French media companies are not particularly large. The argument in favour of greater concentration within the domestic media was that this would allow French companies such as Havas and Hersant to compete on a more level playing field with other European, Japanese and American companies. The dilemma for the French is that the national market is not large enough both to sustain a wide range of domestic media players and, at the same time, provide France with companies which can compete with the global giants on equal terms. The authorities feared that if ownership regulations to protect pluralism at the domestic level were too strict, then French companies might lose out in the international marketplace.

In tackling the issue of concentration of media ownership in 1986 the role of the Constitutional Council was crucial.[25] Stone describes the background to the Council's intervention as follows.

The Chirac government's audiovisual bill was designed to privatise the broadcast industry and to deregulate the communications sector as a whole. The Left, seeking an effective means of structuring privatisation, sought to extend the constitutional politics of press pluralism to the audiovisual industry. The government could respond that broadcasting was unlike the press sector in at least one crucial respect. In 1986 private capital did not pose an existing challenge to pluralism, since the state's longtime broadcasting monopoly constituted the only important concentration in the field. Moreover, because the bill would create wider access to broadcasting rights, its legislative effect, at least at this stage in the development of the industry, could only be to favour pluralism. That said, the government actively sought to encourage the formation of media groups. The French telecommunications industry, the government argued, was far less concentrated and therefore less competitive internationally than the German, Dutch or even the British ones.

Nevertheless, fear of Council censure led the government to include anti-trust provisions. In brief, for television channels, rules were based upon a maximum interest (25 per cent) any one person or group could hold; for radio frequencies, the bill relied on generous fixed ceilings for maximum potential audience. The Socialists argued that the law as written would allow unacceptably high degrees of concentration of ownership and the formation of multi-media conglomerates. On 18 September 1986 the Council agreed and annulled 14 articles of the legislation and provided instructions as to how the bill should be revised . . . a single bill to 'correct' both the press and audiovisual legislation was adopted and promulgated, with the government choosing to incorporate the precise language of the decisions directly into the censured provisions. As a result, an elaborate anti-trust regime governing the whole of multi-media communications, inclusive of cable and satellite broadcasting, emerged with strict limits on the development of multi-media groups.[26]

According to Stone, the supplementary legislation introduced in November to conform with the Constitutional Council's ruling testified to the growing authority of the Council as a specialized, third chamber of Parliament with a growing impact on the legislative process.

In these and many other cases, the Council exercised its veto authority over important legislative priorities. It also, however, demonstrated its creative capacity to recast the policy-making environment, to encourage certain legislative solutions and undermine others and to insert the precise terms of its jurisprudence into legislative provisions. The virtual *constitutionalisation* of anti-trust mechanisms based on fixed market ceilings provides a dramatic example. . . . The Chirac government felt obliged to extend complex and multi-dimensional ceilings to the whole of communications, in spite of the fact that one central priority of its programme was to permit the emerging audiovisual sector to develop free from such shackles. The anti-trust formulas now prevalent in this area have acquired a kind of indirect constitutional value of their own.[27]

The conservative government's desire to keep cross-media ownership provisions flexible was held in check, therefore, not so much by the expected opposition of the Left as by the intervention of the Constitutional Council. The result was a highly complex set of anti-concentration provisions in the media sector, covering the press, broadcasting and the new media at local, regional and national levels. The legislation set ceilings on ownership both within and across different media. For example, no person or group could own more than a 25 per cent stake in any one national television channel or more than a 15 per cent stake in any two. A national press group (already limited under the 1986 press legislation to a maximum of 30 per cent of total daily circulation) could have a stake in a national television company provided that its radio interests did not cover a potential audience of more than 30 million inhabitants and its cable interests more than 6 million inhabitants. Under the same provisions, a national television company could have shares in a national radio company (i.e. one with a potential audience of more than 30 million), provided that its interests in cable did not exceed a potential audience of 6 million and its press interests did not exceed 20 per cent of circulation. However, a national television company could not run another terrestrially transmitted television service at either the local or national level. Yet while these ceilings were precise, they were also extremely generous. No media company had to sell off any of its existing shareholdings. More particularly, the provisions did nothing to prevent the Hersant press group from taking the maximum 25 per cent stake in the consortium which made the successful bid for the channel five franchise.[28]

THE 1989 REFORMS

Mitterrand's second presidential election success in 1988 was followed by the dissolution of Parliament, a general election and the constitution of a minority Socialist government under the premiership of Michel Rocard.[29] Though Mitterrand had been fiercely opposed to the privatization of TF1, the Socialists accepted the new status quo in the balance between the public and commercial sectors of French television. TF1 would remain in the enlarged private sector, leaving Antenne 2 and FR3 as the residual lump of the old state monopoly. There were, however, aspects of the broadcasting system which the Socialists wanted to reform, even if they did not wish to introduce a totally new comprehensive reorganization.

The specific areas of concern targeted by the Socialist government covered, first, the composition and functions of the regulatory authority and, second, the organization and status of the public sector channels. Under the first heading, the main objective was to replace the CNCL with a new regulatory body. The professional credibility and political independence of the CNCL had never been very high. With a total of 13 members it was a larger and more cumbersome decision-making forum than its predecessor, the High Authority. More importantly, a clear majority of its members, including its chairman Gabriel de Broglie, held barely concealed political sympathies for the Right.[30] In fact, some of the CNCL members had been part of the broadcasting establishment under Giscard d'Estaing, Pompidou and de Gaulle.[31] As a result, from the outset the new authority was considered suspect by many media professionals and non-government politicians.

Such suspicions were not dispelled by the manner in which the CNCL went about its business. In December 1986 it appointed to the top managerial posts in the public sector broadcasting companies persons in the main closely identified with the Gaullist party, including Claude Contamine as chairman and director general of Antenne 2.

'The names of the chairmen were proposed by the [Gaullist] party itself,' one of the Commission members said. 'As eight commissioners are connected with the Gaullist party, their appointment was automatic.'[32]

The allocation of the channel five franchise to a consortium led by the former Gaullist deputy Robert Hersant and the channel six franchise to a consortium which included Jérôme Monod in its ranks reinforced the impression of a regulatory authority which sought primarily to accommodate the interests of government supporters. The CNCL's role in the dismissal from TF1 of Michel Polac, the host of a popular late-night discussion programme which often poked fun at the political establishment, brought it into further disrepute. The Commission was also accused of abusing its powers for political purposes in the allocation of local radio frequencies in the Paris region. In short, the functioning of the CNCL did little to boost elite or public confidence in the independence or efficiency of the authority. President Mitterrand's public condemnation of the authority in September 1987 was a clear indication that the CNCL would not survive a change of government in 1988.

The criticisms directed by Mitterrand and the Socialists against the CNCL during the period of *cohabitation* were echoed during the 1988 presidential election campaign. Several candidates, and not just those on the Left, announced that if they were elected the CNCL would be replaced by a new authority. In his *Letter to the French People*, Mitterrand went so far as to demand that the new authority become part of the Constitution, a move which he argued would establish real guarantees of independence for broadcasting *vis-à-vis* the government.[33]

The new regulatory authority, the Higher Audiovisual Council (CSA), was established by new legislation at the beginning of 1989. Like the High Authority, its composition was modelled on that of the Constitutional Council.[34] Jacques Boutet, a former managing director of TF1 in the early months of the first Socialist government, was appointed chairman by Mitterrand. In contrast to the CNCL, the CSA tried to project a non-partisan image, independent of the government. For instance, it did not replace the incumbent director generals of the public sector companies, preferring to keep them in post until the end of their period of appointment. Nor did the CSA reallocate any radio frequency or annul any television franchise awarded by the CNCL. Even the new transmitters granted by the CNCL to La Cinq and M6, but prohibited by the Conseil d'Etat, were given the go-ahead in the interest of presenting an image of non-partisanship.[35]

A division of labour was established by the legislation between the government and the CSA. The former retained responsibility for defining the general rules applicable to both public and private broadcasting companies as part of a conscious attempt to remedy some of the more serious problems in the functioning of the French television system. For example, the government established general rules defining the obligations of the channels in the areas of programme sponsorship, advertising and the screening of feature films, and laid down regulations covering the separation of the functions of producer and broadcaster.

The CSA was given the responsibility of negotiating a contract with the private sector channels within a framework laid down by the legislation and ensuring that the channels observed the terms of the contract. The norms would be more flexible than the old programming obligations and would take account of the economic and financial situation of the channel. The contract covers the amount of time devoted to the transmission of programmes in French and their scheduling; the amount of turnover devoted to the acquiring of broadcast rights for French-language feature films; the transmission of educative and cultural programmes; the maximum amount of time given to advertising and to sponsored programmes, as well as rules governing their insertion in the schedule (new legislation stated that a private channel television programme could be interrupted only once by an advertising break); and measures of support for the French film and television programme production industries. The CSA was also given the responsibility of controlling the respect by Canal Plus of its programme obligations, a task which the CNCL did not have (though Canal Plus did not fall under the aegis of the CSA as far as the pronouncement of sanctions was concerned). The CSA also awards licences for private radio stations.

As far as sanctions were concerned, the CSA would exercise greater powers of sanction in cases of non-respect of the programming obligations than had been enjoyed by the CNCL. The CNCL had recognized that the channels were not respecting the quotas of French production and the regulations governing advertising imposed by the law. However, while La Cinq had been fined, the structural problem had not been satisfactorily resolved. The new law allowed the CSA to reduce the length of time a station was authorized to continue broadcasting and to levy financial sanctions against stations which were in breach of the regulations.[36]

According to Delcros, the functioning of the CSA testifies to the problems the French government has experienced with regulatory authorities in the broadcasting field. The High Authority operated within narrow terms of reference, arguably too narrow, though the limited nature of its role may have been necessary for the new body to gain legitimacy in this highly politicized area of activity. The CNCL suffered from being given too many functions to perform, many of which were politically very controversial, especially the TF1, channel five and channel six franchise allocations. The CSA too has had to assume responsibilities in areas for which it is not really prepared. Moreover, while a great deal of emphasis has been placed on the imposition of specific regulations on the television channels, the CSA has been given very little discretion. The result is that the authority suffers from having to exercise responsibility without possessing sufficient power: it enforces sanctions, but does little to shape the regulations.[37]

In the summer of 1989 the Socialist government addressed the second broadcasting problem it had faced on returning to office: the plight of the public sector channels Antenne 2 and FR3. One of the major consequences of the privatization of TF1 was a radical change in the balance between the public and private sectors in French television. Antenne 2 and FR3 now represented only the public sector component of a much broader range of television channels. The formerly dominant public sector channels were now in the minority numerically and, more importantly, the audience ratings for the public sector channels compared poorly with those of their commercial rivals. In the highly competitive television market of the mid- to late 1980s, the two public sector channels had experienced all sorts of financial and industrial problems as their audience ratings plummeted.

For Antenne 2, the head-to-head competition with the privatized TF1 had proved particularly damaging. Though supposedly providing a public service, Antenne 2 had tried to maximize its audience in a struggle for advertising revenue, which represented 66 per cent of its total income (compared with under 30 per cent from licence revenue). Meanwhile, FR3 was facing similar problems to those of Antenne 2. Though nominally a regional channel, in reality FR3 was a national channel with some regional opt-out programming (notably regional news) and so was also involved in the nationwide competition for viewers and revenue.[38] Worryingly for their management, the public sector channels were notably unattractive to young viewers – the television audience of tomorrow. Antenne 2 and FR3 were experiencing nothing short of a legitimacy crisis, as the values of the public service ethos in broadcasting became devalued and emptied of real substantive content.[39] To put it another way, the public sector channels were in a mess.

The government wanted to rescue the ailing public sector, stop the damaging competition between Antenne 2 and FR3, make their programme schedules complementary and give some sense of coherence to the public sector side of the broadcasting system. In recognition of the common problems facing Antenne 2 and FR3, part of the government's response was the creation of a super-chairman of both channels, who was to be responsible for the harmonization of the two channels' programme output.[40] The first super-chairman, Philippe Guilhaume, appointed by the CSA in August 1989, never enjoyed the full confidence of the government and in the face of growing problems during 1990 resigned at the end of the year to be replaced by the former head of TF1 prior to privatization, Hervé Bourges.[41] The task facing Bourges was first to restore confidence in the public service mission among his broadcasting staff and then recapture a credible market share of the audience without merely imitating the programme formulae and scheduling policies of the commercial channels.

TELEVISION IN THE LIBERAL ERA

The problems faced by Antenne 2 and FR3 in the highly competitive television market of the late 1980s were by no means confined to the public sector channels. All television companies, including the newly privatized TF1, were having to learn to adapt to a new audiovisual environment in which the system had been rebalanced to favour the commercial sector and a market ethos. The conservative government's broadcasting initiatives had led to an even greater emphasis being placed on the need to achieve high audience ratings to bring in advertising revenue. While in theory the competition between the different companies was subject to regulation, in practice the system was driven by an overwhelmingly commercial logic, which led in some cases to regulations being overtly flouted as companies struggled to prosper and even just survive.

The major beneficiary of this competitive environment was TF1. The company was able to take advantage of its nationwide transmission network, its programming know-how and its sheer experience in the business to establish itself as the market leader. While as a public service channel in the early 1980s TF1 had been outgunned by Antenne 2, after privatization it was able to pursue the mass audience subject to fewer regulatory constraints. Since the channel would no longer be part funded from licence revenue, the privatization of TF1 had predictable consequences for the channel's programme output and scheduling, with greater emphasis being placed on maximizing the prime-time viewing audience.

> If MM. Bouygues and Le Lay had had cultural aspirations, the necessity to amortize the purchase price has certainly rapidly dissuaded them. The respect of the programming obligations cannot come at the top of their preoccupations.[42]

In such a competitive market, it is scarcely surprising that Bouygues tried to delay the extension of the transmission zones of both La Cinq and M6 or that he lobbied strongly to prevent the maintenance of advertising on the public sector channels. The commercial success of TF1 had to be secured. It was. By the early months of 1988 the channel was gaining over 50 per cent of market share compared with 38 per cent at the start of 1987. In 1989 it was steadily attracting well over 40 per cent of the audience and had captured about 50 per cent of the television advertising market. With its dominant position in the ratings, TF1 was a naturally attractive choice for advertisers wishing to target a mass nationwide audience. By November 1991 shares in the company had gone up in value by 152 per cent.[43]

TF1's successfully aggressive commercial stance had a knock-on effect on the rest of the television system. The two commercial channels, La Cinq and M6, had not had much time to establish themselves in the market before the privatization of TF1. La Cinq in particular had difficulty in carving out a niche for itself. Its strategy in 1987 of enticing established television stars to join the channel in the hope that audiences would follow the big names had not been a success. Audience ratings for La Cinq remained stubbornly low, while the critical publicity about the huge earnings of television's elite brought the strategy into disrepute. Because of its restricted transmission network, La Cinq's programmes (like those of M6) were not available nationwide and this too was an important drawback for the channel as it struggled to build up its audience share in competition with more established contenders, notably TF1.

La Cinq's miserably poor showing of a 7.4 per cent audience share in 1987 caused Berlusconi to argue that the channel screened too much news emanating from Hersant's press interests and insufficient entertainment.[44] Viewing figures for La Cinq stabilized from 1988 on, hovering between 10 per cent and 12.5 per cent . However, though the channel quickly reached a double-figure percentage audience share, it never succeeded in surpassing 13 per cent over the schedule as a whole. This was despite experimenting with no less than six different types of programme schedule between 1986 and 1992 in an attempt to boost its ratings. These included the 'tele-spaghetti' schedule of the early months under Berlusconi, the 'Coca-Cola schedule' of 1986–87 with its emphasis on US imported programming, the star-centred and news-oriented schedule of 1987–88, a complementary programme schedule to its competitors and a schedule centring on the channel's news provision following its successful 'live' coverage of the events in Romania in late 1989. None of these different scheduling policies succeeded in attracting audiences in sufficiently large numbers or from the socio-economic groups desired by advertisers. Despite some programme successes with serials and telefilms, La Cinq failed to be either a mass audience or a specialist upmarket channel.

In September 1989 the battle for control of La Cinq erupted into open warfare between Hersant and the other shareholders. Hersant was forced to concede defeat and in autumn 1990 he left. The Hachette company, which had lost out in the franchise bid for TF1, now took a 25 per cent stake in La Cinq to join Berlusconi as the joint main shareholder.[45] Between 1989 and 1991, while audience ratings continued to stagnate, advertising revenue dropped by 10 per cent, a loss of 200 million francs. At the same time programming costs increased by almost 30 per cent. A cumulative deficit of 3 billion francs since 1987 was announced. As a result of the channel's deteriorating financial position, 567 redundancies were made in December 1991, only a year after the Hachette takeover. This meant that more than two-thirds of posts in the company were terminated, while among the news staff 77 of the 104 journalists were made redundant. Though La Cinq had never had a clear image in terms of general programming, it had constructed one on the basis of its news provision. To destroy its news output meant that the whole channel was put in jeopardy.

In response, employees and viewers formed a pressure group, Association de défense de La Cinq et du pluralisme de la télévision, which grew from 600,000 members to more than 1,200,000 by the time of the channel's liquidation. According to Chartier, this pressure group activity confirmed the brand image of La Cinq as a channel which since the time of Hersant leant politically towards the Right.[46] The protest was to no avail. Though Berlusconi stepped in at the start of 1992 with a rescue project, he abandoned his plans in March. The massive financial problems of the channel and the difficulty Berlusconi experienced in finding French backers effectively scuppered any hopes of saving the channel from bankruptcy.[47] With a deficit of 4 billion francs by the end of its short life, the first commercial television channel in France ceased broadcasting on April 12 1992. Its transmission network was taken over by the joint Franco-German cultural channel, ARTE. La Cinq thus became the main victim of the liberal, market-oriented television system established in the late 1980s. Its demise also highlighted the way in which economics was becoming as important as politics in determining the fate of French television.

In contrast to the desperate fate of La Cinq, M6 prospered. By the end of 1989 it was attracting an 8 per cent market share. Though in itself this was not a particularly large proportion of the audience, the channel was especially popular among the 15–35 age group, an attractive target group for advertisers. Taking up the mantle inherited from its predecessor (TV6), M6 is obliged to transmit 30 per cent music per day and in fact transmits 35 per cent.[48] Music has become a major ingredient of the programme schedule, with over 100 video-clips being shown per day. Moreover, since the French clips are considered to be French audiovisual works, they count towards the channel's quota of home-produced programming. However, music is not shown at prime time since it does not attract a family audience. The programme strategy of the channel has been based on the notion of counter-programming, i.e. transmitting a product different from that shown on the other channels. For example, at 8pm when its competitors were transmitting news, M6 transmitted *The Cosby Show*. Anglo-American series and comedies became a mainstay of the channel's prime-time output, as did magazine programmes. The channel's news output was largely confined to news flashes/headline news, shown without a presenter. Overall, M6 has benefited from its close links with RTL (one of its two main owners is the CLT), with much of its news staff coming from the Luxembourg broadcasting company. The channel's staff are generally young and not marked by the tradition of public service television.

Alongside TF1, the major television success story of the liberal era has been Canal Plus. The growth in subscriptions since it reached the break-even point of 700,000 in early 1986 has been nothing short of spectacular. By the summer of the same year it had 1 million subscribers; by the autumn of 1987 2 million; by the end of 1988 over 2.5 million; by 1991 over 3 million; and by early 1992 it had 3.3 million subscribers, with the strong upward curve of the 1980s beginning to level off in the early 1990s. In addition, consumer satisfaction with the channel was very high: in 1990 95.4 per cent of subscribers renewed their annual subscription (94 per cent in 1989 and 93 per cent in 1988).[49]

Lunven and Vedel attribute the success of Canal Plus to three factors: favourable conditions surrounding its establishment; an innovative programme output; and what they term the 'club effect'. Canal Plus, they argue, came into existence at a time when demand was appearing for a more diversified television service which had not yet been satisfied either by other television channels or by cable. The channel benefited from a very sympathetic regulatory regime, while it also enjoyed a huge advantage with regard to the transmission of feature films, the central core of its output. At the same time, VCR penetration was less high in France than in Britain. Second, Canal Plus has broadcast a programme output very different from its competitors. Not only has it gained exclusive rights for the transmission of some programme genres (for example, recently released feature films and sports events), but it has also invented a new style of television, very different from that of the public service channels. Finally, Canal Plus has successfully marketed itself as a special club. The channel has fostered good links with its clientele by sophisticated marketing and by promoting the exclusivity of Canal Plus membership. It has emphasized the club element of Canal Plus subscription, appealing to the self-image subscribers have that they are part of a well-defined consumer group and not just viewers of another television channel. None the less, subscribers come from a wide cross-section of French society, with a bias towards young urban-dwelling families. Their importance to the company's commercial success can be gauged by the fact that in 1990 viewer subscriptions represented 85 per cent of total turnover.[50] The importance of Canal Plus's subscription revenue is also demonstrated by the fact that the channel commands only 3.1 per cent of French television advertising revenue, yet is as well funded as TF1, which commands 47.7 per cent of annual French television advertising revenue.[51]

However, the success of Canal Plus cannot be measured by subscription rates alone. Another source of its strength is the way in which the company has become the privileged partner of the French film industry. Canal Plus has become a major source of finance for domestic film production, participating in the financing of the vast majority of films produced in France. It has even created its own subsidiary companies with direct involvement in film production, thus minimizing its dependency on external suppliers. At the beginning of 1991, for example, it took a majority stake in a new venture called Studio, which allowed Canal Plus to intervene in all stages of film production, from the choice of scripts and actors right through to distribution.[52] Since Canal Plus relies on films for a large proportion of its programme output, it was a logical step for the company to become directly involved in movie production if it were not to be left to the vagaries of the market as a mere purchaser of film product.

Canal Plus has expanded its interests greatly since it was established as Europe's first terrestrial pay channel. To ensure its continued success in the television marketplace, Canal Plus has pursued the corporate strategy followed by successful communications groups in the 1980s: a combination of vertical integration, media diversification and internationalization. The company is involved in programme production through its control of assets in subsidiary companies such as Ellipse. It has also diversified into the television hardware business, where its holdings in Tonna and Eurodec have given it a stake in the manufacture and sales of satellite dishes and decoder systems. It is thus involved in every stage of the television process: production, programming and transmission.

In the new media of cable and satellite Canal Plus is also a major player. It possesses shares in the main cable operators such as Lyonnaise Communications; it is the primary shareholder in several cable channels, including Canal Jimmy, Ciné-Cinéma and Ciné-Cinéfil; and it also has a stake in other cable channels such as Canal J (a channel for children), TV-Sport and MCM Euromusique.[53] Canal Plus is also involved in French satellite broadcasting, transmitting on both TDF1 and Télécom 1. At the end of 1992 it set up Canalsatellite to market its thematic channels on the satellite Télécom 2. The range of satellite services provided by Canal Plus was to be targeted at those households which could not receive Canal Plus via terrestrial transmission and those households without access to cable. In this way, Canal Plus could increase the potential audience of its thematic channels and occupy an apparently lucrative market niche in advance of any competitors.[54] Finally, Canal Plus has extended its reach outside France. It has exported its concept to Belgium (Canal Plus TVCF), Spain (Canal Plus Espagne) and Germany (Première), where it has established pay-television channels in partnership with locally based media companies, which have a better knowledge of local conditions, regulations and audience tastes and are more acceptable to the respective national governments.[55] Using its experience in France, Canal Plus is trying to position itself as the leader in Europe in the controlled-access television market. It is also investing in television in Francophone Africa. Prior to the change of franchise holders in 1991, it was also involved in the British ITV system through its holdings in TVS.

In short, in well under a decade Canal Plus has become one of the two main television companies in France. It has succeeded in selling a new type of television to French viewers, in which a televised product is purchased by consumers without the distortions introduced by the licence fee system or a reliance on advertising for income. In this market relationship audience ratings for individual programmes are far less important than monthly subscriptions. The gamble of 1984 has proved to be a winner.

Chapter 8

The new media

Expansion in the provision of terrestrial television in the 1980s was accompanied by developments in the new media of cable and satellite. While the potential industrial and economic benefits to be gained from the communications revolution drove much of policy making in this sector, the decisions taken clearly had important implications for broadcasting. At the heart of the analysis in this chapter lie two major paradoxes. The first is that despite large-scale state investment, neither of these new media has so far been successful in becoming a major supplier of programmes to the television audience in France. Few French viewers receive programmes from cable or direct satellite transmission, with the result that as yet both have spectacularly failed to pose a competitive challenge to the market dominance of terrestrial television.

The second paradox is that, while most of the changes that took place in the French television system during the 1980s were technically independent of – and in many respects wholly unrelated to – the development of cable and satellite, at the same time much of the political debate on the future of French broadcasting centred on these new means of programme delivery. Whatever the limitations of their impact in terms of household subscriptions or audience ratings, they still exercised a significant influence on the media policy agenda. While France was scarcely unique among western European states in this respect, with similar debates taking place in Britain and Germany, two aspects of the French experience are particularly intriguing.[1] First, why was the French state willing to invest so heavily and so directly in the development of new media technology? Second, why have the optimistic predictions of the early 1980s not been realized, with the result that more than a decade later cable and satellite remain relatively marginalized on the French audiovisual scene?

CABLE TELEVISION

Early experimentation

Strictly speaking, cable television is not a new medium. For a long time it has been exploited in the United States, Canada and various parts of Europe to improve the reception of network television in areas where the topography makes terrestrial transmission unsatisfactory. Advances in its technological sophistication, however, have provided cable with an opportunity to change one of the long-standing structural constraints in the supply of television programmes: the finite nature of the frequency spectrum. For much of the postwar period television transmission in western Europe was limited by frequency scarcity, with the result that in each country there was space for only a very restricted number of nationwide terrestrial television channels. This technical constraint was a major factor in influencing many west European governments, including the French, to control entry into the broadcasting market and to regulate programme output. In the French case in particular, it was an important argument used to defend the establishment and maintenance of the state monopoly.

Cable – especially its broadband fibre optic variant – removes this technical impediment. It replaces a system of penury with one of abundance by realizing the previously impossible goal of multi-channel television. As a result, cable has the capacity to make fundamental alterations to the rules which have governed the transmission of television programmes since the establishment of the medium as a means of mass communication. It is not surprising, then, that the development of cable and its many possible ramifications for the traditional television system featured prominently on the audiovisual policy agenda in France during the 1980s.

Yet until the end of the 1960s the French authorities showed scant interest in cable. As a means of delivering programmes to households it was more expensive than terrestrial transmission, while it was also a more sophisticated technology than was required in an era of severely restricted television supply. In addition, the development of cable was opposed by the state broadcasting organization, the ORTF, which jealously guarded its statutory right to monopoly control of the transmission of television signals. In a foretaste of a bureaucratic conflict which was to be a central feature of the media policy debate in the 1980s, the ORTF was unwilling to allow the Ministry of Post, Telegraphy and Telephony (PTT) to trespass on what it regarded as its own sovereign territory.[2]

A more favourable climate for French cable appeared in the early 1970s. The technology was now regarded by many progressive groups in western Europe as an ideal medium to encourage participation in the life of local communities. Nowhere was this role more necessary than in the new towns which had sprung up across France during the previous decade. Here cable was seen by its proponents as a vital means of providing a channel for dialogue and communication in locations where there was no existing sense of community. More generally, its supporters argued that cable could act as a forum for social communication in an industrialized, technocratic society characterized by individual alienation and anomie.[3]

Perhaps most importantly in the French context, cable fitted in with the post-1968 vogue for decentralization and participation through its potential as an 'alternative' medium to pose a direct challenge to hierarchical decision-making structures in general and the centralized control of broadcasting by the state in particular. At the same time, in less idealistic fashion, French industrialists saw in cable a technology ripe for development and lobbied the government for a positive response. For a mix of political and economic reasons, the Gaullist government of President Pompidou was sufficiently persuaded of the possible merits of cable to give the go-ahead to seven small-scale experimental projects, though only the scheme in Grenoble transmitted programmes on a regular basis.

By the middle of the decade, however, the state authorities had become more sceptical about the benefits to be derived from cable and their policy response on the issue was increasingly negative. Particularly after the election of Giscard d'Estaing as President in 1974, the development of cable as a localized competitor to the national television networks was actively discouraged, with even the Grenoble experiment grinding to a halt in 1976. Various factors explain the reluctance of the government to support cable during the Giscard d'Estaing presidency, but above all the political will was lacking. The President was mindful of the different views within his parliamentary coalition on the media issue, with the numerically dominant Gaullist party known to be largely in favour of maintaining centralized state control of broadcasting. The President himself was either personally sympathetic to this stance or did not have the necessary support in his parliamentary majority to oppose it. At the same time, he was afraid that cable could become a political weapon at the local level in the hands of the Socialist–Communist opposition.[4] Consequently, while he was prepared to accept the utility of cable in its minimalist role of relaying the programmes of the terrestrial television channels of the state monopoly, the President was adamant in his opposition to its use as an alternative source of programming.

Giscard d'Estaing's opposition to the development of cable as a local medium was also based on his evaluation of the difficulties such a policy might create for the press and state television, which stood to lose out as suppliers of information and beneficiaries from advertising revenue.

> I think that at the moment we should think about whether we have to keep on multiplying *ad infinitum* the range of mass media. The risk is that the media destroy each other, as we can see happening with the present difficulties of the press. The three state television channels have not yet reached a stage of full development. Therefore, we have to wait for the full use of the present media before asking questions about the future role of alternative media.[5]

The regional press, with its virtual monopoly on local news provision and media advertising, was an important lobby group against cable. Some newspaper owners would have been willing to participate in the new medium's expansion rather than run the risk of being outflanked by a new competitor. However, an official embargo on cable's development undoubtedly made life easier.

Finally, state resources in the communication and media sectors were already committed to the modernization of France's antiquated telephone system, the transition to colour television transmission and the extension of the FR3 network of regional television stations. These areas of state expenditure took priority over cable, whose potential as an interactive medium was not yet fully appreciated. In this unfavourable political climate, cable naturally failed to make much headway. As a result, when Giscard d'Estaing vacated the presidency in 1981, cable penetration was estimated to have attained the far from vertiginous heights of 0.6 per cent of French households.[6]

The Socialist government's 1982 cable plan

Under President Mitterrand and his Socialist government the official attitude to cable changed quite dramatically. Far from being regarded as an unwanted ancillary service or unnecessary competitor, cable was elevated to the status of an essential component in the communications revolution. As such, the implications of its development extended far beyond its capacity to extend viewers' programming choice by acting as the carrier for a multiplicity of television channels. In fact, the television side of cable was viewed as a relatively minor part of a more comprehensive technological shift. In the longer term the development of a whole range of interactive services would be of much greater significance as France embraced the era of new information technology.

Cable was being pushed in France because the development of high technology such as fibre optics was seen as an essential element in France's adjustment to changing economic circumstances. With the downgrading of traditional manufacturing industries such as steel, shipbuilding, textiles and heavy engineering, the French government believed that if France was to compete in the global marketplace it had to concentrate on certain key industrial sectors, notably the new 'sunrise' industries. Information technology became of central importance both for 'positive adjustment – the term coined by the OECD for the process of shifting national resources from "sunset" to "sunrise" sectors – and for the modernization of more traditional industries'.[7] As a result of this governmental initiative, a country which had never fully completed its industrial revolution was seeking to ensure its place in the vanguard of the communications revolution of the late twentieth century.

The industrial thrust behind the Socialists' 1982 cable plan was paramount. The state-of-the-art fibre optic star-switched cable networks would act as a commercial shopwindow for international markets and form an integral part of the modernization of this captive sector of the domestic economy. Cable (and satellite) was part of a wider governmental emphasis on the electronics sector, which was marked out at the start of Mitterrand's first presidential term as an area where the state could play a key role in promoting modernization and growth. State intervention in the *filière électronique* under the Socialists in the early 1980s was ambitious, even if the results of the policy were more debatable.[8]

> the French electronics industry which ranked only third in Europe – and very far behind the world leaders, Japan and the US – argued that France could not afford to repeat its past failures (eg with computers or more recently with VCRs). . . . From July 1982 onwards, the Mitterrand administration decided to systematically promote . . . all high technology industries and services considered as an integrated whole.[9]

> Over 5 years, 140 billion francs was budgeted to redress the commercial imbalance in the [electronics] sector, create 80,000 jobs, and increase production by 9 percent a year. Public orders were used to stimulate technological progress in microelectronics, computers, robots, and office communications.[10]

At the same time, with a national unemployment total of around 2 million in the early 1980s, the installation and operation of cable networks would give a much needed boost to employment. In addition, 'the rapid growth of the telephone industry had diminished after the boom of the 1970s so that French industry began looking for new investment opportunities', of which fibre optics was one.[11]

It is tempting to view the commitment of the French state to cable in terms of the general increase in state interventionism and expansion of the public sector which followed the election of the Socialist government. For example, the early months of Mitterrand's first presidential term witnessed a wave of nationalizations in the financial and industrial sectors of the economy, at the end of which the state owned 13 of the 20 largest firms in France and a controlling share in many other French companies.[12] Nationalization was part of the Socialist government's early economic strategy to use the public sector to boost domestic demand and encourage economic growth – the policy of Keynesianism in one country which was quickly to run up against the constraints of France's integration within the interdependent global economy. More particularly, some nationalization measures – including those affecting Thomson, the tenth largest electronics corporation worldwide, Bull Computers and the Compagnie Générale d'Electricité (CGE) – were specifically intended to aid the implementation of the Socialist government's strategy in the electronics sector.[13]

Yet it would be a mistake to see the cable plan as primarily the consequence of the election of the first government of the Left in the Fifth Republic. In postwar France the propensity to state intervention in the economy was not an exclusive preserve of the Left. The postwar French state has intervened to achieve its industrial goals through a variety of mechanisms and instruments: selective public procurement, investment programmes, provision of cheap credit, financial subsidy, merger promotion, protection of the domestic market, and regulation and planning.

This is not to argue that state intervention has always been successful or coherent. Commentators disagree about the effectiveness and success of state intervention in industrial policy just as much as politicians conflict about its desirability. The fragmentation of the state, the interdependence of economies and the imbalance of public/private power relationships may all act as a constraint on rational, coherent state policy formulation and implementation.[14] Certainly there have been notable failures of intervention, such as the attempt to create an independent French computer industry. Moreover, the *degree* of state intervention has varied during the postwar period, reflecting changing economic circumstances and ideological predispositions.[15] The Giscardian presidency, for example, is frequently viewed as an attempt to introduce a more liberal policy in this sphere, albeit severely hampered by economic crisis which saw the state assisting declining economic sectors such as textiles. While in the very early part of the Mitterrand presidency the role of the state in economic management was undoubtedly enhanced, this should not be perceived as a seismic shift in the parameters of postwar economic policy making.

One area where there seems to be a high level of agreement that state intervention was effective is telecommunications, which was defined as a national priority in the sixth state plan (1971–75). Between 1973 and 1985 the number of mainline subscribers increased fourfold, from over 5 million to over 22 million. This transformation was effected by the General Directorate of Telecommunications (DGT), France's public telecom operator, which grew in power between 1974 and 1984.[16] Rhodes describes the DGT as a 'state within the state' with its own resources and expertise, its own system of recruitment and its own autonomous – and homogeneous – elite which allows a state project to become that of a *corps* and thus to be carried through to a successful conclusion.[17] While officially remaining integral parts of the state machine, state apparatuses like the DGT may operate as 'quasi-autonomous agencies in developing their own strategies and lobbying policy-makers for decisions in their favour'.[18]

Within the state apparatus, technocrats in the PTT ministry were leading lobbyists for the cable plan. Indeed, it was their own pet project, their 'big idea' for the 1980s, which was successfully sold to government ministers. These technocrats intended that the cabling of France would be a worthy successor to the successful modernization of the French telephone network during the previous decade and that it would act as testimony to their commitment to the development of an advanced communications system. Organized within the DGT, they supported a state-backed cable plan which would allow them to dictate norms and standards on the hardware side, thus ensuring the technical compatibility and state-of-the-art sophistication of the networks nationwide.

A state-funded project for cabling France was also part of their attempt to retain policy control of infrastructural developments in the high-profile and fast-moving communications field, where in many respects the telecommunications sector was converging with the historically differentiated broadcasting sector. Their fear was that in the absence of a long-term cable plan under their stewardship, their influence on future policy developments in the communications field would decline and their prestige nationally and internationally would suffer a grievous blow. The cable plan was therefore integral to their self-perception of their status and political influence within the state administration, a test of their insider technocratic power:

> the [PTT] ministry did not see a future for direct broadcasting, having never favoured the direct satellite broadcasting project, TDF1, which was managed by its principal rival, TDF. Second, the PTT was searching for new services to take up a declining rate of growth in the market for telecommunications equipment and services and counteract trends that would undermine employment within the telecommunications industry. Third, many within the PTT saw bright prospects for fibre optics and made this technology a key aspect of its strategic plans.[19]

Another factor enhancing the power of the DGT was the Nora-Minc Report on the computerization of society published in 1978.[20] This report used the development of information technologies and the growing technological convergence of computing, telecommunications and broadcasting to argue that France needed a well-thought-out strategy in this area to prepare for the information society and resist foreign challenges, especially that of IBM. The report argued that the future of computing in France lay in state control of the telecommunications network, further strengthening the role of the DGT. The state was thus assigned the central role in technological innovation and the wiring up of French society.[21]

Indeed, with the aura of a high-profile, state-backed, advanced technology project, the cable plan exemplified an aspect of industrial policy which had been pursued with equal vigour by previous governments of the Right during the Fifth Republic, particularly during the de Gaulle presidency. Technological development as manifested in different industrial sectors (computers, transport, telecommunications, space, nuclear power) has been awarded high status by the state during the Fifth Republic. The Concorde supersonic plane, the *plan calcul* in computers, the Ariane space rocket and the high-speed train (TGV) have been prestigious technological projects used by the state to achieve both the substantive goal of domestic economic growth and the symbolic objective of enhancing the status of France in the international community. This belief in the substantive and symbolic qualities of high technology, which has achieved virtual cult status among various elite groups in France, has not been bound by traditional ideological divisions or partisan affiliations. Rather a faith in state-backed technological advance as the means to attain the goal of economic and social modernization has cut across many of the entrenched battlelines of the French body politic since the Liberation. As Green has commented:

> French governments have traditionally adopted a *non-market* approach to technological development, with the emphasis on supply: the state determines the technology, selects or creates the firm(s) suited to its development, creates guaranteed demand for the product and/or assumes a significant share of the financial burden of development in an initially protected market, then supports the firm by 'economic diplomacy' in the international market.[22]

In particular, the decision to embrace the cable plan was, according to Green,

> typical of the non-market approach to industrial development at which the French excel. The announcement of the plan was in line with the tradition of launching *grands programmes* involving a partnership between the state (as client and provider of funds) and industry, to accelerate the development of a technology and/or industry deemed to be in the national interest. At the same time, it gave the domestic electronics and cable industries a shot in the arm and put money into the development of a potential industrial winner (optic fibre) with a clear export potential . . . the designation of the PTT as the coordinator of plan implementation . . . reaffirmed the state's leadership role in exploiting the industrial potential of this new technology.[23]

Hugely important though it was, the industrial factor was not the only reason that the French state positively backed the development of cable in the early 1980s. Cultural arguments were also deployed. There was the desire to widen opportunities for French programme production and at the same time to protect French culture from external subversion in the form of foreign television output from satellite transmission. It was hoped that the installation of cable would provide new openings for French programme makers whose work was underused or ignored by the state television companies. With more sources of television supply, a thousand creative flowers could now have the chance to bloom and a greater range and diversity of programming could be made available to viewers. At the same time the regulation of programme material on cable services would be relatively straightforward. Against the backcloth of the simultaneous development of satellite broadcasting across Europe, the cabling of French households would obviate the need for each householder to purchase a receiving 'dish' and so the state would be able to continue to exercise a regulatory control over the programming diet of the French audience. In short, cable could be promoted both as a defensive measure against the much derided Anglo-Saxon cultural hegemony in television programming and as a positive vehicle for the dissemination of French culture.

There was also a political factor favouring the cable plan. One of the principal early reform measures of the Socialists – indeed, it had been described by the responsible minister as the 'major issue' of Mitterrand's first presidential term – was the decentralization of power from Paris to regional, departmental and town councils. The cable plan envisaged the active involvement of local authorities at different stages of the process: the decision to install a cable network, the financing of its construction and the running of its services. All this emphasis on local participation could be presented as part of the Socialist government's decentralization policy.

Finally, there was a desire on the part of the government both to look good electorally and to respond to public dissatisfaction with the output of the terrestrial television networks. In terms of the government's electoral image, the cable plan made the Socialists look modern and in touch. In addition, cable could help provide alternative programming to the public service networks, expanding the range and diversity of programmes and providing greater viewer choice. In short, as described by Vedel and Dutton, the cable plan

> aimed at invigorating French industry, complementing other initiatives aimed at dismantling the state's monopoly over programming, maintaining a positive balance of French language programming and promoting the decentralist policies of François Mitterrand's Socialist administration.
>
> It promised new industries to France, new areas of responsibility and authority to local politicians, new markets to telecommunications firms, new areas for creative activity for programme producers and the prospect of more diversity, choice and control to viewers. It was also a political 'coup' for the Socialist Party as it became a symbol of change and liberalization in the aftermath of restrictive policies.[24]

In the autumn of 1982, just a few months after the enactment of the new legislation on terrestrial broadcasting, the Mauroy government announced its strategy on cable.[25] The plan envisaged that 1.5 million households would be linked to a cable system by 1986, with 1 million additional households being connected every year after that. In Paris alone it was hoped that 500,000 households would be hooked up by the end of 1989. The French state was laying out its *dirigiste* strategy on cable in no uncertain terms: an integrated network of switched-star optical fibre interactive cable systems carrying sound, pictures, text and data. The objective was to establish

> an integrated service digital network, integrating all electronic technologies, new (from satellites to home computers) and old (from the telephone to recorded music), so as to serve the communication requirements of business, government and of private citizens.[26]

The scheme would build on France's record in telecommunications in the Fifth Republic, including teletext and videotex projects such as the Minitel telephone directory.

The provisions of the cable plan were set out as follows. Local authorities would take the initiative in asking for their area to be cabled and they would bear a proportion – roughly one-third – of the initial investment costs. The DGT would carry out the installation of the cable network and would be the legal owner of the network infrastructure. In stark contrast to Britain, where the Thatcher government relied on the private sector to put in cable, in France the installation and control of the technology was designated a state responsibility.

On the programming side, the operation of the cable network would be managed by a company in which local authorities could have a 33 per cent stake. Private sector participation was encouraged by the state in 1984. Each participating authority was asked to set up a body specifically designed for this task, composed of representatives from the public and/or private sectors, but usually including members from the state transmission company. A variety of interests could be involved at this stage, including press groups and commercial enterprises intent on securing a stake in the new multimedia future. No person or company, however, could have a financial interest in more than one cable service. In practice, however, local authorities preferred to grant concessions for operating control of the cable networks to private operators – notably the Caisse des dépots et consignation, which provides financial services to local authorities, or to the private water utilities, La Générale des eaux and La Lyonnaise des eaux. In the case of Paris, a major part of the capital was controlled by La Lyonnaise des eaux and the chairman of the operating company was a Paris official.

The announcement of the French cable plan coincided with decisions taken by the British and West German governments also to commit themselves to a high-technology policy on cable.[27] In all three countries the commitment to the 'information revolution' took place in a climate of high expectations surrounding the potential of cable and associated technologies to facilitate the transition from an economic base historically reliant on manufacturing industry to one founded on the service and communications sectors. In France this early mood of optimism was reflected in a pro-active policy by the state to inform local authorities about the benefits of cable and governmental measures announced to encourage audiovisual production and local programming.

Given the role played by the DGT in successfully lobbying for the cable plan, it is not surprising that policy formulation in this field is frequently viewed as being technocratically driven and dominated. Yet Vedel and Dutton are right to suggest that cable policy has also been shaped by a number of other groups and interests, which has resulted in the policy-making autonomy of the telecommunications technocrats being constrained.[28] Policy formulation and implementation have been riven with conflict. At central government level, for example, the PTT and Communication ministries perceived the development of cable within different contexts, with the former concerned more with the telecommunications side of the technology and the latter with its implications for broadcasting.

Vedel and Dutton also point to disagreements between the DGT and the local authorities, centring on issues such as the cost of cable installation (finance) and the type of technology employed (hardware), with the local authorities frequently adopting a more short-term, pragmatic and political view on cable than that taken by the central state officials. Similar disagreements were also evident between the state authorities and the major cable operators. Generally speaking, the DGT emphasized the hardware side of the exercise, while the cable operators were more sensitive to the marketing aspects and so paid greater attention to the software – the programmes. One perennial source of conflict in a field which embraced aspects of both telecommunications and broadcasting was that the PTT objective of constructing an advanced communications network frequently clashed with the cable operators' goal of quickly hooking up as many subscribers as possible through the provision of entertainment television programming; 'a conflict came to exist between a national industrial policy goal – a goal widely accepted beyond the Left – and a framework based on local initiative and private financing'.[29]

One problem was that in order to gain support for its plan in governmental circles, the DGT had to build up support among different players in the policy-making process. These players saw in cable different elements to attract them. For the technofreaks it was a means of constructing an advanced communications network which would be the envy of the world; for the culturophiles it was part of a policy of disseminating artefacts of French culture by strengthening the domestic programme production industry; and for the proponents of 'small is beautiful' cable was part of a wider governmental initiative in favour of the decentralization of power to the local level. The successful way in which a variety of interests combined under DGT guidance ensured that the cable plan was given state backing. Yet at the same time, the coalition of elite groups in favour of cable was a fragile one. The strength of the cable plan in securing support across different ministries, across the public/private divide and across the central/local cleavage was notable. This strength, however, was also a potential weakness when the cable plan failed to meet the high expectations raised in the early 1980s.

As the cable plan ran into problems, the officially sponsored climate of confidence did not endure for long. First, there was the high cost of the advanced fibre optic cable, which had been chosen in preference to the tried-and-tested but technologically more limited coaxial version. Fibre optic cable was both more sophisticated and more expensive than many councils either wanted or needed. It was also a drain on the DGT's budget, already stretched because of commitments in other investment sectors.[30] Second, supply from the manufacturers was unreliable and subject to delays. After much soul searching the telecommunications technocrats gave up their insistence on fibre optic star-switched systems and accepted the conventional coaxial tree and branch systems (or a mixture of the two). Conflict between the local authorities and cable operators on the one hand, and the DGT on the other, further complicated matters, as did divisions within the PTT ministry itself over the implementation of the plan. Finally, the development of cable was held back by the application of stringent programme regulations regarding the amount of local and national programming to be shown on the networks.

In short, a mixture of financial, technical, bureaucratic and regulatory issues combined to break up the initial coalition of interests and sow seeds of dissent among the different players involved in policy formulation and implementation. The Socialist government's cable plan failed to deliver across a range of objectives. Most fundamentally, when the Right returned to power after the 1986 general election, few networks had been commissioned and even fewer were operational. Indeed, the cable plan was so far behind its targets that only two small networks were up and running and cable was available to only a small minority of French households nationwide.

The liberalization of cable policy by the Right

French government policy on cable changed when the Gaullist–Giscardian conservative coalition returned to power in the spring of 1986. New legislation on broadcasting put an end to the state monopoly in the construction of cable networks and technical control of the infrastructure. At the same time greater freedom of manoeuvre was given to local authorities and private cable operators. As a result of this policy shift, since 1986 there have been two sorts of cable networks operating in France: those constructed under the terms of the 1982 cable plan and those which originated under the 1986 provisions. In late 1986 the government announced that private and public sector companies could compete against the DGT in tendering for contracts to equip municipalities with cable infrastructures and that a mixture of cable and optical fibre technology could be employed.

The 1986 legislation gave a greater role to local authorities than the Socialists' cable plan, effectively ending the DGT's monopoly over the installation and technical operation of cable systems. The local authorities could now authorize the construction of cable networks in their area and choose both the technical and commercial operator, subject to approval from the relevant regulatory authority (initially the CNCL and then the CSA). Conversely, the input of the state telecommunications agency in the cabling process was much reduced.

The 1986 law also recognized a new category of players – private cable operators – who could now be responsible for the construction and commercial exploitation of networks. In addition, through a process of vertical integration, these private operators could also supply programmes to the networks, notably in the form of thematic channels. The whole cable operation became less an area for the implementation of technocratic policy and more a commercial battle for subscribers, as the marketing of cable services came to the fore.[31]

Not surprisingly the role of private cable operators has increased since 1986. The major cable operators remain the Caisse des dépots et consignation and the two water companies, while the state-owned electricity company, EDF, has also acquired a small stake in the industry. These private operators run the commercial side of the cable networks through subsidiary companies as part of a corporate diversification strategy. The 'big three' cable companies have two essential advantages: their financial muscle and their privileged relationship with local authorities through their primary business. Since it is a high-risk enterprise requiring large-scale investment over the long term, the cable industry is not an attractive prospect for many companies, particularly as the return on investment is slow and unsure. Because of this, well-known French media companies such as Hachette and Havas have not become involved in the business as cable network operators. Even the 'big three' have encountered problems with the marketing of cable to potential consumers, despite their familiarity as providers of services at the local level.

Since 1989 the regulatory authority for cable has been the Higher Audio-visual Council (CSA). Before authorizing the commercial exploitation of a cable network, the CSA checks that the infrastructure conforms to the technical standards laid down by the state, that the commercial operator is not in breach of the anti-concentration provisions of the 1986 legislation and that the programme plan respects the relevant regulatory obligations, especially those set out in the cable decree of September 1 1992. A complex set of anti-concentration measures was detailed in the 1986 law to prevent a private cable operator exercising monopoly control over the cable industry and to outlaw extensive cross-ownership of cable, terrestrial television, radio and press interests.[32] Programme regulations, especially regarding the showing of feature films and brand advertising, were contained in the 1992 decree. While for general cable channels these regulations are similar to those applicable to terrestrial television, for designated movie channels they are less stringent.[33] In addition, the CSA can impose a 'must carry' rule on cable networks so that they are obliged to transmit the programmes of the terrestrial channels. Regulations imposing a quota on local programming are extremely lenient. Finally, there are provisions to mitigate the practice of vertical integration whereby the cable network operators may gain total control over programme output. These regulations allow the CSA to give subscribers a greater choice of channels than would perhaps be made available by the network operator enjoying a monopoly position in the marketplace.

By the end of March 1992 the three major operators had 3,272,000 households linked to a cable system and a total of 663,000 subscribers.[34] In return for their subscription, households can receive more than 30 channels distributed via cable. These include the output of the French terrestrial channels (TF1, France 2, France 3, etc.); thematic channels such as Canal J, Planète, TV-Sport and Ciné-Cinéma, covering various programme genres including movies, music, children's programmes and sport;[35] satellite channels, usually foreign owned and non-Francophone (for example CNN, MTV Europe, Sat1 and Worldnet), but also including a couple of French-language channels – RTL TV and TV5; local channels, often financed by the local authority, which remain very underdeveloped; and some miscellaneous services, such as pay-per-view and educational programming.[36] The thematic channels are usually subscription channels which require an additional payment on top of the basic service. (This is also the case with CNN and MTV Europe.) Generally the thematic channels have very little of their own production and rely mostly on programming bought in from outside.

To consolidate their control of the cable television market, the major cable operators have established their own channels. In general, however, these have not been a commercial success. Canal Plus has also become involved in cable television as part of a strategy which favours the vertical integration and diversification of the company across many sectors of the media industry. Ownership and control of its own thematic channels are part of a wider expansion in the production and programming functions of the television business. Canal Plus has also agreed a joint strategy with the three main operators, which includes taking a financial stake in each of their cable subsidiaries. Moreover, apart from a couple of exceptions such as Eurosport, share ownership in many of the thematic channels is dominated by Canal Plus and its corporate ally CGV (the cable subsidiary of La Générale des eaux).

The activity of the commercially shrewd Canal Plus in this media sector demonstrates that the cable industry in France is not moribund. Yet nor is it particularly healthy. It is fair to say that over a decade on from the optimistic forecasts of the Socialist government's much heralded hi-tech plan, the impact of cable has been far less than many would have anticipated. Moreover, despite a more liberal technical and regulatory regime since 1986, cable has still failed to make major inroads in the French broadcasting system. By the spring of 1992 there were only 830,000 cable subscribers in total (out of the nearly 4 million households equipped with cable points), of whom 602,000 were individual household subscriptions. This total was nowhere near as many as had been forecast ten years previously. Just as depressingly for the advocates of cable as an interactive technology, most were connected to old-fashioned tree and branch networks using coaxial cable.

These figures mean that a decade on from the announcement of the cable plan only about 4 per cent of all French households subscribed to a cable network. For most this was not a question of choice. Cable was available to only about 20 per cent of all households, even though most towns of more than 100,000 inhabitants (including Paris, Marseilles and Lyons) had a functioning cable system. Even where a network existed, only about 20 per cent of households who could subscribe to cable actually did so, with subscription rates in small localities much higher than in the large towns and cities. The failure of cable to live up to business expecta-tions had by the early 1990s resulted in financial losses in this sector for France Télécom, the major cable operators and the thematic channels. For many involved in the business, cable has been a licence to lose money.

The overall result is that France is one of the least cabled countries in Europe, well behind several of its EU neighbours, most notably Germany (see table 8.1). Even if industry estimates of 2,000,000 subscribers by 1995 were to prove well founded, this would represent only about 10 per cent of French households and would still leave France way behind Germany in terms of cable penetration. The relaunch plan announced in May 1992, which included increasing the share of France Télécom in the financially

Table 8.1 Cable penetration in different European countries, June 1991

Country	Households with TV set (in '000s)	Households with cable link (in '000s)	Households subscribing to cable (in '000s)
Belgium	3,530	3,330	3,262
France	20,250	3,214	647
Germany	31,350	16,597	8,953
Great Britain	21,450	2,059	461
Italy	20,250	0	0
Netherlands	5,870	4,800	4,580

Source: R. Lunven and T. Vedel, *La télévision de demain*, Paris, Armand Colin, 1993, p.93.

squeezed cable operators, has a lot of ground to make up if France is to join the front rank of cabled countries in Europe.

An explanation of the failure of cable to achieve a mass market in France requires a twofold approach. First, why is such a large percentage of the French population still deprived of the choice of subscribing to a cable network? Or, to put it another way, why has the process of constructing cable networks been so slow and so patchy? Second, where a cable network does exist, why do so few French households take out and maintain a subscription?

The small number of cable networks in France is attributable to a variety of factors. Initially, as we have seen, the technology chosen by the telecommunications technocrats was too sophisticated for many local authorities, the installation costs too high and the hardware too unreliable. There were also many instances of conflict between the different players involved in policy implementation. Finally, the incoherence in the government's media policy in the mid-1980s, with a strategy of expansion of all outlets simultaneously (the legalization and growth of local radio, the establishment of Canal Plus, the creation of two new terrestrial television channels and the support for direct broadcasting by satellite), helped undermine the attractiveness of cable to potential operators.

The expansion of terrestrial television is also a major factor in explaining consumer resistance to subscribing to a cable network where one exists. Why should a French viewer receiving half a dozen channels by conventional transmission, including Canal Plus with its diet of feature films and sport, subscribe to cable? Overall, there is not enough attractive programming on cable networks over and above what is already available via terrestrial transmission. In part this is a problem of programme production and supply, with the French programme production industry unable to take advantage of the large increase in the number of television channels coming on stream during the 1980s. The failure of the major operators' own thematic channels has led to greater cooperation between them in an attempt to achieve much needed economies of scale. Their attempts to persuade consumers to subscribe to cable will also be helped by new lighter-touch regulations which have been introduced for programming, for example on the transmission of feature films.

A second restraining factor on consumer demand is the financial outlay involved. The cost of cable subscription – around 135 francs per month for the basic service – is clearly a disincentive for many households. Moreover, the cost of cable subscription cannot be treated as an isolated variable. It must be considered within the context of the potential expenditure of French households in the field of audiovisual entertainment as a whole. Non-cable expenditure might include capital costs (the purchase of a television set, video recorder, satellite dish and decoding equipment) and running costs (the annual television licence fee and subscription to Canal Plus). Given the cost and the range of programming available on cable, it is not wholly surprising that in those areas where a network exists, the French public have frequently been less than enthusiastic. The result is that despite the establishment of a more liberal and less *dirigiste* regime since 1986, consumer use of cable is still a minority activity in France.

SATELLITE BROADCASTING

If the first consequence of new media technology was the opening up of the possibility of multi-channel television, the second is the end of national boundary restrictions on television supply and reception. In the past the output of most national television systems in Europe was confined to the country of transmission. The notable exceptions to this general rule were those countries with a small surface area, such as Belgium and Luxembourg, and certain regions close to national frontiers. This restriction is no longer in evidence, as satellite broadcasting has enabled transnational television transmission to become a reality. The footprints of broadcast satellites in geostationary orbit above the earth overspill national frontiers. As a result, national governments and regulatory authorities can no longer control television programme output as easily as in the past. In addition,

> if signals are propagated over a wide geographical area, for example over Western Europe, an integrated advertising market and audience of an unprecedented size and structure is potentially available. Such a potentiality is attractive to interests such as the European Commission, charged with the creation of a single EEC market by 1992, and threatening to those who, like Jack Lang, ex-Minister of Culture and Communication in France, fear the erosion of existing communities and cultures.[37]

As with cable, the French government's commitment to satellite broadcasting has not been without its problems and the result in terms of audience figures has been extremely disappointing. Since the late 1970s the debate concerning the development of satellite television has been riddled with disagreement and dissension. Politicians, often of the same party, have taken opposing stances, government ministers have fallen out with each other, the administration has been divided, commercial media companies have competed for governmental favours and France has frequently found itself in conflict with fellow EU member states, most notably Luxembourg, over satellite policy. At the same time, techno-industrial goals have often been at odds with cultural objectives. As a result, the strategy set out in the late 1970s has been questioned and re-examined at various stages in the light of technological advances, developments in terrestrial television and changes in the composition of the governing majority. In short, France has not pursued the satellite television option single-mindedly or without controversy.[38]

Before one can assess the impact of satellite broadcasting in France, it is first of all necessary to analyse the reasons why the state embarked on such a scheme in the first place and to outline the key steps in its development. The launch of French direct broadcasting by satellite (DBS) in 1988 marked the culmination of a policy whose origins can be traced back to the presidency of Mitterrand's immediate predecessor, Giscard d'Estaing. At the beginning of the 1970s the possibility of transmitting television programmes directly from a satellite to individual households started to become a reality. In Europe, the West Germans were the first to elaborate a coherent development strategy for this new technology when, in 1976, the federal authorities decided to make direct broadcasting by satellite the principal axis of their space policy and pursued the construction of their own satellite, TV-Sat.[39] Meanwhile, in France the state transmission company TDF seized on the opportunity created by Germany to persuade the government to pursue its own DBS project, supporting its case largely on technical and economic grounds. DBS, it was argued, would complement the French space project, which at the time centred on the development of the launch rocket Ariane. At the same time, DBS would ensure that France remained at the forefront of the audiovisual technology revolution as a major export contender in a potentially lucrative global satellite market. Finally, it was hoped that the French DBS would act as a hi-tech vehicle for French programming, a window for viewers in other European countries to sample the delights of French culture. However, industrial considerations clearly predominated over broadcasting or cultural ones.

Yet TDF also recognized that the research and development costs of a purely national DBS scheme would be high and accepted the desirability of cooperation with a European partner. At the 32nd Franco-German summit in October 1979, President Giscard d'Estaing and Chancellor Schmidt announced that their two countries would cooperate on DBS, abandoning the option of a wider European project under the aegis of the European Space Agency. 'At stake were the development of an independent satellite industry, the complementary Ariane rocket project and Europe's place as an independent player in the world space industry.'[40] French cooperation with Germany would help keep down investment costs, as well as effectively removing a potential competitor from the field. The technical hardware would be constructed mainly by French and German companies.[41] The agreement foresaw the launching in the mid-1980s of two DBS satellites, the French TDF1 and the German TV-Sat, plus a back-up satellite in case either of the two main satellites broke down.

As in the case of the ambitious cable plan, the French DBS project did not have to seek out problems in the 1980s. The first arose as a result of fierce rivalry within the upper ranks of the French state apparatus involving different government ministries and administrative agencies. It was not apparent to everyone in government and in the upper echelons of the administration that the simultaneous pursuit of two high-technology objectives in audiovisual communications was essential or even desirable. At one level this dispute was a purely technical one, centring on the relative merits of two types of satellite: high-powered broadcasting satellites versus lower-powered telecommunications satellites. TDF, the Ministry of Industry and the Ministry of Communication among others supported government backing for the former, while the PTT ministry and the telecommunications agency favoured the development of the latter.

The telecommunications technocrats within the PTT ministry questioned whether DBS was technically necessary if France was adopting cable in any case. They argued that the less expensive and technically complicated telecommunications satellites could be used to transmit programmes to headends from which the programmes could be transmitted to subscribers via the cable networks. This type of satellite transmission would complement the cable plan rather than compete with it. Moreover, cable would be able to retransmit programmes from different satellites, thus avoiding individual consumers in the extra expense of separate dishes and decoders. At the same time, a control on output could be exercised at the headend by the relevant authorities, acting as a regulatory intermediary between satellite transmission and viewer reception. If these arguments were considered insufficiently convincing, the PTT had others. For example, a leaked PTT report in 1984 criticized the TDF1 project as too expensive and too technologically sophisticated in an era where medium-powered satellites would be able to transmit more channels at lower cost to individual households. Naturally, such arguments were opposed by TDF, which regarded the French DBS as its own prestige project, and the PTT spoiling operation failed.

The substance of this technical disagreement masked a more fundamental antagonism between the broadcasting and telecommunications technocrats over control of French policy in the communications field. This was more than a conflict of policies; it was a battle for growth, perhaps even survival, between rival administrative empires. Historically TDF and the DGT (now called France Télécom) have had a relationship marked more by conflict than cooperation. Though they were both state agencies, in several areas they had developed mutually competitive services and followed conflicting policy objectives, as in the field of satellite development. In the 1980s TDF sought to defend its historical legacy and maintain technical control of an autonomous broadcasting sphere. In sharp contrast, the telecommunications agency wanted to pursue a more holistic policy which recognized the increasing convergence of telecommunications and broadcasting technology, no better exemplified than in the area of the new media.[42]

This conflict within the upper echelons of the French administration was largely fought out between technocrats. Ministers also became involved as representatives of their respective departments, but the issue never became one of intense public controversy. Compared to the furore surrounding the establishment of channels five and six or the privatization of TF1, the debate about new audiovisual technology hardware was largely conducted by insider specialists. The highly technical nature of the controversy helped keep it out of the public political domain for much of the time. But this was not the only factor. The issue also cut across party political divisions, with both Right and Left backing in a general fashion France's commitment to high-technology research and development.

Faced with conflicting technocratic advice and incapable of deciding which horse to back, the French government chose the soft option by supporting both types of satellite development: TDF's DBS project and the DGT's telecommunications scheme. For industrial reasons the government decided to maintain its interest in operating a direct broadcasting satellite for fear of leaving this potential export market to its rivals. It also wanted to ensure that France would be present in the skies above Europe. At the same time, a lower-powered telecommunications satellite, Télécom 1, was also developed.

The government's inability or unwillingness to choose between the two projects was facilitated by the widely held view that the two types of satellite were more complementary than competitive. For a while it was considered that the telecommunications satellite was not suitable for direct broadcasting to households and that, therefore, it was not a rival to TDF1. With the benefit of hindsight, it is now clear that the arguments of the telecommunications technocrats have gained the ascendancy. TDF1 is a more sophisticated transmission system than is necessary, yet paradoxically is able to deliver a very restricted service in terms of the number of television channels. The French telecommunications satellites have given France Télécom the opportunity to demonstrate that DBS has been overtaken by events, while the integration of TDF within the France Télécom group in 1988 is a mark of their bureaucratic victory in the domestic satellite war.[43]

Télécom 1 has had a notable impact in the audiovisual field. It is used by the mother stations of private local radio networks such as NRJ, Europe 2 and Skyrock to feed their affiliated stations. In addition, after 1986 La Cinq and M6 used Télécom 1 to transport their programmes to terrestrial TDF transmitters. The telecommunications satellites have also transported the programmes of cable channels to headends for onward transmission to individual households. By 1992 more than two-thirds of the capacity of Télécom 1 satellites was being given over to broadcasting transmissions and the competition between Télécom 1 and TDF1 had become even more bitter. One of the recent converts to telecommunications satellites is Canal Plus, which established Canalsatellite in November 1992 and entered a new domain of pay-satellite television, using Télécom 2A for the transmission of a cluster of encrypted thematic channels.[44]

The second problem that the French DBS project had to contend with in the 1980s was competition from France's media-active neighbour

– Luxembourg. Luxembourg had been allocated satellite transmission frequencies for its own use in 1977, with its satellite footprint covering a large area of north-eastern France.[45] Interested in pursuing a DBS option for economic reasons, the Luxembourg government allowed the official Luxembourg broadcasting agency, the Compagnie Luxembourgeoise de Télédiffusion (CLT) to announce in 1979 that it would be launching a DBS satellite, Lux-Sat. At the same time, the CLT displayed its interest in being allocated a channel on the French DBS. The French Socialist government after 1981 was at first sympathetic to the CLT claim, subject to its programmes conforming to French regulations.

When it came to power the Socialist government was anxious to preserve and foster as much as possible the role of French broadcasting as a disseminator of the national culture. It was, therefore, strongly opposed to a free-for-all in the development of the new media in Europe, which in its eyes would lead to European broadcast outlets being used as channels for the transmission of low-quality output, notably from the United States. The opposition to France becoming a dumping ground for American programming was strongly articulated in ministerial pronouncements in the early period of the first Mitterrand presidential term, while the fear of a Luxembourg satellite acting as a clearing house for such television product was omnipresent in the bilateral government negotiations during the first half of the 1980s. At the same time, in recognition of the changing international dimension, the Socialist government called for a European solution to the problems posed by DBS, including the creation of a European support fund for the television programme industry and greater emphasis on coproductions at the European level.

France feared that Luxembourg would launch its own DBS in competition with the French satellite, thereby compromising the latter's commercial viability. At the same time, the Socialist government in France regarded a Luxembourg satellite as an undesirable alien which would bombard French viewers with US programming. France wanted cooperation from Luxembourg (i.e. no competition) in this domain. Through its important shareholding in the CLT, the French government applied pressure on the Luxembourg authorities to abandon their own project. As a *quid pro quo*, Luxembourg would be given one or two channels on TDF1. Simultaneously, the Luxembourg government continued to pursue other avenues, including a scheme entitled the Coronet project which was based on the launching of a telecommunications satellite with both more channels (16) and lower running costs than DBS. When in early 1985 President Mitterrand announced his plan to establish privately owned terrestrial television channels, the CLT made a bid for one of the new franchises. The CLT's lack of success brought relations between the two countries to a new low ebb.

The Luxembourg government continued to support the Coronet project and in December 1988 the multi-channel medium-powered Astra satellite was launched, which, among other services, transmits Murdoch's BSkyB channels to audiences in Britain.[46] While the reallocation of the franchises of channels five and six at the start of 1987 gave control of channel six to a group which included the CLT, France had failed in its attempt to keep Luxembourg out of the satellite broadcasting race. The French government decided to proceed with its own four-channel DBS in any case. Meanwhile, the conflict with the Luxembourg government was partly resolved when it agreed not to show any French-speaking output on its satellite. None the less, the success of the French DBS could not be taken for granted, given the huge costs involved and the fluid situation in European satellite broadcasting generally.

Faced with opposition at home and competition abroad, the French DBS project encountered a third problem common to high-technology ventures: ever-spiralling research and development costs. The expenditure required persuaded the French government to review its commitment to the DBS scheme on various occasions during the 1980s. Successive governments of Left, Right and Left again maintained their support for the French DBS, including the go-ahead for the construction and launching of a second satellite, TDF2. However, it was clear that grave reservations were being expressed in ministerial quarters about the growing cost and technological importance of the project. While public finance was still made available, the continuation of the scheme was being backed with increasing reluctance.[47] The state sought private backers for the scheme as well as programme companies who wanted to lease channels on the satellite, but private sector enthusiasm and finance were both in short supply. By the end of the decade it was evident that the project was in a mess. It appeared to have definitively escaped the control of policy makers and was existing on the dynamic created in the early years of optimism.[48]

It was more in an atmosphere of relief than celebration, therefore, that TDF1 was finally and successfully launched on October 28 1988 from Ariane's launch site in Kourou in French Guyana.[49] The satellite had the capacity to transmit five television channels, two more than envisaged almost a decade previously and one more than had been anticipated in the middle of the 1980s. Under the current regulatory regime, the CSA authorizes the provision of commercial television services on the French DBS, just as it does in the case of private terrestrial channels. (It is the government, however, which decides to grant public service channels a transmission frequency on DBS.) The authorization is for ten years. The regulatory provisions on satellite television cover issues such as ownership, advertising and the screening of French and European Union feature films.[50]

Which channels would transmit on the DBS satellite had been the subject of much media speculation throughout the decade, with different possibilities dropping in and out of favour. Initially it was thought that the satellite might transmit programmes of the public service channels TF1 and Antenne 2 to aid reception in areas poorly served by terrestrial transmission. Later it was proposed that Robert Maxwell might have a channel, while still later a European commercial television consortium including Berlusconi among its backers was provisionally allocated two channels. Several French and a few foreign media companies expressed an interest in a channel on TDF1 from time to time.

The Socialist government of the mid-1980s was keen that one satellite channel should be used to provide a cultural television service. It asked Pierre Desgraupes to undertake a preliminary study for programming and he proposed an upmarket channel in cooperation with other European television companies who would share the capital expenses. This project, which in a different form came to fruition in the television channel known as La Sept, 'added a cultural and political dimension to the DBS project, symbolizing the Left government's desire to foster greater European identity, and create a "global village" – a unifying link between the many local communities'.[51] La Sept was subsequently replaced by the Franco-German cultural channel ARTE.[52] In 1992 the French DBS satellites transmitted the programme output of four channels: ARTE, Antenne 2, Canal Plus and Euromusique. Of these, the first three were also available to viewers through terrestrial transmission.

By the early 1990s satellite television had made little impact on the French broadcasting system. In March 1992 a meagre 180,000 households were equipped with a satellite dish, representing 0.8 per cent market penetration. Only about 50,000 dishes were sold in the whole of 1991. The French have been reluctant to purchase the necessary receiving equipment to enable them to receive satellite television transmissions. In comparison with Germany and Britain, therefore, France is well behind in the satellite television race and there seems little prospect of it ever making up the lost ground (see table 8.2).

Table 8.2 Satellite penetration in different European countries, June 1991

	Households with TV set (in '000s)	Households with satellite dish (in '000s)	Satellite as % of TV households
Belgium	3,530	35	0.4
France	20,250	40	0.2
Germany	31,350	2,300	7.5
Great Britain	21,450	2,000	9.3
Italy	20,250	0	0
Netherlands	5,870	150	2.6
Spain	10,935	100	0.9

Source: R. Lunven and T. Vedel, La télévision de demain, Paris, Armand Colin, 1993, p.157.

There are various reasons why French viewers have not as yet taken to satellite television. One factor is the cost, with a fixed dish costing about 4,000 to 5,000 francs. Another is consumer confusion. By the end of March 1992 11 Francophone channels were broadcast over French territory via four satellite systems: Astra, TDF, Télécom and Eutelsat. With different satellites transmitting to French audiences, many viewers are prepared to wait and see who emerges as the market leader before taking the plunge. Perhaps most importantly, satellite television has so far offered little that is new. The private terrestrial television channels established in the 1980s, most notably Canal Plus, have already largely fulfilled viewer expectations regarding television programme supply, notably in the areas of film and sport. There are few new satellite channels in comparison with what is already available via terrestrial transmission.

Two conclusions about the French satellite television experience stand out. First, though given state backing, the whole DBS scheme was racked by political and administrative infighting at the highest levels of decision making as government ministers and technocratic agencies fought a prolonged internecine war of attrition. In the end, despite serious misgivings in various quarters, the French DBS project went ahead because its backers convinced the government that the project was in the national interest in various policy fields: technological, industrial and cultural. At the same time there is little doubt that the French DBS, like Concorde 20 years previously, benefited from the interpretation that it was never the right moment to cut government losses and run. This was particularly true after the second DBS satellite had been authorized at the end of 1984.

Second, the French DBS plan failed because it was too technologically sophisticated. This in itself had various consequences. It was expensive to develop, prone to delay and functionally unreliable. At the same time it could broadcast only a very limited number of channels in comparison to the output of lower-powered satellites. This in itself made it an unattractive option both to television channels and to viewers. Television companies were averse to taking the risk of using DBS in a highly competitive broadcasting market until there was evidence of audience demand, the technology was proven and the regulatory regime allowed them to compete with an inbuilt advantage over terrestrial broadcasters. Meanwhile, the audience was unwilling to make the necessary financial outlay until there was evidence of new television programming. To a British observer the story had echoes of the BSB project, with the difference that in Britain it was private sector companies and their shareholders, not the state, which bore the brunt of the investment miscalculation.

The history of the French DBS project illustrates the problems policy makers experience in conditions where information is imperfect, the stakes are high and the risks incalculable. For much of the 1980s the French policy-making process on satellite television resembled a battleground in which conflicting armies of technocratic experts fought themselves to a standstill. In these circumstances, once a policy has been embarked upon, government ministers find it increasingly difficult to call a halt to a process which has gained a self-sustaining momentum.

In Fifth Republic France this danger has been exacerbated by the tradition of state intervention in key industrial and technological sectors. While such a policy of huge state investment has had outstanding successes, most recently the high-speed train (TGV), it is equally prone to spectacular failures if the technocrats offer what turns out to be the wrong advice. In highly specialist fields of activity, where technological progress rapidly renders projects obsolescent, there is always the risk that state officials will make errors of judgement in investment decisions. Such a risk is compounded when the officials have a natural tendency to perceive the pursuit of the national interest and the advancement of their own professional group interests as synonymous. The case of satellite (and cable) development in France serves as a reminder of the fallibility of technical expertise at the heart of the policy-making process and of the limitations of technocracy in controlling the policy environment.

Conclusion

In the fifty years since the Liberation, France has become a media-rich society, whose citizens have access to a wide range of newspapers, radio stations and television channels for their information and entertainment. While there have been aspects of continuity in the French media system during this period, change has frequently been more apparent. Indeed, some of the changes, notably in the audiovisual media during the 1980s, have been radical and profound. These elements of change and continuity have been analysed and assessed in the previous chapters, where the material has been organized under the heading of different media sectors: press, radio, television and the new media respectively. However, some postwar developments in the French media show certain shared characteristics which cut across sectorial divisions. The aims of this concluding chapter are to draw together some common threads from the preceding analysis and to highlight key issues on the media policy agenda in the 1990s. To help contextualize this material, we begin with a brief retrospective overview of some of the key developments in the structure of the French media system since the Liberation.

THE POSTWAR MEDIA

The single most notable structural development in the French media during the postwar period has been the rise of television from a position of insignificance to the prime role it exercises today. Television's growing importance can be illustrated in a number of ways. First, ownership of sets and associated hardware has expanded as French households have become increasingly geared to the demands of the audiovisual age. By the early 1990s around 95 per cent of French households possessed a television set (about 30 per cent possessed two or more), while over 30 per cent had a video cassette recorder. A growing proportion also subscribed to Canal Plus, necessitating additional consumer expenditure on decoding equipment. Second, there has been a huge expansion in the amount of television programming supplied to viewers. The number of television channels has increased, particularly since the abolition of the state monopoly at the beginning of the 1980s. Whereas in the 1950s France had only one channel, by the early 1990s there were at least six terrestrial networks plus an assortment of cable and satellite channels. Meanwhile, programme schedules have also lengthened considerably. As a result, the annual number of programme hours transmitted has shot up from under 2,800 in 1960 to over 48,000 by 1990. Third, television's share of media advertising expenditure has grown. From 0 per cent before 1968 it has increased to an estimated 29 per cent in 1992, which in monetary terms represented a total in excess of 14,000 million francs. Finally, the popularity of television viewing as a leisure activity has reached its highest ever levels. The average amount of time spent watching television has grown from 57 minutes per person per day in 1964 to 130 minutes in 1975, and then after a decade of relative stagnation to 190 minutes in 1990. Moreover, whereas for much of the postwar period the increase in viewing time per person was largely because *more people* were watching television, since the mid-1980s it has largely been the result of people watching *more television.*[1]

The press and radio have both had to adapt to the pressures of the television age. By many criteria the press has been on the decline since the highpoint of 1946. The postwar years have seen a reduction in the number of newspaper titles (from 203 in 1946 to 73 in 1990), a decrease in total circulation (from a print run of over 15 million in 1946 to under 10 million in 1990) and a drop in the share of media advertising expenditure (from 79 per cent in 1967 to an estimated 51 per cent in 1992). Paris-based newspapers have suffered particularly badly, while the provincial daily press has proved to be more resilient.

Fears that radio would be eclipsed by television have proved unfounded. Two initiatives in particular have helped radio during the postwar period. The first was the invention of the transistor, which allowed radio to capitalize on its advantage as a portable medium. The second was the legalization of private stations in the 1980s. Private networks have followed in the tradition of the peripheral stations in tapping new markets for the medium among younger listeners and have built up a solid following in the 15–34 age group. Radio as a whole has benefited from its relative cheapness to produce and from the emphasis on music in its programming.

Finally, the new media of cable and satellite have promised much in terms of greater viewing choice, better technical quality and the myriad possibilities of interactive television. By the early 1990s, however, their impact on the media system remained marginal, as many French viewers either could not receive their programme output or, where they could, chose not to subscribe to it. Yet, despite the setbacks of the 1980s, the new media may well make more of an impression in the years to come as their benefits become more evident to consumers searching for ever more diversity in their television consumption.

A COMPETITIVE MARKET?

As the French media system has grown since the Liberation, it has become a much more competitive environment in the 1990s than it was 50 years ago. Fierce rivalry for audiences and revenue takes place both between and within the different media sectors, as newspapers, radio stations and television channels fight for market supremacy or just plain survival. Such competition has produced winners (for example, the provincial press, TF1, Canal Plus and NRJ) and losers (the Paris newspapers, the public sector television channels, La Cinq and the peripheral radio stations). The disappearance of dozens of newspaper titles since the war, the failure of many private radio stations in the late 1980s and the collapse of a national commercial television channel in the early 1990s, all testify to the downside of media competition for some players. Conversely, the huge success of Canal Plus and NRJ demonstrates that innovative programming combined with sophisticated marketing can reap their own rewards.

Yet even among the survivors, the effects of competition can be very damaging. Underfunded, poorly managed and demoralized by the success of its commercial rivals, public sector television for example has struggled since the mid-1980s. The values of public service broadcasting have been called into question over the past decade as the rump of the previously all powerful state monopoly has been compelled to redefine its mission in a television market increasingly geared towards the needs of advertisers. The structural reorganization of the second and third channels in the wake of the privatization of TF1 has not succeeded in resolving the crucial question of the role of public sector television in a competitive market system. In particular, the policy debate continues in the 1990s on the dilemma facing the public sector channels: should they seek to compete head-on with the commercial sector at the cost of losing their distinctiveness or should they complement the latter's output at the risk of low audience ratings and a loss of legitimacy?

The emphasis on greater competition among producers is, however, only one aspect of the relationship between the media in the postwar period. Competition has sometimes been offset by cooperation, as in the sharing of printing facilities and the creation of common advertising agencies by different newspapers. In addition, provincial press groups often respect each other's territory and do not seek to expand their regional empires for fear of disturbing the status quo. Perhaps the most significant constraint on competition is audience usage of the media. For consumers, the media are frequently perceived as complementary rather than competitive in the services they provide. To many French citizens the press represents their primary source of local and regional information, while television is preferred for its coverage of national and international events. Radio remains a popular medium in the morning and in the car, while television dominates the domestic scene in the evening. Finally, newspapers such as *Le Figaro*, *Libération* and *Le Monde* are used by their readers for in-depth background analysis to the frequently superficial news content of television and radio. In short, French consumers use a combination of print and audiovisual media to satisfy their many needs. This would suggest that they regard the media as performing complementary roles and consequently that there are limits to the extent of competition between, if not within, the different media sectors.

THE MIXED IMPACT OF NEW TECHNOLOGY

One common element running through the picture of postwar media change is the impact of new technology. Technological advances have revolutionized working practices in the press, facilitated the entry of new players into the radio and television markets and underpinned ambitious state-backed projects in cable and satellite broadcasting. In the print media new technology has contributed to every stage of the newspaper production process, cutting labour costs and easing the task of producing separate localized editions of provincial papers. In the audiovisual media two of the big success stories of the 1980s, Canal Plus and NRJ, have benefited from technological developments. The pay channel relies on programme scrambling and decoding equipment to maintain the integrity of its service, while the private radio network uses satellite to transmit its programmes to its franchise stations. Local cable systems across France provide television channels not available via terrestrial transmission, while telecommunications and broadcasting satellites have improved the quality of radio and television signals.

The impact of new technology has also made itself felt on the media policy agenda, especially in the audiovisual sector. One of the main features of media policy debates in France during the 1980s was the emphasis placed on the potential role of new programme delivery systems and their possible destabilizing consequences for established broadcasting structures and practices. This resulted in highly confused policy-making environments in which government ministers, state technocrats and media practitioners embarked on what was to become a steep and bumpy learning curve as they strove to formulate and implement policy in conditions of highly imperfect information.

Yet while new technology has radically altered many aspects of the functioning of the contemporary media, it is also important to emphasize the limitations of the technological revolution. The introduction of new technology in the print media has tended in the main to reinforce pre-existing patterns of ownership and control. Of itself, it has not produced greater diversity of titles, nor stemmed declining circulations. Most of the expansion in television supply since the Liberation, including the new channels set up in the 1980s, has come from additional terrestrial transmission networks. It is terrestrial broadcasters such as TF1 who continue to dominate the television market. Moreover, new technology played no part in key developments in the television sector in the 1980s such as the establishment of commercial channels or the privatization of TF1. Both of these initiatives are best explained with reference to political factors whereby electoral and ideological considerations exerted a powerful influence on policy making. Even the new media of cable and satellite have so far failed to capture public attention. Their penetration remains constrained partly because of the high investment costs and partly because of consumer resistance to their product. In any case, many cable systems are not using the advanced state-of-the-art technology originally proposed in the 1982 cable plan, while conversely the French DBS has proved more technologically sophisticated than has been found necessary. Overall, therefore, the impact of technological change on media developments has been more muted than seemed likely at the start of the 1980s.

CHANGE AND INNOVATION

As the media system has expanded since the war, new players have entered the market while others have dropped out. As a result, many of the names which now dominate the French media scene were unknown in the early postwar years. In the print media the change of ownership has largely resulted from the interplay of *economic* factors. In the audiovisual sector the transformation of the system owes more to the *legislative* innovations of the main broadcasting and communications statutes.

The French press had been virtually rebuilt from scratch immediately after the Liberation, with few pre-war press groups or titles surviving. Since then, the press has continued to undergo change. While several newspaper titles established after the war still survive in the 1990s, there have been important new entrants into and departures from the market in the intervening period. Several newspaper titles have managed to do both: going from launch to liquidation in the space of a few years or even less. More importantly, there have been major changes in the ownership of newspapers. Some press groups, such as the Prouvost group, have seen their power decline, while others, most notably Hersant, have risen to national prominence.

In radio, the state monopoly service inherited from the wartime Vichy regime found itself in competition for audiences with Radio Luxembourg. New peripheral stations, including Europe 1, were later set up and tolerated by the French state which had major shareholdings in them. The legalization of private radio in the 1980s allowed a whole host of new local and community radio stations to come into being. While many of these did not survive into the 1990s, the legacy of that era is still present. It is best embodied in the NRJ network which has grown from modest beginnings, successfully challenged the authority of the state and now ranks as one of the most popular radio stations in France.

Television has undergone the most fundamental changes in the postwar period as wave after wave of reform has resulted first in the structural reorganization of the public sector, and then in the establishment of new commercially run channels. The dismantling of the monolithic ORTF represented a move away from the model of an omnicompetent, unitary broadcasting corporation. In its place came separate production, transmission and programme companies, including three new state television channels: TF1, Antenne 2 and FR3. Liberalization policies in the 1980s following the abolition of the state monopoly saw the birth of Canal Plus, La Cinq and M6 (formerly TV6) and the privatization of TF1. The demise of La Cinq in 1992 demonstrated that it was just as possible for television channels as for newspapers to enter and leave the market in a remarkably short space of time. Meanwhile, the cultural channel, La Sept, also set up in the late 1980s, was replaced by ARTE only a few years later. Cable has encouraged the creation of a host of thematic channels, which, with their emphasis on a single programme genre (such as films, sport or music), represent an innovation in French television provision. Overall, the simplicity of the RTF public service monopoly in the 1950s has been replaced by a complex, multilayered system of channels operating under different regulatory regimes and offering different types of programme schedules. The functions of production and programming have become increasingly differentiated since the ORTF gave up its production monopoly in the 1960s. At the same time a system of highly restricted, producer-dominated supply has given way to one in which consumers have greater possibility of registering their viewing preferences.

Another notable change in the functioning of the postwar media has been in the realm of funding. One aspect of this is the growing importance of advertising as a source of income, with the total advertising budget for the media going up from 18,000 million francs in 1982 to over 50,000 million in 1990. Its percentage share in the turnover of the press has increased as the share from sales revenue has declined. Most of French radio is now financed through advertising. So too is much of French television, including the public sector channels, as advertising has burst through the barriers of a previously forbidden and then highly regulated market. In the television sector new means of funding have also been introduced, notably subscription and programme sponsoring. The success of subscription in the case of Canal Plus suggests a previously untapped reservoir of direct consumer payment for television at a time when the traditional licence fee system has come under renewed attack as anachronistic in an age of multichannel competition.

Finally, the growth of the media in general and the liberalization of the audiovisual sector in particular have opened up this sector of the economy to new actors. In the immediate postwar period the media formed a comparatively closed system. The print sector was dominated by newly created press groups and political parties emanating from the Resistance, while broadcasting was a state monopoly entrusted to the public service broadcasting organization, the RTF. Since the Liberation the political parties have, with the odd exception, long lost their direct controlling interest in the press. The state remains a major player, though its role has changed, as we shall see below. Public service broadcasting is now only part of a diverse radio and television provision. The audiovisual sector has seen the entry (and sometimes exit) of hitherto excluded players, including local authorities, utility companies, banks and finance houses, construction giants, private entrepreneurs and voluntary associations. As a result of these changes, the media system of the 1990s appears more open and pluralistic than its predecessor of 50 years previously.

CROSS-MEDIA OWNERSHIP

Or have the changes merely allowed for the emergence of powerful communications groups with interests across the different media sectors? Has cross-media ownership undermined diversity and choice for the consumer, with a few multimedia companies dominating the market?

The possibility for companies to have concurrent interests in the press, radio, television and new media dates only from the early 1980s when private radio and commercial television appeared on the scene. Prior to then, the state had a monopoly of ownership in television and a dominant position in radio (where the simplicity of the monopoly was confused only by the presence of peripheral stations), while the new media of cable and satellite had not yet begun to make their presence felt. Inasmuch as cross-media ownership has become an issue on the policy agenda, therefore, it is one which dates from relatively recently. During this period various media companies have followed complementary strategies of diversification, vertical integration and internationalization which has involved the spread of their interests and risks as they attempt to build up their position across traditional sectorial divisions and in different national markets. It is important to note that this is a fast-changing environment in which companies position and reposition themselves for maximum commercial advantage as technology develops, regulations change and new economic opportunities present themselves.

The three main multimedia companies in France since the early 1980s have been Hachette, Havas and Hersant. Of these, the largest is Hachette, which has a long history of media interests. Founded as a book publisher in 1829, Hachette became involved in newspaper distribution in the 1890s. Eliminated from participating in the media at the Liberation, it re-entered the press sector with a 49 per cent stake in what was to become the main newspaper distribution enterprise in France, Nouvelles messageries de la presse parisienne. Until 1976 the company had a stake in *France-Soir*, which it then sold to Hersant. Under its managing director, Jean-Luc Lagardère, Hachette's turnover grew impressively in the 1980s: from 7.8 billion francs in 1981 to 30 billion in 1990, in large part due to the company's expansion abroad, particularly in the United States. In 1988 the group's activities covered book and newspaper distribution (36.9 per cent of turnover); publishing (22.9 per cent), with stakes in Livre de Poche, Grasset and Fayard among others; broadcasting and advertising billboards (6.6 per cent), including a 40 per cent holding in Europe 1; and the press (33.6 per cent), including interests in newspapers such as *Les Dernières Nouvelles d'Alsace* (sold to the Hersant group in 1993), *Le Provençal*, *L'Echo républicain* and *Le Journal du Dimanche*, a string of weekly and monthly magazines including *Elle*, *France-Dimanche*, *Ici Paris*, *Le Nouvel Economiste*, *Parents* and *Fortune* and various television listings magazines including one of the market leaders, *Télé-7 jours*, and the newsaper supplement, *TV Hebdo*. Hachette also owned 25 per cent of *Le Parisien* and the sporting daily *L'Equipe*, as well as printing works and airport and railway station newspaper kiosks. The company has strong links with the Filipacchi press group, which owns various magazines including *Paris-Match*. Filipacchi also has a controlling interest in the Skyrock radio network. In the autumn of 1990 Hachette finally realized one of its goals in obtaining a controlling interest in a national television channel, La Cinq.[2]

The second major multimedia group in France is Havas, with a turnover of 26.5 billion francs in 1991. Privatized in 1987, Havas controls the largest advertising group in France, with about 20 per cent of market share. The group also has interests in publishing, tourism and in freesheet newspapers, the last through its participation in the Comareg company. In the audiovisual sector Havas has long had an interest in Audiofina (30 per cent in the early 1990s), which is the majority shareholder in the Luxembourg broadcasting company, the CLT. The CLT in turn runs Radio Luxembourg and is a major shareholder in the French commercial television channel M6. Finally, Havas is the principal shareholder in Canal Plus. Of the three major media groups which diversified into television ownership in the 1980s and early 1990s, the experience of Havas with Canal Plus was by far the most successful.

The third multimedia group in the 1980s was that run by Robert Hersant. Hersant built up a huge stake in the French press during the 1970s and early 1980s, mostly by buying up existing titles rather than starting those of his own. By the end of the decade the Hersant press group, organized round the central core company Socpresse, controlled an estimated 26.4 per cent of the total circulation of French daily newspapers and around 25 different daily titles.[3] His group also owned numerous magazines, particularly in the leisure interests sector (cooking, motoring, gardening, fishing and knitting, among others), a successful television listings weekly, *TV magazine*, various printing works and advertising agencies. In the late 1980s Hersant moved into the burgeoning audiovisual sector, taking a 25 per cent holding in La Cinq in 1987 and running the Fun-Chic private radio network which controlled around 30 stations by the early 1990s.

As we have already noted in chapter 7, the process of diversification by press groups into other media sectors gave rise to political concern in the mid-1980s, leading to the introduction of cross-media ownership legislation to prevent undue concentration both within and across the different sectors. In practice, however, limits on the extent of cross-media ownership have largely been the result of economic factors rather than legislative impediments. For example, several newspaper groups which sought to expand their interests into radio and television found the experience fell far short of their expectations. In November 1984, for instance, the Communist *L'Humanité* and the Socialist *L'Unité* left the Fréquence Presse radio station which since June 1982 had grouped these two titles together with *Le Parisien libéré*, *Le Matin* and the Bayard press group. In June 1985 Radio-Libération, launched a year earlier by the *Libération* newspaper, was abandoned.[4] In the provinces, too, several regional papers took a stake in local radio, only to get their fingers badly burnt. Meanwhile, attempts by newspapers in cooperative ventures to become involved in commercial television ownership were notably unsuccessful.

Even the three multimedia groups mentioned above have experienced significant failures in the pursuit of cross-media diversification. Hachette failed in its bid to win the TF1 franchise in 1987 and pulled out of La Cinq at the end of 1991, barely over a year after acquiring its television holding. Its plans to broaden its press interests by launching a new national popular daily newspaper (the *Omega* project) were abandoned.[5] The Havas group too has had its setbacks, notably its withdrawal from the Hachette-led consortium which bid for the TF1 franchise. Finally, the Hersant group, plagued by financial problems, reduced its shareholding in La Cinq in 1990 (selling to Hachette) and in early 1993 sold the Fun Radio network to the CLT. The Hersant group appeared to be moving away from diversification in the 1990s and concentrating on its original interests in the press.

INTERNATIONALIZATION

During the period since the Liberation the French media have been affected by a process of internationalization, whereby the domestic media have become increasingly integrated within, first, a European media system and, second, a global one. By highlighting the breakdown of national boundaries in various areas of contemporary media activity, internationalization emphasizes the inadequacy of an analysis which limits itself solely to the national dimension. There is a need, therefore, to situate postwar French media developments within wider European and global contexts.[6]

In certain respects internationalization is not a recent phenomenon for the French media. At no time during the whole of the postwar period have the French press, radio and television ever been totally isolated from media developments elsewhere. For instance, technological innovations in the means of production, transmission and reception have found their way into France from outside. So too have media formats. In the print media, for example, American weekly news magazines such as *Newsweek* and *Time* were clearly the model for their French variants, *L'Express* and *Le Point*. Media content has also been taken in from abroad. In the audiovisual sector French television has long used imported programmes, particularly from the United States, while French radio has depended on Anglo-American pop music to help fill its schedules.

Moreover, even where there is little evidence of a conscious decision to import a model from abroad, developments in the French media have frequently run in parallel with those in other countries. This was the case, for example, with the traditional postwar organization of French television. Despite its quintessentially national characteristics, the French television system between 1945 and 1982 was far from being a purely idiosyncratic system. Rather it shared many of the organizational and normative features of other national European broadcasting systems and so could easily be categorized as a variant of the dominant postwar European model: a geographically centralized, licence-fee-funded state monopoly, embodying a public service ethos.

These postwar manifestations of internationalization have been accentuated and supplemented in the past decade or so, as the process has spread and taken on new forms. The first of these, the transnational transmission of television programmes, is a consequence of advances in media technology. Satellite broadcasting, either direct to households or via cable networks, allows programme channels to cross previously well-defined national boundaries. This means that European viewers outside France have the possibility of watching French television output (for example through the programming of the Francophone channel TV5 available on Eutelsat), while French viewers hooked up to cable are exposed to the programming of other European broadcasters.

A second facet of internationalization is to be found in the field of media ownership. Ever more complex ownership patterns are being established, especially within Europe, as companies move out from strong domestic bases to acquire interests in foreign media markets. This is a two-way process: while the French media have been opened up to outside investors, French companies have sought to build up their media holdings abroad. The privatization and liberalization of the French audiovisual sector in the 1980s and growing European economic and political integration have accelerated this process. Recent examples of foreign companies which have acquired a stake in the French media include: Berlusconi's foray into the French commercial television sector in the late 1980s; Maxwell's holding in the privatized TF1; the shares in M6 held by the Luxembourg media group, CLT; the takeover of the financial newspaper *Les Echos* by the Pearson group, and of the women's magazine *Marie-France* by the German press group, Bauer; and the impressive penetration by the German media giant Bertelsmann, with a list of successful titles managed in France by the Prisma Presse group, including *Femme Actuelle*, *Prima* and *Télé loisirs*. French sorties into international media markets have also been in evidence. Canal Plus has a stake in pay-television channels in various European and African countries; the Chargeurs group is a shareholder in the satellite broadcaster BSkyB, which is currently expanding its audience reach in Britain; the Hersant group has extensive newspaper holdings in Belgium, Spain and several countries in eastern Europe; and Hachette has important publishing and audiovisual interests in the USA and Spain, with roughly half its turnover coming from its foreign holdings. Finally, the Franco-German cultural television channel ARTE, jointly funded by the two governments, is a new example of transnational cooperation in European television management.

A third facet of internationalization can be seen in media content. In the print media different national editions of the French magazines *Elle* and *Marie-Claire* are available in several countries. Indeed, sales of the foreign editions of the latter represent a quarter of the total turnover of the Marie-Claire Album group. Conversely, in the audiovisual sector the balance sheet is clearly negative. While France imports a large amount of audiovisual product from abroad, especially American films, detective series and soap operas, French programme exports are much more limited. Although steps have been taken at various times to promote the sale of French television programmes abroad, language and cultural mores remain a formidable barrier outside of Francophone areas. The hugh US market has proved a particularly difficult one for the French to exploit, as can be seen from the fact that while in 1990 France *imported* 600 million francs' worth of television programming from North America, it *exported* only 35 million francs' worth.[7]

Fourth, there has been an internationalization of media formats. The soap opera format has been adapted to French tastes (for example, *Châteauvallon*); the role of the US television news anchorperson has been imitated (for example Roger Gicquel on TF1 in the 1970s); American game shows such as *The Wheel of Fortune* have been copied in France, where they have gained nothing in the translation (*La roue de la fortune*); and *Le Muppets* has been transformed into a hugely popular political satire, the *Bébête Show*. Thematic channels on French cable networks have frequently imitated American equivalents, while in its use of pop music video-clips TV6 strongly evoked the approach of MTV.

The final recent feature of internationalization lies in the growing competence of the European Union in media matters. The EU has taken regulatory initiatives 'to establish common standards for satellite television transmission, to establish the single broadcasting market and to establish a programme of support for audiovisual production and distribution'.[8] By exploiting the supranational ramifications of the new audiovisual technology, the *Television Without Frontiers* directive, published in 1989, aimed to harmonize regulations in certain areas to help achieve a single broadcasting market across the EU member states. The provisions of the directive include, *inter alia*, the regulation of television advertising and programme sponsorship, a European content quota, steps to promote independent production and distribution companies, measures to defend the European cinema industry and steps to protect minors from violent or pornographic programming. Provisions also inhibit member states from restricting retransmission on their territory of television broadcasts from other member states.[9] Meanwhile, though the consequences for the print media have received less coverage, the creation of the single European market has meant that practices such as state aid to the French press are also no longer issues on a purely national political agenda.[10]

Does the internationalization of technology, ownership, content, formats and regulation mean that the French media are becoming less French? The authorities have long shown themselves to be conscious of this danger. In the eyes of French policy makers the values of French culture and civilization are constantly under threat from Anglo-American domination. Fears that the French language is being contaminated by the introduction of English expressions, that French cinema is being destroyed by the products of Hollywood, that French television may become a conduit for foreign programming and that the French media as a whole may lose their distinctive national identity are staple items in the political debate on the media, uniting politicians right across the party spectrum. During the General Agreement on Tariffs and Trade (GATT) negotiations in 1993 the French government typically fought long and hard to protect its audiovisual and cinema industries from what it regarded as unfair American competition in the proposed international free market of goods and services.

Through a combination of protectionism and pro-active measures the state has sought to promote French media product for cultural and economic reasons. For example, statutory regulations contained in the operating conditions of the television channels have included obligations to show quotas of programmes of French origin. Currently the precise nature of these regulations varies from channel to channel, with the public sector channels subject to the most onerous requirements. These programme quotas are a traditional method in France of protecting national programme production in the audiovisual sector. A variety of financial aid schemes has also been established over the years to encourage domestic programme production, particularly in the documentary and fiction genres.

The problem the French face in the audiovisual sector is self-evident. With the development of more television channels and the expansion in programme schedules, there has been a huge upsurge in demand for product to fill air time. French production companies, encouraged by the state, clearly want to maximize their share of this expanding market. For their part, the television channels want to keep their programming costs down to remain competitive. Since it is generally cheaper to import programmes from the United States, where production costs have been amortized in the domestic market, than to purchase programmes 'made in France', there is a natural conflict of interests between French producers and programmers. (This conflict is exacerbated if the imported programmes also prove popular with the audience, since then there are two factors – cost and ratings success – working in favour of imports. Conversely, the tension is mitigated if the audience prefer French productions.) The aim of the state has been to reconcile this conflict through regulation. The dilemma for programmers has been whether to abide by the regulations and risk losing audience share or to breach the regulations for commercial reasons and risk being sanctioned by the regulatory authority. To what extent the various measures taken by the state will be sufficient to protect and promote certain genres of programming (notably fiction) on French television channels in the future remains a matter of debate. It is also unclear how successful the measures will be in helping provide a solid base for French production industries to conquer new European programme markets outside France in competition with other national production industries such as those of the UK.

In any event, despite the different features of internationalization in the contemporary French media, the extent of this process should not be exaggerated, nor its consequences overstated. The low levels of cable and satellite penetration have so far effectively cut off the vast majority of French viewers from being exposed to foreign product via the internationalization of new media technology. For example, by the spring of 1992 only an estimated 650,000 French viewers had access to the channels transmitted from the Astra satellite.[11] In terms of ownership, most of the press, radio and television are still in the hands of French companies. Indeed, by the early 1990s foreign media moguls like Berlusconi and Maxwell had relinquished their holdings in French television ownership. Much media content is produced in France and reflects French tastes and sensibilities. The healthy circulation of many provincial newspapers provides striking evidence of the negligible impact of internationalization in this key media sector. Finally, the EU provisions on transnational television, though less stringent than the French government would have wished, do not undermine the capacity of the French state to impose regulations on its own national broadcasters. In short, the ramifications of internationalization for the French media and culture have so far proved less profound than anticipated.

THE STATE AND THE MEDIA

The measures taken by the authorities to defend and promote indigenous audiovisual production demonstrates that the French state continues to play an active role in media matters. The liberalization and privatization policies followed by French governments of Left and Right in the 1980s have not resulted in a powerless state. In fact, the performance of some functions by the state has continued largely unaltered throughout the post-war period, including the fixing of the level of the licence fee for public sector television and the provision of financial assistance to the press.

Undoubtedly other aspects of the state's relationship with the media have decreased in importance. For example, the state no longer directly controls and censors television news output the way it did during the de Gaulle presidency in the 1960s. The Ministry of Information no longer determines television's news agenda. In addition, state ownership of the media has fallen sharply in the wake of the privatization measures of the 1980s which saw TF1, Havas and Europe 1 sold off to the private sector. As a result, the extent of state ownership of the media in the 1990s is considerably reduced when compared with the era of the broadcasting monopoly. In the light of these changes it is tempting to speak of a notable weakening of the state's relationship with the media.

However, this would be too simplistic. While there has certainly been a transformation in the nature of the ties between the state and the media, this should not be equated with a relinquishing by the state of its interests in media content or performance. It is the manner in which that interest manifests itself, rather than the interest itself, which has changed profoundly since the early 1980s. For instance, while crude partisan political control of the media may be less evident than in the past, this is not synonymous with a depoliticization of output. Instead, state representatives have adapted to a multi-channel environment and a more sophisticated audience by seeking to get their message across with greater subtlety than in the past, coopting rather than controlling the media. The importance of the media as a political tool has not been rejected. However, now politicians place greater emphasis on image projection and agenda structuring rather than crude manipulation. As a primary definer of issues the state has become more sophisticated in its use of the media to ensure that the official version of events dominates press, radio and television coverage.

Meanwhile the role of the state as regulator has increased. During the 1980s there was an upsurge of legislative activity, affecting all media sectors: the press, radio, television and the new media. In an environment in which economic, technological and political factors combined to produce conditions of extreme turbulence, the state was obliged to define the rules on a whole variety of policy issues from concentration of ownership to the status of public service television. In the audiovisual sector the need to draft new regulations for a multi-channel system led to a flourishing of official reports, policy statements and legislative proposals. While the question of deregulation was central to the media debate in the 1980s, the same decade saw the establishment by the state of no fewer than three successive regulatory authorities for radio and television. As well as drafting the rules, the state also controlled the procedure of appointment to these new authorities. In short, developments in the media in the 1980s, particularly the major changes in the audiovisual sector, necessitated active state involvement as policy was formulated, implemented, reformulated and reimplemented in quick succession.

While it is impossible to predict the future relationship between the state and the media in France, it seems safe to assume that the state will remain a major actor in this field. Many of the issues which dominated the policy debate in the 1980s have not been fully resolved, while new issues (and old ones in new forms) will no doubt come on to the media policy agenda in the years to come. Cross-media ownership, financial aid to the press, the dissemination of French cultural products via the media, the balance of party political coverage and the future of France's audiovisual industries – these topics among others seem certain to be part of the media policy debate well into the third millenium. Whatever the precise terms of that debate, it is one in which the state seems likely to play a central, influential role.

Notes

INTRODUCTION

1 P. Albert, *La presse française*, Paris, La documentation française, 1990, pp.22–23.

2 For an overview of the debate on media effects see D. McQuail, *Mass Communication Theory*, London, Sage, 1987, pp.249–295.

3 Ibid., p.69. For some interesting comments on the media functions debate see McQuail, op. cit., pp.68–72.

4 For an alternative typology of media functions see McQuail, op. cit., p.71.

5 Press coverage of an alleged corruption deal involving the former Prime Minister, Pierre Bérégovoy, may have led to the latter's suicide in May 1993. This case illustrates the fine line to be drawn between investigative journalism and character assassination when the media act as a public watchdog.

6 The most durable regime – the Third Republic – survived for 70 years (1870–1940). Other political systems such as the Vichy state (1940–44) and the Fourth Republic (1946–58) lasted for only a few years.

7 A notable example of press power in this respect is the leading role played by journalists in 1830 and 1848 in overthrowing the government. For instance, the practice of state interference in the press contributed to the Revolution of 1830, which began when groups of liberal journalists protested against Charles X's abrogation of press freedom. See A. Smith, *The Newspaper: An international history*, London, Thames and Hudson, 1979, p.112.

8 For much of French political history these divisions have been not just concurrent, but also superimposed on each other, creating cross-cutting cleavages in French society. These in turn have usually been reflected in parliamentary representation. Consequently, French politics has often presented a complex mosaic to the Anglo-American observer more accustomed to a simple dualistic political conflict. As Philip Williams writes, 'where Britain had two major political attitudes, France never had fewer than three. The clerical and conservative Right was opposed by a socialist Left (itself, since the rise of the Communist party, internally divided by the deepest fissure of all). But between these rivals was a great amorphous mass of peasants and small businessmen, who were social and economic conservatives yet ardent Republicans and anticlericals' (P. M. Williams, *Crisis and Compromise*, London, Longman, 1964, 3rd edn, p.4).

9 On the historical bases of the ideological and social divisions in France see D. Thomson, *Democracy in France since 1870*, Oxford, Oxford University Press, 1969, 5th edn.

10 Political parties have ranged from representatives of the extreme Right (for example, Action Française, Pétainists, Poujadists and most recently supporters of the National Front) to those of the extreme Left (various Trotskyist, Maoist, Anarchist and other left-wing groups) and have included a variety of mainstream political forces occupying the ideological terrain between these two poles. The mainstream parties have themselves been divided, not just *between* Right and Left but *within* both of these broad camps as well. The French Centre too has usually embraced numerous different parties.

11 On the concept of polarized pluralism see G. Sartori, 'European political parties: the case of polarized pluralism', in J. Lapolambara and M. Weiner (eds), *Political Parties and Political Development*, Princeton, Princeton University Press, 1966, pp.137–176.

12 For example, notwithstanding the formation of the Union of the Left in the early 1970s, the Communist and Socialist parties have at best been friendly rivals, at worst implacably warring enemies. The Right has been split between Gaullist and non-Gaullist forces, despite the apparent emergence of a catchall Gaullist party in the early 1970s. The Centre parties (the Radicals and the Christian Democrats among others) have found it difficult to resist the bipolarizing pressures engendered by the existence of a powerful presidential office and a two-ballot electoral system, while at the same time they have been fearful of losing their identity by being totally subsumed within one of the larger, fragile coalitions of Left or Right. In addition, the emergence of post-industrial issues on the political agenda has found political expression in new social and political movements, such as the Greens. Left-wing fringe parties have flitted around the edges of the mainstream Left, achieving prominence most notably during the 1968 'events' and then either retreating into oblivion or being incorporated into the new Socialist party of François Mitterrand in the 1970s. Finally, on the extreme Right, Jean-Marie Le Pen's National Front achieved international prominence in the 1980s with its impressive electoral scores based on a platform of racism against ethnic minorities, support for tough law and order measures and virulent condemnation of the established mainstream parties of both Left and Right. On the Left in the postwar period see R. W. Johnson, *The Long March of the French Left*, London, Macmillan, 1981. On the Right see J. Charlot, *The Gaullist Phenomenon*, London, Allen and Unwin, 1971.

13 The most notable exception to this presidential dominance in media policy making was the period of *cohabitation* from 1986 to 1988 when the Prime Minister and his office at Matignon took over responsibility for domestic policy from the President and his staff at the Elysée.

14 For an alternative typology of the links between the state and the media in France see J. W. Freiberg, *The French Press: Class, state and ideology*, New York, Praeger, 1981, pp.155–205.

15 A. de Tarlé, 'The press and the state in France', in A. Smith (ed.), *Newspapers and Democracy*, Cambridge, Mass., MIT, 1980, pp.127–148.

16 Freiberg, op. cit., pp.199–203.

17 According to Palmer and Tunstall, some commentators go even further than this and have observed that in the broadcasting sector 'perhaps the period 1945–81, of a state monopoly of transmission networks and of programming, was a hiatus, an aberration in the tradition of French broadcasting' (M. Palmer and J. Tunstall, *Liberating Communications: Policy-making in France and Britain*, Oxford, Blackwell, 1990, p.75).

1 THE PRESS: HISTORY AND ECONOMICS

1 Service Juridique et Technique de l'Information (SJTI), *Tableaux statistiques de la presse 1990*, Paris, La documentation française, 1992, p.9. The 2,913 titles were made up of 97 dailies, 22 Sundays, 895 weeklies, 1,141 monthlies, 726 quarterlies and 32 others (ibid., p.47). The corresponding total for 1989 was 2,880 titles.
2 See the Conclusion for more information on this phenomenon.
3 H. Gough, *The Newspaper Press in the French Revolution*, London, Routledge, 1988, p.44; A. Smith, *The Newspaper: An international history*, London, Thames and Hudson, 1979, p.88. Gough writes that 'by the end of 1789 Paris had seen over 130 new political newspapers come on to the market, to replace or rival the six that can be described as political, which had been in circulation at the beginning of the year' (p.26).
4 M. Mathien, *La presse quotidienne régionale*, Paris, PUF, 1986, 2nd edn, p.3.
5 See, for example, Y. Guillauma, *La presse en France*, Paris, La Découverte, 1988, pp.13–15.
6 Gough, op. cit., p.231.
7 Whereas 'by 1850 only some 3,000 kilometres of line were open to traffic, another 14,500 kilometres were added during the Second Empire, and then by 1890 that figure was more than doubled again.' (D. Thomson, *France: Empire and Republic, 1850–1940*, New York, Walker, 1968, p.8).
8 Gough comments that 'the beginnings of industrialisation and steady economic growth from the 1830s onwards opened the way to large-scale advertising and commercial exploitation of the press's potential' (Gough, op. cit., p.231).
9 T. Zeldin, *France 1848–1945, Volume Two: Intellect, taste and anxiety*, Oxford, Oxford University Press, 1977, p.526.
10 Ibid., p.527.
11 See chapter 2 for details on the 1881 press statute.
12 'The extension of the franchise also brought more people into the political net and extended the potential readership to almost the entire adult population by the end of the century' (Gough, op. cit., p.231).
13 Zeldin, op. cit., p.535.
14 N. Hewitt, 'The birth of the glossy magazines: the case of *Paris-Match*', in B. Rigby and N. Hewitt (eds), *France and the Mass Media*, Basingstoke, Macmillan, p.111.
15 See chapter 2 for information on state censorship of the press by the Vichy regime.
16 R. Aron, *The Vichy Regime 1940–44*, London, Putnam, 1958, pp.198–200.
17 See chapter 3 for information on the role of radio during the Second World War.
18 On the clandestine press in wartime France see C. Bellanger, *Presse Clandestine 1940–1944*, Paris, Armand Colin, 1961.
19 H. R. Kedward, *Occupied France*, Oxford, Blackwell, 1985, p.52.
20 H. R. Kedward, *Resistance in Vichy France*, Oxford, Oxford University Press, 1978, p.45.
21 Kedward, *Occupied France*, p.52.
22 Aron, op. cit., pp.142 and 200.
23 Kedward, *Resistance*, p.244.
24 P. Bilger and P. Lebedel, *Abrégé du droit de la presse*, Paris, CFPJ, 1991, p.28.
25 See chapter 2 for information on the party political press after the Liberation.
26 J.-M. Charon, *La presse en France de 1945 à nos jours*, Paris, Seuil, 1991, p.53.
27 Smith, op. cit., p.176.
28 P. Albert, *La presse française*, Paris, La documentation française, 1990, p.96.

29 L. Guéry, *La presse régionale et locale*, Paris, CFPJ, 1992, p.23.

30 D. J. Hart, 'Changing relationships between publishers and journalists: an overview', in A. Smith (ed.), *Newspapers and Democracy*, Cambridge, Mass., MIT, 1980, p.276; SJTI, op. cit., pp.84 and 86.

31 Guillauma, op. cit., p.123; Guéry, op. cit., p.23.

32 V. Lalu, 'Redresser les quotidiens', *Médiaspouvoirs*, no.19, Paris, 1990.

33 E. Lambert, 'Prix de vente des quotidiens: le lecteur français est-il défavorisé?', *Médiaspouvoirs*, no.8, Paris, 1987.

34 P. Todorov, *La presse française à l'heure de l'Europe*, Paris, La documentation française, 1990, p.18.

35 Guillauma, op. cit., p.124.

36 Note, however, that the situation is different with magazine reading. According to certain estimates, within the European Community France had the highest penetration rate of magazines at 1,354 per 1,000 inhabitants in 1985. This compared with 1,183 for Belgium, 1,055 for the Netherlands, 1,018 for West Germany, 711 for Italy, 656 for Great Britain and 218 for Spain (see Todorov, op. cit., pp.18 and 118).

37 In 1990 it was estimated that 19 million French people over the age of 15 regularly read a regional daily, 83 per cent of them every day, a much higher figure than the readership of the Paris dailies (Guéry, op. cit., p.89).

38 As the text makes clear, this trend in favour of the provincial over the Paris press pre-dates the Second World War. See Guéry, op. cit., p.16.

39 Albert, op. cit., p.36.

40 A. Pedley, 'The media', in M. Cook (ed.), *French Culture since 1945*, London, Longman, 1993, p.150.

41 Other local mayors who have played an important role in national politics during the Fifth Republic include Jacques Chaban-Delmas (Bordeaux), Pierre Mauroy (Lille) and Gaston Defferre (Marseilles).

42 V. Wright, *The Government and Politics of France*, London, Unwin Hyman, 1989, 3rd edn, ch. 12, especially pp.319–323.

43 Perhaps to compensate for their poor consumption of daily newspapers, Parisians are greater users of radio than inhabitants of the provinces. See N. Doucant, 'Le public de la radio', *Médiaspouvoirs*, no.21, Paris, 1991, p.161.

44 Albert, op. cit., p.96.

45 Charon, op. cit., pp.97–104.

46 C. Conso, 'Un quotidien populaire national: une idée neuve?', *Médiaspouvoirs*, no.19, Paris, 1990.

47 Albert, op. cit., p.73.

48 It is worth noting that concentration as measured by the decline in the number of titles is not apparent in every sector of the French press. For example, weekly and monthly magazines have been much less affected, even if there has been a turnover in specific titles. In fact, daily newspapers constitute the only sector of the press where there has been a marked decline in the number of titles.

49 On the short life of *La Truffe* see M. Scriven and F. Kierszenbaum, '*La Truffe* est remise en terre', *Modern and Contemporary France*, no.49, Portsmouth, 1992.

50 Other market failures have included *Le Matin de Paris, J'informe, Vingt-quatre heures* and a whole assortment of fringe papers. *Le Quotidien de Paris* launched in April 1974 continues to survive but only with great difficulty.

51 Guéry, op. cit., p.17; Mathien, op. cit., pp.17–18.

52 Hart, op. cit., p.276; Guillauma, op. cit., pp.57–59.

53 Georges Vedel quoted in Mathien, op. cit., pp.27–28.

54 Guéry, op. cit., pp.18–19.

55 Albert, op. cit., p.91. Hersant's press interests include: *Le Figaro, France-Soir, Paris-Turf*, various magazines and the following provincial titles: *Nord-Eclair, Nord-Matin, Havre libre, Le Havre-Presse, Paris-Normandie, La Liberté du Morbihan, Presse-Océan, L'Eclair, Centre-Presse, Le Dauphiné libéré, Lyon-Matin, Le Progrès, La Tribune, L'Espoir, Loire-Matin, Lyon-Figaro, Le Bien public, Les Dépêches* and *L'Union*, as well as shares in *Midi libre, L'Indépendant, Le Courrier de Saône-et-Loire, L'Est républicain* and *L'Ardennais*. See Guéry, op. cit., p.17.
56 Todorov, op. cit., p.12.
57 SJTI, op. cit., p.20.
58 Ibid.
59 Y. Lorelle, *La presse*, Paris, Retz, 1992, pp.137–142. See also Guéry, op. cit., p.90. According to Guéry it is unusual in the regional press sector for advertising to exceed 50 per cent of total income. Revenue from sales is usually higher than that from advertising.
60 Todorov, op. cit., pp.19–20.
61 Albert, op. cit., p.78.
62 Ibid, p.81.
63 See chapter 2 for an analysis of the multifaceted role of the state in press matters.
64 N. Toussaint Desmoulins, 'Les effets pervers des aides à la presse', *Médias-pouvoirs*, no.8, Paris, 1987, p.107.
65 Ibid., p.108.
66 Albert, op. cit., pp.44 and 73.
67. A. de Tarlé, 'The press and the state in France', in A. Smith (ed.), *Newspapers and Democracy*, Cambridge, Mass., MIT, 1980, p.135. De Tarlé's chapter provides a useful account of the conflict at *Le Parisien libéré* which I have drawn upon in this section.
68 Albert, op. cit., pp.62 and 68.
69 Charon, op. cit., p.146.
70 E. Ducarroir, 'Evolution de la diffusion des quotidiens et principaux périodiques français de 1988 à 1991', *Médiaspouvoirs*, no.28, Paris, 1992, p.155.
71 Guéry, op. cit., pp.104–105. See the Conclusion for an assessment of cross-media ownership in France.

2 THE PRESS: POLITICS

1 P. Todorov, *La presse française à l'heure de l'Europe*, Paris, La documentation française, 1990, p.30.
2 I. Collins, *The Government and the Newspaper Press in France 1814–1881*, Oxford, Oxford University Press, 1959, p.xiv.
3 A. Smith, *The Newspaper: An international history*, London, Thames and Hudson, 1979, p.87.
4 H. Gough, *The Newspaper Press in the French Revolution*, London, Routledge, 1988, pp.154–155.
5 Collins, op. cit., p.183.
6 D. Thomson, *France: Empire and Republic, 1850–1940*, New York, Walker, 1968, p.108.
7 Smith, op. cit., p.110.
8 This summary is based on accounts in the following: Smith, op. cit., p.114; Collins, op. cit., pp.181–183; and Thomson, op. cit., p.108.
9 Smith, op. cit., p.114.
10 Thomson, op. cit., p.108.

11 T. Zeldin, *France 1848–1945, Volume Two: Intellect, taste and anxiety*, Oxford, Oxford University Press, 1977, pp.548–549.

12 A. Cobban, *A History of Modern France, Volume 3: 1871–1962*, Harmondsworth, Penguin, 1965, p.24. On this aspect of the abuse of the freedoms enshrined in the 1881 law, see J. F. McMillan, *Twentieth-Century France*, London, Edward Arnold, 1992, p.90.

13 Thomson, op. cit., p.108.

14 J.-C. Asselain, 'Les nationalisations 1944–1945', in *Etudes sur la France de 1939 à nos jours*, Paris, Seuil, 1985.

15 Y. Guillauma, *La presse en France*, Paris, La Découverte, 1988, p.19.

16 J.-M. Charon, *La presse en France de 1945 à nos jours*, Paris, Seuil, 1991, Introduction and section 1, especially pp.70–71.

17 Guillauma, op. cit., p.21.

18 P. Albert, *La presse française*, Paris, La documentation française, 1990, p.170.

19 A. Stone, *The Birth of Judicial Politics in France*, Oxford, Oxford University Press, 1992, pp.176–177.

20 F.-O. Giesbert, *Le Président*, Paris, Seuil, 1990, pp.235–237.

21 Stone, *Birth of Judicial Politics*, p.180.

22 S. C. Labrousse and P. Robinet (eds), *Paris et enjeux de la presse de demain*, Grenoble, Presses Universitaires de Grenoble, 1987, pp.78-79; Albert, op. cit., p.43.

23 Stone, *Birth of Judicial Politics*, p.186.

24 A. Stone, 'Where judicial politics are legislative politics: the French Constitutional Council', *West European Politics*, vol.15, London, 1992, p.40.

25 Stone, *Birth of Judicial Politics*, p.192.

26 See chapter 7.

27 See Stone, *Birth of Judicial Politics*, ch. 7, pp.173–208 for a detailed account of the legislative process of the 1984 and 1986 press reforms (and the 1986 audiovisual reform), with particular emphasis on the rulings of the Constitutional Council in all three cases.

28 Albert, op. cit., p.43.

29 See chapters 3–7 on radio and television.

30 Zeldin, op. cit., p.493.

31 Smith, op. cit., p.89. Robespierre personified the change in approach. From being a defender of the freedom of the press during the lifetime of the Constituent Assembly, he later 'accepted the practical necessity for the government to exercise control over the opinions of the people, and abandoned the liberty of the press, which he had formerly defended so often and with such ardour'. (A. Cobban, *Aspects of the French Revolution*, St Albans, Paladin, 1971, p.174).

32 Gough, op. cit., p.83.

33 Ibid., p.100.

34 Ibid., p.154.

35 Collins, op. cit., p.82.

36 Ibid., pp.114–115.

37 On the 1852 legislation see Collins, op. cit., pp.116–135 and Thomson, op. cit., pp.107–108.

38 Smith, op. cit., pp.112-113.

39 Collins, op. cit., p.136.

40 On censorship of the press in the First World War, see McMillan, op. cit., p.68, and J.-M. Charon, '1914–1918: la presse française dans la grande guerre', *Médiaspouvoirs*, no.23, Paris, 1991.

41 H. R. Kedward, *Resistance in Vichy France*, Oxford, Oxford University Press, 1978, pp.187–188.
42 A. Horne, *A Savage War of Peace*, Harmondsworth, Penguin, 1979, p.232; J. Talbott, *The War Without a Name*, London, Faber and Faber, 1981, p.211. Talbott writes that 'Throughout the war it [the government] freely indulged in what *The Economist* called "squeezing the press." For some editors, visits from the police became as routine as visits from the mailman. . . . No government tried to establish a formal apparatus of censorship. But each did its best to prevent the press from publishing certain kinds of information, especially allegations or revelations of the use of torture. Nothing was more likely to invite the attention of the authorities than charging the army with misconduct' (Talbott, op. cit., pp.106–107).
43 P. Knightley, *The First Casualty*, London, Pan, 1989, p.362.
44 J. Keane, *The Media and Democracy*, Oxford, Polity Press, 1991, p.97.
45 H. Alleg, *The Question*, London, John Calder, 1958, pp.7–9.
46 P. Brooks and A. Hayling, 'Drowning by bullets', *Secret History*, Channel 4 television, London, July 13 1992.
47 Talbott, op. cit., p.112.
48 Knightley, op. cit., p.370.
49 On the concept of primary definer see S. Hall, C. Critcher, T. Jefferson, J. Clarke and B. Roberts, *Policing the Crisis*, London, Macmillan, 1978, ch.3.
50 For example, between 1792 and 1794 Robespierre, who had previously viewed with suspicion all governmental authority and placed his faith in the unfettered operation of public opinion, 'came to believe in the duty of government not only to control, but also to create, public opinion. For this purpose he became ready to call every agency that could influence opinion into action' (Cobban, *Aspects of the French Revolution*, p.175).
51 After the end of the Second World War the state set up Agence France-Presse (AFP) as the major French news agency to take over the information-gathering functions of the pre-war Havas agency. The AFP soon became the nerve centre of the French press system, with all major French newspapers largely dependent on its services for information provision. Between 1944 and 1957 the AFP had such extremely close links with the French government that the credibility of the agency abroad was severely undermined. While in 1957 the agency's links with the authorities were somewhat relaxed, the French state continued to enjoy an important role in the funding and management of the AFP.
52 McMillan, op. cit., p.91.
53 Zeldin, op. cit., p.524.
54 C. Seymour-Ure, *The Political Impact of Mass Media*, London, Constable, 1974, pp.157–159.
55 Ibid., pp.160 and 173.
56 J.-P. Rioux, *La France de la Quatrième République, Volume 2: L'expansion et l'impuissance 1952–1958*, Paris, Seuil, 1983, p.336.
57 Seymour-Ure, op. cit., p.168.
58 Ibid., pp.164–165.
59 Ibid., p.172.
60 Ibid., pp.156–176.
61 See C. Monnot and X. Ternisien, '*Le Figaro*: Sans la liberté de changer . . .', *Médiaspouvoirs*, no.13, Paris, 1989.
62 See table 1.7 for circulation figures.
63 J. Curran and J. Seaton, *Power Without Responsibility: The press and broadcasting in Britain*, London, Routledge, 1991, 4th edn, p.124. Curran and Seaton

argue that in Britain in 1987 the Conservative Party had the support of 72 per cent of national daily circulation but only 43 per cent of the vote.

3 RADIO

1 Lewis and Booth write that 'radio is marginalised in policy debates in favour of the newer media, and has been displaced by television from its former command of the domestic hearth' (P. M. Lewis and J. Booth, *The Invisible Medium*, Basingstoke, Macmillan, 1989, p.xii).

2 C. Méadel, 'The arrival of opinion polls in French radio and television 1945–60', in B. Rigby and N. Hewitt (eds), *France and the Mass Media*, Basingstoke, Macmillan, 1991, p.150.

3 J. Bourdon, *Histoire de la télévision sous de Gaulle*, Paris, Anthropos/INA, 1990, p.90.

4 Ibid., pp.207–208.

5 P. Desgraupes, *Hors antenne*, Paris, Quai Voltaire, 1992, pp.80 and 83. See also Bourdon, op. cit., pp.147–159.

6 Bourdon, op. cit., p.154.

7 A. Werth, *De Gaulle*, Harmondsworth, Penguin, 1967, p.269.

8 L. Bernard, *Europe 1: La grande histoire dans une grande radio*, Paris, Centurion, 1990, p.118.

9 A.-J. Tudesq, 'La radio, les manifestations, le pouvoir', in Comité d'Histoire de la Télévision, *Mai 68 à l'ORTF*, Paris, La documentation française, 1987, p.142.

10 These were: Le Poste Parisien, Radio-Agen, Radio-Béziers, Radio-Bordeaux-Sud-Ouest, Radio-Juan-les-Pins, Radio-LL, Radio-Lyon, Radio-Mont-de-Marsan, Radio-Montpellier, Radio-Nîmes, Radio-Toulouse, Radio-Vitus and Radio-Paris. Radio-Normandie officially joined this list in 1933. See F. Cazenave, *Les radios libres*, Paris, PUF, 1980, 1st edn, p.19.

11 P. Miquel, *Histoire de la radio et de la télévision*, Paris, Perrin, 1984, p.35.

12 Ibid., p.32.

13 Cazenave, op. cit., p.12.

14 Miquel, op. cit., pp.32–33.

15 Cazenave, op. cit., pp.19–20.

16 Ibid., p.20.

17 A. Briggs, *The History of Broadcasting in the United Kingdom*, vol. 2, *The Golden Age of Wireless*, London, Oxford University Press, 1965, pp.350–352.

18 R. H. Coase, *British Broadcasting: A study in monopoly*, London, Longmans, 1950, ch. 5.

19 Briggs, *Golden Age of Wireless*, p.352.

20 Ibid., p.365.

21 Ibid.

22 Miquel, op. cit., pp.32–33; Cazenave, op. cit., p.20.

23 Miquel, op. cit., p.75.

24 Ibid., p.77. See also Cazenave, op. cit., pp.20–21.

25 R. Thomas, *Broadcasting and Democracy in France*, London, Crosby Lockwood Staples, 1976, p.3.

26 P. Amaury, *Les deux premières expériences d'un ministère de l'information en France*, Paris, Pichon et Durand-Auzias, 1969, pp.409–422; and H. Eck (ed.), *La guerre des ondes*, Paris, CRPFL, 1984.

27 A. Briggs, *The History of Broadcasting in the United Kingdom*, vol. 3, *The War of Words*, London, Oxford University Press, 1970, p.173.

28 Ibid., p.227.

29 Ibid., pp.178, 180, 239 and 251.
30 A. Smith, *The Shadow in the Cave*, London, Allen and Unwin, 1973, p.157.
31 A. Briggs, *War of Words*, p.5. See C. de Gaulle, *Mémoires de guerre*, Paris, Plon, 1954, pp.89 and 108.
32 Werth, op. cit., p.103.
33 M. Anderson, *Government in France*, Oxford, Pergamon, 1970, p.44.
34 J. Lacouture, *De Gaulle The Rebel 1890–1944*, London, Collins Harvill, 1990, p.225. The reference in the original French version is J. Lacouture, *De Gaulle le rebelle 1890–1944*, Paris, Seuil, 1984, p.370. The text of de Gaulle's appeal of June 18 1940 may be found immediately before the cited quotation from Lacouture's biography.
35 H. R. Kedward, *Occupied France*, Oxford, Blackwell, 1985, p.48.
36 Briggs, *War of Words*, p.242.
37 J. Charlot, *The Gaullist Phenomenon*, London, Allen and Unwin, 1971, p.92.
38 Kedward, op. cit., p.53.
39 Briggs, *War of Words*, p.251.
40 Ibid.
41 H. Coston, *Dictionnaire de la politique française*, Paris, La Librairie Française, 1967, p.901.
42 H. Eck, 'Radio, culture and democracy in France in the immediate postwar period 1944–50', in B. Rigby and N. Hewitt (eds), *France and the Mass Media*, Basingstoke, Macmillan, 1991, p.130.
43 Miquel, op. cit., pp.146–147.
44 Ibid., p.148.
45 Briggs, *War of Words*, pp.736–737.
46 B. Voyenne, *L'information en France*, London, McGraw-Hill, 1972, p.126; and Thomas, op. cit., pp.2–5.
47 Eck, 'Radio, culture and democracy', p.131.
48 The best general work on the politics of the Fourth Republic is P. M. Williams, *Crisis and Compromise*, London, Longman, 1964, 3rd edn.
49 J. Montaldo, *Dossier ORTF 1944–1974: Tous coupables*, Paris, Albin Michel, 1974, pp.29, 43, 49, *passim*.
50 Eck, op. cit., p.132.
51 Ibid., p.136.
52 P. M. Williams, *The French Parliament 1958–1967*, London, Allen and Unwin, 1968, p.91; and Thomas, op. cit., pp.5–10.
53 Thomas, op. cit., pp.102–107; Voyenne, op. cit., pp.131–134; and J. E. Ray and M. Ray, *Corsaires des ondes*, Paris, Cerf, 1978.
54 Cazenave, op. cit., p.23.
55 Bernard, op. cit., p.387.
56 C. Durieux, *La télécratie*, Paris, Tema, 1976, p.45.
57 Miquel, op. cit., p.16; and Bernard, op. cit., p.506.
58 Bernard, op. cit., pp.409, 627 and 630.
59 Miquel, op. cit., pp.150-152.
60 C. Méadel, 'L'information à France-Inter', in Comité d'Histoire de la Télévision, *Mai 68 à l'ORTF*, Paris, La documentation française, 1987.
61 Tudesq, op. cit., p.146.
62 Bernard, op. cit., p.265; Cazenave, op. cit., p.30; and Lewis and Booth, op. cit., p.147.
63 Lewis and Booth, op. cit., p.139.
64 M. Siegel, *Vingt ans ça suffit*, Paris, Plon, 1975; and Bernard, op. cit., pp.357–380.
65 Bernard, op. cit., p.498.

66 Ibid., pp.408 and 418.
67 Ibid., pp.523–538 and 588.
68 Ibid., pp.545–546.
69 Ibid., pp.634 and 639.
70 On the pirate radio phenomenon in France see F. Ténot, *Radios privées, radios pirates*, Paris, Denoel, 1978; Cazenave, op. cit.; and A. Cojean and F. Eskenazi, *FM: La folle histoire des radios libres*, Paris, Grasset, 1986.
71 D. Sassoon, 'Political and market forces in Italian broadcasting', in R. Kuhn (ed.), *Broadcasting and Politics in Western Europe*, London, Frank Cass, 1985.
72 F. Chassaing, *Radio Fil Bleu*, Dunkirk, Westhoek, 1980.
73 C. Collin, *Ecoutez la vraie différence*, Claix, La pensée sauvage, 1979.
74 The decision may have been the responsibility of the Prime Minister, Pierre Mauroy. See Lewis and Booth, op. cit., p.152.
75 See chapter 6 for more details on the composition and responsibilities of the High Authority.
76 On private local radio in the early 1980s see R. Prot, *Des radios pour se parler*, Paris, La documentation française, 1985.
77 Lewis and Booth, op. cit., p.154.
78 Prot, op. cit., p.38, and Lewis and Booth, op. cit., p.154.
79 P. Petit, 'L'âge de raison des réseaux FM', *Médiaspouvoirs*, no.24, Paris, 1991, p.103.
80 Lewis and Booth, op. cit., pp.155–157.
81 B. Clarens, 'Parcours sans faute de Jean-Paul Baudecroux, entrepreneur de radio', *Médiaspouvoirs*, no.15, Paris, 1989.
82 P. Vittet-Philippe and P. Crookes, *Local Radio and Regional Development in Europe*, Manchester, European Institute for the Media, n.d., p.85.
83 Prot, op. cit., pp.55–58.
84 Bernard, op. cit., p.486.
85 D. Hamelin, 'Décentralisation de Radio France', *Médiaspouvoirs*, no.18, Paris, 1990, p.120.
86 Ibid., p.118.
87 G. Hare, 'The law of the jingle, or a decade of change in French radio', in R. Chapman and N. Hewitt (eds), *Popular Culture and Mass Communication in Twentieth Century France*, Lampeter, The Edwin Mellen Press, 1992, p.34.
88 N. Doucant, 'Le public de la radio', *Médiaspouvoirs*, no.21, Paris, 1991, p.161.
89 Ibid., p.165.
90 See chapter 7 for more details on the composition and responsibilities of the CNCL and the CSA.
91 Lewis and Booth, op. cit., p.155.
92 Petit, op. cit., p.103.
93 Radio France enjoys a different status with the CSA and is provided with frequencies to ensure its public service mission.
94 Petit, op. cit., pp.105–107.
95 Ibid., p.107.
96 Hare, op. cit., p.28.
97 R. Méjan, 'Stratégies et concurrence dans la radio', *Médiaspouvoirs*, no.16, Paris, 1989.
98 Hamelin, op. cit., p.118.
99 As has already been mentioned in the text, some networks have targeted an older audience. At least one has aimed at a younger age group. Superloustic is targeting children between 8 and 12 years old, using one of the few FM formats not imported from the USA. The station, which is a *de facto* national network, emphasizes interactivity between its listeners and presenters, using a format

which rejects non-stop music. The problem for Superloustic is not so much how to attract its target audience as how to persuade advertisers that the audience represents an important consumer group. For more details see P. Petit, 'Superloustic: le copain des enfants sur la bande FM', *Médiaspouvoirs*, no. 25, Paris, 1992.
100 P. Petit, 'Trop de réseaux en France?', *Médiaspouvoirs*, no.25, Paris, 1992.
101 The *Independent*, August 29 1992.
102 Hare, op. cit., p.44.
103 Lewis and Booth, op. cit., p.162.

4 TELEVISION UNDER DE GAULLE

1 On reasons for France's backwardness in the market penetration of television see R. Thomas, *Broadcasting and Democracy in France*, London, Crosby Lockwood Staples, 1976, pp.6–7.
2 On the hostility of many French intellectuals to mass culture see B. Rigby, *Popular Culture in Modern France*, London, Routledge, 1991.
3 On the origins of French television see P. Miquel, *Histoire de la radio et de la télévision*, Paris, Perrin, 1984, pp.190–198.
4 Rigby, op. cit., p.42.
5 J. Durand, 'L'évolution des audiences de la radio et de la télévision au cours des quarante dernières années', *Médiaspouvoirs*, no.21, Paris, 1991, p.138. By 1983 94 per cent of French households had a television set.
6 Ibid.
7 J. Bourdon, *Histoire de la télévision sous de Gaulle*, Paris, Anthropos/INA, 1990, p.164.
8 J.-P. Rioux, *The Fourth Republic 1944–1958*, Cambridge, Cambridge University Press, 1987, p.443.
9 L. Wylie, *Village in the Vaucluse*, Cambridge, Mass., Harvard University Press, 1974, 3rd edn, p.348.
10 J.-L. Missika and D. Wolton, *La folle du logis*, Paris, Gallimard, 1983, p.40.
11 De Gaulle's vision of how the new institutions should operate had been spelled out in 1946 in a speech at Bayeux. The political immobility of the Fourth Republic had done nothing to temper that vision – on the contrary, for de Gaulle the party-dominated regime of the 1950s had been responsible for many of the social, economic and political problems which France had experienced during the 1950s. In his view, chronic governmental instability and party bickering had resulted in a lack of political direction at home and a loss of reputation abroad. The absence of strong effective leadership at the apex of the political system was for him a particularly crucial defect. This was to be remedied after 1958. Under the provisions of the new Constitution the power of the executive was enhanced at the expense of the legislature, while within the executive a sharing of power seemed to be envisaged between the President as head of state and the Prime Minister as head of government. In practice, however, the presidency under de Gaulle emerged as the primary source of executive authority. In fact, the powerful office of the presidency was the single most important difference between the Fifth Republic and its predecessor. It represented the most significant institutional development in postwar French politics. See C. de Gaulle, *Mémoires d'espoir*, Paris, Plon, 1970, ch. 1 and ch. 7.
12 M. Palmer and J. Tunstall, *Liberating Communications: Policy-making in France and Britain*, Oxford, Blackwell, 1990, p.76.
13 G. Dupuis and J. Raux, *L'ORTF*, Paris, Armand Colin, 1970, p.7.

14 M. Anderson, *Government in France*, Oxford, Pergamon, 1970, p.175.

15 P. Viansson-Ponté, *Histoire de la République Gaullienne*, vol. 1, Paris, Fayard, 1970, pp.266–267.

16 Palmer and Tunstall, op. cit., p.81.

17 P. M. Williams, *French Politicians and Elections 1951–69*, London, Cambridge University Press, 1970, p.118.

18 Anderson, op. cit., p.49; J. C. Maitrot and J. D. Sicault, *Les conférences de presse du Général de Gaulle*, Paris, PUF, 1969.

19 A. Werth, *De Gaulle*, Harmondsworth, Penguin, 1967, p.361; see also P. Viansson-Ponté, *Les gaullistes*, Paris, Seuil, 1963, p.52.

20 In pre-war France the political system of the Third Republic, with its democratic base in the provinces rather than Paris, its numerous small, self-contained constituencies and its weak party organization, resulted in an emphasis on local political personalities and issues. This emphasis was already shifting during the 1950s as post-war economic reconstruction, the demands of indicative planning and the growth of the state pushed national political issues more firmly to the top of the political agenda. Television further amplified this trend towards *national* political debate. See P. M. Williams, *Crisis and Compromise*, London, Longman, 1964, 3rd edn, pp.60–62.

21 C. Durieux, *La télécratie*, Paris, Tema, 1976.

22 On the public service tradition in British broadcasting see R. Negrine, *Politics and the Mass Media in Britain*, London, Routledge, 1989, ch. 5.

23 Viansson-Ponté, *Histoire de la République Gaullienne*, vol. 1, p.70.

24 J. Montaldo, *Dossier ORTF 1944–74: Tous coupables*, Paris, Albin Michel, 1974, pp.124–125.

25 Bourdon, op. cit., pp.82–83 and p.123.

26 Ibid., p.52.

27 An extreme but not necessarily atypical example of this one-sided coverage of politics in the early years of the regime occurred 'during de Gaulle's visit to the United States in April 1960, [when] the French radio seemed to think it quite natural to start one of its news bulletins with the words: "In the absence of General de Gaulle, there is no political news in France today"' (A. Werth, *The De Gaulle Revolution*, London, Robert Hale, 1960, p.396).

28 Williams, *French Politicians and Elections*, p.98.

29 Viansson-Ponté, *Histoire de la République Gaullienne*, vol. 1, p.71; see also Werth, *De Gaulle*, pp.247–248.

30 Williams, *French Politicians and Elections*, p.139; see also Anderson, op. cit., p.184.

31 Bourdon, op. cit., p.99.

32 Ibid., p.90.

33 A. Smith, *The Shadow in the Cave*, London, Allen and Unwin, 1973, pp.158–59.

34 On the background to and content of the 1964 ORTF statute see Thomas, op. cit., pp.14–19.

35 Bourdon, op. cit., pp.212–215.

36 F. Cazenave, *Les radios libres*, Paris, PUF, 1980, p.23.

37 The chapter on the media in *Le mal français* presents an account of the liberalizing measures Peyrefitte introduced as Minister of Information and an explanation for the lack of greater progress in this domain. It is an apologia for his ministerial term in office, the claims of which ring hollow when compared against the record. See A. Peyrefitte, *Le mal français*, Paris, Plon, 1976.

38 The 1964 statute did go some way to moving the state broadcasting organization further away from the mentality and functioning of a civil service department in which many employees clung to civil service attitudes and work practices. A

significant move in this direction had already been made in 1960 with a new staff statute. It is important not to confuse the appointment of *énarques* at the top of the ORTF hierarchy with the maintenance of a civil service mentality lower down. At the same time as the former was becoming a feature of the system, the latter was beginning to wane.

39 Bourdon, op. cit., pp.44–45.

40 Ibid., p.69. Bourdon gives the example of the imposition of the terms of the minimum service to be provided by ORTF staff in case of industrial action.

41 Ibid., p.104.

42 P. Viansson-Ponté, *Histoire de la République Gaullienne*, vol. 2, Paris, Fayard, 1971, pp.183–184.

43 Cahiers de la Fondation Nationale des Sciences Politiques, *L'élection présidentielle des 5 et 19 décembre 1965*, Paris, Armand Colin, 1970.

44 J. Ardagh, *The New France*, Harmondsworth, Pelican, 1973, 2nd edn, p.611.

45 J. Thibau, *Une télévision pour tous les français*, Paris, Seuil, 1970, pp.273–282.

46 C. Debbasch, *Traité du Droit de la Radiodiffusion: radio et télévision*, Paris, Librairie générale de droit et de jurisprudence, 1967, p.106.

47 For example, in 1963–64 the state blocked the credits necessary for the launching of the second channel. See Bourdon, op. cit., p.219. Bourdon argues that *a posteriori* financial control did not really come into existence until 1974, after partial improvements in 1964 and 1969 (ibid., p.28).

48 The debate about the financial autonomy enjoyed by the ORTF is a complex one. For example, while a parliamentary committee of inquiry published in 1968 condemned the excessive powers of the state controller in matters such as staff recruitment and promotion, it concluded that, for much of the ORTF's operational budget, there was no external *a priori* control. Some progress had been made, therefore, after 1964 in reducing the control of the Ministry of Finance over broadcasting expenditure. Diligent Report, *Documents Sénat* no.118, Paris, Journaux Officiels, 1968, pp.74–76.

49 The annual debate in Parliament on the approval of the licence fee was often the pretext for a wide debate about political control of the ORTF. Opposition deputies used the opportunity to criticize government manipulation of the corporation. Parliamentarians of all parties also frequently used the occasion to condemn the waste and financial mismanagement which they alleged was rife within the ORTF.

50 Up until 1968 the only form of advertising allowed on state television was of the generic kind, which encouraged viewers to buy a certain produce (e.g. chicory) without reference to a particular brand name. This type of advertising (*la publicité compensée*) had been introduced as early as 1951 with the aim of boosting the consumption of domestic agricultural produce. It had grown from 0.7 per cent of the RTF budget in 1960 to 3.3 per cent in 1966. The politically controversial issue, however, was whether to allow the introduction of brand advertising (*la publicité de marques*) on to state television.

51 For further details on the role of the commercial television lobby in the late 1960s see Thomas, op. cit., pp.110–122; Thibau, op. cit., pp.134–137 and pp.149–153; and the Diligent Report, op. cit., pp.210–256.

52 The phrase 'the brute force of monopoly' was used by the first director general of the BBC, John Reith, in his opposition to the establishment of commercial television in Britain. See I. McIntyre, *The Expense of Glory: A life of John Reith*, London, HarperCollins, 1993, p.301.

53 Rigby, op. cit., p.131.

54 Bourdon, op. cit., p.125.

55 Missika and Wolton, op. cit., pp.34–35.
56 Bourdon, op. cit., pp.129–133.
57 J. Beaulieu, *La télévision des réalisateurs*, Paris, La documentation française, 1984.
58 Bourdon, op. cit., pp.65–66.
59 Ibid., pp.164–169.
60 Ibid., pp.160–164.
61 Ibid., p.73.
62 Missika and Wolton, op. cit., p.23. Missika and Wolton portray the period between 1945 and 1953 as one in which policy making in the television field was dominated by technicians and engineers.
63 Bourdon, op. cit., pp.217–219.
64 Ibid., p.227. For the terms of the Franco-Soviet agreement see Dupuis and Raux, op. cit., pp.95–96.
65 Bourdon, op. cit., pp.225–231.
66 The May events have been variously interpreted as psychodrama, a crisis of the techno-bureaucratic state, a crisis of modernization and a crisis of a stalemate society. See R. Aron, *La révolution introuvable*, Paris, Fayard, 1968; A. Touraine, *The May Movement, Revolt and Reform*, New York, Random House, 1971; B. Brown, *Protest in Paris*, Morristown, General Learning Press, 1974; and M. Crozier, *La société bloquée*, Paris, Seuil, 1970.
67 C. Manigand and I. Veyrat-Masson, 'Les journalistes et la crise', in Comité d'Histoire de la Télévision, *Mai 68 à l'ORTF*, Paris, La documentation française, 1987.
68 J.-P. Filiu, 'Le gouvernement et la direction face à la crise', in Comité d'Histoire de la Télévision, *Mai 68 à l'ORTF*, Paris, La documentation française, 1987, p.165.
69 On the 1968 events at the ORTF see R. Louis, *L'ORTF un combat*, Paris, Seuil, 1968; C. Frédéric, *Libérer l'ORTF*, Paris, Seuil, 1968; J.-P. Manel and A. Planel, *La crise de l'ORTF*, Paris, Pauvert, 1968; A. Astoux, *Ondes de choc*, Paris, Plon, 1978; and Comité d'Histoire de la Télévision, *Mai 68 à l'ORTF*, Paris, La documentation française, 1987. Short summaries in English can be found in Thomas, op. cit., pp.26–30, and A. Smith, *The Shadow in the Cave*, London, Quartet, 1976, pp.82–86.
70 Manigand and Veyrat-Masson, op. cit., p.83.
71 Y. Guéna, *Le temps des certitudes*, Paris, Flammarion, 1982, p.280, quoted in Filiu, op. cit., p.192.
72 Comité d'Histoire de la Télévision, op. cit., pp.218–219.
73 Bourdon, op. cit., p.267.
74 Ibid., p.269.
75 L'Année Politique, Paris, 1968, pp.369–372.
76 Diligent Report, op. cit., p.260.
77 Viansson-Ponté, *Histoire de la République Gaullienne*, vol. 1, p.151.

5 TELEVISION: THE DECLINE AND FALL OF THE ORTF

1 J. Durand, 'L'évolution des audiences de la radio et de la télévision au cours des quarante dernières années', *Médiaspouvoirs*, no.21, Paris, 1991, p.138.
2 Ibid.
3 On the extent of Pompidou's reformist commitment see G. Pompidou, *Le nœud gordien*, Paris, Plon, 1974.
4 R. W. Johnson, *The Long March of the French Left*, London, Macmillan, 1981.

5 De Gaulle called a referendum in April 1969, nominally on the question of Senate and regional reform, but in fact on the central issue of his presidential leadership. On this occasion, however, the French electorate failed to accept the traditional Gaullian dichotomy of himself or chaos. The skilful handling of the government negotiations by Prime Minister Pompidou at the height of the 1968 protest had shown that a vote against de Gaulle in the referendum would not necessarily lead to regime instability and collapse. Moreover, the opposition to de Gaulle of some leading right-wing politicians, including Giscard d'Estaing, broke the fragile unity of the Gaullist-dominated governing coalition. In these circumstances, de Gaulle's attempt to re-establish his special link with the French people failed and he immediately resigned the presidency.

6 Poher was President of the Senate and interim President of the Republic after de Gaulle's resignation. In contrast to 1965, the Socialists and Communists put up separate candidates in the 1969 election. For the first and only time in direct elections to the presidency during the Fifth Republic, Mitterrand shrewdly chose not to stand. While the Communist vote held up reasonably well, the Socialist candidate was humiliated. Neither of the two candidates of the Left secured enough first ballot support to be represented at the second ballot run-off in which Pompidou defeated Poher with relative ease.

7 *Le Monde*, May 27 1969.

8 *L'Express*, no.936, June 9–15 1969.

9 *Le Monde*, May 17 1969.

10 On this aspect of the 1969 reform see J. Ardagh, *The New France*, Harmondsworth, Pelican, 1973, 2nd edn, pp.612–613; J. Thibau, *La télévision, le pouvoir et l'argent*, Paris, Calmann-Lévy, 1973, pp.17–46; and G. Martinet, *Le système Pompidou*, Paris, Seuil, 1973, pp.120–131.

11 J. Chaban-Delmas, *L'Ardeur*, Paris, Stock, 1975, ch. 31.

12 Desgraupes later described one incident which in his opinion illustrated the poor relationship between the channel one news team and the Elysée in the early 1970s:

> I can quote you an example which was at the origins of my conflict with Pompidou and which, in the end, caused my departure shortly soon after. He had travelled to the east of France and his visit had been covered by. . . Hervé Chabalier. . . . He had filmed the visit objectively. Pompidou had been booed by some young people, as happens quite frequently to Presidents of the Republic on visits. Perhaps we gave too much coverage to this . . . anyway, the report went out on a Friday evening, and on the Saturday morning the telephone rang early, at around 8 o'clock. It was Pompidou's press officer. He said that he found the report disgraceful, that we had given far too much importance to the demonstrations. I went to see him at the Elysée. I asked him what he wanted me to do. It wasn't worth asking me to sack Chabalier, I wouldn't have done it. He told me quite simply that he would no longer be accredited at the Elysée. . . . My relationship with Pompidou gradually deteriorated when he realized that the television programmes I was making were not those which served him the best.
> (P. Desgraupes, *Hors antenne*, Paris, Quai Voltaire, 1992, pp.123–24)

13 D. Bombardier, *La voix de la France*, Paris, Robert Laffont, 1975, pp.88–91. Evident in their disagreement over broadcasting policy, the widening rift between President Pompidou and Prime Minister Chaban-Delmas ended in the total breakdown of their relationship at the executive heart of the state. Despite a huge vote of confidence accorded the Prime Minister in Parliament in May, Pompidou dismissed him from the premiership barely a month later. The

political lesson of 1972 showed that presidential dominance of the institutions of the Fifth Republic had been institutionalized; it was not just a feature of General de Gaulle's tenure of the office. The 1972 ORTF statute can thus be interpreted as one sign of the consolidation of presidential power under Pompidou.

14 Diligent Report, *Documents Sénat, 1971–1972, no.165*, Paris, Journaux Officiels, and Le Tac Report, *Documents Assemblée Nationale, 1971–1972, no.2291*, Paris, Journaux Officiels. Both parliamentary reports were published in April 1972.

15 Paye Report, *Rapport de la commission d'étude du statut de l'ORTF*, Paris, La documentation française, 1970.

16 For an exposition of Malaud's political views and his opinions on the broadcasting issue see P. Malaud, *La révolution libérale*, Paris, Masson, 1976, esp. pp.13–32.

17 *Le Monde*, July 19 1972.

18 On the 1972 statute see R. Thomas, *Broadcasting and Democracy in France*, London, Crosby Lockwood Staples, 1976, pp.39–44, and J. Chevallier, *La radio-télévision française entre deux réformes*, Paris, Librairie Générale de Droit et de Jurisprudence, 1975, pp.9–121.

19 For an account of the events leading up to Conte's dismissal see A. Conte, *Hommes libres*, Paris, Plon, 1973, pp.300–326.

20 A. Smith, *The Shadow in the Cave*, London, Quartet, 1976, p.95.

21 A graduate of the prestigious Ecole Nationale d'Administration and the Ecole Polytechnique and a brilliant technocrat, Giscard d'Estaing had been Minister of Finance under both de Gaulle (1962–65) and Pompidou (1969–74). His Independent Republican party had generally supported the Gaullist government in Parliament without ever being integrated within the Gaullist party. Thus, in the 1974 campaign, Giscard d'Estaing could emphasize both continuity with the Gaullist tradition in the Fifth Republic and at the same time maintain a distance from the unpopular aspects of Gaullist policy. On the Giscardian presidency in general see J. Frears, *France in the Giscard Presidency*, London, Allen and Unwin, 1981; V. Wright (ed.), *Continuity and Change in France*, London, Allen and Unwin, 1984; and M. Larkin, *France since the Popular Front*, Oxford, Oxford University Press, 1988, ch. 18.

22 A radical reorganization of state broadcasting at the beginning of his presidential term was only one of a series of early reforms designed to set the tone for the Giscardian presidency. Giscard d'Estaing's election victory was immediately followed by the introduction of various measures designed to give the new President a liberal, humanitarian image in the eyes of the public. These included the suppression of widely abused telephone tappings, the lowering of the age of majority from 21 to 18, liberalization of the laws on contraception, improvements in the penal system and promised changes on the controversial issues of abortion and divorce.

23 Chinaud Report, *Documents Assemblée Nationale, 1973–74*, no.1072, Paris, Journaux Officiels. For a summary of the contents of the Chinaud Report see Thomas, op. cit., pp.74–77.

24 Interview on Radio Europe 1, May 13 1974.

25 H. Mercillon (ed.), *ORTF l'agonie du monopole?*, Paris, Plon, 1974, pp.80–98; M. Poniatowski, *Cartes sur table*, Paris, Fayard, 1972, p.113.

26 See ch. 7 on the privatization and liberalization of television.

27 See ch. 3 on radio.

28 See ch. 8 on the new media.

29 For a detailed exposition of the provisions of the 1974 broadcasting statute see

Chevallier, op. cit., pp.123–322. For a briefer summary see Thomas, op. cit., pp.63–67.
30 V. Giscard d'Estaing, *Démocratie française*, Paris, Fayard, 1976, p.99.
31 When the broadcasting companies were affected by strikes in 1979, new legislation was introduced to limit the capacity of the broadcasting unions to disrupt programming.
32 In a letter written by President Giscard d'Estaing to the heads of the programme companies in January 1975, the President asserted that:

> The authorities do not intend to run [name of the company] through you. They delegate this role to you in its entirety until the end of your term of office. That is why they must establish relations with your company, as they do with the other important media of press and information, that is to say by a periodic exchange of views on their initiative or yours regarding the most important problems in the life of [name of the company], but without ever interfering in your managerial and news broadcasting responsibilities. If you come across any exception to this principle which I regard as fundamental, I ask you to bring it to my attention personally.
>
> (M. Jullian, *Courte supplique au roi pour le bon usage des énarques*, Paris, Mazarine, 1979, pp.20–21)

33 Under the terms of the legislation the new director generals (who also chaired their respective board of governors) were guaranteed a minimum three-year term of office.
34 M. Jullian, *La télévision libre*, Paris, Gallimard, 1981, pp.137–140.
35 A. de Tarlé, 'France: the monopoly that won't divide', in A. Smith (ed.), *Television and Political Life*, London, Macmillan, 1979, pp.62–65.
36 C. Durieux, *La télécratie*, Paris, Tema, 1976, pp.82–85, and J. Diwo, *Si vous avez manqué le début*, Paris, Albin Michel, 1976, pp.264–265.
37 Jullian recounts the story in both the books previously cited. See Jullian, *Courte supplique au roi*, pp.21–22 and *Télévision libre*, pp.141–142.
38 J.-J. Ledos, J.-P. Jézéquel and P. Régnier, *Le gâchis audiovisuel*, Paris, Editions ouvrières, 1986, p.173.
39 F. Giroud, *La comédie du pouvoir*, Paris, Fayard, 1977, p.174.
40 J.-L. Missika and D. Wolton, *La folle du logis*, Paris, Gallimard, 1983, pp.71–72.
41 For a strong critique of the effects of the system of competition on programme policy between 1974 and 1981 see Ledos *et al.*, op. cit., pp.111–157.
42 Missika and Wolton, op. cit., pp.70–71.
43 For Averty's account of this meeting see J. Siclier, *Un homme averty*, Paris, Jean-Claude Simoen, 1976, pp.192–201.
44 *Le Monde*, April 24 1976.
45 *Rapport fait au nom de la commission d'enquête sur les conditions de l'information publique . . .*, *Documents Assemblée Nationale,* no.1289, Paris, Journaux Officiels, 1979, p.28.
46 G. Lavau and J. Mossuz-Lavau, 'The Union of the Left's defeat: suicide or congenital weakness', in H. Penniman (ed.), *The French National Assembly Elections of 1978*, Washington, American Enterprise Institute, 1980, pp.110–143.
47 A. Duhamel, *La république giscardienne*, Paris, Grasset, 1980, p.100.
48 Television news could not avoid covering the allegations that Giscard d'Estaing had accepted a personal gift of diamonds from the Central African tyrant, but the issue was raised cautiously and with due deference to presidential sensibilities.
49 C. Ockrent, *Duel*, Paris, Hachette, 1988.

50 Giscard d'Estaing's antagonism towards the Gaullists, which had helped bring
    about de Gaulle's downfall in the 1969 referendum, was repaid in kind during
    the 1981 presidential elections when Chirac gave only muted support to Giscard
    d'Estaing before the second ballot, thus helping to secure his defeat and
    Mitterrand's victory.

6 TELEVISION: THE END OF THE STATE MONOPOLY

1   For an analysis of the abolition of the state monopoly in radio see ch. 3.
2   F. Mitterrand, *Ici et maintenant*, Paris, Fayard, 1980, pp.99–13.
3   On the Italian broadcasting system in the 1980s see D. Sassoon, 'Political and
    market forces in Italian broadcasting', in R. Kuhn (ed.), *Broadcasting and
    Politics in Western Europe*, London, Frank Cass, 1985; and G. Mazzoleni, 'Is
    there a question of vulnerable values in Italy?', in J. Blumler (ed.), *Television
    and the Public Interest*, London, Sage, 1992.
4   M. Palmer and J. Tunstall, *Liberating Communications: Policy-making in
    France and Britain*, Oxford, Blackwell, 1990, p.183.
5   Quoted in F.-O. Giesbert, *Le Président*, Paris, Seuil, 1990, p.153.
6   R. Kuhn, 'The presidency and the media, 1974-82' in V. Wright (ed.), *Continuity
    and Change in France*, London, Allen and Unwin, 1984, pp.178–201.
7   For an insider view of the transition by an Antenne 2 journalist, see N. Mamère,
    Telle est la télé, Paris, Mégrelis, 1982.
8   *Le Monde*, September 29 1981.
9   T. Pfister, *La vie quotidienne à Matignon au temps de l'union de la gauche*, Paris,
    Hachette, 1985, pp.132–133.
10 See, for example, the critique put forward by Alain Peyrefitte in *Quand la rose
    se fanera . . .* , Paris, Plon, 1983, especially ch. 19.
11 See, for instance, the views put forward by a former Giscardian minister, Michel
    d'Ornano, in *La manipulation des médias*, Paris, Albatros/Veyrier, 1983.
12 Moinot Report, *Pour une réforme de l'audiovisuel, Rapport au Premier ministre
    de la Commission de réflexion et d'orientation présidée par Pierre Moinot*, Paris,
    La documentation française, 1981.
13 In 1979 92.7 per cent of French households possessed a television set. By 1983
    this figure had increased only slightly to 94.0 per cent (J. Durand, 'L'évolution
    des audiences de la radio et de la télévision au cours des quarante dernières
    années', *Médiaspouvoirs*, no.21, Paris, 1991, p.138).
14 Moinot recommended that another three would be drawn from top judicial bod-
    ies such as the Cour de Cassation and the Conseil d'Etat and a further three per-
    sons would be coopted from a list of names put forward by the National Council
    for Broadcasting (a proposed consultative assembly on broadcasting matters).
    Moinot also recommended that the chairperson should be elected by the mem-
    bers of the High Authority, who would all enjoy a guaranteed six-year non-
    renewable term of office.
15 Ironically, this method of appointing the members of the High Authority was a
    carbon copy of that employed to nominate the members of the Constitutional
    Council, despite the fact that the latter body had been severely criticized by the
    Socialist government for its alleged political bias in holding up the nationaliza-
    tion legislation.
16 M. Cotta, *Les miroirs de Jupiter*, Paris, Fayard, 1986, pp.157–191.
17 Ibid., p.118.
18 Ibid., p.238.
19 Besides having a stake in Radio Télévision Luxembourg, Havas was also active

in the fields of advertising and travel. Other original shareholders in Canal Plus included a banking consortium, a privately run water authority, a property company, two insurance companies and a regional press group.

20 One of the former chairmen of Havas, Yves Cannac, had previously been a member of President Giscard d'Estaing's *cabinet* at the Elysée and had participated in the drafting of the 1974 broadcasting reform.

21 Previously, Rousselet had been Mitterrand's *chef de cabinet* during the Fourth Republic and had managed the financial side of his first two presidential election campaigns.

22 For a short biography of Rousselet see J. Tunstall and M. Palmer (eds), *Media Moguls*, London, Routledge, 1991, pp.158–159.

23 C. Pastiaux, 'Les recettes de Canal Plus', *Médiaspouvoirs*, no.14, Paris, 1989, p.110.

24 B. Schmutz and M. Glayman, 'Canal Plus: le verrouillage', *Médiaspouvoirs*, no.23, Paris, 1991, p.95.

25 Ibid., p.98.

26 R. Lunven and T. Vedel, *La télévision de demain*, Paris, Armand Colin, 1993, p.204.

27 Tunstall and Palmer, op. cit., p.159.

28 On the early months of Canal Plus see B. Guillou, *Les stratégies multimédias des groupes de communication*, Paris, La documentation française, 1985, pp.19–23.

29 Pastiaux, op. cit., p.111.

30 Schmutz and Glayman, op. cit., p.98.

31 See ch. 8 on the new media for an analysis of the development of cable television in France.

32 This phrase was part of the terms of reference of the Bredin committee as set out in the letter of January 14 1985 from Prime Minister Laurent Fabius to Jean-Denis Bredin. See J.-D. Bredin, *Les nouvelles télévisions hertziennes*, Paris, La documentation française, 1985, p.5.

33 Ibid., pp.160–166.

34 On the Berlusconi media empire in Italy see G. Mazzoleni, 'Media moguls in Italy', in Tunstall and Palmer (eds), op. cit., pp.162–183.

7 PRIVATIZATION AND LIBERALIZATION

1 For a critical commentary on the 1986 statute see B. Delcros and B. Vodan, *La liberté de communication: Loi du 30 septembre 1986, analyse et commentaire*, Paris, La documentation française, 1987.

2 On the *cohabitation* period in general see J. Tuppen, *Chirac's France, 1986–88*, London, Macmillan, 1991.

3 See D. Swann, *The Retreat of the State*, London, Harvester Wheatsheaf, 1988, ch. 4, pp.128–163; and P. Dunleavy and B. O'Leary, *Theories of the State*, London, Macmillan, 1987, ch. 3, pp.72–135.

4 P. Fysh, 'Gaullism and the Liberal Challenge', University of London, unpublished Ph.D. thesis, 1990. Fysh argues that, during the first half of the 1980s, the Gaullist party abandoned the state interventionism which had been the party's traditional economic policy while it was the dominant force in French politics during the 1960s in favour of a liberalism which stressed individual responsibility and the free play of market forces. He argues that the party's ideological development can be explained less with reference to organizational, generational or electoral factors, than by long-run changes in the climate of ideas in society generally, which acted as the source of a synthesis that could articulate the

interests of an alliance of technocrats and the party's business friends who exerted considerable influence on the drafting of the new party programmes (P. Fysh, op. cit., p.2).

5 Swann, op. cit., p.13.

6 M. Bauer, 'The politics of state-directed privatisation: the case of France, 1986–88', *West European Politics*, vol.11, London, 1988, p.49.

7 Ibid., p.51. Apart from Havas and TF1, firms with an interest in communications which were privatized included the Compagnie Générale d'Electricité (CGE) and the defence firm Matra.

8 Tuppen, op. cit., p.186.

9 Bauer, op. cit., p.58.

10 M. Palmer and J. Tunstall, *Liberating Communications: Policy-making in France and Britain*, Oxford, Blackwell, 1990, p.192.

11 Le Monde dossiers et documents, *La télévision en 1987: le grand chambardement*, Paris, Le Monde, 1988, p.54.

12 For a partisan insider account of this successful strategy see H. Bourges, *Une chaîne sur les bras*, Paris, Seuil, 1987.

13 The *Guardian*, January 19 1987.

14 Bourges, op. cit., p.197. Tuppen argues that Léotard wanted the transfer of at least two channels to the private sector, while Chirac preferred to settle for one. According to Tuppen, it was Chirac who won this ministerial conflict of wills and in May it was announced that TF1 would be privatized, 'a surprise choice and again one originally not favoured by Francois Léotard' (Tuppen, op. cit., p.191).

15 Le Monde dossiers et documents, op. cit., p.20.

16 T. Bower, *Maxwell: The outsider*, London, Mandarin, 1991, p.450.

17 Ibid., ch. 15, pp.447–487.

18 Ibid., p.454.

19 Jean-François Lacan, in Le Monde dossiers et documents, op. cit., p.23.

20 Palmer and Tunstall, op. cit., p.195.

21 N. Davies, *The Unknown Maxwell*, London, Pan, 1993, p.245.

22 The *Independent*, February 8 1991.

23 The respective jurisdictions of the government and the CNCL are set out in Palmer and Tunstall, op. cit., p.190. The roles of the High Authority and the CNCL are contrasted in Delcros and Vodan, op. cit., pp.15–18.

24 E. Ballaguy, 'Le Figaro, France-Soir et La 5', *Médiaspouvoirs*, no.8, Paris, 1987.

25 The Constitutional Council had played a key role on a similar issue two years previously, when it had ruled on the Socialist government's 1984 press reform. See ch. 2.

26 A. Stone, 'Where judicial politics are legislative politics: the French Constitutional Council', *West European Politics*, vol.15, London, 1992, p.41.

27 Ibid., pp.41–42.

28 For detailed tables giving the different cross-media ownership combinations permitted by the 1986 legislation see Delcros and Vodan, op. cit., pp.95–98.

29 On the 1988 presidential elections see J. Gaffney (ed.), *The French Presidential Elections of 1988*, Aldershot, Dartmouth, 1989.

30 The 13 members of the CNCL were appointed as follows. The President of the Republic, the President of the National Assembly and the President of the Senate each chose two members. The Conseil d'Etat, the Cour de Cassation and the Cour des Comptes, the highest administrative and judicial bodies in the country, chose one member each, as did the Académie Française. The ten members appointed then coopted three proven professionals, one in

telecommunications, one from the print media and the last from the creative sector of broadcasting (Le Monde dossiers et documents, op. cit., pp.6–7).

31 Palmer and Tunstall, op. cit., p.190.

32 The *Guardian*, January 19 1987.

33 C. Mauriat, *La presse audiovisuelle*, Paris, CFPJ, 1989, p.15.

34 Three members including the chairman were appointed by the President of the Republic, three by the President of the National Assembly and three by the President of the Senate. For the membership see Mauriat, op. cit., p.18.

35 Mauriat, op. cit., p.19.

36 J.-P. Delivet, 'Une nouvelle instance de régulation: le Conseil supérieur de l'audiovisuel', *Médiaspouvoirs*, no.14, Paris, 1989.

37 See articles by Bertrand Delcros and Francis Balle on the CSA in *Médiaspouvoirs*, no.29, Paris, 1993.

38 B. Cousin, 'Quel avenir pour France 3?', *Médiaspouvoirs*, no.29, Paris, 1993.

39 D. Mehl, 'Audiovisuel: le service public, naufrage d'une notion', *Médiaspouvoirs*, no.19, Paris, 1990. On the notion of vulnerable values in French television see D. Wolton, 'Values and Normative Choices in French Television', in J. Blumler (ed.), *Television and the Public Interest*, London, Sage, 1992, pp.147–160.

40 In 1992 in recognition of their joint public sector status, Antenne 2 and FR3 were renamed France 2 and France 3 respectively.

41 For a bitter denunciation of the CSA and the Socialist government's handling of the crisis at Antenne 2 and FR3 see P. Guilhaume, *Un président à abattre*, Paris, Albin Michel, 1991.

42 E. Lambert, 'TF1: la mauvaise affaire de Francis Bouygues?', *Médiaspouvoirs*, no.11, Paris, 1988, p.7.

43 The *Independent*, November 23 1991.

44 R. Collins, *Satellite Television in Western Europe*, London, John Libbey, 1990, p.89.

45 I. Astier, 'Le mystère de La Cinq', *Médiaspouvoirs*, no.30, Paris, 1993.

46 L. Chartier, 'Quand La Cinq se déchaîne', *Médiaspouvoirs*, no.27, Paris, 1992, p.58.

47 Ibid., p.55.

48 M. Dagnaud, 'M6: le guide de la contre-programmation', *Médiaspouvoirs*, no.19, Paris, 1990, p.75.

49 R. Lunven and T. Vedel, *La télévision de demain*, Paris, Armand Colin, 1993, p.205.

50 Ibid., p.208.

51 Collins, op. cit., p.53.

52 B. Schmutz and M. Glayman, 'Canal Plus: le verrouillage', *Médiaspouvoirs*, no.23, Paris, 1991, pp.104–105.

53 Lunven and Vedel, op. cit., pp.209–210.

54 Ibid., p.145.

55 Canal Plus has entered into partnerships with Bertelsmann and Kirch in Germany; Prisa in Spain; and RTBF in Belgium. As yet, none of these foreign ventures has been as commercially successful as Canal Plus in France.

8 THE NEW MEDIA

1 On new media policy in western Europe in the 1980s see K. Dyson and P. Humphreys, *Broadcasting and New Media Policies in Western Europe*, London, Routledge, 1988.

2 R. Lunven and T. Vedel, *La télévision de demain*, Paris, Armand Colin, 1993, p.16.

3 See, for example, F.-R. Barbry, *La télévision par câbles: vers la communication horizontale*, Paris, Cerf, 1975.

4 T. Vedel and W. H. Dutton, 'New media politics: shaping cable television policy in France', *Media, Culture and Society*, vol.12, London, 1990, p.494.

5 R. Kuhn, 'France: the end of the government monopoly', in R. Kuhn (ed.), *The Politics of Broadcasting*, Beckenham, Croom Helm, 1985, p.33.

6 Lunven and Vedel, op. cit., p.19.

7 M. Rhodes, 'Industry and modernisation: an overview', in J. Gaffney (ed.), *France and Modernisation*, Aldershot, Gower, 1988, p.66.

8 On the aims of the Socialist government's policy in the electronics sector and constraints on its successful implementation see Rhodes, op. cit., pp.79–89. See also J.-L. Moynot, 'The Left, industrial policy and the *filière électronique*', in G. Ross, S. Hoffmann and S. Malzacher (eds), *The Mitterrand Experiment*, Cambridge, Polity Press, 1987, p.264. This chapter gives an overview of the 1981–86 Socialist government's policy in the electronics field.

9 C.-J. Bertrand, 'Cable television in France', in R. Negrine (ed.), *Cable Television and the Future of Broadcasting*, London, Croom Helm, 1985, p.138.

10 P. Hall, *Governing the Economy: the politics of state intervention in Britain and France*, Cambridge, Polity Press, 1986, p.209.

11 J.-M. Guehenno, 'France and the electronic media', in Ross, Hoffmann and Malzacher (eds), op. cit., p.283.

12 Hall, op. cit., p.204.

13 Moynot, 'The Left, Industrial Policy and the *filière électronique*', in Ross, Hoffmann and Malzacher (eds), op. cit., p.264.

14 See Rhodes, op. cit., for an overview of state industrial policy in the Fifth Republic and a critique of the coherence and effectiveness of state action in this field.

15 For example, Palmer and Tunstall state that 'the historian of France's industrial policy for the electronics industry . . . considers that – with the exception of the telecommunications sector – French government policy between the 1960s and 1981 was relatively liberal and non-interventionist' (M. Palmer and J. Tunstall, *Liberating Communications: Policy-Making in France and Britain*, Oxford, Blackwell, 1990, p.112).

16 On the growing power and then declining influence of the DGT in telecommunications policy in the 1970s and 1980s, see Palmer and Tunstall, op. cit., ch. 6, pp.135–161. They write that 'The DGT. . . sought to fashion long-term industrial policy. The sums at its disposal to transform the telecommunications infrastructures of France turned it into France's leading national investor (1975–79), and the powerhouse of government policy across the whole of the electronics industries', p.114.

17 Rhodes, op. cit., p.71, based on the views expressed in E. Cohen and M. Bauer, *Les grandes manœuvres industrielles*, Paris, Belfond, 1985.

18 Ibid., p.71.

19 Vedel and Dutton, op. cit., p.495.

20 S. Nora and A. Minc, *L'informatisation de la société*, Paris, Seuil, 1978.

21 On the Nora-Minc Report see Palmer and Tunstall, op. cit., pp.118–121.

22 D. Green, 'The political economy of information technology in France', in Gaffney (ed.), op. cit., p.126.

23 Ibid., p.130.

24 Vedel and Dutton, op. cit., pp.492 and 496.

25 INA, *Dossiers de l'Audiovisuel no.3: trois plans pour le câble*, Paris, La documentation française, 1985.

26 C.-J. Bertrand, 'Cable television in France', in Negrine (ed.), *Cable Television*, pp.139–140.

27 In Britain legislation was introduced in 1984 following the recommendations of the Information and Technology Advisory Panel (ITAP) and the Hunt Report, both of which argued that cable was an essential element of industrial modernization. In West Germany the federal government embarked on an ambitious state-funded cable scheme in 1982 under the control of the Bundespost.

28 Vedel and Dutton, op. cit., p.504.

29 Guehenno, 'France and the electronic media', in G. Ross, Hoffmann and Malzacher (eds), op. cit., p.284.

30 Lunven and Vedel, op. cit., p.22.

31 Vedel and Dutton, op. cit., p.502.

32 Lunven and Vedel, op. cit., p.32.

33 Ibid., p.33.

34 Ibid., p.46.

35 R. Collins, *Satellite Television in Western Europe*, London, John Libbey, 1990, pp.88–89.

36 Lunven and Vedel, op. cit., pp.69–75.

37 Collins, op. cit., p.3.

38 R. Kuhn, 'Satellite broadcasting in France', in R. Negrine (ed.), *Satellite Broadcasting: The politics and implications of the new media*, London, Routledge, 1988, p.182.

39 Lunven and Vedel, op. cit., p.111.

40 Guehenno, 'France and the Electronic Media', in Ross, Hoffmann and Malzacher (eds), op. cit., p.281.

41 Lunven and Vedel, op. cit., p.114.

42 On DGT/TDF rivalry in communications policy see Palmer and Tunstall, op. cit., pp.115–116.

43 Lunven and Vedel, op. cit., p.134.

44 Ibid., pp.138 and 145. Another French-language channel using a telecommunications satellite for programme delivery is TV5-Europe. Transmitting from one of the Eutelsat satellites, TV5-Europe began operating in 1984. It draws on television programmes from the main French network channels and from Belgium, Canada and Switzerland. TV5 aims to strengthen the position of the French-speaking world and to give people a Francophone perspective. It reaches 5.5 million cable homes in 20 countries. As a French-language channel, its realistic potential audience in Europe is concentrated in France and the Francophone parts of Belgium and Switzerland (Collins, op. cit., p.92).

45 The French DBS footprint would cover the French mainland, Corsica, Belgium, Switzerland, Northern Italy and a part of the former West Germany. For a map of the Astra footprint see Collins, op. cit., p.19.

46 Channels from the Astra satellite are not widely viewed in France.

47 Lunven and Vedel, op. cit., p.121.

48 Ibid., p.123.

49 French Guyana is an overseas department close to the equator, a location which gives Ariane a competitive advantage over other launch systems (Collins, op. cit., p.39). A second DBS satellite, TDF2, was put into service in July 1990.

50 Lunven and Vedel, op. cit., p.130.

51 Guehenno, 'France and the electronic media', in Ross, Hoffmann and Malzacher (eds), op. cit., p.282.

52 F. Mariet, 'L'audience d'ARTE', *Médiaspouvoirs*, no.30, Paris, 1993, pp.35–44.

CONCLUSION

1 For relevant statistics see F. Truffart, *Guide des télévisions en Europe*, Paris, *Médiaspouvoirs*, 1991, p.30; D. Bahu-Leyser, 'Histoire des équipements et des pratiques télévisuelles en France', *Médiaspouvoirs*, nos.31–32, Paris, 1993, pp.297–302.

2 P. Albert, *La presse française*, Paris, La documentation française, 1990, p.90; Y. Lorelle, *La presse*, Paris, Retz, 1992, pp.74–78.

3 Lorelle, op. cit., pp.79–80.

4 Y. Guillauma, *La presse en France*, Paris, La Découverte, 1988, p.97.

5 1991 was a very tough financial year for Hachette with the news of its first financial deficit for ten years. This led to the announcement of a merger with the defence firm Matra and a reduction in the stock owned by Lagardère.

6 On the phenomenon of the internationalization of the media see R. Negrine and S. Papathanassopoulos, *The Internationalisation of Television*, London, Pinter, 1990, and A. Smith, *The Age of Behemoths*, New York, Priority Press, 1991.

7 R. Lunven and T. Vedel, *La télévision de demain*, Paris, Armand Colin, 1993, p.187.

8 R. Collins, *Audiovisual and Broadcasting Policy in the European Community*, London, University of North London Press, 1993, pp.5–6.

9 Ibid., p.13.

10 On the possible ramifications of the single market for the French press see P. Todorov, *La presse française à l'heure de l'Europe*, Paris, La documentation française, 1990.

11 Lunven and Vedel, op. cit., p.140.

Select bibliography

Albert, P. (1979) *La presse française* (Paris: La documentation française).
Albert, P. (1990) *La presse française* (Paris: La documentation française).
Alleg, H. (1958) *The Question* (London: John Calder).
Amaury, P. (1969) *Les deux premières expériences d'un ministère de l'information en France* (Paris: Pichon et Durand-Auzias).
Ambler, J. (1985) *The French Socialist Experiment* (Philadelphia: ISHI).
Anderson, M. (1970) *Government in France* (Oxford: Pergamon).
Année Politique, L' (1968) (Paris).
Ardagh, J. (1973, 2nd edn) *The New France* (Harmondsworth: Pelican).
Ardagh, J. (1977, 3rd edn) *The New France* (Harmondsworth: Pelican).
Aron, R. (1958) *The Vichy Regime 1940–44* (London: Putnam).
Aron, R. (1968) *La révolution introuvable* (Paris: Fayard).
Asselain, J.-C. (1985) 'Les nationalisations 1944–1945' in L'histoire, *Etudes sur la France de 1939 à nos jours* (Paris: Seuil).
Astier, I. (1993) 'Le mystère de La Cinq', *Médiaspouvoirs* (Paris: no.30).
Astoux, A. (1978) *Ondes de choc* (Paris: Plon).
Avril, N. and Elkabbach, J.-P. (1982) *Taisez-vous, Elkabbach* (Paris: Flammarion).
Bahu-Leyser, D. (1993) 'Histoire des équipements et des pratiques télévisuelles en France', *Médiaspouvoirs* (Paris: nos.31–32).
Ballaguy, E. (1987) 'Le Figaro, France-Soir et La 5', *Médiaspouvoirs* (Paris: no.8).
Balle, F. and Eymery, G. (1984) *Les nouveaux médias* (Paris: PUF).
Barbry, F.-R. (1975) *La télévision par câbles: vers la communication horizontale* (Paris: Cerf).
Bauer, M. (1988) 'The politics of state-directed privatisation: the case of France, 1986–88', *West European Politics* (London: vol.11).
Beaulieu, J. (1984) *La télévision des réalisateurs* (Paris: La documentation française).
Bellanger, C. (1961) *Presse Clandestine 1940–1944* (Paris: Armand Colin).
Bernard, L. (1990) *Europe 1: La grande histoire dans une grande radio* (Paris: Centurion).
Bertrand, C.-J. (1985) 'Cable television in France', in R. Negrine (ed.), *Cable Television and the Future of Broadcasting* (London: Croom Helm).
Bilger, P. and Lebedel, P. (1991) *Abrégé du droit de la presse* (Paris: CFPJ).
Blumler, J. (ed.) (1992) *Television and the Public Interest* (London: Sage).
Bombardier, D. (1975) *La voix de la France* (Paris: Robert Laffont).
Bourdon, J. (1990) *Histoire de la télévision sous de Gaulle* (Paris: Anthropos/INA).
Bourges, H. (1987) *Une chaîne sur les bras* (Paris: Seuil).
Bower, T. (1991) *Maxwell: The outsider* (London: Mandarin).

Bredin, J.-D. (1985) *Les nouvelles télévisions hertziennes* (Paris: La documentation française).

Briggs, A. (1965) *The History of Broadcasting in the United Kingdom*, vol. 2, *The Golden Age of Wireless* (London: Oxford University Press).

Briggs, A. (1970) *The History of Broadcasting in the United Kingdom*, vol. 3, *The War of Words* (London: Oxford University Press).

Brooks, P. and Hayling, A. (1992) 'Drowning by bullets', *Secret History*, July 13 1992 (London: Channel 4 television).

Brown, B. (1974) *Protest in Paris* (Morristown: General Learning Press).

Cahiers de la Fondation Nationale des Sciences Politiques (1970) *L'élection présidentielle des 5 et 19 décembre 1965* (Paris: Armand Colin).

Cayrol, R. (1991) *Les médias* (Paris: PUF).

Cazenave, F. (1980) *Les radios libres* (Paris: PUF).

Cazenave, F. (1984, 2nd edn) *Les radios libres* (Paris: PUF).

Chaban-Delmas, J. (1975) *L'Ardeur* (Paris: Stock).

Chapman, R. and Hewitt, N. (eds) (1992) *Popular Culture and Mass Communication in Twentieth Century France* (Lampeter: The Edwin Mellen Press).

Charlot, J. (1971) *The Gaullist Phenomenon* (London: Allen and Unwin).

Charon, J.-M. (1991a) *La presse en France de 1945 à nos jours* (Paris: Seuil).

Charon, J.-M. (1991b) '1914-1918: la presse française dans la grande guerre', *Médiaspouvoirs* (Paris: no.23).

Charon, J.-M. (1991c) *L'Etat des médias* (Paris: La Découverte).

Chartier, L. (1992) 'Quand La Cinq se déchaîne', *Médiaspouvoirs* (Paris: no.27).

Chassaing, F. (1980) *Radio Fil Bleu* (Dunkirk: Westhoek).

Chevallier, J. (1975) *La radio-télévision française entre deux réformes* (Paris: Librairie Générale de Droit et de Jurisprudence).

Chinaud Report (1974) *Documents Assemblée Nationale, no.1072* (Paris: Journaux Officiels).

Clarens, B. (1989) 'Parcours sans faute de Jean-Paul Baudecroux, entrepreneur de radio', *Médiaspouvoirs* (Paris: no.15).

Coase, R. H. (1950) *British Broadcasting: A study in monopoly* (London: Longman).

Cobban, A. (1965) *A History of Modern France, Volume 3: 1871-1962* (Harmondsworth: Penguin).

Cobban, A. (1971) *Aspects of the French Revolution* (St Albans: Paladin).

Cojean, A. and Eskenazi, F. (1986) *FM: La folle histoire des radios libres* (Paris: Grasset).

Collin, C. (1979) *Ecoutez la vraie différence* (Claix: La pensée sauvage).

Collins, I. (1959) *The Government and the Newspaper Press in France 1814-1881* (Oxford: Oxford University Press).

Collins, R. (1990) *Satellite Television in Western Europe* (London: John Libbey).

Collins, R. (1993) *Audiovisual and Broadcasting Policy in the European Community* (London: University of North London Press).

Comité d'Histoire de la Télévision (1987) *Mai 68 à l'ORTF* (Paris: La documentation française).

Commission nationale de la communication et des libertés (1987) *Douze ans de télévision 1974-1986* (Paris: La documentation française).

Conso, C. (1990) 'Un quotidien populaire national: une idée neuve?', *Médiaspouvoirs* (Paris: no.19).

Conte, A. (1973) *Hommes libres* (Paris: Plon).

Cook, M. (ed.) (1993) *French Culture since 1945* (London: Longman).

Coston, H. (1967) *Dictionnaire de la politique française* (Paris: La Librairie Française).

Cotta, M. (1986) *Les miroirs de Jupiter* (Paris: Fayard).

Cousin, B. (1993) 'Quel avenir pour France 3?', *Médiaspouvoirs* (Paris: no.29).

Crozier, M. (1970) *La société bloquée* (Paris: Seuil).

Curran, J. and Seaton, J. (1991, 4th edn) *Power without responsibility: The press and broadcasting in Britain* (London: Routledge).

de Gaulle, C. (1970) *Mémoires d'espoir* (Paris: Plon).

de Gaulle, C. (1954, 1956, 1959) *Mémoires de guerre* (Paris: Plon).

d'Ornano, M. (1983) *La manipulation des médias* (Paris: Albatros/Veyrier).

de Tarlé, A. (1979) 'France: the monopoly that won't divide', in A. Smith (ed.), *Television and Political Life* (London: Macmillan).

de Tarlé, A. (1980) 'The press and the state in France', in A. Smith (ed.), *Newspapers and Democracy* (Cambridge, Mass.: MIT).

Dagnaud, M. (1990) 'M6: le guide de la contre-programmation', *Médiaspouvoirs* (Paris: no.19).

Davies, N. (1993) *The Unknown Maxwell* (London: Pan).

Debbasch, C. (1967) *Traité du Droit de la Radiodiffusion: Radio et Télévision* (Paris: Librairie Générale de Droit et de Jurisprudence).

Delcros, B. and Vodan, B. (1987) *La liberté de communication: Loi du 30 septembre 1986, analyse et commentaire* (Paris: La documentation française).

Delivet, J.-P. (1989) 'Une nouvelle instance de régulation: le Conseil supérieur de l'audiovisuel', *Médiaspouvoirs* (Paris: no.14).

Desgraupes, P. (1992) *Hors antenne* (Paris: Quai Voltaire).

Diligent Report (1968) *Documents Sénat no.118* (Paris: Journaux Officiels).

Diligent Report (1972) *Documents Sénat no.165* (Paris: Journaux Officiels).

Diwo, J. (1976) *Si vous avez manqué le début* (Paris: Albin Michel).

Doucant, N. (1991) 'Le public de la radio', *Médiaspouvoirs* (Paris: no.21).

Ducarroir, E. (1986) 'L' évolution du marché publicitaire', *Médiaspouvoirs* (Paris: no.2).

Ducarroir, E. (1989) 'Le marché publicitaire français en 1988', *Médiaspouvoirs* (Paris: no.15).

Ducarroir, E. (1990) 'Le marché publicitaire français en 1989', *Médiaspouvoirs* (Paris: no.19).

Ducarroir, E. (1991a) 'Le marché publicitaire français en 1990', *Médiaspouvoirs* (Paris: no.23).

Ducarroir, E. (1991b) 'Evolution de la diffusion des quotidiens et principaux périodiques français de 1987 à 1990', *Médiaspouvoirs* (Paris: no.24).

Ducarroir, E. (1992a) 'Le marché publicitaire français en 1991', *Médiaspouvoirs* (Paris: no.28).

Ducarroir, E. (1992b) 'Evolution de la diffusion des quotidiens et principaux périodiques français de 1988 à 1991', *Médiaspouvoirs* (Paris: no.28).

Duhamel, A. (1980) *La république giscardienne* (Paris: Grasset).

Dunleavy, P. and O'Leary, B. (1987) *Theories of the State* (London: Macmillan).

Dunnett, P. (1990) *The World Television Industry: An economic analysis* (London: Routledge).

Dupuis, G. and Raux, J. (1970) *L' ORTF* (Paris: Armand Colin).

Durand, J. (1991) 'L'évolution des audiences de la radio et de la télévision au cours des quarante dernières années', *Médiaspouvoirs* (Paris: no 21).

Durieux, C. (1976) *La télécratie* (Paris: Tema).

Dyson, K. and Humphreys, P. (1988) *Broadcasting and New Media Policies in Western Europe* (London: Routledge).

Eck, H. (ed.) (1984) *La guerre des ondes* (Paris: CRPFL).

Eck, H. (1991) 'Radio, culture and democracy in France in the immediate postwar period 1944-50', in B. Rigby and N. Hewitt (eds), *France and the Mass Media* (Basingstoke: Macmillan).

Flower, J. E. (ed.) (1977, 3rd edn; 1987, 6th edn; 1993, 7th edn) *France Today* (London: Methuen, 3rd edn; Routledge, 6th edn; Hodder and Stoughton, 7th edn).

Frears, J. (1981) *France in the Giscard Presidency* (London: Allen and Unwin).

Frèches, J. (1985) *La télévision par câble* (Paris: PUF).

Frèches, J. (1986) *La guerre des images* (Paris: Denoel).

Frédéric, C. (1968) *Libérer l'ORTF* (Paris: Seuil).

Freiberg, J. W. (1981) *The French Press: Class, state and ideology* (New York: Praeger).

French Embassy (1986) *Act on Reforming the Legal System Governing the Press (1986)* (London: French Embassy).

Funès, N. (1991) 'Qui écoute la radio? Une comparaison internationale', in J.M. Charon (ed.), *L'Etat des médias* (Paris: La Découverte).

Fysh, P. (1990) 'Gaullism and the liberal challenge', (University of London: unpublished Ph.D. thesis).

Gaffney, J. (ed.) (1988) *France and Modernisation* (Aldershot: Gower).

Gaffney, J. (ed.) (1989) *The French Presidential Elections of 1988* (Aldershot: Dartmouth).

Gaillard, J.-M. (1990) *Zappons, enfants de la patrie* (Paris: Fayard).

Giesbert, F.-O. (1990) *Le Président* (Paris: Seuil).

Giroud, F. (1977) *La comédie du pouvoir* (Paris: Fayard).

Giscard d'Estaing, V. (1976) *Démocratie française* (Paris: Fayard).

Gough, H. (1988) *The Newspaper Press in the French Revolution* (London: Routledge).

Green, D. (1988) 'The political economy of information technology in France', in J. Gaffney (ed.), *France and Modernisation* (Aldershot: Gower).

Guehenno, J.-M. (1987) 'France and the electronic media', in G. Ross, S. Hoffmann and S. Malzacher (eds), *The Mitterrand Experiment* (Cambridge: Polity Press).

Guéry, L. (1992) *La presse régionale et locale* (Paris: CFPJ).

Guilhaume, P. (1991) *Un président à abattre* (Paris: Albin Michel).

Guillauma, Y. (1988) *La presse en France* (Paris: La Découverte).

Guillou, B. (1985) *Les stratégies multimédias des groupes de communication* (Paris: La documentation française).

Hall, P. (1986) *Governing the Economy: The politics of state intervention in Britain and France* (Cambridge: Polity Press).

Hall, S., Critcher, C., Jefferson,T., Clarke, J. and Roberts, B. (1978) *Policing the Crisis* (London: Macmillan).

Hamelin, D. (1990) 'Décentralisation de Radio France', *Médiaspouvoirs* (Paris: no.18).

Hare, G. (1992) 'The law of the jingle, or a decade of change in French radio' in R. Chapman and N. Hewitt (eds), *Popular Culture and Mass Communication in Twentieth Century France* (Lampeter: The Edwin Mellen Press).

Hart, D. J. (1980) 'Changing relationships between publishers and journalists: an overview', in A. Smith (ed.), *Newspapers and Democracy* (Cambridge, Mass.: MIT).

Hewitt, N. (1991) 'The birth of the glossy magazines: the case of *Paris-Match*', in B. Rigby and N. Hewitt (eds), *France and the Mass Media* (Basingstoke: Macmillan).

Horne, A. (1979) *A Savage War of Peace* (Harmondsworth: Penguin).

INA (1985) *Dossiers de l'Audiovisuel no.3: trois plans pour le câble* (Paris: La documentation française).

Johnson, R. W. (1981) *The Long March of the French Left* (London: Macmillan).

Jouanno, B. (1988) 'L'Europe en chiffres', *Médiaspouvoirs* (Paris: no.12).

Jullian, M. (1979) *Courte supplique au roi pour le bon usage des énarques* (Paris: Mazarine).

Jullian, M. (1981) *La télévision libre* (Paris: Gallimard).

Keane, J. (1991) *The Media and Democracy* (Oxford: Polity Press).

Kedward, H. R. (1978) *Resistance in Vichy France* (Oxford: Oxford University Press).

Kedward, H. R. (1985) *Occupied France* (Oxford: Blackwell).

Keeler, J. T. S. and Stone, A. (1987) 'Judicial-political confrontation in Mitterrand's France', in G. Ross, S. Hoffmann and S. Malzacher, *The Mitterrand Experiment* (Cambridge: Polity Press).

Knightley, P. (1989) *The First Casualty* (London: Pan).

Kuhn, R. (1984) 'The presidency and the media, 1974–82', in V. Wright (ed.), *Continuity and Change in France* (London: Allen and Unwin).

Kuhn, R. (ed.) (1985a) *The Politics of Broadcasting* (Beckenham: Croom Helm).

Kuhn, R. (ed.) (1985b) *Broadcasting and Politics in Western Europe* (London: Frank Cass).

Kuhn, R. (1988a) 'The modernisation of the media', in J. Gaffney (ed.), *France and Modernisation* (Aldershot: Gower).

Kuhn, R. (1988b) 'Satellite broadcasting in France', in R. Negrine (ed.), *Satellite Broadcasting: The politics and implications of the new media* (London: Routledge).

Labrousse, S. C. and Robinet, P. (eds) (1987) *Paris et enjeux de la presse de demain* (Grenoble: Presses Universitaires de Grenoble).

Lacouture, J. (1984) *De Gaulle Le rebelle 1890–1944* (Paris: Seuil).

Lacouture, J. (1990) *De Gaulle The Rebel 1890–1944* (London: Collins Harvill).

Lalu, V. (1990) 'Redresser les quotidiens', *Médiaspouvoirs* (Paris: no.19).

Lambert, E. (1987) 'Prix de vente des quotidiens: le lecteur français est-il défavorisé?', *Médiaspouvoirs* (Paris: no.8).

Lambert, E. (1988) 'TF1: la mauvaise affaire de Francis Bouygues?', *Médiaspouvoirs* (Paris: no.11).

Lapolambara, J. and Weiner, M. (eds) (1966) *Political Parties and Political Development* (Princeton: Princeton University Press).

Larkin, M. (1988) *France since the Popular Front* (Oxford: Oxford University Press).

Ledos, J.-J., Jézéquel, J.-P. and Régnier, P. (1986) *Le gâchis audiovisuel* (Paris: Editions ouvrières).

Le Monde dossiers et documents (1988) *La télévision en 1987: le grand chambardement* (Paris: Le Monde).

Le Tac Report (1972) *Documents Assemblée Nationale no.2291* (Paris: Journaux Officiels).

Lewis, P. M. and Booth, J. (1989) *The Invisible Medium* (Basingstoke: Macmillan).

Lorelle, Y. (1992) *La presse* (Paris: Retz).

Louis, R. (1968) *L'ORTF un combat* (Paris: Seuil).

Lunven, R. and Vedel, T. (1993) *La télévision de demain* (Paris: Armand Colin).

McIntyre, I. (1993) *The Expense of Glory: A life of John Reith* (London: HarperCollins).

McMillan, J. F. (1992) *Twentieth-Century France* (London: Edward Arnold).

McQuail, D. (1987) *Mass Communication Theory* (London: Sage).

Maitrot, J. C. and Sicault, J. D. (1969) *Les conférences de presse du Général de Gaulle* (Paris: PUF).

Malaud, P. (1976) *La révolution libérale* (Paris: Masson).

Mamère, N. (1982) *Telle est la télé* (Paris: Mégrelis).

Manel, J.-P. and Planel, A. (1968) *La crise de l'ORTF* (Paris: Pauvert).

Mariet, F. (1993) 'L'audience d'ARTE', *Médiaspouvoirs* (Paris: no.30).

Martinet, G. (1973) *Le système Pompidou* (Paris: Seuil).

Mathien, M. (1986, 2nd edn) *La presse quotidienne régionale* (Paris: PUF).

Mattelart, A. (1990) *La publicité* (Paris: La Découverte).

Mauriat, C. (1989) *La presse audiovisuelle* (Paris: CFPJ).

Méadel, C. (1987) 'L'information à France-Inter', in Comité d'Histoire de la Télévision, *Mai 68 à l'ORTF* (Paris: La documentation française).

Méadel, C. (1991a) 'Mesures de la radio', *Médiaspouvoirs* (Paris: no.24).

Méadel, C. (1991b) 'The arrival of opinion polls in French radio and television 1945–60' in B. Rigby and N. Hewitt (eds) *France and the Mass Media* (Basingstoke: Macmillan).

Mehl, D. (1990) 'Audiovisuel: le service public, naufrage d'une notion', *Médiaspouvoirs* (Paris: no.19).

Méjan, R. (1989) 'Stratégies et concurrence dans la radio', *Médiaspouvoirs* (Paris: no.16).

Mercillon, H. (ed.) (1974) *ORTF l'agonie du monopole?* (Paris: Plon).

Michel, H. (1989) *La télévision en France et dans le monde* (Paris: PUF).

Miquel, P. (1984) *Histoire de la radio et de la télévision* (Paris: Perrin).

Missika, J.-L. and Wolton, D. (1983) *La folle du logis* (Paris: Gallimard).

Mitterrand, F. (1980) *Ici et maintenant* (Paris: Fayard).

Moinot Report (1981) *Pour une réforme de l'audiovisuel, Rapport au Premier ministre de la Commission de réflexion et d'orientation présidée par Pierre Moinot* (Paris: La documentation française).

Monnot, C. and Ternisien, X. (1989) 'Le Figaro: sans la liberté de changer . . .', *Médiaspouvoirs* (Paris: no.13).

Montaldo, J. (1974) *Dossier ORTF 1944–1974: Tous coupables* (Paris: Albin Michel).

Moynot, J.-L. (1987) 'The Left, industrial policy and the *filière électronique*', in G. Ross, S. Hoffmann and S. Malzacher (eds), *The Mitterrand Experiment* (Cambridge: Polity Press).

Negrine, R. (ed.) (1985) *Cable Television and the Future of Broadcasting* (London: Croom Helm).

Negrine, R. (ed.) (1988) *Satellite Broadcasting: The politics and implications of the new media* (London: Routledge).

Negrine, R. (1989) *Politics and the Mass Media in Britain* (London: Routledge).

Negrine, R. and Papathanassopoulos, S. (1990) *The Internationalisation of Television* (London: Pinter).

Ockrent, C. (1988) *Duel* (Paris: Hachette).

ORTF (1973) *ORTF 73* (Paris: Presses de la Cité).

Palmer, M. and Tunstall, J. (1990) *Liberating Communications: Policy-making in France and Britain* (Oxford: Blackwell).

Pastiaux, C. (1989) 'Les recettes de Canal Plus', *Médiaspouvoirs* (Paris: no.14).

Paye Report (1970) *Rapport de la commission d'étude du statut de l'ORTF* (Paris: La documentation française).

Pedley, A. (1993) 'The media', in M. Cook (ed.), *French Culture since 1945* (London: Longman).

Penniman, H. (ed.) (1980) *The French National Assembly Elections of 1978* (Washington: American Enterprise Institute).

Petit, P. (1991) 'L'âge de raison des réseaux FM', *Médiaspouvoirs* (Paris: no.24).

Petit, P. (1992a) 'Trop de réseaux en France?', *Médiaspouvoirs* (Paris: no.25).

Petit, P. (1992b) 'Superloustic: le copain des enfants sur la bande FM', *Médias-pouvoirs* (Paris: no.25).

Peyrefitte, A. (1976) *Le mal français* (Paris: Plon).

Peyrefitte, A. (1983) *Quand la rose se fanera . . .* (Paris: Plon).

Pfister, T. (1985) *La vie quotidienne à Matignon au temps de l'union de la gauche* (Paris: Hachette).

Pompidou, G. (1974) *Le nœud gordien* (Paris: Plon).

Poniatowski, M. (1972) *Cartes sur table* (Paris: Fayard).

Prot, R. (1985) *Des radios pour se parler* (Paris: La documentation française).

Ray, J. E. and Ray, M. (1978) *Corsaires des ondes* (Paris: Cerf).

Redfern, W. D. (1977, 3rd edn; 1987, 6th edn) 'The press' in J. E. Flower (ed.), *France Today* (London: Methuen, 3rd edn; Routledge, 6th edn).

Rhodes, M. (1988) 'Industry and modernisation: an overview', in J. Gaffney (ed.), *France and Modernisation* (Aldershot: Gower).

Rigby, B. (1991) *Popular Culture in Modern France* (London: Routledge).

Rigby, B. and Hewitt, N. (eds) (1991) *France and the Mass Media* (Basingstoke: Macmillan).

Rioux, J.-P. (1980 and 1983) *La France de la Quatrième République* (Paris: Seuil).

Rioux, J.-P. (1987) *The Fourth Republic 1944–1958* (Cambridge: Cambridge University Press).

Ross, G., Hoffmann, S. and Malzacher, S. (1987) *The Mitterrand Experiment* (Cambridge: Polity Press).

Sartori, G. (1966) 'European political parties: the case of polarized pluralism', in J. Lapolambara and M. Weiner (eds), *Political Parties and Political Development* (Princeton: Princeton University Press).

Sassoon, D. (1985) 'Political and market forces in Italian broadcasting', in R. Kuhn (ed.), *Broadcasting and Politics in Western Europe* (London: Frank Cass).

Schmutz, B. and Glayman, M. (1991) 'Canal Plus: le verrouillage', *Médiaspouvoirs* (Paris: no.23).

Scriven, M. and Kierszenbaum, F. (1992) '*La Truffe* est remise en terre', *Modern and Contemporary France* (Portsmouth: no.49).

Seymour-Ure, C. (1974) *The Political Impact of Mass Media* (London: Constable).

Siclier, J. (1976) *Un homme averty* (Paris: Jean-Claude Simoen).

Siégel, M. (1975) *Vingt ans ça suffit* (Paris: Plon).

Service Juridique et Technique de l'Information (SJTI) (1992) *Tableaux statistiques de la presse 1990* (Paris: La documentation française).

Smith, A. (1973) *The Shadow in the Cave* (London: Allen and Unwin).

Smith, A. (1976) *The Shadow in the Cave* (London: Quartet).

Smith, A. (1979) *The Newspaper: An international history* (London: Thames and Hudson).

Smith, A. (ed.) (1979) *Television and Political Life* (London: Macmillan).

Smith, A (ed.) (1980) *Newspapers and Democracy* (Cambridge, Mass.: MIT).

Smith, A. (1991) *The Age of Behemoths* (New York: Priority Press).

Société Française de Télédistribution (1974) *Pour une télédistribution française* (Paris: Société Française de Télédistribution).

Stone, A. (1989) 'In the shadow of the Constitutional Council: the "juridicisation" of the legislative process in France', *West European Politics* (London: vol.12).

Stone, A. (1992a) *The Birth of Judicial Politics in France* (Oxford: Oxford University Press).

Stone, A. (1992b) 'Where judicial politics are legislative politics: the French Constitutional Council', *West European Politics* (London: vol.15).

Swann, D. (1988) *The Retreat of the State* (London: Harvester Wheatsheaf).

Talbott, J. (1981) *The War Without a Name* (London: Faber and Faber).

Ténot, F. (1978) *Radios privées, radios pirates* (Paris: Denoel).

Thibau, J. (1970) *Une télévision pour tous les français* (Paris: Seuil).

Thibau, J. (1973) *La télévision, le pouvoir et l'argent* (Paris: Calmann-Lévy).

Thomas, R. (1976) *Broadcasting and Democracy in France* (London: Crosby Lockwood Staples).

Thomson, D. (1968) *France: Empire and Republic, 1850–1940* (New York: Walker).

Thomson, D. (1969, 5th edn) *Democracy in France since 1870* (Oxford: Oxford University Press).

Todorov, P. (1990) *La presse française à l'heure de l'Europe* (Paris: La documentation française).

Touraine, A. (1971) *The May Movement, Revolt and Reform* (New York: Random House).

Toussaint Desmoulins, N. (1987) 'Les effets pervers des aides à la presse', *Médiaspouvoirs* (Paris: no.8).

Truffart, F. (1991) *Guide des télévisions en Europe* (Paris: Médiaspouvoirs).

Tudesq, A.-J. (1987) 'La radio, les manifestations, le pouvoir', in Comité d'Histoire de la Télévision, *Mai 68 à l'ORTF* (Paris: La documentation française).

Tunstall, J. and Palmer, M. (eds) (1991) *Media Moguls* (London: Routledge).

Tuppen, J. (1991) *Chirac's France, 1986–88* (London: Macmillan).

Vedel, T. and Dutton, W. H. (1990) 'New media politics: shaping cable television policy in France', *Media, Culture and Society* (London: vol.12).

Viansson-Ponté, P. (1963) *Les gaullistes* (Paris: Seuil).

Viansson-Ponté, P. (1970) *Histoire de la République Gaullienne*, vol.1 (Paris: Fayard).

Viansson-Ponté, P. (1971) *Histoire de la République Gaullienne*, vol.2 (Paris: Fayard).

Vittet-Philippe, P. and Crookes, P. (n.d.) *Local Radio and Regional Development in Europe* (Manchester: European Institute for the Media).

Voyenne, B. (1972) *L'information en France* (London: McGraw-Hill).

Werth, A. (1960) *The De Gaulle Revolution* (London: Robert Hale).

Werth, A. (1967) *De Gaulle* (Harmondsworth: Penguin).

Williams, P. M. (1964, 3rd edn) *Crisis and Compromise* (London: Longman).

Williams, P. M. (1968) *The French Parliament 1958–1967* (London: Allen and Unwin).

Williams, P. M. (1970) *French Politicians and Elections 1951–69* (London: Cambridge University Press).

Wolton, D. (1992) 'Values and normative choices in French television', in J. Blumler (ed.), *Television and the Public Interest* (London: Sage).

Wright, V. (ed.) (1984) *Continuity and Change in France* (London: Allen and Unwin).

Wright, V. (1989, 3rd edn) *The Government and Politics of France* (London: Unwin Hyman).

Wylie, L. (1974, 3rd edn) *Village in the Vaucluse* (Cambridge, Mass.: Harvard University Press).

Zeldin, T. (1977) *France 1848–1945, Volume Two: Intellect, taste and anxiety* (Oxford: Oxford University Press).

Index

Printed in the United States
by Baker & Taylor Publisher Services